Theodor Lessing's Philosophy of History in Its Time

Philosophy of History and Culture

Edited by

Michael Krausz (*Bryn Mawr College*)

Advisory Board

Annette Baier† (*University of Pittsburgh*)
Purushottama Bilimoria (*Deakin University, Australia*)
Cora Diamond (*University of Virginia*)
William Dray† (*University of Ottawa*)
Nancy Fraser (*New School for Social Research*)
Clifford Geertz† (*Institute for Advanced Study, Princeton*)
Peter Hacker (*St. John's College, Oxford*)
Rom Harré (*Linacre College, Oxford*)
Bernard Harrison (*University of Sussex*)
Martha Nussbaum (*University of Chicago*)
Leon Pompa (*University of Birmingham*)
Joseph Raz (*Balliol College, Oxford*)
Amélie Rorty (*Harvard University*)

VOLUME 38

The titles published in this series are listed at *brill.com/phc*

Theodor Lessing, Hanover, June 14th, 1926
DRAWING BY EMIL STUMPP (1886–1941)

Theodor Lessing's Philosophy of History in Its Time

By

Herman Simissen

BRILL

LEIDEN | BOSTON

Library of Congress Cataloging-in-Publication Data

Names: Simissen, H. G. J. M., author.
Title: Theodor Lessing's philosophy of history in its time / by Herman Simissen.
Description: Leiden ; Boston : Brill, [2021] | Series: Philosophy of history and culture, 0922-6001 ; volume 38 | Includes bibliographical references and index. | Summary: "This study–the first full-length monograph in English on the subject–discusses the genesis of Theodor Lessing's philosophy of history as mainly expressed in his books "Geschichte als Sinngebung des Sinnlosen" (1919 and 1927), as well as its philosophical implications. Lessing on the one hand vehemently denies that historians can know the past as it actually happened. On the other hand, and rather surprisingly, he emphasizes the exceptional importance of history within a culture, because of what he calls its religious function. His penetrating analysis of history is remarkably relevant for ongoing debates on the very nature of history"–Provided by publisher.
Identifiers: LCCN 2021015559 (print) | LCCN 2021015560 (ebook) | ISBN 9789004464766 (hardback) | ISBN 9789004464773 (e-book)
Subjects: LCSH: Lessing, Theodor, 1872-1933–Political and social views. | Germany–Intellectual life–20th century. | History–Philosophy. | Lessing, Theodor, 1872-1933. Geschichte als Sinngebung des Sinnlosen.
Classification: LCC B3286.L44 S56 2021 (print) | LCC B3286.L44 (ebook) | DDC 901–dc23
LC record available at https://lccn.loc.gov/2021015559
LC ebook record available at https://lccn.loc.gov/2021015560

Typeface for the Latin, Greek, and Cyrillic scripts: "Brill". See and download: brill.com/brill-typeface.

ISSN 0922-6001
ISBN 978-90-04-46476-6 (hardback)
ISBN 978-90-04-46477-3 (e-book)

Copyright 2021 by Herman Simissen. Published by Koninklijke Brill NV, Leiden, The Netherlands. Koninklijke Brill NV incorporates the imprints Brill, Brill Hes & De Graaf, Brill Nijhoff, Brill Rodopi, Brill Sense, Hotei Publishing, mentis Verlag, Verlag Ferdinand Schöningh and Wilhelm Fink Verlag. All rights reserved. No part of this publication may be reproduced, translated, stored in a retrieval system, or transmitted in any form or by any means, electronic, mechanical, photocopying, recording or otherwise, without prior written permission from the publisher. Requests for re-use and/or translations must be addressed to Koninklijke Brill NV via brill.com or copyright.com.

This book is printed on acid-free paper and produced in a sustainable manner.

In memory of my parents
> Bets Simissen-Rasker (1920–2014)
> and Theo Simissen (1916–1974)

•••

...daß auf Erden das Leiden der Menschen ende und Gerechtigkeit und Wahrheit werde.
> Theodor Lessing, *Gerichtstag über mich selbst* (1925)

•••

...so that on earth the suffering of humans will end and justice and truth will be.
> Theodor Lessing, *Judgement Day over myself* (1925)

•••

lo bechail, welo bekoach, ki im beruach

•••

neither with force, nor the power of arms, only with the strength of the mind

Ein Seelenforscher hat geschrieben: 'Die Eigenliebe des Menschen hat dreimal eine tiefe Kränkung erlitten. Die kosmologische Kränkung, die den Glauben zerstörte, daß die Erde Mittelpunkt der Welt sei. Die biologische Kränkung, die die Illusion beseitigte, daß der Mensch im Unterschiede gegen Pflanze und Tiere eine göttliche Seele habe, und die psychologische Kränkung, die mit der Vorstellung aufräumte, daß unser bewußtes Ich frei und Herr im eigenen Hause sei.' ... Getrost kann ich hinzufügen, daß diese drei Kränkungen der menschlichen Selbstgerechtigkeit fast belanglos sind im Vergleich zu der vierten Kränkung: der geschichtlichen, welche klar macht, daß Geschichte ein für das Leben der Menschen notwendiger Mythos ist und welche dieses klar macht einem Geschlechte, daß die Kraft zum Mythos verloren hat.

Theodor Lessing, *Geschichte als Sinngebung des Sinnlosen* (1927)

A psychologist wrote: 'Three times, human self-love suffered a deep blow. The cosmological blow, which destroyed the belief that the earth were at the centre of the world. The biological blow, which disposed of the illusion that, in contrast to plants and animals, humans have a divine soul, and the psychological blow, which cleaned up the idea that our conscious self were free and master of its own house.'... I may confidently add that these three blows of human self-righteousness are almost insignificant as compared to the fourth blow: the historical, which makes clear that history is a myth which is indispensable for human life and which makes this clear to a generation that has lost the power for myth.

Contents

Preface XI
Abbreviations XIII

1 **Introduction** 1
  1 A Philosopher and His Reputation 1
  2 Historiography 11
  3 Approach and Aims 17

2 **'Ein Aus Eignem Blut Gereiften Weltsystem'** 28
  1 Childhood and Schooldays 31
  2 Wandering Years, and Back to Hanover 44
  3 Turning for Philosophy 67
  4 Philosophy of Need: Notes towards a Reconstruction 80

3 **'Et Si Omnes, Non Ego'** 102
  1 "The Spirit of 1914" 104
  2 German Intellectuals and the "Spirit of 1914" 108
  3 Justifying the War Historically 116
  4 Theodor Lessing on the Great War 128

4 **'Aber Wir Benötigen Geschichte, Um Geschichte Zu Machen'** 153
  1 Preliminary Observations on History 154
  2 Lessing's Critique of Historical Reason 161
  3 Epistemological Questions 166
  4 Psychological Questions 182
  5 History as an Ideal 199
  6 Conclusion 209

5 **'Den Früheren Auflagen Gegenüber Ein Völlig Neues Werk'** 212
  1 What Is History? 213
  2 Historian of Hanover 219
  3 Reply to His Critics 226
  4 A New Light on His Own Writings 232
  5 Pre-logical Reflections 239
  6 Logical Reflections 251
  7 Para-logical Reflections 272

6 'Es Wird Zum Denken Anregen'   284
   1   *Geschichte als Sinngebung des Sinnlosen* Reviewed   288
   2   Lessing's Philosophy of History Discussed   304

Conclusion   327

Bibliography   335
Index of Names   348
Index of Subjects   352

Preface

This study originated in 1985. Just having finished my study of history at the Katholieke Universiteit Nijmegen and looking for an occupation, I discussed my options with my former teacher in philosophy of history, Dr. W.J. van der Dussen. He suggested to consider the possibility of doing research in philosophy of history, and mentioned the German philosopher Theodor Lessing as a most interesting thinker who had been hardly discussed, and whose ideas on history as expounded in his book with the fascinating title *Geschichte als Sinngebung des Sinnlosen* might well be an interesting subject to study. Theodor Lessing's philosophy of history has been on my mind ever since, even though there have been years I could barely spend any time to study it, because of teaching obligations and other projects I got involved with. But I was never inclined to abandon the project – and Dr. Van der Dussen, who meanwhile became a professor and, moreover, both my head of department at the Dutch Open Universiteit and a valued friend, showed truly exceptional patience with supervising it over all these years. I am most grateful for his encouragement and help over these many years; for the completion of this study, I owe him more than anyone else. Only when the then dean of the Faculteit van Cultuur- en Rechtswetenschappen van de Open Universiteit, Prof. Mr. E. Stamhuis, granted me time off from my regular tasks to complete this study, I managed to do so. I am much obliged to Prof. Stamhuis for this support. When I first started this project in 1985, Prof. Dr. H.W. von der Dunk was a most friendly and very helpful adviser; I am grateful for his stimulating observations.

Over the years, a great number of colleagues and friends helped me, by providing information or texts or by encouraging me. For their help and encouragement, I want to thank Dr. Lawrence Baron, Dr. Leo van Bergen, Drs. Paul van den Boorn, my godfather the late Prof. J.A. Huisman, Dr. A.E.M. Janssen, Mr. Manfred Küchler, Prof. J. van Marle, Dr. Rob Meens, Father G.W. Pieterse scj, Drs. Ruud van de Plassche, Mr. Martin Rethmeier, Prof. Guido Vanheeswijck, Drs. Cees Willemsen, and my colleagues at the Faculteit van Cultuur- en Rechtswetenschappen van de Open Universiteit.

This study was almost completely written in the Reading Room of the University Library of my alma mater, which in the meantime changed its name into Radboud Universiteit. I thank the staff of the Reading Room for their always warm hospitality.

Incorporated in this study are the findings of a number of essays in Dutch on Theodor Lessing, which I published between 2001 and 2015 in the monthly *Streven*. I thank the editors of this monthly – indeed, my fellow-editors, as I have been involved with *Streven* since 1998 –, both for publishing the articles, and for the boost writing these texts proved to be in continuing paying attention to Lessing. Generally, discussions in the board of editors of *Streven* have proved to be very informative and valuable for me. Hence, I thank Father Jan Koenot SJ for inviting me to join the board of editors of this monthly and, subsequently, to succeed him as editor-in-chief.

For their unrelenting support over the years, I especially thank my closest and highly esteemed colleagues Dr. Toon Bosch, Dr. Femke Kok and Dr. Jeroen Vanheste at the Studiecentrum Nijmegen of the Open Universiteit; and my sister Brechtje and my brother George.

I dedicate this book to my parents, Bets Simissen-Rasker and Theo Simissen, in loving memory. Both of them had a keen interest in history; my father did only just live long enough to see me developing the wish to study history when I still was a schoolboy; my mother did not live to see me finishing this study on Lessing. I am sure both of them would have greatly enjoyed seeing the completion of this work.

Nijmegen / Heerlen, April 2017

Addendum

I would like to express my special thanks to Jennifer Pavelko, Fenja Schulz, Emma de Looij and Christina Sargent of Brill for their professional and friendly support in publishing this book.

Herman Simissen
April 2021
Nijmegen / Heerlen

Abbreviations

In references to Lessing's works, the following abbreviations will be used:

BEK	*Der Bruch in der Ethik Kants: Wert- und willenstheoretische Prolegomena* (Bern 1908)
BiS	*Bildung ist Schönheit. Autobiographische Zeugnisse und Schriften zur Bildungsreform*, ed. by Jörg Wollenberg (*Ausgewählte Schriften*, vol. 1, Bremen 1995)
DjS	*Der jüdische Selbsthaß* (Berlin 1930)
DusJ	*Deutschland und seine Juden* (Prag - Karlin 1933)
DvK	*Die verfluchte Kultur. Gedanken über den Gegensatz von Leben und Geist* (Munich 1921)
EuA	*Europa und Asien* (Berlin 1918)
Eunw	*Einmal und nie wieder. Lebenserinnerungen* (Gütersloh 1969)
GSS	*Geschichte als Sinngebung des Sinnlosen* (Munich 1919)
GSS4	*Geschichte als Sinngebung des Sinnlosen oder die Geburt der Geschichte aus dem Mythos* (Leipzig 1927)
IFEG	*Ich warf eine Flaschenpost ins Eismeer der Geschichte. Essays und Feuilletons*, ed. by Rainer Marwedel (Darmstadt and Neuwied 1986)
PaT	*Philosophie als Tat* (Göttingen 1914)
Spir	*African Spir's Erkenntnislehre* (Phil. Diss. Erlangen, Gießen 1900)
S-W-N	*Schopenhauer - Wagner - Nietzsche. Einführung in moderne deutsche Philosophie* (Munich 1906)
SzW	*Studien zur Wertaxiomatik. Untersuchungen über Reine Ethik und Reines Recht* (Leipzig 1914)
Th-STM	*Theater-Seele und Tomi melkt die Moralkuh. Schriften zu Theater und Literatur*, ed. by Jörg Wollenberg et.al., (*Ausgewählte Schriften*, vol. 3, Bremen 2003)
WeU	*Wortmeldungen eines Unerschrockenen. Publizistik aus drei Jahrzehnten*, ed. by Hans Stern (Leipzig and Weimar 1987)
Wmnm	*Wir machen nicht mit! Schriften gegen den Nationalismus und zur Judenfrage*, ed. by Jörg Wollenberg (*Ausgewählte Schriften*, vol. 2, Bremen 1997)

CHAPTER 1

Introduction

1   A Philosopher and His Reputation

On Wednesday August 30, 1933, the German philosopher Theodor Lessing returned from the Eighteenth Zionist Congress in Prague to the city of Marienbad, also in Czechoslovakia, where he lived in exile.[1]

Earlier that year, on March 1, Lessing, accompanied by his daughter Ruth, had fled Hanover, Germany, where he – being a fighting spirited pacifist, socialist and Zionist – could no longer feel safe after the National-Socialists had overtaken power on January 31. Lessing indeed had every reason to feel seriously and immediately threatened. Early in January 1933, three members of the SA harassed him in a tram in Hanover, yelling that Hitler would hang all Jews, and that he, Lessing, himself should be "immediately removed" ("unverzüglich entfernen").[2] Some weeks later, during one of his stage appearances in Hanover, the controversial clairvoyant Erik Jan Hanussen (1889–1933),[3] prompted by members of the SA, predicted for 1933 not only a new world war and a further devaluation of the *Reichsmark*, but also that "a scholar, very well-known in Hanover, about whom there is much talk in Hanover, will die this year".[4] This prediction referred to Lessing – as many in the audience during Hanussen's stage appearance, Lessing himself included, understood all too well. So Lessing decided to flee to Marienbad. Despite his promise to his wife Ada to keep a low profile in exile, and although he realised that he had to take the fate of those still living in Germany into consideration – "I do indeed have to bear in mind that I do not harm the brothers in Germany, nor the comrades in prisons and labour camps"[5] –, Lessing continued his struggle against

---

1   Rainer Marwedel, *Theodor Lessing 1872–1933. Eine Biographie* (Darmstadt and Neuwied 1987) 361.
2   O.c., 345.
3   Hanussen, a Czech Jew, was born as Hermann Steinschneider. For a short portrait, see Mel Gordon, 'Hitler's Jewish Psychic', in: *Guilt and Pleasure* 3 (Summer 2006) 58–69. Later in 1933, Hanussen himself was killed, presumably by the SA.
4   'ein in Hannover sehr bekannter Gelehrter, über den in Hannover viel gesprochen wird, wird in diesem Jahr den Tod erleiden'; Lessing himself described Hanussen's prediction in the essay 'Mein Tod' ('My death') in the *Prager Tagblatt*, February 5th, 1933; the quotation is from this essay. Cfr. Marwedel, o.c., 342.
5   '[...] ich habe wohl zu bedenken, daß ich den Brüdern in Deutschland nicht schade, nicht den Genossen in Gefängnissen und Arbeitslagern'; *DusJ*, reprinted in: *Wmnm*, 217–240; there 218.

the National-Socialist regime by writing passionate articles that were read not only in Germany, but in several other European countries as well, and by lecturing on the political situation in Germany, and especially on the position of the German Jews. Because of these activities, National-Socialists threatened Lessing in his exile as well. In June 1933, several German language journals in Czechoslovakia published the story that a price of 80 000 *Reichsmark* was put on Lessing's head. Lessing responded, quite characteristically, by writing a satire entitled "Mein Kopf" ('My head'). In this satire – it was not published until 1983[6] –, Lessing professed that all through his life there was something the matter with his head:

> My God! The things I have had to hear about my head all through a long life. At school, it was said it was no head for studying. At university, it were muddle-headed. The colleagues said, it was headstrong. A critic wrote, it was no political head. Another one: no historical head. Yet others: my head lacked certain organs. The organ for metaphysics. For myth. For comedy. For mathematics. In short everything about my head was negative. I puzzled my head and never made any money. And now eighty thousand Reichsmark! And this good fortune others have with my head.[7]

Yet, despite this mockery, Lessing did indeed feel seriously threatened. He asked for, and was granted, protection by the Czech police. When Lessing left Marienbad to attend the Zionist Congress in Prague, he signed out to the police. However, when he returned prematurely to Marienbad on August 30 – the Zionist Congress lasted until September 4 –, Lessing failed to report to the Marienbad police.

Thus, Lessing's house in Marienbad, "Villa Edelweiß", was not watched by the police when he returned to the city on August 30. In the evening of that very day, about half past nine, an attempt on Lessing's life was made. – Police investigations later showed that Lessing's assaulters had been spying on him for some time, and did indeed know that he had returned to Marienbad,

---

6   Theodor Lessing, 'Mein Kopf', in: *Uni Hannover. Zeitschrift der Universität Hannover* 10 (1983) Heft 1, 29 *ff*; reprinted in: *BiS*, 69–71.

7   'Mein Gott! Was habe ich ein langes Leben über meinen Kopf hören müssen. Auf der Schule hieß es, er sei kein Lernkopf. Auf der Universität, er sei ein Wirrkopf. Die Kollegen sagten, er sei ein Querkopf. Ein Kritiker schrieb, er sei kein politischer Kopf. Ein anderer: Kein historischer Kopf. Wieder andere: Meinem Kopfe fehlten gewisse Organe. Das Organ für Metaphysik. Für den Mythos. Für das Komische. Für Mathematik. Kurz alles an meinem Kopf war negativ. Ich zerbrach mir den Kopf und verdiente nichts damit. Und nun Achtzigtausend Reichsmark! Und dies Glück haben andere mit meinem Kopf.' ; o.c., quoted from *BiS*, 70.

whereas the police did not. – Two assaulters had placed a ladder against the backside of "Villa Edelweiß", in between the two windows of Lessing's study. Standing on the ladder, both of them fired a shot, hitting Lessing in the head. His wife Ada, who some weeks after his escape from Germany had joined him in exile, found him, severely bleeding. Lessing was rushed to a local hospital, where some hours later he succumbed to his wounds.

The murder of Theodor Lessing prompted protests by the Czech labour movement against further toleration of National-Socialist groups in Czechoslovakia. Lessing was mourned for in articles in several European papers and journals.[8] But in his native Hanover, the National-Socialist *Niederdeutsche Zeitung* wrote in triumph: "Now this miserable spook too has been wiped out",[9] and the *Hannoversche Anzeiger* stated that Lessing had not assured himself a good reputation in Hanover.[10] On August 31, the novelist Thomas Mann (1875–1955) wrote in his diary: "News of the murder of Th. Lessing in Marienbad by National-Socialists".[11] The next day, he noted:

> No further news on Th. Lessing's end yet. The intended deterring effect will not hold off. Prague, Paris, Amsterdam may be safer than Marienbad or Basel, but Schwarzschild and the people from the Weltbühne will hardly feel their life is safe. I shrink at such an end, not because it is the end, but because it is so miserable and may be fitting for a Lessing, but not for me.[12]

– In July 1934, Mann, writing on the influence Jewish authors in his view had had on the anti-liberal turn in German politics, again wrote about Lessing's murder:

> The – otherwise really appalling Lessing, who was obtusely murdered, did write a book against the mind – why did one have to kill him. He

---

8   For an overview, see Jörg Wollenberg, 'Schönheit durch Bildung – Theodor Lessing als Bildungsreformer und Volkshochschulgründer', in: *BiS*, note 7, 195–196.
9   'Nun ist auch dieser unselige Spuk weggewischt'; quoted from Marwedel, o.c., 368.
10 Ibidem.
11 'Nachricht von der Ermordung Th. Lessings in Marienbad durch Nationalsozialisten'; Thomas Mann, *Tagebücher 1933–1934*, ed. by Peter de Mendelssohn (Frankfurt am Main 1977) 165.
12 'Über Th. Lessings Ende noch keine weiteren Nachrichten. Die beabsichtigte erschreckende Wirkung wird nicht ausbleiben. Prag, Paris, Amsterdam mögen sicherer sein als Marienbad oder Basel, aber Schwarzschild und die Leute der Weltbühne werden sich kaum ihres Lebens sicher fühlen. Mir graust vor einem solchen Ende, nicht weil es das Ende, sondern weil es so elend ist und einem Lessing anstehen mag, aber nicht mir.'; ibidem.

admittedly committed all kinds of weakly and pseudo-lyrical tactlessness and did call himself a socialist. But in the main, he shared the persuasions of his murderers.[13]

–. On September 2, at the first Nuremberg NSDAP Party rally following Hitler's takeover of power, Joseph Goebbels gave an address on "Rassenfrage und Weltpropaganda" ('The Racial Question and World Propaganda'). In this speech, Goebbels alluded to Lessing's murder:

> For a time, it was difficult to persuade the people of this, for public opinion was entirely in his hands. [*i.e.*, the hands of the Jew, HS]. He had ensured himself well in advance of the rule over the big press organs and enviously saw to it that his name was not mentioned, neither positively nor negatively, in public debates. There was no paper that had the character to back out of this anonymous influence, no party that had the courage to protest against it, no parliament in which a public statement about it was tolerated.
> On a Berlin stage run by the Jews, with the words "Away with the filth!" a steel helmet was swept into the dust heap. The Jew Gumbel called the dead of the war "those who fell on the field of dishonour." The Jew Lessing compared Hindenburg with the mass murderer Haarmann. [...]
> Is it surprising that the German Revolution also broke this spiritual yoke?[14]

---

13 'Der – übrigens recht widerwärtige Lessing, der stumpfsinniger Weise ermordet wurde, hatte ein Buch gegen den Geist geschrieben – warum mußte man den ermorden. Er hatte zwar allerlei weichliche und pseudo-lyrische Taktlosigkeiten begangen und nannte sich einen Sozialisten. In der Hauptsache aber war er einer Gesinnung mit seinen Mördern.'; idem, 474.

14 'Zwar war es zu gewissen Zeiten schwer, das dem Volke verständlich zu machen; denn die öffentliche Meinung lag ausschließlich in seiner Hand [*i.e.*, der Hand des Juden, HS]. Er hatte sich beizeiten die Herrschaft über die großen Presseorgane gesichert und wachte eifersüchtig darüber, das sein Name weder im Guten noch im Bösen in der öffentlichen Diskussion genannt wurde. Keine Zeitung, die den Charakter hatte, sich diesem anonymen Einfluß zu entziehen, keine Partei, die den Mut aufbrachte, dagegen Sturm zu laufen, kein Parlament, in dem ein offenes Wort darüber geduldet wurde.
Auf einer Berliner Bühne, die von Juden geleitet wurde, fegte man einen Stahlhelm mit den Worten: „Dreck, weg damit!" auf den Kehrichthaufen. Der Jude Gumbel nannte die Toten des Krieges „Auf dem Felde der Unehre Gefallenen". Der Jude Lessing verglich Hindenburg mit dem Massenmörder Haarmann [...]
Ist es da verwunderlich, daß die deutsche Revolution auch eine Abschüttelung dieses geistigen Jochs mit sich brachte?'; Joseph Goebbels, 'Rassenfrage und Weltpropaganda', in: Joseph Goebbels, *Signale der neuen Zeit. 25 Ausgewählte Reden* (Munich 1934) 212–213.

Even the left-wing publicist Kurt Hiller (1885–1972), who was much more sympathetic towards Lessing's ideas, contended that Lessing himself had helped to shape the bullet that eventually killed him.[15]

The much-discussed murder of Theodor Lessing made a cruel end to his highly eventful life. In 1932, Theodor Lessing himself – then sixty years old, living in his birthplace Hanover, where he was professor in the philosophy of science at the *Technische Hochschule* ('University of Technology') – had started to describe this life in his memoirs. It was his third attempt to do so: the results of both earlier attempts did not satisfy the author, and he destroyed almost a thousand of pages of manuscripts.[16] This third attempt, however, proved to be more of a success: Lessing did complete the first part of his autobiography, in which he described his youth, although he does insert some descriptions of later events. It was posthumously published as *Einmal und nie wieder* in 1935.

In the introductory pages of this autobiography Lessing expresses his scepticism with regard to historical writing:

> Anyone who has ever tried to put to paper the most important events of his days, has to discover with amazement how uncertain, yes how doubtful all history and biography is that not only calls forth from the vaults what is past according to its various states and situations, but also gives a new sound to weather-beaten words, yes even seems to know whether the moon shone over those past words or the sun. [...][17]

Yet in between the abortive attempts to write an autobiography and the completion of *Einmal und nie wieder*, Lessing published several autobiographical essays. In one of them, "Gerichtstag über mich selbst" ('Judgment Day over Myself'), written on request of the journal *Junge Menschen* and published in 1925, Lessing pointed at the divergence between the reputation he had in the Germany of his days and his self-image:

> Just that I am not, what the public opinion judges me as: a fighting nature, polemic, practical man, activist. It always occurred to me, to take all the

---

15 Kurt Hiller, 'Der Denker im Spiegel', in: Kurt Hiller, *Köpfe und Tröpfe. Profile aus ein Vierteljahrhundert* (Hamburg 1950) 305; this essay was first published in *Die neue Weltbühne* in 1936.
16 Theodor Lessing, 'Ein Mensch schreibt Erinnerungen', in: *Die Kritik* 2 (1934), nr. 10; reprinted in: *IFEG*, 411–414.
17 'Wer je den Versuch gemacht hat, die wichtigsten Ereignisse seiner Tage zu Papier zu bringen, der muß mit Verwunderung entdecken, wie ungewiß, ja wie zweifelhaft alle Historik und Biographik ist, die nicht nur das Vergangene nach Lagen und Zuständen aus den Grüften hervorruft, sondern auch verwehrte Worte neu tönen macht, ja sogar zu wissen scheint, ob zu jenen Worten von einst der Mond leuchtete oder die Sonne [...]'; *Eunw*, 12.

human ants' existence, and my own too, not very seriously and only with humour. Every kind of watching and knowing sounded more familiar to my nature than practice, politics, dialectics, pathos or polemics. Now how is it possible that the public delusion looks so differently?[18]

Nevertheless, the image of Lessing as a fighting nature, polemic and activist prevails in the literature written on the man and his ideas, even some seventy-five years after his death; this induced the American historian Lawrence Baron to conclude that "Theodor Lessing [...] is remembered more for the political controversies surrounding his career than for his philosophy".[19]

All through his life, Lessing indeed was mixed up with all kinds of scandals and conflicts. The first of these was when he – then in his early twenties – was concerned in the scandal in connection with the play *Das Liebeskonzil* ('The Council of Love'; 1894) by the German playwright Oskar Panizza (1853–1921). This play is a radical satire, and extremely critical of the catholic church. It describes how in 1495 syphilis was introduced in the world by the devil, executing an order from God himself, who wanted to punish humanity, and especially Pope Alexander VI and his retinue in the Vatican, for its loose manners and sexual misbehaviour. Because of it, Panizza – charged with blasphemy – was sentenced to a term of imprisonment of one year. Although he had not read the play, Lessing responded to this sentence by writing a pamphlet entitled *Der Fall Panizza. Eine kritische Betrachtung über 'Gotteslasterung' und künstlerische Dinge vor Schwurgerichten* ('The Panizza case. A critical reflection of 'blasphemy' and artistic matters before courts with a jury'). In this pamphlet, he argued that "the public should, however, at long last learn from these processes that literary and artistic counts and offences in general are not suitable

---

18   'Gerade das bin ich nicht, als was die Öffentlichkeit mich beurteilt: Kämpfernatur, Polemiker, Praktiker, Aktivist. Immer lag es mir nahe, das ganze menschliche Ameisendasein und auch das eigene nie so ganz ernst und nur mit Humor zu nehmen. Jede Art Schauen und Wissen klang meinem Wesen vertrauter entgegen als Praktik, Politik, Dialektik, Pathos oder Polemik. Wie nun ist es möglich, daß das öffentliche Wahnbild so anders aussieht?'; Theodor Lessing, 'Gerichtstag über mich selbst', in: *Junge Menschen* 6 (1925), Heft 10, 238–244; reprinted in: *BiS*, 57–68; there 62. In 1926, Lessing published a shorter essay entitled 'Gerichtstag über mich selbst' as well in the *Prager Tagblatt*, on June 13 1926; reprinted in: *Eunw*, 316–322.
19   Lawrence Baron, 'Discipleship and Dissent: Theodor Lessing and Edmund Husserl', *Proceedings of the American Philosophical Society* 127 (1983) no. 1, 32.

to public prosecution".[20] After the publication of this pamphlet, the police searched Lessing's house; several of his manuscripts were confiscated, and for some time the police kept a close watch on him.

In 1910, Lessing was in the centre of yet another scandal. In his satire 'Samuel zieht die Bilanz' ('Samuel draws up the balance'), he poked fun at the literary critic Samuel Lublinski (1868–1910) because of his book *Bilanz der Moderne* ('Balance of the Modern'; 1904). Lublinski was defended by no one less than Thomas Mann in his 'Der Doktor Lessing'[21] – hence Mann's description of Lessing as 'really appalling' quoted above –, because Lublinski was the first critic to praise Mann's *Buddenbrooks* (1901) as a masterpiece. Thereupon followed a polemic between Lessing and Mann[22] – which gave the Mann-scholar Hans Wysling reason to conclude that nowadays Lessing would be largely unknown, had he not managed to enter Thomas Mann's biography through this very affair.[23]

In August 1914, at the outbreak of the First World War, Theodor Lessing did not share in the enthusiasm with which it was greeted by the vast majority of German intellectuals. On the contrary: he tried to gather a group of likeminded thinkers to draw up a statement in protest against the war, but to no effect. Even some friends whom he had always seen as kindred spirits, supported the war with unqualified enthusiasm. But the longer the war lasted, the quicker this enthusiasm died out. Nevertheless, Lessing's critical attitude during the first months of the war made him into a controversial, if not suspect figure in the eyes of right-wing politicians and of the right-wing press, during the war but no less afterwards: he allegedly lacked patriotism.[24]

In 1924, Lessing again made the headlines. As a reporter, from December 4th till December 19th he followed the trial of the homosexual sex murderer

---

20 'das Publikum aber sollte aus solchen Prozessen endlich lernen, das literarische und künstlerische Klagepunkten und Vergehen überhaupt für staatliche Gerichtsbarkeit ungeeignet sind'. Theodor Lessing, *Der Fall Panizza. Eine kritische Betrachtung über 'Gotteslasterung' und künstlerische Dinge vor Schwurgerichten* (München 1895) 35.
21 Thomas Mann, 'Der Doktor Lessing, followed by Berichtigungen, followed by An die Redaktion der „Staatsbürgerzeitung"', in: Thomas Mann, *Gesammelte Werken in Zwölf Bänden*, ed. by Hans Bürgin, vol. 11. *Reden und Aufsätze* 3 (s.l. [Frankfurt a.M.] 1960) 719–731.
22 The polemic, including Mann's contributions to it, is documented in Theodor Lessing, *Samuel zieht die Bilanz und Tomi melkt die Moralkuh oder Zweier Könige Sturze. Eine Warnung für Deutsche, Satiren zu schreiben* (Hannover 1910); reprinted in *Th-STM*.
23 Hans Wysling, '„Ein Elender". Zu einem Novellenplan Thomas Manns', *Quellenkritische Studien zum Werk Thomas Manns*, ed. by P. Scherrer and H. Wysling (Bern and Munich 1967) 110. See below, chapter 2, for a more detailed description.
24 See below, chapter 3, for a more detailed description.

Fritz Haarmann (1879–1925), who between 1918 and 1924 killed more than twenty boys in Hanover. Haarmann was eventually sentenced to death. Lessing strongly criticized the judicial process, in which the police tried to conceal it had used Haarmann as an informant. Because of his criticisms, expressed in a series of articles, mainly published in the *Prager Tagblatt*,[25] which was eventually compiled in the book *Haarmann*,[26] the judge denied Lessing access to the court – in his view Lessing lacked a sense for objectivity. In his book, Lessing argues that society as a whole shared responsibility for Haarmann's behaviour.

A few months later, on April 25 1925, on the eve of the presidential elections in Germany, Lessing published a short satirical masterpiece "Hindenburg" in the *Prager Tagblatt*, a character study of the presidential candidate, field marshal Paul von Hindenburg (1847–1934). Hindenburg, the former Chief of the General Staff of the German Army, had retired from public life in 1919, but returned when he was asked to stand for the presidency.

Hindenburg accepted, as he believed he was the only one who could "save" Germany, even if he was not really interested in holding a public office. Lessing described Hindenburg as someone who, as a military man, was used to follow orders, and not at all suited to lead. He concluded his essay with the statement – the most often quoted sentences of his entire *oeuvre*! – that

> According to Plato, philosophers should be the rulers of peoples. With Hindenburg, a philosopher would just not be ascending the throne. Only a representative symbol, a question mark, a zero. One can say: "Better a zero than a Nero". Unfortunately history shows that behind a zero always a future Nero is hidden.[27]

A partial reprint of Lessing's article, mixed with comments by the editor, was published in the local newspaper *Hannoversche Kurier* on May 8, the very day Hindenburg's victory in the elections was celebrated in Hanover where both the field marshal and Lessing lived. This gave rise to furious reactions, especially from right wing students' organisations. The windows of Lessing's house were smashed, he and his family were physically threatened, and his lectures

---

25   Lessing was a regular contributor to the *Prager Tagblatt*. At the time, it was considered to be one of the best newspapers in German language.
26   Theodor Lessing, *Haarmann. Die Geschichte einer Werwolfs* (Berlin 1925).
27   'Nach Plato sollen die Philosophen Führer der Völker sein. Ein Philosoph würde mit Hindenburg nun eben nicht den Thronstuhl besteigen. Nur ein repräsentatives Symbol, ein Fragezeichen, ein Zero. Man kann sagen: 'Besser ein Zero als ein Nero'. Leider zeigt die Geschichte, daß hinter einem Zero immer ein künftiger Nero verborgen steht'; Theodor Lessing, ' Hindenburg', in: *Prager Tagblatt*, 25.4.1925; reprinted in: IFEG, 69.

were disturbed. The students formed a so-called "Kampfausschuss gegen Lessing" ('Committee to fight Lessing'), and even threatened to leave the *Technische Hochschule* and to continue their studies in Braunschweig if Lessing was not sacked. Both local authorities and dignitaries at the *Technische Hochschule* feared for such a massive departure of students: it would do great harm to the local economy and to the *Technische Hochschule* itself. The protesting students were financially supported by the extremely right wing politician and businessman Alfred Hugenberg (1865–1951), who was to be a member of Adolf Hitler's first cabinet in 1933 but was already forced to resign in June of that very same year. Lessing eventually got support from the civil authorities, if only reluctantly. The conflict over this article, which drew attention from newspapers all over Germany and even abroad, dragged itself along for over a year. In the end, the parties involved compromised. Lessing was not officially sacked, but had to promise not to lecture anymore; in exchange for this promise, he was granted a meagre scholarship, to enable him to do research in the philosophy of culture.

This research kept him occupied for the following years. Moreover, he continued his comments on the political developments of his time, by contributing regularly to several newspapers. In these years, Lessing was very critical of the rising National-Socialism. He wrote, for example, about Hitler as "the man, who is called 'the man with the drum' by 'world history', like at one time it called Luther 'the man with the battle-axe'. For the believers in the 'Third Reich', Adolf Hitler is already a myth. For the unbelieving, however, 'half fool, half comedian, and complete megalomaniac'".[28] He kept writing articles like this one even after he went into exile in Marienbad. Indeed, in his exile he became more and more preoccupied with warning against Hitler and National-Socialism. A characteristic example is the following complaint, in his essay "Vermächtnis an Deutschland" ('Bequest to Germany'), which was published in the Czech pacifist journal *Die Wahrheit* ('Truth') that supported German exiles:

> Everyone who does not say yes to the current situation of the world, who does not see in the accidental changes of power of the so-called world history commands of God and splendid ideals, yes, in the end everyone

---

28　'der Mann, den die "Weltgeschichte" den "Mann mit der Trummel" genannt hat, wie sie einst Luther nannte "der Mann mit der Streitaxte". Adolf Hitler ist für die Gläubigen des "Dritten Reiches" schon Mythos geworden. Für die Ungläubigen aber "halb Dummkopf, halb Komödiant, und gänzlich ein Gernegroß"'; Theodor Lessing, 'Wie es kommen wird', in: *General-Anzeiger für Dortmund*, 19.6.1932; reprinted in: IFEG, 109.

who criticises in general, who thinks and expresses his thoughts, is an enemy of the state and a betrayer of this time and its ideas.[29]

In March, April and May 1933, Lessing lectured on the social and political situation of the Jews in Germany. The text of this lecture was published as *Deutschland und seine Juden*;[30] it was the last of Lessing's publications to appear during his lifetime. In this lecture, Lessing was, again, highly critical of the National-Socialist government of Germany: he was very outspoken in his rejection of its racist policy. Typical examples are the following statements:

> But the way in which one solves questions of blood and race in Germany today, is as clumsy as it is stupid, as presumptuous as vile. It seems as if the Germans have no other dignity left but the dignity that they are not Jews.[31]
>
> But what is happening in Germany today – a cruelty that exceeds all atrocities of the Middle Ages! – , is a false and treacherous game, through which Germans and Jews alike are humiliated and demoralised. I am willing to assume that the authorities who want to talk the German people into this hate, are quite honest, yes, full of a holy love of their country. Many an outsider sees in them a troop of desperados, gamblers, lansquenets, vehmic murderers, whereas perhaps only a poor education, stupidity, indolence, fanaticism, mental narrow-mindedness can explain Germany's rage.[32]

---

29 'Jeder, der nicht zum gegenwärtigen Weltzustand ja sagt, der nicht in den Machtwechselzufällen sogenannter Weltgeschichte Fügungen Gottes und herrliche Ideale sieht, ja, schließlich jeder, der überhaupt kritisiert, der denkt und seine Gedanken äußert, ist ein Staatsfeind und Verräter an der Zeit und ihre Ideen.'; Theodor Lessing, 'Vermächtnis an Deutschland', in: *Die Wahrheit* (1933) Heft 19; reprinted in: *WeU*, 367–372; and in: *BiS*, 75–80; there 77.

30 Theodor Lessing, *Deutschland und seine Juden* (Prag - Karlin 1933), reprinted in: *Wmnm*, 217–240.

31 'Aber wie man heute in Deutschland die Blut- und Rassenfragen löst, das ist ebenso stümperhaft wie dumm, ebenso selbstüberheblich wie niederträchtig. Es scheint so, daß die Deutschen keine andere Würde mehr hätten, als die Würde, daß sie eben keine Juden sind.'; o.c., 227.

32 'Aber was heute in Deutschland vor sich geht – eine Grausamkeit, die alle Greuel des Mittelalters überbietet!-, das ist ein falsches, betrügerisches Spiel, wodurch Deutsche und Juden in gleicher Weise erniedrigt und entsittlicht werden. Ich will annehemen, daß die Gewalthaber, welche diesen Haß dem deutschen Volke einreden wollen, guten Glaubens sind, ja erfüllt, von einer heiligen Vaterlandsliebe. Manch Außenstehender sieht in ihnen eine Horde Desperados, Hazardspieler, Landsknechte, Femmemörder, wo doch vielleicht nur aus Halbbildung, Dumpfheit, Herzensträgheit, Veranntheit, geistiger Borniertheit Deutschlands Raserei erklärt werden kann.'; o.c., 228.

Similarly pronounced condemnations of the National-Socialist government, and especially of its persecution of the Jews, by an author who was well-known in Germany during the Weimar republic certainly may have provoked the National-Socialist authorities in having Lessing murdered. That Lessing indeed was well-known during the Weimar republic may for instance be inferred from the fact that he was, for example, invited to contribute to the German edition of the controversial book *La maîtresse légitime* by the French author Georges Anquetil. Included in the German edition of this book were the answers to a questionnaire on the subject of marriage and polygamy that was sent out by the editor, with the intention of obtaining "a cross section of the view of the spiritual Germany with regard to this question".[33] Lessing apparently was that well-known that his opinion was considered to be part of the vision of the 'spiritual Germany' on the subject. Likewise, he was invited to share his opinions on other social or political matters, such as what he thought about Mussolini – in a supplement to the Christmas edition of the *Prager Tagblatt* in 1925, under the heading "Bedeutende Zeitgenossen über Mussolini",[34] what annoyed him,[35] the legal ban on homosexuality,[36] the position of intellectuals,[37] and conservative tendencies within social democracy.[38] Only public figures with a certain repute were invited to give their views on these subjects.

2   Historiography

In 1971, the German historian of literature Hans Mayer observed that a suspicious silence surrounded Lessing.[39] At the time, Mayer was certainly right:

---

33   'einen Querschnitt der Ansicht des geistigen Deutschlands zu dieser Frage'; Georges Anquetil, *Ehen zu Dritt. Das Recht auf die Geliebte*, translated and edited by L. Steinfeld (Berlin 1928) 229.

34   Theodor Lessing, 'Antwort auf die Rundfrage: Wie Sie Mussolini sehen', in: *Prager Tagblatt*, 25.12.1925.

35   Theodor Lessing, 'Worüber ich mich immer wieder ärgere. Antwort auf eine Enquête', in: *Das Stachelschwein* 2 (1925), Heft 14, 15–22; reprinted in: *IFEG*, 145–154.

36   Theodor Lessing, '§ 297: Gewerbsmäßige Unzucht. Antwort auf eine Rundfrage', in: *§ 297: 'Unzucht zwischen Männern'? Ein Beitrag zur Strafgesetzreform*, ed. by R. Linsert (Berlin 1929); reprinted in: Theodor Lessing, *Haarmann. Die Geschichte einer Werwolfs und andere Gerichtsreportagen*, ed. by Rainer Marwedel (Frankfurt a.M. 1989).

37   Theodor Lessing, 'Antwort auf die Rundfrage: 'Die Intellektuellen haben das Wort'', in: *Die Linkskurve*, September 1930; reprinted in: *WeU*, 346–347; and in: *Wmnm*, 107–108.

38   Theodor Lessing, 'Konservative Tendenzen in der Sozialdemokratie? Eine Rundfrage', in: *Mitteilungsblatt des sozialdemokratischen Intellektuellenbundes*, Juli 1930, Heft 5, 9–13; reprinted in: *IFEG*, 96–102; and in: *Wmnm*, 109–115.

39   Hans Mayer, 'Berichte über ein politisches Trauma', in: Hans Mayer, *Der Repräsentant und der Märtyrer. Konstellationen der Literatur* (Frankfurt a.M. 1971) 96.

not much was written on Lessing, and what was written reflected the image sketched above – the image of someone who was well-known, not in the least because he was always involved in conflicts and scandals. This very same image is dominant in the articles written in remembrance of Lessing – of which quite a number exists. The emphasis time and again is on Lessing's biography, on the controversies surrounding him.

A first important impetus to more in-depth inquiry in both Lessing's biography and his ideas was given by Ekkehard Hieronimus (1926–1998), a pastor in the Evangelical Lutheran State Church of Hanover, with his study *Theodor Lessing, Otto Meyerhof, Leonard Nelson. Bedeutende Juden in Niedersachsen* ('Theodor Lessing, Otto Meyerhof, Leonard Nelson. Important Jews in Lower Saxony'),[40] published in 1964. In this study itself, the emphasis is not so much on Lessing's ideas, but on his life. The same holds for the complementing study that Hieronimus published in 1972, on occasion of the hundredth birthday of Lessing, with the title *Theodor Lessing. Eine Lebensskizze* ('Theodor Lessing. A Sketch of his Life').[41] This sketch, which was published by the city of Hanover, contains a bibliography of Lessing's writings by Luitger Dietze. This bibliography forms an important first step towards a complete inventory of Lessing's writings, but since its publication many more essays and articles have been rediscovered. In between both publications by Hieronimus, in 1970, Hans Eggert Schröder (1905–1985) published his book *Theodor Lessing's autobiografischen Schriften. Ein Kommentar* ('Theodor Lessing's Autobiographical Writings. A Comment').[42] Schröder, the biographer of the German philosopher and psychologist Ludwig Klages (1872–1956), was at the time caretaker of Klages' legacy. His book, written as a response to the republication of Lessing's autobiography *Einmal und nie wieder* in 1969,[43] is a not very tidy effort to clear Klages – during their youth Lessing's very best friend – from every responsibility for the end of their friendship, and especially from charges of anti-Semitism in his behaviour towards Lessing. In 1978, Herbert Poetzl promoted on his dissertation *Confrontation with Modernity: Theodor Lessing's Critique of German Culture*.[44] Poetzl discusses both Lessing's life and his ideas. He describes Lessing as "an anti-modernist critic of German culture" and

---

40　Ekkehard Hieronimus, *Theodor Lessing, Otto Meyerhof, Leonard Nelson. Bedeutende Juden in Niedersachsen* (Hanover 1964).
41　Ekkehard Hieronimus, *Theodor Lessing. Eine Lebensskizze* (Hanover 1972).
42　Hans Eggert Schröder, *Theodor Lessing's autobiografischen Schriften. Ein Kommentar* (Bonn 1970).
43　*Eunw.*
44　Herbert Poetzl, *Confrontation with Modernity: Theodor Lessing's Critique of German Culture* (unpublished Ph.D.-thesis, University of Massachusetts 1978).

"a frustrated late-Romantic" – qualifications that are highly disputable.[45] The study of Lessing's biography found in 1987 its culmination in the monograph *Theodor Lessing 1872–1933. Eine Biographie* by Rainer Marwedel.[46] Marwedel offers a thorough and lengthy discussion of the political and social background of Lessing's life and work. In this respect, the book is excellent. Marwedel does, however, not pay much attention to Lessing's philosophical ideas and views. As one reviewer put it: "For the most important works of Lessing, his biographer often has hardly a page of comment as regards content to spare".[47] Lessing's youth, and especially his friendship with Ludwig Klages, was studied in depth by Elke-Vera Kotowski in her book *Feindliche Dioskuren* ('Hostile Dioscuri');[48] her study is relevant for understanding the genesis of Lessing's ideas as well. In 2009, Kotowski published a short, very fine, introductory portrait of Lessing: *Theodor Lessing (1872–1933): Philosoph - Feuilletonist – Volksbildner* ('Theodor Lessing (1872–1933): Philosopher-Columnist-Popular Educator').[49]

One of the few who – already when Lessing still was alive: in 1930 – seriously paid attention to Lessing's ideas was the German philosopher Wolf Goetze, in his dissertation *Die Gegensätzlichkeit der Geschichtsphilosophie Oswald Spenglers und Theodor Lessing* ('The Contrast between the Philosophy of History of Oswald Spengler and Theodor Lessing').[50] This comparison between Spengler and Lessing is generally considered as an interesting and reliable study, but Goetze only discusses Lessing's most well-known books. A discussion of his less well-known books and articles can add, however, to the understanding of Lessing's ideas. Shortly after Lessing's death, a former student of his, Herbert L. Kaufmann who played an important part in efforts to save Lessing's legacy from destruction by the National-Socialists by smuggling a box with miscellaneous paper work to France,[51] published his dissertation *Essai sur l'anti-progressisme et ses origines dans la philosophie allemande moderne* ('Essay on

---

45 E.g., o.c., vii.
46 Rainer Marwedel, *o.c.*.
47 'Für die wichtigsten Arbeiten Lessings hat sein Biograph manchmal kaum eine Seite inhaltsbezogenen Kommentars übrig [...]'; Ulrich Horstmann, 'Im Irrsinnsurwald der Geschichte. Dilettant, Polemiker, Feuilletonist: R. Marwedel legt die Biographie Theodor Lessings vor', in: *Die Welt*, Samstag 13-6-1987, nr. 135, 5.
48 Elke-Vera Kotowski, *Feindliche Dioskuren. Theodor Lessing und Ludwig Klages: Das Scheitern einer Jugendfreundschaft* (Berlin 2000).
49 Elke-Vera Kotowski, *Theodor Lessing (1872–1933): Philosoph - Feuilletonist – Volksbildner* (Berlin 2009).
50 Leipzig 1930.
51 Cfr. Elke-Vera Kotowski et.al., *"Ich warf eine einsame Flaschenpost in das unermessliche Dunkel". Theodor Lessing 1872–1933* (Hildesheim 2008) 197.

anti-progressivism and its origins in modern German philosophy'),[52] that was dedicated to the memory of Theodor Lessing. Kaufman tries to understand Lessing's philosophical ideas from the context of contemporary developments within the tradition of the so-called *Lebensphilosophie* ('philosophy of life'). In 1961 yet another dissertation on Lessing's philosophy was published: *Geschichtsphilosophie und Kulturkritik Theodor Lessings* ('Theodor Lessing's philosophy of history and criticism of culture')[53] by Hans Dieter Hüsgen. Hüsgen describes Lessing as a "a mystic-romantic visionary" and "a complete hymnographer of ecstasy"[54] – a description that is, to say the least, questionable. Manfred Küchler made a next contribution to the literature on Lessing, in his *Die literarische und philosophische Entwicklung Theodor Lessings* ('Theodor Lessing's literary and philosophical development').[55] Küchler discusses, in chronological order, the literary and the philosophical books Lessing wrote – he does not discuss Lessing's numerous essays and articles. Nevertheless, Küchler does give a short but handy overview of Lessing's ideas. The political aspects of Lessing's philosophy are discussed in *Theodor Lessing – Politische Aspekte seiner Philosophie und Publizistik in der Zeit der Weimarer Republik 1918–1933* ('Theodor Lessing – Political Aspects of his Philosophy and Publications during the Era of the Weimar Republic 1918–1933') by Martin Rethmeier.[56] In this excellent study from 1984 that regrettably remained unpublished, the author focuses on the political aspects of Lessing's publications, but, moreover, he discusses Lessing's philosophical ideas and their background as well. Two years later, Peter Böhm's *Theodor Lessings Versuch einer erkenntnistheoretischen Grundlegung von Welt. Ein kritischer Beitrag zur Aporetik der Lebensphilosophie* ('Theodor Lessing's Attempt of an Epistemological Basis of the World. A Critical Contribution to the Aporia of the Philosophy of Life') [57] was published. In this rather inaccessibly written study, Böhm discusses Lessing's ideas on epistemology, which the latter developed during the first decade of the twentieth century. In the aftermath of the publication of Marwedel's biography of Lessing, several studies appeared that mainly concentrated on one aspect of his thinking. The first of these was *Kulturerkenntnis und Kulturbewertung bei*

---

52   Diss. Sorbonne, Paris 1936.
53   Diss. Mainz 1961.
54   'mystisch-romantischen Visionär' and a 'totalen Hymniker des Rausches'; o.c., 28.
55   Staatsexamensarbeit Technische Hochschule Hannover, Hanover 1976. Mr. Küchler at my request kindly sent me a copy of his *Staatsexamensarbeit* and a number of texts, for which I greatly thank him.
56   Schriftliche Hausarbeit RWTH, Aachen 1984. Mr. Rethmeier at my request kindly sent me a copy of his *Hausarbeit*, for which I greatly thank him.
57   Amsterdam 1986.

Theodor Lessing ('Knowledge and Judgment of Culture with Theodor Lessing') by Bernward Baule,[58] a fine study of Lessing's ideas on culture and the study of culture. Maja I. Siegrist wrote a subsequent study, *Theodor Lessing – Die entropische Philosophie. Freilegung und Rekonstruktion eines verdrängten Denkers* ('The Entropic Philosophy. Exposition and Reconstruction of a Repressed Thinker'),[59] a valuable attempt to reconstruct Lessing's philosophical system that he himself never published as such but that underlies next to all of his philosophical publications. An interesting study of Lessing's views on the – and his! – Jewish identity was published by Jochen Hartwig: *'Sei was immer du bist'. Theodor Lessings wendungsvolle Identitätsbildung als Deutscher und Jude* ('Be Whoever You Are. Theodor Lessing's Changing Forming of Identity as German and Jew').[60] In 2004, Uwe Kemmler published *Not und Notwendigkeit. Der Primat der Ethik in der Philosophie Theodor Lessings* ('Need and Necessity. The Primacy of Ethics in Theodor Lessing's Philosophy'),[61] a most interesting study that underlines the pivotal place of ethics within Lessing´s philosophy. In the same year, Johannes Henrich published a study, in which he compared the philosophical ideas of Theodor Lessing with those of Friedrich Nietzsche, who has obviously profoundly inspired him.[62] Apart from these books, numerous articles on Lessing were published in all kinds of journals.

The increasing interest in Lessing's biography and ideas does not only show from the growing number of studies dedicated to his life and thought, but also from the fact that he was the subject of three exhibitions. In 1995, on occasion of the seventy-fifth anniversary of the *Volkshochschule Hannover*, the invaluable contributions Ada and Theodor Lessing made to this institution were celebrated in the exhibition *Wissen ist Macht, Bildung ist Schönheit. Ada & Theodor Lessing und die Volkshochschule Hannover.*[63] In 1920, Ada and Theodor Lessing founded this *Volkshochschule*; Ada Lessing was its managing director until 1933, when the new, National-Socialist authorities had her sacked.[64] Theodor Lessing was for many years one of the principal teachers

---

58 Hildesheim 1992.
59 Bern 1995.
60 Oldenburg 1999.
61 Frankfurt a.M. 2004.
62 Johannes Henrich, *Friedrich Nietzsche und Theodor Lessing. Ein Vergleich* (Marburg 2004).
63 Cfr. the catalogue accompanying the exhibition: *Wissen ist Macht, Bildung ist Schönheit. Ada & Theodor Lessing und die Volkshochschule Hannover.* Katalog zur Ausstellung des Stadtarchivs zum 75 jährigen Bestehen der VHS. 26.1. – 4.3.1995 in der VHS Hannover (Hannover 1995).
64 After the Second World War, she vainly tried to get her job back; see Jörg Wollenberg, 'Ada und Theodor Lessing: Rückkehr unerwünscht', in: *Sozial. Geschichte* 21 (2006) 52–66.

at the *Volkshochschule Hannover*, lecturing on a variety of subjects. In 2005, another exhibition dealt with the connections between Albert Einstein and Theodor Lessing, documenting their struggle against National-Socialism, their short but direct acquaintance in exile, and the attempts by Lessing, and after he was murdered, by his widow Ada, to seek Einstein's help in their efforts to build a new life in exile after their escape from Germany.[65] A third exhibition, in 2008, supervised by Elke-Vera Kotowski, recalling the murder of Lessing seventy-five years previously, tried to give an overview of both Lessing's life and thought; as such, it is an excellent introduction to Theodor Lessing.[66] It was organised in the *Volkshochschule Hannover* that nowadays is called the *Ada-und-Theodor-Lessing-Volkshochschule*.

Five years before, in 2003, Elke-Vera Kotowski was instrumental in organising a conference on the life and thought of Theodor Lessing, seventy years after his murder. This conference was not only attended by academics studying the man and his writings, but by some descendants of his as well. The proceedings of this conference were published under the title *"Sinngebung des Sinnlosen"*.[67]

Finally, the growing interest in Lessing shows from the reissue of several of his books over the last three decades, for instance *Die verfluchte Kultur. Gedanken über den Gegensatz von Leben und Geist* (1981); *Geschichte als Sinngebung des Sinnlosen* (1983); *Der jüdische Selbsthaß* (1984); *Blumen* (2004); and *Meine Tiere* (2004). Two anthologies with writings by Lessing were published, *Ich warf eine Flaschenpost ins Eismeer der Geschichte. Essays und Feuilletons*, edited by Rainer Marwedel 1986) and *Wortmeldungen eines Unerschrockenen. Publizistik aus drei Jahrzehnten*, edited by Hans Stern 1987).[68] In both anthologies, some essays were included that are hard to find otherwise. In addition, the German publisher Donat Verlag started a series of Lessing's *Ausgewählte Schriften*, three volumes of which have been published thus far.[69] Lastly, in the collection *Nachtkritiken* (2006),[70] Rainer Marwedel gathered the reviews Lessing wrote in 1906 and 1907 as a theatre critic for the *Göttinger Zeitung*, with some other

---

65   Cfr. the catalogue accompanying the exhibition: Wolf D. Mechler, *Albert Einstein und Theodor Lessing: Parallelen. Berührungen. Begleitband zur Ausstellung des Historischen Museums Hannover* (Hannover 2005).
66   Cfr. the catalogue accompanying the exhibition: Elke-Vera Kotowski et.al., *"Ich warf eine einsame Flaschenpost in das unermessliche Dunkel". Theodor Lessing 1872–1933* (Hildesheim 2008).
67   Elke-Vera Kotowski (ed.), *"Sinngebung des Sinnlosen". Zum Leben und Werk des Kulturkritikers Theodor Lessing (1872–1933)* (Hildesheim 2006).
68   IFEG, and *WeU*.
69   *BiS*; *Wmnm*; and *Th-STM*.
70   Theodor Lessing, *Nachtkritiken. Kleine Schriften 1906–1907*, ed. by Rainer Marwedel (Göttingen 2006).

short writings from the same period. At the time, Lessing was pursuing further academic studies at Göttingen university, and had a sideline job as theatre critic with this paper. His interest in the theatre did not stop with this job: he wrote two books on the subject, *Theater-Seele* (1907) and *Der fröhliche Eselsquell* (1914), and in later years as well occasionally published on the theatre.

In conclusion, one could say that over the last twenty-five years the interest in the life and thought of Theodor Lessing has steadily increased. As a result, serious attention has been paid to specific aspects of Lessing's philosophy – notably his philosophy of history by Goetze and Huesgen, his ideas on epistemology by Böhm, his view of culture by Baule, the underlying philosophical system of his publications by Siegrist, and the central place of ethics in his thinking by Kemmler. In spite of that, the conclusion still remains justified that as a thinker Lessing has been neglected. For the controversies surrounding him have all too often distracted the attention from his thinking. As a result - as for instance put forward by Böhm - Lessing's philosophy did not yet get the attention it deserves.[71] For all that, several authors have pointed out that some of Lessing's ideas still have topical value. The German philosopher Peter Sloterdijk, for example, claims in his *Kritik der zynischen Vernunft* (1983) that Lessing laid the foundations of an "ecological-philosophical critique of the Western predatory industry".[72] One could also refer to certain similarities between Lessing's ideas and those of the French anthropologist and philosopher Claude Lévi-Strauss (1908–2009). For they both share an aversion for the horrors of history and time that destroyed an idealised state of nature – for Lessing Asia, for Lévi-Strauss the America's of the Indians. This shared aversion should be seen as a radical critique of the, according to both men destructive, influences of European civilization on the world outside Europe. Moreover, Herbert Poetzl points out similarities between Lessing's philosophy of history and the ideas of the well-known American philosopher of history Hayden White, especially with regard to the attention paid by both of them to the "poetics of history".[73]

3 Approach and Aims

From this overview of the literature on Lessing one may infer that there are several reasons that justify another inquiry into his philosophy. First of all,

---

71 Böhm, o.c., 7.
72 'ökologisch-philosophische Kritik der westlichen Raubindustrie'; Peter Sloterdijk, *Kritik der zynischen Vernunft* (Frankfurt a.M. 1983) vol. 2, 641.
73 Poetzl, o.c., 168.

this subject until now did not get the attention it deserves, despite the suggestion made by several authors that some of Lessing's ideas do still have topical value. In the second place, one can observe remarkable contradictions in existing interpretations of Lessing's ideas. Huesgen and Poetzl, for example, emphasize the alleged irrationalism in Lessing's philosophy, and Hans Mayer characterizes him as a thinker of the counter-Enlightenment,[74] whereas Marwedel strongly denies that even a hint of irrationalism can be found in his philosophy. Marwedel claims that Lessing "lived a philosophy of practical reason and looked for the effectiveness of his ideas in the light of public controversy".[75] Furthermore, the reception of Lessing's ideas thus far has been limited: not all aspects of his philosophy have been discussed, nor has there been an in-depth discussion of the aspects of his philosophy to which attention has been paid. Finally, there is far more evidence available for a study of Lessing's philosophy than was used by most authors on the subject. A number of Lessing's essays, articles and serials shed light on the ideas he expressed in his books, but these were only sparingly used for this purpose. The same holds for his legacy.

In this study, I will concentrate on Lessing's philosophy of history. I do agree with Baule that Lessing's philosophy of history got more attention than other aspects of his philosophy, but I do not think this means that Lessing's philosophy of history has been amply discussed.[76] On the contrary, there is more reason to endorse Hayden White's statement, calling Lessing's book *Geschichte als Sinngebung des Sinnlosen* "brilliant but neglected".[77] For this book has indeed been neglected, despite the fact that it's fascinating title has been often alluded to. Moreover, in both dissertations dedicated to Lessing's philosophy of history, the authors – Goetze and Huesgen – neither use his essays and articles nor his legacy, whereas this could help to improve our understanding of Lessing's philosophy of history. To this should be added that in Lessing's view historiography and philosophy of history are of special importance. For that matter, Lessing rejected a sharp distinction between historiography and philosophy of history. In his opinion, in all historiography a philosophy of history is implicitly present. This opinion has become fashionable in current debates in philosophy of history: it was put forward, for instance, by Hayden White in his

---

74   Hans Mayer, o.c., 118.
75   'lebte eine Philosophie der praktischen Vernunft und suchte die Wirksamkeit seiner Ideen im Licht öffentlicher Kontroversen'; Rainer Marwedel, '„Ich warf eine Flaschenpost ins Eismeer der Geschichte". Einleitung', in: *IFEG*, 13.
76   Baule, o.c., 23.
77   Hayden White, 'Foucault decoded: notes from underground', in: Hayden White, *Tropics of Discourse. Essays in cultural criticism* (third edition Baltimore and London 1985) 257.

Metahistory,⁷⁸ by Haskell Fain in his *Between philosophy and history*,⁷⁹ and by Peter Munz in his *The Shapes of Time*,⁸⁰ According to Lessing, historiography and philosophy of history should pre-eminently be seen as efforts of Western civilization to justify its nationalism, capitalism and imperialism. For that very reason, an analysis of historiography and philosophy of history – exposing their underlying standards and values, and the way they are expressed – can plainly show what Western civilization is really like.

Historiography and philosophy of history are, in Lessing's view, distinguishing marks of Western civilization. They are closely connected with the importance that is attached to the ideas of change, development, and progress in Western civilization. Lessing relates these concepts with the Western, linear conception of time, which in his view is the product of Judaeo-Christian religion. He contrasts this conception of time with the circular conception of time, which, he contends, is typical for Asian civilization, a civilization he idealised. He appreciated this Asian conception of time much more than the Western one, hence the subtitle of the second edition of his book *Europa und Asien*: '6 Bücher wider Geschichte und Zeit' ('Six books against history and time').⁸¹

Lessing's writings on history and historiography span a period of about forty years. He first mentioned the subject in 1895, in *Der Fall Panizza*:

> – that the whole of so-called history of the world, on close inspection, is the family-chronicle of the nobility and the private experience of the courts, that every war between two nations eventually was the war of their cabinets, that is something only wilfully blind forgery of history can want to deny. – ⁸²

In his autobiography *Einmal und nie wieder*, published posthumously in 1935, forty years after *Der Fall Panizza*, Lessing repeatedly returned to his ideas on history. Lessing's most elaborate statement on history was his book *Geschichte*

---

78   Hayden White, *Metahistory: the historical imagination in nineteenth-century Europe* (Baltimore 1973).
79   Haskell Fain, *Between philosophy and history: the resurrection of speculative philosophy of history within the analytic tradition* (Princeton 1970).
80   Peter Munz, *The shapes of time. A new look at the philosophy of history* (Middletown CT 1977).
81   *EuA*; *EuA2*.
82   - 'daß die ganze sogenannte Weltgeschichte, bei Lichte besehen, die Familienchronik des Junkerstandes und das Privaterlebnis der Höfe ist, daß jeder Krieg zweier Naturnationen in letzter Instanz der Krieg ihrer Kabinette war, das kann nur absichtlich blinde Geschichtsfälschung leugnen wollen -'; Theodor Lessing, *Der Fall Panizza*, 33.

als Sinngebung des Sinnlosen, first published in 1919.[83] A fourth, completely revised edition of this book was published in 1927.[84]

Until now, discussions of Lessing's philosophy of history – in so far as it has been discussed – mainly concentrated on the ideas expressed in both editions of *Geschichte als Sinngebung des Sinnlosen* and in *Europa und Asien*. However, by including his other writings in a discussion of his philosophy of history, a better understanding of this subject may be obtained. A suchlike approach of Lessing's philosophy of history can, first of all, be justified with an observation by Lessing himself in the 'Vorrede' of the fourth edition of *Geschichte als Sinngebung des Sinnlosen*:

> I may expect that my books will be seen as continuing traces and diaries of a life, so that the one will be clarified by the other.[85]

Moreover, this does not only hold for Lessing's books, but for his numerous essays, articles and serials as well: some of these do indeed shed light on the ideas expressed in his books. An example is his essay 'Es ist nur ein Übergang' ('It is only a transformation'),[86] a reading of which helps to understand his criticisms of the Western idea of progress.

In addition, certain aspects of Lessing's thinking which are of importance in his philosophy of history he developed in earlier writings. An example is his idea that man is disposed to try to give meaning to events retrospectively – *logificatio post festum*, as Lessing calls it. This notion Lessing developed in his *Studien zur Wertaxiomatik*, first published in two parts in the journal *Archiv für systematische Philosophie* in 1908 and as a separate book in 1914.[87] Likewise, in the *Studien zur Wertaxiomatik* Lessing laid the foundations for later analyses of the notion of causality. A third and last example is his essay 'Psychologie der Ahmung', first published in 1912, in which Lessing developed his idea of pre-conscious knowledge.[88]

---

83   GSS.
84   GSS4.
85   'Ich darf erwarten, daß meine Bücher als fortlaufende Spuren und Tagebücher eines Lebens betrachtet werden, so daß immer eines aus den anderen Licht empfängt.'; GSS4, 26.
86   Theodor Lessing, 'Es ist nur ein Übergang', in: *Prager Tagblatt*, 28.5.1926; reprinted in: *IFEG*, 346–349.
87   Theodor Lessing, 'Studien zur Wertaxiomatik', in: *Archiv für systematische Philosophie*, Neue Folge, 14 (1908), 58–93, 226–257 and *SzW*.
88   Theodor Lessing, 'Psychologie der Ahmung', in: *Archiv für systematische Philosophie*, Neue Folge, 18 (1912), 209–223; reprinted in: *PaT*, 127–151.

Any student of Lessing's philosophy of history should keep in mind that it should only be judged – and, indeed, can only be understood – in the light of his idea of philosophy. Lessing exposed his view on philosophy in his *Philosophisches Antrittskolleg* 'Philosophie als Tat',[89] that he delivered at the *Technische Hochschule* in Hanover in December 1907. The starting-point of this *Antrittskolleg* are the conclusions of the *Probevorlesung* 'Wissenschaft als Kraftökonomie'[90] that he had delivered in November of the same year. This *Probevorlesung* was a meditation on a well-known statement by the English scientist Isaac Newton: "maximus effectus minimo sumptu" – an effect as large as possible with an expenditure of energy as small as possible. According to Newton, this is a law of nature that underlies all natural processes: all natural processes tend to an effect as large as possible with an expenditure of energy as low as possible. Lessing contends that we know now, ever since the *Kritik der reinen Vernunft* (1781) by Immanuel Kant was published that this is not a law of nature: "What one saw in the past as a law of nature, now appears as a the self-definition of the mind that builds the world".[91] For this reason, Newton's statement eventually is not a statement about nature, but about the way man knows nature. In other words, Newton's statement is, in Lessing's view, a statement about the working of the human mind. Or, the human mind itself tends to an effect as large as possible with an expenditure of energy as low as possible.

Now in 'Philosophie als Tat', Lessing contends that this argument is applicable to philosophy as well: as a product of the human mind, philosophy too tends to an effect as large as possible with an expenditure of energy as low as possible. That is to say that philosophy will use the energy at its disposal ever more effectively, ever more rationally, ever more efficiently. Philosophy will ever more confine itself to its essence, and dispose of questions that are not necessary. In actual fact this means, Lessing avers, that philosophy will leave behind metaphysical questions, and will develop into ethics. This does not imply that Lessing was opposed to metaphysics – on the contrary, he saw metaphysics as a necessary and indispensable preparatory phase for the idea of philosophy he himself propagated. According to Lessing, the correctness of his idea of philosophy was confirmed by the insight that "eventually already

---

89   Theodor Lessing, 'Philosophie als Tat', in: *Archiv für systematische Philosophie*, Neue Folge, 15 (1909), 23–39; reprinted in: *PaT*, 1–29.
90   Theodor Lessing, 'Wissenschaft als Kraftökonomie', in: *PaT*, 30–73.
91   'Was man früher für Naturgesetz hielt, das erscheint nun als die Selbstsetzung des die Welt aufbauenden Geistes'; o.c., 34.

experience is something thought and the whole of our existence an act".[92] This insight radicalizes Kant's view that building up knowledge is not a matter of passive reception, but of active shaping by the human mind. Lessing supports the idea that ethics should be at the centre of philosophy as follows: "without any doubt we know that life was not given us as provision for fine feelings or for guessing futile knight's moves, but as heavy task for everyday work".[93] This means "that amongst general human misery and glaring distress for large sections of the population, it can be a direct crime if the individual dedicates himself to an attitude of reflection and passivity".[94]

Thus, Lessing laid the foundation for his view that philosophy should concentrate on ethics. Now, if ethics is to be the centre of philosophy, the next question is, of course, does a guiding principle for ethics, for man's actions exist, and if so, what is it? According to Lessing, this guiding principle does indeed exist, and can be phrased as the injunction "to make the best of a given situation".[95] Lessing often phrased this principle in English: "Make the best of it!", a quotation from the sixth scene of the fifth act from *Coriolanus* by William Shakespeare. As a former theatre critic, Lessing was very familiar with the theatre classics, including Shakespeare's works. According to Lessing, however, the philosopher cannot and, indeed, may not confine himself to phrasing this principle – he must verify it. Eventually, "not what I know is philosophy, but my act!".[96] This idea of philosophy implies that the philosopher and his philosophy are inextricably connected: in the end, the philosopher will be judged by his acts, by the question whether he succeeded in practising what he preached. Lessing always remained true to the idea of philosophy that he brought to the fore in this *Philosophisches Antrittskolleg*. He repeatedly put it forward in his later writings, the guiding principle "make the best of it" then usually being phrased as "diminish the need" ('Mindere die Not').

The injunction "to make the best of a given situation" demands a continuous analysis of the situation the acting person finds himself in, an analysis that has to serve as a basis for acting. Lessing himself expressed his continuous reflection on his situation as an acting person at two different levels and in two different ways. At a general level, he expressed the assessment of his situation

---

92 'zuletzt schon Erfahrung ein Gedachtes und all unser Dasein Tat ist'; o.c., 11.
93 'unzweifelhaft wissen wir, daß das Leben uns nicht als Gelegenheit zu schönen Gefühlen oder zum Herumraten an müssigen Rösselprüngen gegeben ist, sondern als schwere Aufgabe einer täglichen Arbeit'; o.c., 17.
94 'inmitten des allgemeinen Menschenelends und der gröbsten Bedürftigkeit des breiten Volkes es direkt zum Verbrechen werden kann, wenn der Einzelne sich rein beschaulicher und passiver Lebensbehaltung verschreibt'; o.c., 17.
95 'aus der uns gegebenen Konstellation das Bestmögliche herauszuschlagen'; o.c., 18.
96 '[n]icht mein Wissen ist Philosophie, sondern meine Tat'; o.c., 28.

through his cultural criticism, that is, a criticism of Western civilization. In Lessing's criticism of Western civilization, one can distinguish several themes. First of all, he criticizes the way people treat each other in Western civilization. He was concerned with the way women were treated, and very much in favour of the emancipation of women. But his greatest concern was the treatment of the labouring classes. They were locked away in ghetto's, spending their life in dirt and noise. They were raised in a tradition of nationalism, and because of that they lost sight of their international solidarity, and allowed themselves to be abused and slaughtered in wars. Immediately in line with these criticisms of Western civilization is his criticism of the conduct of European nations in international politics. Lessing condemned nationalism, and the wars that result from it, out of a deeply felt pacifism. A second theme in his criticism of Western civilization regards his assessment of the influence it had outside of Europe. Lessing judged this influence negatively:

> The history of the European colonies, of the British in Further India, on Ceylon, Singapore, in Canada and Hongkong, on Gibraltar, Malta, Cyprus and Egypt; of the Latin, Spanish and French in Mexico, Cayenne, Peru, Bolivia and Algeria; of the German on Samoa and in Southwest-Africa; what is it? A chain of ruthless violations and extortions under the cloak of culture.[97]

Lessing's judgement implied, of course, a condemnation of colonialism and imperialism. A third and last theme in criticism of Western civilization regards the way nature is treated. According to Lessing, a ruination of nature threatens if Western man continues to abuse nature. The results of the attitude of Western man towards nature are already devastating:

> What is shot of from the surface of the earth in Germany within 100 years? Aurochs, tarpan, wisent, bear, badger, wolf, elk, wild cat, beaver, otter, marten, mink. Before long wild boar, weasel, badger and fox. From several thousands of species of birds only a few hundred remain.[98]

---

97 'Die Geschichte der Siedelungen Europas, der britischen in Hinterindien, auf Ceylon, Singapore, in Kanada und Hongkonk, auf Gibraltar, Malta, Cypern, und in Ägypten; der lateinischen, spanischen und französischen in Mexiko, Cayenne, Peru, Bolivia, Algier; der deutschen auf Samoa und in Südwest-Afrika; was ist sie? Eine Kette rücksichtsloser Vergewaltungen und Erpressungen unter dem Deckmantel: Kultur.'; *DvK*, 24.
98 'Was ist in Deutschland binnen 100 Jahren von Erdboden weggeknalt? Auerochs, Tarpan, Wisent, Bär, Lux, Wolf, Elch, Wildkatze, Biber, Otter, Marder, Nerz. - Demnächst auch Eber, Wiesel, Dachs und Fuchs. Von mehreren tausend Vogelarten blieben wenige hundert übrig.'; o.c., 17.

At a more specific level, Lessing expressed his assessment of his situation through his comments on political developments in Germany. The most famous of these was, of course, his satirical masterpiece on Hindenburg, to which reference was already made. Especially after the First World War, Lessing wrote numerous comments on political developments, in which he, for instance, warned against the rise of National-Socialism. But he also wrote about malpractices in the German legal system, as in the process against the homosexual sex murderer Fritz Haarmann – whose trial was not fair because the police tried to conceal it had used Haarmann as an informant.

According to Lessing, a philosopher should not confine to phrasing his philosophy, but he has, moreover, to verify it – a second way in which he expressed his assessment of the situation he was in. Lessing himself tried to practice what he preached: he was involved in a variety of activities, to verify his philosophy. These activities link up with his continuous reflection on his situation. Lessing was involved in women's liberation and in a movement against prostitution.[99] He tried to further the elevation of the labouring classes. In this respect, one can mention first of all his political preference: he opted for solidarity with the oppressed and the poor, calling himself a socialist at one time, a communist at another, although he was highly critical of the ideas of Karl Marx. In the second place, he tried to support the labouring classes by teaching courses. In the winter of 1904–1905, for example, he taught courses for labourers in a room in the railway station of Dresden on the philosophy of Schopenhauer, Wagner and Nietzsche, and on ethical and social problems respectively.[100] After the First World War, Lessing was for a number of years, together with his second wife Ada, the moving force behind the *Volkshochschule Hannover*.[101] In this respect his battle against noise should be mentioned as well: in the years before the First World War, Lessing was the moving spirit behind the German anti-noise league, the *Anti-Lärm Verein*.[102] Lessing's pacifism induced him to participate

---

99 Cfr. Rainer Marwedel, *o.c.*, 79–84.
100 Cfr. o.c., 77–78; Lessing published his lectures on Schopenhauer, Wagner and Nietzsche: SWN.
101 Cfr. Jörg Wollenberg, 'Schönheit durch Bildung – Theodor Lessing als Bildungsreformer und Volkshochschulgründer', in: *BiS, 10–50*; and Ruth Schwake, 'Von den Volkstümlichen Hochschulkursen zur Gründung der Freien Volkshochschule Hannover Theodor Lessing in Linden', in: *BiS*, 85–98.
102 Cfr. Lawrence Baron, 'Noise and Degeneration: Theodor Lessing's Crusade for Quiet', *Journal of Contemporary History* 17 (1982), 165–178; Matthias Lentz, '"Ruhe ist die erste Bürgerpflicht". Lärm, Großstadt und Nervosität im Spiegel von Theodor Lessings „Antilärmverein"', *Medizin, Gesellschaft und Geschichte* 13 (1994) 81–105; and John Goodyear, 'Viel Lärm um Theodor Lessing', in: *Angermion* 4 (2011), 95–112.

in the peace movement. After the outbreak of the First World War, he tried to gather a group of intellectuals, to launch a common protest against the war.¹⁰³ This initiative failed, however: even people whom Lessing considered as kindred spirits allowed themselves to be carried away with the enthusiasm with which the war was welcomed. This meant that Lessing broke with some of them; an example is Max Scheler, as Lessing indicates in his autobiography:

> The position towards the war, however, became the criterion that I used to establish authenticity and falseness, truth and lie with all those people, whom I until then considered as kindred souls. Scheler however was lost. He inflamed like everyone at the big flush of fire of the fatherland. He did not want to miss the finest hour. He wrote a gory revolting book that dialectically justifies the world historical massacre and seemed to me worse than murder. Only then we severed.¹⁰⁴

Lessing's pacifism certainly was intensified by his experiences during the First World War; during the first months of the war he worked as an army doctor. He published a series of articles on his experiences in the army hospital.¹⁰⁵ Meanwhile, his once idealist pacifism had taken a more realistic shape; his later view is at its best summarized with the title of an essay of his: 'Nur wer die Waffen hat, kann Frieden schaffen' ('Only the one who controls the weapons can bring about peace').¹⁰⁶ In this respect, it is very remarkable indeed that Lessing already in 1927 warned against military utilization of nuclear fission. He recommended to bring this technique under international control, to make sure it would not produce an arms race.¹⁰⁷ His protests against colonialism and imperialism drove him to attend international conferences on the subject; in

---

103   Cfr. Hans Stern, 'Theodor Lessing (1872–1933)', in: *WeU*, 23.
104   'die Stellungnahme zum Krieg [wurde] der Maßstab, nach dem ich Echtheit und Unechtheit, Lebenswahrheit und Lebenslüge abmaß an all den Menschen, denen bis dahin ich mich geistig verbunden fühlte. Scheler aber entfiel. Er entbrannte wie allen am großen Flammenrausch des Vaterlandes. Er wollte die große Stunde nicht verpassen. Er schrieb ein bluttriefendes widriges Buch, das die weltgeschichtliche Metzelei dialektisch rechtfertigt und mir schlimmer schien als ein Mord. Damals erst gingen wir endgültig auseinander.'; *Eunw*, 344.
105   Theodor Lessing, 'Das Lazarett', *Prager Tagblatt*, 10.2.1929; 17.2.1929; 2.3.1929; 7.3.1929; 23.3.1929; 6.4.1929; 19.41929; reprinted in: *IFEG*, 354–386; and in: *Wmnm*.
106   Theodor Lessing, 'Nur wer die Waffen hat, kann Frieden schaffen', *General-Anzeiger für Dortmund*, 2.3.1932.
107   Theodor Lessing, 'Die ‚Kulturmission' der abendländischen Völker', in: *Das Flammenzeichen vom Palais Egmont*, published by the Liga gegen Imperialismus und für nationale Unabhängigkeit (Berlin 1927); reprinted in: *WeU*, 257.

1927 he himself addressed an international conference in Brussels.[108] Finally, Lessing's criticisms of the way Western civilization abused nature induced him to be active in the protection of nature.

Lessing's idea of philosophy and his attempts to practice what he preached imply that his writings and his social and political activities are closely connected or, indeed, form a unity. For my approach to his philosophy of history this means that I will try to understand Lessing's philosophy of history within the context of the unity of his writings and activities. That is to say, one cannot understand Lessing's writings on the philosophy of history *per se*, but one should always relate them to his idea of philosophy in general and to the unity of his other writings and activities. Only such an approach can, in my opinion, do justice to Lessing's philosophy of history.

From this line of approach, I will try to answer the question what the gist of Lessing's philosophy of history is. What are its main aspects, and how do they relate to his other writings and to his social and political activities? This includes a comparison of the first and the fourth editions of his *Geschichte als Sinngebung des Sinnlosen*. In addition, I will try to identify influences on Lessing's philosophy of history – asking for political and social developments that urged him to phrase his views the way he did, as well as for other authors that inspired him in expressing his philosophy of history. Finally, I will try to evaluate Lessing's philosophy of history: how should we judge it, in the light of current debates in philosophy of history? In answering this question, I will try to take the history of the reception of his philosophy of history into consideration.

By answering these questions on Theodor Lessing's philosophy of history, I hope, on the one hand, to contribute both to a better understanding of the man and his ideas, and of the time he lived in. On the other hand, I hope to make a contribution to the reflection on the social role and significance of historiography and history teaching in general.

The plan of the book is as follows. In chapter two I will sketch Lessing's formative years, in which he developed the philosophical system of his own, as this system is the expression of his most inner experiences. Roughly this is the period up to 1914. Subsequently, I will discuss both Lessing's formal and informal education. In the concluding section of this chapter, I will sketch the outlines of Lessing's philosophical system.

---

108   O.c., 248–259.

In the third chapter I will go into Lessing's response to the outbreak of the First World War, as this was instrumental in the elaboration of his philosophy of history. Lessing's response differed completely from the one of an overwhelming majority of German intellectuals. As Lessing's reaction to the war was in part a response to their reaction, in particular to the way they appealed to history to justify their position, I will first sketch the response of the majority of German intellectuals, and next Lessing's immediate reaction.

Lessing's more detached reaction to the war was his philosophy of history as expressed in the first edition of *Geschichte als Sinngebung des Sinnlosen*, which was published in 1919. This book will be discussed in chapter four. First, I will look into Lessing's utterances on history prior to the publication of the book. Next, I will discuss the argument of the book in detail.

In 1927, Lessing published a fourth, completely revised edition of the book – actually, it is a new book bearing the same title. This will be discussed in chapter five. I will start with looking into Lessing's publications on history in between the appearance of both editions of the book. Then I will discuss Lessing's reports on the Haarmann-trial, which may be read as a contemporary history of early twentieth-century Hanover. Next, I will discuss the major differences between the 1919 and 1927 editions of the book, starting from Lessing's own observations on the matter. Subsequently, the 1927 edition itself will be discussed in detail.

In the sixth and final chapter, I will sketch the reception of Lessing's philosophy of history. First, I will go into the reviews of both editions of *Geschichte als Sinngebung des Sinnlosen*. In the second section of this chapter, I will make a first step towards a full-scale treatment of the relevance of Lessing's philosophy of history for contemporary debates within this discipline.

CHAPTER 2

'Ein Aus Eignem Blut Gereiften Weltsystem'

Lessing's development until the First World War

As we saw in chapter one,[1] Lessing conceived the life of a philosopher and his philosophy as being closely connected.[2] The philosopher, in his view, should accordingly verify his ideas through his activities:

> I want to keep awake the awareness of the fact that philosophy is the commitment of the entire man, that with the philosopher one has to ask for his life, his character, his small, smallest habits, his attitude to woman, to friendship, to students, as much as for the contents of the problems that he thought through.[3]

But there is yet another way, in which – at least according to Lessing himself – the life of the philosopher and his philosophy are closely connected. Lessing used to distinguish between philosophy as such, and philosophy as taught at universities or academic philosophy – a distinction that was, indeed, quite common among German philosophers of the nineteenth and twentieth centuries and that was held by, for instance, Arthur Schopenhauer and Friedrich Nietzsche as well. It seems to go back to the German philosopher Friedrich Schlegel (1782–1829), who distinguished between philosophy of life and philosophy of school (or academic philosophy), the latter being at best some kind of preparation for the former, the former being philosophy in the true sense of the word and thus far more important.[4] In Lessing's view, the relation of academic philosophy to philosophy as such is similar to the relation of literary history to literature – novels, stories, poetry, and essays. Experts in literary history write about literature, but what they write is not itself literature. Likewise, academic

---

1 Cfr. Chapter one, 20 *ff.*
2 A translation of the chapter title is, 'A world system ripened out of my own blood'.
3 '[I]ch [will] das Bewußtsein dafür wach halten [...] daß Philosophie ein Einsetzen des Gesamtmenschen ist, daß man beim Philosophen genau so gut nach seinem Leben, seinem Charakter, seinen kleinen, kleinsten Lebensgewohnheiten, seiner Stellung zur Frau, zur Freundschaft, zur Schülerschaft zu fragen hat, wie nach dem Inhalt der Probleme, die er durchdachte'; Theodor Lessing, 'Philosophie als Tat', in: *Archiv für systematische Philosophie*, Neue Folge, 15 (1909), 23–39; reprinted in: *PaT*, 1–29; there 29.
4 Cfr. Robert Josef Kozljanič, *Lebensphilosophie. Eine Einführung* (Stuttgart 2004) 32–34.

philosophers write about philosophy, but their writings are not itself philosophy, or, in other words, they do not themselves philosophize.[5] For this reason, Lessing used to call academic philosophy 'Über-Philosophie'.[6] His main problem with this 'Über-Philosophie' is that it is completely arbitrary: its characteristic disagreements on the interpretation of a particular passage in, say, the work of Plato might just as well be on the work of Aristotle, Kant or Hegel. Already in 1906, in his book *Schopenhauer-Wagner-Nietzsche*, Lessing, quite characteristically, mocked this tendency: "Yes, he who knows especially the German university system is tempted to believe that at every single one of our colleges two ordinary professors of philosophy are paid to this end that always the one may "refute" what the other one writes – which both mostly manage to do".[7] Both these professors as well as the problems they argued about, usually are completely forgotten within a few years after their death... According to Lessing, such disagreements over interpretations of the works of past philosophers or such disputes between contemporaries, almost always lack the inner necessity that is a feature of all true philosophy: all true philosophy stems from an inner necessity. As such, it, in one way or another, reflects the life of the philosopher:

> But the entire subject-matter of the philosopher is a life that with him was born into the world. Not life, not experience, but his life and his experience.[8]

Or, as Lessing wrote in his autobiography:

> Because my philosophy was *my* philosophy. In order to create it, I had to be born and to die living.[9]

This phrase echoes, if not exactly, an idea that Lessing already expressed in his book *Schopenhauer-Wagner-Nietzsche* (1906):

---

5 Cfr. Lessing, o.c., 25.
6 This term is untranslatable; it is a pun that unites the meanings of 'philosophy about' and 'meta-philosophy'.
7 'Ja, wer speziell deutsches Universitätswesen kennt, der ist versucht, zu glauben, daß an jeder unserer Hochschulen zwei ordentliche Professoren der Philosophie zu dem Zwecke besoldet werden, damit immer der eine das, was der andere schreibt, "widerlegen" könne, - was auch meistens beiden gelingt'; *S-W-N*, 427.
8 'Aber der ganze Stoff des Philosophen ist ein Leben, das mit ihm zur Welt geboren ist. Nicht das Leben, nicht die Erfahrung, sondern sein Leben und seine Erfahrung'; *PaT*, l.c..
9 'Denn meine Philosophie war *meine* Philosophie. Ich mußte, um sie schaffen zu können, geboren werden und lebend ersterben'; *Eunw*, 87.

What kind of philosophy, thus, a thinker has, depends on what he primarily sees with his first look at the world. That is, it depends on the inclination of his attention. And this, again, on the nature of his feelings and valuations, that is, of the make-up of his "personality".[10]

And again: "Because metaphysical views – as much as they seem to be the results of measured calculations and objective deliberations – without exception are acts of will and revelations of psychological tendencies implied in our predispositions".[11] In other words, for Lessing himself his philosophy was, in a sense, nothing but the meditation on his own life, and the reflection of his own personality. This idea of philosophy fits perfectly well within the tradition of the so-called *Lebensphilosophie*, or philosophy of life. This, mainly German, tradition began with Friedrich Schlegel; other well-known representatives are Arthur Schopenhauer, Carl Gustav Carus, Friedrich Nietzsche, and Ludwig Klages. Within this tradition, several closely connected conceptions of philosophy were developed, for instance philosophy as the sum of an individual's outlooks on God, ethics and social life; or philosophy as the reflection on the various stages of a human's life; or philosophy as a guide to everyday life.[12] Lessing's view of philosophy as being, in a sense, a reflection on a philosopher's own life is very similar to, if not identical with, the one used by the German psychologist Philipp Lersch (1898–1972) in his overview *Lebensphilosophie der Gegenwart* ('Contemporary philosophy of life'; 1932). Lersch defines philosophy of life as the kind of philosophy "that is concerned with the philosophical reflection on the contents of experience, or, more precisely, with the question whether, and to what extent, experience is able to open up the realm of reality for us".[13] Experience in this sense refers both to the way man experiences himself, and to the way he experiences the world. Although this reflection on the contents of experience always is a reflection on the personal, individual

---

10   'Was also ein Denker für eine Philosophie hat, das hängt davon ab, was er beim ersten Blick in der Welt vornehmlich sieht. Das heißt, es hängt ab von der Inklination seiner Aufmerksamkeit. Und diese wieder von der Art seines Fühlens oder Wertens, d.h. von der Konstitution seiner „Persönlichkeit"'; *S-W-N*, 175.

11   'Denn metaphysische Weltbilder, – so sehr sie Produkte überlegenden Kalkuls [sic!] und objektiver Erwägungen zu sein scheinen – sind ausnahmslos Taten des Willens und Offenbarungen der in unserer Anlage mitgebrachten psychischen Tendenz...'; o.c., 180.

12   For an overview, see Kozljanič, o.c., 14–15.

13   'in der es sich handelt um die philosophische Besinnung auf die Inhalte des Erlebens, genauer gesprochen um die Frage, ob und wieweit das Erleben imstande ist, uns den Bereich der Wirklichkeit aufzuschließen'; Philipp Lersch, *Lebensphilosophie der Gegenwart* (Berlin 1932) 3.

experience of the philosopher, nevertheless, according to Lessing, the insights gained through this meditation on his own life are generally valid:

> Because the precious wonder exists that he who manages to penetrate to the most inner point of his merely personal, merely single conscience, in doing so reaches the general, ever-valid as well.[14]

If we do indeed consider Lessing's own philosophy as a meditation on his life and experience, in trying to understand his philosophy, and following his own directions, we have to take his life and experience into consideration, and especially his formative years[15] – the years in which he developed his philosophical system, which he described as "a world system ripened out of my own blood".[16] Lessing claimed his first notes toward his philosophical system date from 1895,[17] and, moreover, to have completed thinking out this system in 1914. He was all prepared to commit it to paper, even declaring "[f]or that end I was born", when the outbreak of the First World War prevented him from doing so.[18] In other words, Lessing's philosophical publications prior to the First World War should be considered as preliminaries for a philosophical system of his own that was never written, however. But this very system does underlie all of his subsequent post-war publications. For this reason, the years during which he lived through the experiences that induced him to develop this philosophical system of his own will be discussed in the following.

1 Childhood and Schooldays

Lessing himself described his youth and early development extensively in his autobiography *Einmal und nie wieder*, which covers his life until about

---

14 'Denn es besteht das köstliche Wunder, daß, wer in den innersten Punkt des nur persönlichen, nur einmaligen Gewissens vordringt, damit auch das Allgemeine, Ewiggültige erreicht'; Theodor Lessing, o.c., 16.
15 I use the term 'formative years' loosely here, alluding to Lessing's childhood, schooldays, years of study, first jobs, and his turn toward philosophy – indeed his life up to 1914, i.e. the period in which he developed the philosophical system that would be the postulate of his post-war writings.
16 'eines aus eignem Blut gereiften Weltsystem'; Theodor Lessing, 'Vorrede', in: *PaT*, VIII.
17 Theodor Lessing, 'Meine Beziehungen zu Ludwig Klages', reprinted in: *Eunw*, 413–446, see 438.
18 'Dazu war ich geboren'; Theodor Lessing, 'An den Nerven krank und dem Zusammenbruch nahe – Tagebuchnotizen August 1914', in: *Wmnm*, 21–25, there 21; and Theodor Lessing, 'Gerichtstag über mich selbst', *Junge Menschen* 6 (1925), Heft 10,9 238–244; reprinted in: *Eunw*, 391–411, see 404.

1900 – although Lessing sometimes does insert descriptions of later events and developments, for instance his reaction to the outbreak of the First World War and the way it influenced his relations with others like for instance Max Scheler. Indeed, together with Rainer Marwedel's biography,[19] Lessing's autobiography is the most important evidence we have for understanding his early development.

Be that as it may, one should read Lessing's autobiography critically. As both Hans Eggert Schröder[20] and Hans-Dieter Schmid[21] claimed, *Einmal und nie wieder* is not trustworthy as a factual record. – The example discussed by Schmid is revealing. In his autobiography, Lessing describes at length the difficulties he had at school. According to this account, in an attempt to help him overcome these problems, he was sent to the Israelite horticultural college Ahlem. Ahlem was, however, not founded until 1893, when Lessing had for some time already finished his secondary school education and was studying at university. Why, then, did Lessing include this apparently fictional account of his stay at Ahlem in *Einmal und nie wieder*? As Schmid points out, from a literary point of view it does indeed make sense to include this episode in the autobiography. For this reason, Schmid aptly suggests that Lessing's autobiography should not be read as an attempted historical reconstruction, but rather as a description of his psychological development: it is an autobiographically inspired *Bildungsroman* rather than a history book.[22]

Moreover, Lessing himself was involved in various movements that aimed for a reform of education in Germany, and this may have given him yet another reason to include this episode in the book. From 1901 until 1903 he worked as a teacher at the country boarding school Haubinda that was founded by a friend of his, the at the time well-known pedagogue and school reformer Hermann Lietz (1868–1919). In 1903, Lessing resigned because of growing anti-semitism at Haubinda: he fiercely opposed Lietz's decision to allow only a limited number of Jewish students to attend the school in years to come.[23] It brought an end to his friendship with Lietz. Lessing continued his career as a

---

19 Rainer Marwedel, *Theodor Lessing 1872–1933. Eine Biographie* (Darmstadt and Neuwied 1987).
20 Hans Eggert Schröder, *Theodor Lessing's autobiografischen Schriften. Ein Kommentar* (Bonn 1970), *passim*.
21 Hans-Dieter Schmid, 'Theodor Lessing und die Israelitische Gartenbauschule Ahlem - eine Legende', in: *Hannoversche Geschichtsblätter*, Neue Folge 52 (1998), 289–295, *passim*.
22 O.c., 294–295.
23 For a detailed description of this so-called 'Haubinder Judenkrach' ('Haubinda Jewish rumpus'), see Jorg Wollenberg, 'Schönheit durch Bildung – Theodor Lessing als Bildungsreformer und Volkshochschulgründer', in: *BiS*, 16–17.

reform teacher at Laubegast, a similar school in the vicinity of Dresden,[24] in 1904 and 1905. Even after he stopped working as a teacher, in order to pursue further academic studies with the philosopher Edmund Husserl (1859–1938) in Göttingen,[25] Lessing always kept a keen interest in ideas on the reform of education. He published on the subject,[26] and continued his membership of the *Bund entschiedener Schulreformer* ('League of resolved school reformers'). Lessing's work for the Folk High School in Hanover, from 1919 until 1933, should also been seen in the light of his ideas on the reform of education. And in 1933, after his escape from Germany, Lessing intended, together with his wife Ada, to start a girls boarding school in Marienbad; indeed, a number of the necessary preparations had already been made when Lessing was assaulted. Their ideas about this school were influenced by the experiences Lessing had had in Haubinda and Laubegast. So it is quite likely that he wanted to pay homage to the very idea of school reform, and of country boarding schools especially, by including a description of Ahlem in the book, it being, though, a fictional account. Lessing's interest in ideas on school reform most probably stemmed from his own horrific experiences at school[27] – as he wrote in 1930 in his essay on 'German composition', he "only by chance escaped the axe of pedagogy".[28]

However, an even more important question is whether Lessing in writing his autobiography was actually aiming for factual trustworthiness; the 'Preface' in *Einmal und nie wieder* at least suggests he was not:

> Because the most beautiful of the autobiographies we know, those of Plato, Xenophon, Augustine, Dante's Vita Nuova, Goethe's Wahrheit und Dichtung, Nietzsche's Ecce Homo, Hebbel's diaries, Rousseau's confessions, the confessions by August Strindberg, Leo Trotsky's 'My Life' - are they not all the creation of a myth? [...] Is it not more important to fictionalise a life than to confess it?[29]

---

24 At the time, Laubegast was still a village; in 1921, it was incorporated in Dresden, of which it is now a district.
25 See Lawrence Baron, 'Discipleship and Dissent: Theodor Lessing and Edmund Husserl', in: *Proceedings of the American Philosophical Society* 127 (1983), no. 1, 32–49.
26 Some of his essays on the subject are now published in *BiS*.
27 See below, 39*ff*.
28 'Nur durch Zufall entrann ich den Schlachtbeil der Pädagogik'; Theodor Lessing, 'Der deutsche Aufsatz', in: *Die neue Erziehung* 13 (1930), 904–909; reprinted in: *BiS*, 184–191; there 185.
29 'Denn die schönsten der uns bekannten Eigenlebensgeschichten, die des Plato, Xenophon, Augustinus, Dantes Vita Nuova, Goethes Wahrheit und Dichtung, Nietzsches Ecce Homo, Hebbels Tagebücher, Rousseaus Konfessionen, die Geständnisse August Strindbergs, Leo

In a latter chapter of his autobiography, Lessing again discusses this theme. He maintains that

> we cannot write down experiences without shaping. The dance of the images of life will become comprehensible and understandable, narratable and countable only in so far as our shaping force, or should I say, our lying force gets over it, because arranging according to connecting points, yes even every division according to years and life stages already is delicate forgery.[30]

Lessing continues:

> What we call the story of our life, that would in consequence be the fictionalisation or explanation of that life from the side of our spiritual man, that haughty and self-righteous self that, creating connections, floats over the ever varying stream, like a light that now shines too glaring, then too dim and projects into linear sequence what in fact was at once more diverse and more simple.[31]

And from all this Lessing concludes:

> At these pages, I may seem to picture my life, but would someone else write down what I write, then I would deny, I would writhe with injury, I would repudiate the truth. What is truth? – [32]

Trotzkis 'Mein Leben' -, sind sie nicht allesamt Schöpfungen eines Mythos? [...] Ist es nicht wichtiger, Leben zu dichten als zu beichten?'; *Eunw*, 13.

[30] 'wir können Erlebnisse nicht niederschreiben, ohne zu gestalten. Greifbar und begreiflich, erzählbar und zählbar wird des Lebens Bildertanz nur gerade so weit, als unsre gestaltende, oder soll ich sagen, unsre lügende Kraft über ihn herkommt, denn schon die Gliederung nach Beziehungspunkten, ja schon jede Einteilung nach Jahren und Lebensaltern ist zartes Fälschertum'; o.c., 118.

[31] 'Was wir unsere Lebensgeschichte nennen, das wäre demnach Dichtung oder Deutung des Lebens von Seiten unseres geistigen Menschen, dieses hochmütigen und selbstgerechten Ichs, welches die Zusammenhänge erschaffend, über dem ewig wechselvollen Strome schwebt, wie ein Licht, das bald zu grell und bald zu matt beleuchtet und auf lineare Abfolge projiziert, was doch eigentlich zugleich vielfältiger, zugleich einfältiger war'; l.c..

[32] 'Ich kann auf diesen Seiten scheinbar mein Leben schildern; würde aber ein anderer niederschreiben, was ich schreibe, dann würde ich widersprechen, würde verletzt zusammenzucken, würde die Wahrheit nicht anerkennen. Was ist Wahrheit? – '; l.c..

Taking all this into consideration, I think we should follow Schmid's suggestion, and read Lessing's autobiography not so much as a history book, but rather as an autobiographically inspired novel about the psychological development of its principal character. If we do so, we may draw conclusions from it only with some reserve. Especially with regard to matters of fact, these conclusions should be tentative. – However, this should not lead us to conclude, as Schröder does, that Lessing is in general unreliable as a witness; if Lessing in *Einmal und nie wieder* was not aiming for factual exactness, it is a category mistake to dismiss the book or its author because of a lack of factual exactness. – Nevertheless, *Einmal und nie wieder* does give an indication of the way in which Lessing experienced his formative years, even if it does not give an exact factual record. And if one tries to understand Lessing's philosophy, judging from his own idea that all true philosophy eventually is nothing but a meditation by the philosopher on his own life, his own experience, *Einmal und nie wieder* still is a very important source for comprehending Lessing's philosophy. After all, his philosophy was not prompted by the actual facts of his life, but by the way he experienced these facts.

Theodor Elchanan Lessing was born on February, 8, 1872 in Hanover, Germany, where he would spend most of his life. Only in between 1891, when he was sent to school in Hameln – the start of a wandering through Germany as a student and a teacher – and 1907, when he reluctantly[33] returned to habilitate at the *Technische Hochschule*, Lessing did not live in Hanover. As he wrote in 1926:

> I got hung up for life on this spot on the crust of the earth. I know there are more beautiful countries and more sympathetic people. But it happened to be my country and my fate. And therefore I loved it. And hate as well was love.[34]

---

[33] 'Enttäuschter ist nie ein Kind in der Heimat zurückgekehrt' - 'never did a child more disappointedly return to his homeland', Lessing wrote in 1925; in 1907 for him Hanover still was a place he first and foremost connected with his troublesome youth, 'wo auf jedem Pflastersteine eine Träne und ein Seufzer meiner Jugend lag' ('where on every paving stone there was a tear and a sob from my youth'). See Theodor Lessing, 'Gerichtstag über mich selbst', reprinted in: *Eunw*, 391–411, there 402.

[34] 'Ich bin ein Leben lang an dieser Stelle der Erdrinde haftengeblieben. Ich weiß, daß es schönere Länder gibt und wohlwollendere Menschen. Aber dies war nun mal mein Land und mein Schicksal. Und so habe ich es geliebt. Und auch der Haß war Liebe'; Theodor Lessing, 'Jüdisches Schicksal' , in: *Der Jude* (1926), Sonderheft 3 – Judentum und Deutschtum, 11–17, reprinted in: *Wmnm*, 121–128, there 121.

Lessing expressed his love for the people of Hanover, especially for the dialect they spoke, in the booklet *Jää. Studienblätter* ('Yeah. Studies')[35] – a witty study of the customs and language of the inhabitants of his native city that he published under the name Théodore Le Singe (Theodore The Monkey).

His paternal ancestors had been living in Hanover for over two hundred years. Originally, the family name was not Lessing, but Leiser. It was only Theodor's grandfather who adopted the name Lessing, calling himself Levy Leiser Lessing, as an homage[36] to Gotthold Lessing (1729–1781), the famous playwright from the Enlightenment who, both through his play *Nathan der Weise* (1779) and through his friendship with the Jewish philosopher Moses Mendelssohn (1729–1786) was so very important for the emancipation of the Jews in late eighteenth- and nineteenth-century Germany, and even in all of Europe. Both of Lessing's parents were of Jewish descent, but they were assimilated to a large extent. As Lessing wrote in 1933: "I grew up without any connection to Judaism, never ever visiting a synagogue as a boy nor learning more from Hebrew than necessarily the alphabet at school".[37] Indeed, in his autobiography, Lessing claims he never knew he was Jewish until classmates of his told him at school.[38] In 1895, when he was twenty-three, he formally left the Jewish community, only to re-join five years later, "when I got to know Zionism and had understood that only through this the solution of the in my opinion unsolvable Jewish question might be possible".[39] Lessing identified with the Jewish community in Germany ever since, even the more so when this community was more and more discriminated against in the nineteen twenties and thirties.

Theodor's father, Sigmund Lessing (1838–1896), was a popular society doctor, his mother, Adèle Ahrweiler (1848–1926), the daughter of a banker. Their marriage was not a happy one. In fact, Lessing's father was in love with Antoni Ahrweiler, the younger sister of his wife, but he married Adèle because his

---

35   Hanover 1919.
36   Cfr Lessing, *Eunw*, 34.
37   'Ich bin ohne jede Beziehung zum Judentum aufgewachsen, habe als Knabe weder je eine Synagoge besucht noch vom Hebräischen mehr erlernt als im Schulunterricht notdürftig das Alphabet.' ; Theodor Lessing, 'Gnade dem Maultier', in: *Selbstwehr*, 31.8.1933; reprinted in: *Wmnm*, 129–134, there 130.
38   *Eunw*, 112.
39   'als ich den Zionismus kennenlernte und begriffen hatte, daß durch ihn allein die Lösung der meines Erachtens unlöslichen Judenfrage zu ermöglichen sei.'; Theodor Lessing, 'Gnade dem Maultier', now in: *Wmnm*, 129–134, there 130. Lessing's vision on Jewish identity is the topic of Jochen Hartwig, *'Sei was immer du bist'. Theodor Lessings wendungsvolle Identitätsbildung als Deutscher und Jude* (Oldenburg 1999).

father-in-law promised him a higher dowry if he chose the elder girl. But, as Lessing tells in *Einmal und nie wieder*, even when his wife was already pregnant with Theodor, Sigmund Lessing allegedly tried to persuade his father-in-law to allow him to divorce Adèle, and marry Antoni instead. But Antoni was by now engaged, and wanted to marry her fiancé, so nothing came of Sigmund's plan. Consequently, Sigmund stayed with Adèle, a wife he did not love, nor did he, according to his son in *Einmal und nie wieder*, love the child she bore him, "because in me he definitely saw the image of my mother and the Ahrweiler family that he hated".[40] A year and a half later, a second child was born, Lessing's sister Sophie, who resembled her father and to whom he took more kindly. But the birth of Sophie did not improve the relation between Sigmund and Adèle either. It is telling that Sigmund Lessing baptised the family dog 'Ahrweiler', the surname of his wife's family.[41] Moreover, when he was angry with his wife, Sigmund Lessing used to shout 'Ahrweiler' at her, and it took young Theodor several years before he realised that 'Ahrweiler' was not a term of abuse, but his mother's family name.[42] Growing up with a father who hated him, and with a mother who was no match at all for his father, meant Lessing's childhood was not a happy one.

The relationship between Theodor Lessing and his father is the subject of the third chapter of *Einmal und nie wieder*, but, moreover, it is a dominant theme all through the book. In this third chapter, simply but aptly entitled 'Mein Vater', Theodor Lessing tries to analyse both his father's personality and the most difficult, indeed painful relation the two of them had. According to Theodor Lessing, the overriding feature of his father's personality was his extreme directedness towards himself: "This man was for himself the centre of the cosmos, and the centre of this centre was his stomach".[43] A second important feature of Sigmund Lessing's personality was, according to his son, the fluctuation of his moods: one moment he was cheerful and charming, the next angry and unapproachable. Hence, both for his wife and children he was completely unpredictable,[44] which made living with him so very difficult. In his angry moods, he often was violent, beating both wife and son. Indeed, when

---

40   'weil er in mir durchaus das Abbild der Mutter und der ihm verhaßten Familie Ahrweiler sah'; *Eunw*, 77. Lessing describes his father's alleged attempt to divorce his mother in the third chapter of this book, entitled 'My father', 54–57. Cfr. Rainer Marwedel, *Theodor Lessing 1872–1933. Eine Biographie* (Darmstadt and Neuwied 1987), 18.
41   R. Marwedel, l.c..
42   *Eunw*, 135.
43   'Dieser Mann war sich Mittelpunkt des Kosmos, und der Mittelpunkt dieses Mittelpunktes war sein Magen'; o.c., 61.
44   O.c., 61–62.

Theodor Lessing was about fifteen years old, one day his father allegedly beat him so severely that he damaged his back permanently: afterwards, Theodor was never again able to straighten his back completely, and walked somewhat bowed.[45] A third and last feature of his father's personality that Theodor Lessing mentions, was his directedness towards sensual experiences: he completely lived by the moment, and had no sense at all for reflection or abstract thinking.[46] The relationship between father and son put so much pressure on Theodor Lessing that even as an adolescent – as he confesses in his autobiography – he one day inadvertently thought, when he saw his father slumbering: "Now you could do it. Strangle him, and all would be freed".[47]

Although Lessing did not confess similar murderous thoughts with regard to his mother, his relationship with her was hardly better. It is the subject matter of the fourth chapter of his autobiography, entitled 'My Mother'. It is noteworthy that it contains only six pages of the book, whereas the chapter on his father contains over thirty. Lessing portrays his mother as an innocent and helpless personality, as someone who meekly underwent the sufferings of life. She allegedly was completely dependent on her husband, and, according to her son, "that kind of a slave's soul that is satisfied, if one diligently gilds its chain."[48] In conflicts between father and son, she always took side with the father – even when the son tried to intervene when his father was beating her. She was, according to her son, neither good nor evil: she just was the mouthpiece of forces outside her that were stronger than she was – mainly her husband.[49]

Hence, the way Theodor Lessing eventually assesses both of his parents is truly debunking: "As long as I recall, I have suffered from my parents."[50] Given all this, it is tempting to read an observation Lessing makes in his book *Der jüdische Selbsthaß* ('Jewish Self-hatred'; 1930) as an autobiographically inspired lament:

> Do you know what it means to curse the soil on which you have to grow? To drink poison from its roots instead of nourishment? Do you know what it means to be born badly in a marriage of convenience or superficial self-interest? To be born badly, be it neglected or be it coddled, be it enfeebled or be it beaten up? And then hate for life, completely

---

45 O.c., 100.
46 O.c., 62–63.
47 'Jetzt könntest du es tun. Erwürge ihn, und alle waren befreit'; o.c., 101.
48 'jene Sklavenseele, die zufrieden ist, wenn man ihre Ketten fleißig vergoldet'; o.c., 75.
49 O.c., 76.
50 'Ich habe, so lange ich zurückdenke, an meinen Eltern gelitten'; o.c., 73.

pointlessly hate the father, the mother, the schoolmasters, the teachers, all those who made and shaped us according to their own horrible image, without us ever wanting to be born in this world, like this, and in this world.[51]

At school, Lessing did not fare much better. According to his teachers, he was, although intelligent, "not suitable for school".[52] Lessing characterised his school as a "dumbing-people-institution", with "patriotism, Latin and Greek" as principal subjects, and above all as "boring, boring until obtuseness".[53] Elsewhere, when discussing education in Germany, he speaks of "the common use of the German school of drilling minds".[54] The educational system in nineteenth century Germany was dominated by values like obedience, discipline, diligence and good behaviour, which were strictly enforced by teachers who did not hesitate to resolve to corporal punishment if they deemed it necessary. There was not much understanding for a boy like Theodor Lessing, who was far more guided by the things he took an interest in himself, than by what the curriculum demanded of him. Hence, his school record was poor, especially in German language and German composition. In a chapter in *Einmal und nie wieder*, Lessing refers to his home and his school as "the two hells"[55] in which he spent his youth. In the book, Lessing repeatedly and at length describes the troubles he had had at school, both at elementary school and at his secondary school, the *Lyceum I* (which later was known as the *Ratsgymnasium*) in Hanover. A typical example can be found in the chapter on his early youth:

> I cannot at all imagine that ever for a human being scholastic learning became as sour as it was for me. Although I did like to improvise and haggle at the piano for hours in confused tones, learning notes and finger exercises were nothing but inexpressible torment to me. I did let lie

---

51 'Wißt Ihr, was es bedeutet: dem Boden fluchen, darauf man wachsen muß? Aus seiner Wurzel Gift trinken anstatt der Nahrung? Wißt Ihr, was es heißt: Schlechtgeborensein aus dem Ehebette der Berechnung und der oberflächlichen Selbstsucht? Schlechtgeborensein, sei es verwahrlost oder sei es verzärtelt, sei es verweichlicht oder sei es verprügelt? Und nun ein Leben lang hassen, ganz sinnlos hassen, den Vater, die Mutter, die Lehrer, die Bildner, alle, die uns nach ihrem eigenen widrigen Bilde gezeugt und geprägt haben, ohne daß wir doch zur Welt kommen wollten, so zur Welt und in eine solche Welt?'; *DjS*, 45.
52 'nicht schulgemäß'; e.g., *Eunw*, 111.
53 'Menschenverdummungsanstalt'; 'mit Patriotismus, Latein und Griechisch als Hauptfächer'; 'langweilig, langweilig bis zum Stumpfsinn'; o.c, 109.
54 'allgemein übliche Verstandesdressur der deutschen Unterrichtsschule'; Theodor Lessing, 'Georg Simmel. Betrachtungen und Exkurse', in: *PaT*, 305.
55 O.c., chapter 8, 135–150, 'Die zwei Höllen'.

fallow all of this potentiality of my nature, probably only because music would have dislocated me completely. Drawing copies as well as copying texts, learning vocabularies by heart and most of all counting and arithmetic were inexpressibly horrible to me. Yes, all of this remained closed to me. Impossible, ever to accomplish a set school task otherwise than with misery and inner resistance. These difficulties continued until well in the twenty-first year of my life [...][56]

His only comfort in these days was his close friendship with Ludwig Klages, a classmate of his. Probably because of the very sad way it ended, the friendship between Lessing and Klages has often been discussed; it was, for example, the subject-matter of studies by F. Wiersma-Verschaffelt[57] and E.-V. Kotowski,[58] and it is absolutely central in H.E. Schröder's *Theodor Lessings autobiografische Schriften* ('Theodor Lessing's Autobiographical Writings').[59] Lessing himself gives an almost lyrical description of this friendship in the chapter "The friend" in his autobiography.[60] Already in 1928, he had published an essay on the subject, entitled "My connections with Ludwig Klages".[61] This 1928 essay, written in a more or less neutral tone of voice, is a defence against accusations that he took almost all of his philosophical ideas from Klages. Lessing's approach is very factual and, although the subject must have been very painful for him – after their break, he grieved over the loss of his friend for the rest of his life –, he shows no disrespect whatsoever for Klages. But he is very outspoken in his refutation of the accusations against him: though he admits that the discussions Klages and he had had on all kinds of books and subjects inspired him, he denies having ever made Klages' ideas his own. In her very balanced

---

56 'Ich kann mir gar nicht vorstellen, daß jemals einem Menschen ein schulgemäßes Erlernen so sauer geworden ist wie für mich es war. Obwohl ich stundenlang am Klavier in wirren Tönen phantasieren und klimpern mochte, war doch Notenlernen und die Finger üben mir nichts als unsägliche Pein. Ich habe diese ganze Möglichkeit meiner Natur brach liegen lassen, vielleicht nur darum, weil Musik mich völlig zerrüttet hätte. Das Zeichnen nach der Vorlage, das Auswendiglernen von Vokabeln und vollends gar Zählen und rechnen war mir unsagbar widerwärtig. Ja, das alles blieb mir verschlossen. Unmöglich, jemals eine geforderte Schulleistung anders als mit Qual und innerem Widerstreben abzuleisten! Diese Schwierigkeiten dauerten bis ins einundzwanzigste Lebensjahr [...]'; o.c., 94–95.
57 F. Wiersma-Verschaffelt, *Een tragische vriendschap. Ludwig Klages en Theodor Lessing* (Leiden 1968).
58 Elke-Vera Kotowski, *Feindliche Dioskuren. Theodor Lessing und Ludwig Klages. Das Scheitern einer Jugendfreundschaft (1885–1899)* (Berlin 2000).
59 Hans Eggert Schröder, o.c., *passim*.
60 Theodor Lessing, o.c., chapter 12, 172–187, 'Der Freund'.
61 Theodor Lessing, 'Meine Beziehungen zu Ludwig Klages', reprinted in: *Eunw*, 413–446

book on the subject, based on, among other things, letters Lessing and Klages exchanged in their youth, E.-V. Kotowski is inclined to follow Lessing in his conclusions. If one of the two is to be considered as the more original and leading thinker of the two, it is most probably Lessing – in fact, Klages usually was for the greatest part of his intellectual career more of a follower than a leader, Kotowski argues.[62] In *Einmal und nie wieder*, however, Lessing is not concerned with these kinds of questions: in this book, he tries to recall the meaning his friendship with Klages had had for him in his youth. The opening sentence of the chapter on his friendship with Klages sets the tone for his discussion of the subject:

> Ludwig Klages..., every time I heard or read this name – (and with increasing years I heard and read it more and more) –, then a bright ray of joy went through me, as if I glanced at an eternal youth and knew everything fulfilled that I desired and expected of my life.[63]

Lessing describes, how Klages and he used to spend their days together, talking and talking, completely taken up with conversations no adult would have understood. He captures their relation in a beautiful image:

> Our homeward ways would take peculiar shape. I always brought Klages the little stretch to his home. But having arrived there, we were so much involved in such huge subjects that now he, again, came back with me to the fence of our garden. There we stayed, really wanted to say 'bye', but fell into such enormous topics that now once again I had to come with him to his house, and so we shuttled back and forth between the two homes [...].[64]

---

62 E.-V. Kotowski, o.c., 278–286.
63 'Ludwig Klages..., so oft ich diesen Namen gehört oder gelesen habe – (und mit zunehmenden Jahren habe ich ihn immer häufiger gehört und gelesen) –, da durchzuckte mich ein heller Strahl von Freude, als blicke ich in eine ewige Jugend und wußte alles erfüllt, was ich von meinem Leben begehrt und erwartet habe'; *Eunw*, 172.
64 'Unsre Heimwege gestalteten sich merkwürdig. Immer brachte ich Klages noch das kleine Stück bis zu seinem Haus. Aber dort angelangt, waren wir in so gewaltiger Gegenstände vertieft, daß nun er wieder mit zurückging zum Gitter unsres Hofes. Dort blieben wir stehen, wollten eigentlich "Djüs" sagen, aber gerieten in so gewaltige Sachen, daß nun ich nochmals bis zu seiner Haustür mitgehen mußte, und so pendelten wir zwischen den zwei Häusern her und hin [...]'; o.c., 181–182.

Lessing and Klages discussed the books they read – and they read all kinds of books, from classical authors to contemporary literature. And, as Klages wrote, "every reading was the starting-point for critical conversations on lyric poetry, epic, drama, novel, novellas etc., intertwined with meditations as apprehending as confused on God, the world and mankind, and coupled with rather failed efforts to penetrate into the so-called philosophy that generally was dismissed as 'failed poetry'".[65] An author Lessing and Klages especially favoured was the writer and politician Wilhelm Jordan (1819–1904), who with his writings wanted to renew the German national epic. A particular favourite of Lessing was Johannes Scherr (1817 1886), historian of art and culture. Apart from the books they read, Lessing and Klages discussed their own writings, mainly poetry that in part was published when they were older.

Apart from Klages, Lessing found solace as well with the actress Margarethe Ehrenbaum (1831–1901), a friend of his family, who took care of him from when he was fourteen. To her, "my sad childhood owed its meagre happiness", Lessing wrote in 1911, she was "the best person I had".[66] And in his autobiography he observed "[w]ithout her, I would not have stayed alive".[67] In this book, he even refers to her as his foster mother. Fritz, the younger brother of Margarethe, had been a close friend of Sigmund Lessing in their youth. In fact, the Ehrenbaum family visited the Lessing family in Hanover when they made a stopover on their way to Fritz's wedding party. Ever since that visit, Margarethe Erenbaum stayed in close contact with the Lessing family. Sigmund Lessing held her in high esteem, and for his wife Adèle she was, in Theodor Lessing's words, "an incontestably valid oracle".[68] Thus, Margarethe was in an ideal position to mediate between both Sigmund and Adèle, and between Sigmund and Theodor, becoming "the good genius in our wretched house".[69] Theodor would stay with her at her home in Berlin-Charlottenburg during his school vacations, or they would travel together, people often taking him for her son. Grete Ehrenbaum introduced him to the world of the theatre, and to literary circles

---

65   'An jede Lektüre knüpften sich kritische Gespräche über Lyrik, Epos, Drama, Roman, Novelle usw., durchflochten mit ebenso ahnungsvollen wie verworrenen Meditationen über Gott, Welt und Menschheit und begleitet von ziemlich erfolglosen Versuchen, einzudringen in die sogenannte Philosophie, die im allgemeinen als "missglückte Dichtung" abgetan wurde'; Ludwig Klages, 'Aufzeichnungen von Klages aus den Jahren 1943–54', quoted from E.-V. Kotowski, o.c., 127.
66   'der meine traurige Kindheit ihr karges Glück zu danken habe', 'der beste Mensch, den ich besessen habe'; Theodor Lessing, 'Ferdinand Lasalle', in: *PaT*, 397.
67   'Ohne sie wäre ich nicht am Leben geblieben'; *Eunw*, 150.
68   'unumstößlich gültige Orakel'; o.c., 156.
69   'der gute Genius unseres unseligen Hauses'; loc.cit..

she was friendly with. In the chapter he wrote on her in his autobiography,[70] Lessing suggests she might even have been in love with him, despite being over forty years older than he was. Be that as it may, according to Lessing she saved his life.

One of the results of the close friendship between Lessing and Klages was that both neglected their school work: their school record deteriorated. Because of this, Lessing's father forbade their companionship. This did not, however, bring an end to their friendship: henceforth, they would meet in secret, and exchange letters to keep their interchange of ideas going. Because Lessing's school record did not improve, in 1891 his father eventually transferred him to a school in Hameln, the *Städtischen Gymnasium* (currently the *Schiller-Gymnasium*), to make sure he would at long last pass his final exam and get a school diploma. As a result, Lessing and Klages hardly ever met, but they continued their exchange of letters until the time both of them were studying at university in Munich, where they could meet again without parental restrictions. In Hameln, one of Lessing's teachers was the classicist Max Schneidewin (1843–1931), at last a teacher who understood the young Lessing and managed to encourage him in his studies, with the desired result, and who, moreover, introduced him to the philosophy of Arthur Schopenhauer that would prove to be such an important influence on him, and to the work of Eduard von Hartmann. Schneidewin "was for me the only teacher whom I loved", Lessing later wrote.[71] Schneidewin for his part in later years contributed a number of times to the *Anti-Rüpel* ('The Anti-Rowdy'), the monthly of the *Antilärm Verein* ('Anti-Noise Society'), when Lessing was its editor.[72] Moreover, he supported Lessing in 1925, when he was in difficulties over his infamous satire on Hindenburg.[73]

All his reading, all his conversations with Klages, all the letters to and from Klages helped Lessing to develop a philosophy of his own. Indeed, he claims that what he calls "my most personal primordial idea of my philosophy"[74] – the very idea that was of central importance in his mature philosophy, the

---

70 'Meine Pflegemutter'; o.c., 155–161.
71 'Er ist mir der einzig liebe Lehrer gewesen'; Theodor Lessing, 'Gerichtstag über mich selbst', 394.
72 Max Schneidewin, 'Lärm im Schulunterricht', in: *Der Anti-Rüpel 1* (1908–1909), nr. 7, 128; Max Schneidewin, 'Über den Willensentschluß als Hilfe gegen peinigende Lärmempfindung – Schullärm', in: *Der Anti-Rüpel 1* (1908–1909), nr. 8, 50; and Max Schneidewin, 'Vom Lärm in der Schule', in: *Der Anti-Rüpel 1* (1908–1909), nr. 9, 166.
73 See chapter one, 7–8.
74 'der mir eigenste Urgedanke meiner Philosophie'; *Eunw*, 248.

so-called "three spheres theory"[75] that he himself considered to be the foundation of his world view[76] – shot up in his consciousness in a flash, during a walk in Hanover with Klages, when he was only seventeen.[77]

Not surprisingly, living in two hells shaped Lessing's worldview:

> Hence, desperation had to awake, as soon as I overcame the first stuffy sleep of childhood. The world appeared to me only as a place of suffering. Men as tormentors or tormented.[78]

And it changed him: "I had to become a fighter out of the need of my situation."[79]

Now, if we do take seriously Lessing's idea that all true philosophy eventually is nothing but the meditation on his own life by the philosopher; and if we do infer from *Einmal und nie wieder* that he experienced his youth as nothing but suffering, it is hardly surprising that, according to Lessing, to be human is to suffer. Or, in other words, the human condition is to be in need – and hence Lessing called his philosophy "the philosophy of need".[80]

2   Wandering Years, and Back to Hanover

Having at long last successfully finished his secondary school, Theodor Lessing continued his education at university. His father pressured him to read medicine, expecting his son to succeed him eventually in his practice in Hanover.[81] Thus, Theodor Lessing was not free to choose what he wanted to read at university, but he was, however, allowed the choice at which university he wanted to study. He preferred Freiburg im Breisgau, being "the remotest, where it would not be easy for someone from the family to keep a check on me".[82] Lessing wanted to get away from his family as far as possible, not only because of his still

---

75 'Dreisphärentheorie'.
76 Cfr. *GSS4*, 117.
77 *Eunw*, 248–249.
78 'So mußte Hoffnungslosigkeit erwachen, sobald ich über den ersten dumpfen Schlaf der Kinderjahre hinaus kam. Die Welt erschien mir nur als Leidensstätte. Die Menschen als Quäler oder Gequälte.'; o.c., 101.
79 'Ich mußte zum Kämpfer werden aus der Not meiner Lage heraus.'; o.c., 95.
80 'die Philosophie der Not'; e.g., o.c., 251.
81 Theodor Lessing, 'Gerichtstag über mich selbst', 395.
82 'die entfernteste, wo nicht leicht einer von der Familie mich beaufsichtigen konnte'; *Eunw*, 246.

troublesome relation with his parents, especially his father, but also because he had quite different things in mind, apart from reading medicine. First and foremost, he wanted to pursue his literary ambitions, and besides to immerse himself in every subject that interested him. He set himself a tight daily timetable, rising early and going to bed early, doing physical exercises every morning and evening, hoping all this would help him both to meet the demands his study set him, and to write prose and poetry and read widely. After a year in Freiburg, Lessing decided to move to Bonn, to continue his studies at the local university. In late nineteenth century Germany, it was not at all unusual for students to change universities once or even several times during their study; Lessing's decision to leave Freiburg was prompted by the behaviour of members of student societies in the streets of the city, which frequently annoyed him. However, in this respect Bonn was hardly better: university life there as well was dominated by student societies. In Freiburg and especially Bonn, the curriculum for students of medicine very much focused on subjects like anatomy, physiology, and chemistry. In Bonn, Lessing concentrated far more on his study than he had done in Freiburg. His study results were excellent, but he had to work extremely hard to obtain them. Indeed, after a year in Bonn, he was exhausted and had to take a break. But as he passed his exams *summa cum laude*, even his father was very pleased with him, and offered him a break in the autumn and winter of 1894, a time Lessing mainly spent in the Bavarian mountains around Gartenkirchen. During this break, out of the poems he had been writing since his youth he compiled a volume of poetry, *Laute und leise Lieder* ('Loud and Soft Songs') that was to be published in 1896.

By that time, Theodor Lessing had already managed to find a publisher for his first book: under the pen-name Theodor Lensing, in 1893[83] his debut-novel *Comödie* was issued, in two parts, by Wilhelm Friedrich in Leipzig. As this publisher demanded a contribution to the costs of printing the book, Lessing saved on his livelihood, for instance by abstaining from eating meat and by cutting back his consumption of wine, to collect the necessary money. But he still needed some financial support, which was offered by both Grete Ehrenbaum and Ludwig Klages. In a nutshell, *Comödie*, set in the second half of the nineteenth century, tells the story of a conflict over a wood, in which a German forester's family lives quite happily. But a rich Jewish factory owner, who is only guided by his desire for money, wants to stub the wood, as he needs the space to be able to enlarge his business. Because he can spend lots of money in legal procedures, in the end the factory owner manages to get his way. The

---

83   Library catalogues give 1894 as year of publication, whereas for instance Marwedel gives 1893; Lessing himself, in his autobiography, gives 1893 as year of publication as well.

underlying theme of the novel is a criticism of capitalism, of a world that is ruled by money, by those who have money. In contrast, the life of the forester's family is idealised and romanticised. With his portrait of a rich, greedy Jew, only guided by the wish for even more money, Lessing fitted well into a trend in nineteenth century German literature, and German and even West-European culture at large: it was not at all uncommon to criticise capitalism, nor to blame Jews for the increasing influence of capitalism. For his part, Sigmund Lessing, Theodor's father, took deep offence with the novel: not without reason, he thought he recognised himself to a large extent in the portrait of the Jew obsessed with making money. At the time, Theodor Lessing himself thought very highly of his book and had great – even excessive – expectations of the reception it would get, anticipating it would do nothing less than change the world, or at least his own position in it. However, the result was quite different:

> And what happened? Nothing at all. No approval, no disapproval. Everything remained as it was.[84]

Afterwards, Lessing's view of the book changed completely: in his autobiography he mockingly described it as "the thick world redemption piece" and dismissed it as "the silliest of child's work".[85]

The almost complete lack of response to his novel was the main reason Lessing changed his attitude towards his study of medicine, and explains why in Bonn he concentrated far more on it than he had done earlier in Freiburg. All his hard work and his excellent study results had brought him a position as an assistant during lectures by one of his professors. Moreover, through his anatomical and physiological studies Lessing developed enough knowledge of the process of breathing to be able to use it in later years as a metaphor to describe an important aspect of his philosophy of need. In a sense, in the process of breathing, man, or for that matter every creature that is breathing, poisons himself. This is, however, not fatal, as through a spontaneous reversal that is part of the very same process, the poison is emitted. Likewise, to be in need is potentially fatal, but a spontaneous reversal that is part of the process of being in need can and often will prevent fatalities. In other words, the need usually stems itself.[86]

---

84 'Und was geschah? Gar nichts. Kein Zuspruch, kein Widerspruch. Es blieb alles beim Alten'; Theodor Lessing, o.c., 271.
85 'das dicke Welterlösungswerk'; 'die albernste Kinderei' ; o.c., 246.
86 See o.c., 249–250.

Although his year in Bonn had been very fruitful indeed, after his break in the second half of 1894, Lessing decided not to return, but to move to Munich instead, where he wanted to complete his studies and to start research into the working of the human gland, with the prospect of rounding it off with a dissertation on this subject. Most likely, this was not, however, the main reason for Lessing's decision to move to Munich. Ludwig Klages, then studying in Leipzig, had informed Lessing in a letter that he as well would be moving to Munich. Lessing hoped that, once they were living in the same city again, they could resume their close and treasured friendship, like in the days they were classmates in Hanover.

Munich at the time was a true centre of cultural renewal, where all kinds of writers, poets, playwrights, actors, painters, and philosophers lived. Especially the quarter of Schwabing, a former village only recently incorporated in the city, was notorious for the bohemianism of the artists, would-be artists and their following who took up residence there. In a reminiscence of the former socialist leader Ferdinand Lassalle (1825–1864) and his erstwhile wife, the writer Helene von Dönniges (1846–1911), Lessing gave an impression of the bohemians of Munich:

> [...] young men, writing poems and novels, carrying "humanity" toward heaven on their drooping shoulders. Young women from Schwabing in reform clothes, with plaits, practising arts and crafts and landscape painting [...] those poets, who with the gown of prophets and the gestures of tired aesthetes covered all kinds of cravings and defects, and love poetry together with good food. Also those who needed comfort, who take their comfort as the formula for solving the riddle of the world. Armchair anarchists who cannot bear the smell of the poor and that crowd of those philosophers who take philosophy for their couch or loitering bed. Thus, one chattered and wrote away one's life, spent one's days most agreeably, socialized Germany during tea at five o'clock, enjoyed oneself in the name of "psychology" with spiritual gossip and coquetted, quoting spirits, with Napoleon or with Shelley.[87]

---

87 '[...] Gedichte- und Romeschreibende Jünglinge, die auf abfallenden Schultern die „Menschheit" himmelan tragen. Schwabinger Jungfrauen mit Reformkleidern und Schneckerlfrisuren, Kunstgewerbe oder Landschaftsmalerei kultivierend [...] jene Dichter, die mit dem Talar des Prophetentums oder der Geste müder Ästheten allerhand Gelüst oder Defekt verdecken und Poesie in Verbindung mit guten Essen lieben. Auch jene Trostbedürftigen, die ihres Trostes Formel für die Lösung des Welträtsels halten. Salonanarchisten, die keinen Armeleutegeruch vertragen können und die Schar jener Philosophen, die unter Philosophie ihr Ruhe- oder Lungerbett verstehn. So verredete und

A well-known satirical description of life in Schwabing was given by an acquaintance of Lessing's, countess Franziska zu Reventlow (1871–1918) in her roman à clef *Herrn Dames Aufzeichnungen* ('Mr. Lady's Notes'; 1913), a minor classic in early twentieth century German literature that contains descriptions of amongst others Ludwig Klages. Fanny zu Reventlow had a most complicated love life, but for Ludwig Klages she was most probably the love of his life, although the two of them never married.[88] Theodor Lessing went into lodgings in Schwabing, living in the house of an elderly widow, in the noisiest of rooms. – Afterwards, from 1908, when he, being the founder of the German *Anti-Noise Society*, was deeply involved in the battle against all kinds of noise that disturb the life of a human being, he would refer to his stay in these lodgings as the very origin of his involvement in the fight against noise. They were situated in the entertainment district of Schwabing, and its noise often kept him awake all night, and as a result he could get hardly any work done during the day.[89] – Lessing continued his studies, but being nearby so many writers and poets resumed writing poetry, and started writing stage plays.

Oddly enough, Lessing's literary reputation got a real boost when, in the aftermath of the scandal surrounding the playwright Oskar Panizza,[90] his lodgings were searched by the local police and some of his manuscripts were even impounded. His hasty defence of the playwright in his lampoon *Der Fall Panizza* ('The Panizza case'), written when he had not even read Panizza's play *Das Liebeskonzil* that caused all the commotion, threw police suspicion on him. Even after his lodgings were searched, he was under police surveillance for some time, as he was suspected of adhering to "atheism or communism or some other –ism".[91] But through the very fact that his lodgings were searched by the police, Lessing came to the notion of literary circles in Munich. Suddenly, magazines and journals, especially of course those based in the Bavarian capital, were open to his contributions. Initially, he mainly wrote reviews

---

zerschrieb man das Leben, verbrauchte seine Tage auf das angenehmste, sozialisierte Deutschland beim Fünfuhrtee, vergnügte sich unter dem Namen „Psychologie" an geistvoller Médisance und kokettierte, Geister zitierend, mit Napoleon oder mit Shelley'; Theodor Lessing, 'Ferdinand Lasalle' in: *PaT*, 403.

88 Lessing described some of his reminiscences of Fanny zu Reventlow in his essay 'Zwei Gräber', in: *Prager Tagblatt*, 29.7.1928; reprinted in: *IFEG* , 402–406.
89 See Lawrence Baron, 'Noise and Degeneration: Theodor Lessing's Crusade for Quiet', *Journal of Contemporary History* 17 (1982), 165–178; Matthias Lentz, '"Ruhe ist die erste Bürgerpflicht". Lärm, Großstadt und Nervosität im Spiegel von Theodor Lessings „Antilärmverein"', *Medizin, Gesellschaft und Geschichte* 13 (1994), 81–105; and John Goodyear, 'Viel Lärm um Theodor Lessing', in: *Angermion* 4 (2011), 95–112.
90 See Chapter 1 above, 6.
91 'des Atheismus oder Kommunismus oder sonst eines –ismus verdächtig'; *Eunw*, 294.

of books and stage plays, but gradually his output broadened, and he started writing essays and articles as well. As a result, Lessing cheerfully took his leave from his studies and of medical sciences: "Goodbye studies and medicine", he recalled in his autobiography.[92]

Living in the same city with Klages again did not bring what Lessing had hoped for: they did not resume the close friendship of their schooldays. Indeed, their friendship loosened and loosened, one of the reasons being that Klages joined the informal circle surrounding the poet Stefan George (1868–1933). At the time, Klages was completely fascinated by George's personality and presentation: for him, George had become the archetype of the true artist and poet. But until then, Lessing himself had for Klages been the archetype of the true poet, and not surprisingly Lessing suffered from the impression that Klages was about to exchange him for George as his bosom friend, and thus felt rejected. From his part, Lessing could not take George completely serious: in *Einmal und nie wieder* he described him as a snob and a poseur who "strode through the pub like the bishop through the middle of Saint Peter's".[93] According to Lessing, George behaved as if he was the pontiff of poetry. Moreover, Lessing did not at all understand George's rather esoteric and inaccessible poetry, although later in life he would learn to appreciate it more. Indeed, later, in his book *Schopenhauer–Wagner–Nietzsche* (1906) he did quote poetry by George.[94] But all in all, Lessing never felt at ease with the circle surrounding George – to which Klages, on the contrary, felt increasingly attracted –, and he never really wanted to link up with it. Hence, Lessing and Klages gradually alienated, although there was not yet a complete rupture between the two. They did, for example, attend lectures by the psychologist and philosopher Theodor Lipps (1851–1914) together.

In March 1896 Sigmund Lessing, who for several weeks had been severely ill with heart problems, died. According to Theodor Lessing, who for some weeks watched by his father but was not with him when he eventually died, his deathbed was horrible, as his father was overcome by a great fear of death. Despite all the problems and arguments they had had, and deeply impressed by his difficult death, Theodor Lessing truly pitied his father. He discussed the difficult deathbed of his father with his maternal grandfather, Leopold Ahrweiler (1818–1898). Ever since Sigmund Lessing and Adèle Ahrweiler married, the relation between Sigmund Lessing and Leopold Ahrweiler had been most difficult. Even during the last years of Sigmund Lessing's life, when he was

---

92   'Ade Studium und Medizin'; o.c., 294–295.
93   'schritt [...] durch das Café, wie der Bischof durch die Mitte von Sankt Peter'; o.c., 305.
94   S-W-N, 107.

suffering from a bad health and, moreover, had severe financial problems, Leopold Ahrweiler refused to help his son-in-law financially, although he had all the means to do so. But because Sigmund Lessing was too proud to ask for help, Leopold Ahrweiler refused to give it – even though he knew all too well his own daughter was suffering from those very financial problems. But after Sigmund Lessing died, presumably out of a sense of guilt, Leopold Ahrweiler promised to take care of his daughter and two grandchildren. Sophie Lessing, Theodor's sister, received a quite large lump sum, but Theodor himself was granted a monthly allowance of 500 *Reichsmark*, and, moreover, his grandfather promised him to remember him generously in his will. Hence, once all the formalities of the funeral were over, Theodor Lessing returned to Munich, thinking he was financially independent, and one day would even be rich. So he could feel free to pursue his intellectual and literary ambitions without the need to earn a living.

But about the same time, Theodor Lessing started to doubt his future as a poet and an author – he no longer knew what he really wanted to do with his life. For two years, he travelled a lot, spending, for instance, a large part of 1897 in South-Tirol. There he rented rooms close to Omar al Raschid Bey (1839–1911), with whom he had become friends in Munich. Al Raschid Bey was of German-Jewish descent, but born in Russia, as Friedrich Arnd.[95] For some time, he had lived in Turkey, where he converted to Islam, and where he changed his name into Omar al Raschid Bey. His conversion offered him the opportunity to divorce his wife under Islamic law, and to marry the writer Helene Böhlau (1856–1940). Al Raschid Bey had a great interest in Asian philosophy and religion, of which he developed a thorough knowledge. He introduced Theodor Lessing to Asian philosophy and religion; as Lessing put it in his autobiography: "through him I first made my acquaintance with Asian wisdom".[96] According to Lessing, al Raschid Bey and he were worried by the very same question:

> The enigma of knowledge itself. Why, whence, did the element wake up in us? For what the will that moulds history? Why timeline and end? And what is the end?[97]

---

95   Lessing gives his name as Arndt-Kürnberg; cfr. o.c., 363.
96   'durch ihn lernte ich zuerst die Weisheit Asiens kennen'; o.c., 364. In 1912, Lessing wrote a study of Omar al Raschid Bey, which he included in his *Philosophie als Tat*; see Theodor Lessing, 'Omar al Raschid Bey', in: *PaT*, 374–395.
97   'Das Rätsel des Wissens selbst. Warum, woher, ist das Element in uns wach geworden? Wozu der Geschichte bildende Wille? Warum Zeitlinie und Ziel? Und was ist das Ziel?'; *Eunw*, 364.

Ever since al Raschid Bey introduced Asian wisdom to Lessing, it remained very important to him – in later years, he would express many of the central ideas of his own philosophy of need in the terminology of Asian wisdom as well as in the terminology of Western philosophy, claiming his philosophy of need could be equally well expressed in the language of both traditions. But one should not, I think, overestimate the importance of Asian wisdom for the development of Lessing's own philosophy. After all, in *Einmal und nie wieder* he repeatedly claims that the basic ideas of his philosophical system date from his youth and schooldays, when he was not yet familiar with Asian wisdom. During his stay in South-Tirol, Lessing began writing a philosophical text, "Spiele und Freuden im Garten Epikurs" ('Plays and joys in Epicurus' garden'), parts of which he would include, in 1928, in his book *Dämonen* ('Demons'), the third part of his nature trilogy.[98] But eventually, Lessing got enough of the life he was leading:

> I felt the need for a turning point, sensed the danger of dissolving myself in pointless dreams and passively vegetating my life and in eternal occupation with my own self. I longed for a task and for action [...] For where was my end? Where the substance of my life? For what reason was I living at all?[99]

At the very same time Lessing was passing through this crisis, early in 1898, he received a letter, signed by a certain 'Maria'. She wrote to tell him she had read everything he had written, but was worried about the direction he had recently taken with the publication of the booklet *Weiber! 301 Stoßseufzer über das 'schönere' Geschlecht* ('Women! 301 sighs on the fair sex'; 1897), a collection of satirical poems on the weaker sex. Lessing himself described his poems, in the epilogue of the booklet, as "three hundred and one contributions to the study of woman".[100] Even if some of these poems are at best amusing, most of them express popular prejudices about women, or about the perpetual battle between the sexes. To give but one example:

---

98   The other parts were *Meine Tiere* (My Animals, 1926) and *Blumen* (Flowers, 1928).
99   'Ich fühlte die Notwendigkeit eines Wendepunktes, spürte die Gefahr der Selbstauflösung, in zwecklosen Träumen und passivem Dahinvegetieren und ewigem Beschäftigen mit dem eigenen Ich. Mich verlangte nach Aufgabe und Tat. [...] Denn wo war mein Ziel? Wo mein Lebensinhalt? Wofür lebte ich eigentlich?'; Theodor Lessing, o.c., 368.
100 'dreihunderteins Beiträge zur Frauenkunde'; Theodor Lessing, *Weiber! 301 Stoßseufzer über das 'schönere' Geschlecht* (Berlin 1897), 115.

> The stuff of a single rib of one man
> Sufficed for the whole of women's army.
> O God! From the fair sex set us free,
> And give me back my rib again!¹⁰¹

Lessing answered his correspondent in a very long letter, almost a confession. This was the start of an exchange of letters, resulting in a rendezvous, a love affair and, eventually, in 1900, a marriage. Her full name was Maria Stach von Goltzheim (1876–1948); her family belonged to the Prussian nobility, and was distantly related to the Hohenzollern. Her parents opposed a relation between their daughter and Lessing, most likely because of his Jewish descent, but this did not stop her – on the contrary, it made her even more determined to marry him, even if it meant she was disinherited by her family. "In the shape of Maria, for the first time love […] came on my path", Lessing wrote in his autobiography.¹⁰²

In 1898, Lessing's grandfather Leopold Ahrweiler died. Despite his promise to remember Theodor Lessing generously in his will, he left him nothing at all. Moreover, with the death of his grandfather, the monthly allowance Lessing received abruptly stopped. Hence, his grandfather's broken promise left Theodor Lessing not only without the fortune he had expected to inherit, but also without his monthly income, without a regular job – although every now and then he managed to make some money with his writings in journals and magazines –, with an incomplete medical education, and about to marry a wife who herself had been disinherited because of the very fact that she wanted to marry him. Not surprisingly, Lessing experienced all this as an enormous change in his life – looking back, he described it as the true end of his youth,¹⁰³ as the moment the boy Theodor Lessing was forced to change into the man Theodor Lessing.

Moreover, his friendship with Ludwig Klages came to an unhappy end. His relation with Maria Stach von Goltzheim definitely contributed to the break with Klages, as she and Klages simply detested each other, much to Lessing's surprise: "Never did I understand in depth, why both poles of my life, the friend

---

101   'Der Stoff von einer einzgen Männerrippe
      Genügte für das ganze Weiberheer.
      O Gott! Befrei uns von der edlen Sippe
      Und gieb mir meine Rippe wieder her!'
      Theodor Lessing, o.c., 11.
102   'Unter Marias Gestalt trat zum erstenmal die Liebe […] in meinen Weg'; *Eunw*, 369.
103   Loc. cit..

and the wife, Ludwig Klages and Maria, had to repel and to exclude each other".[104] Apart from that, Klages moved further and further away from Lessing, engaging himself in circles where Lessing was not at all at ease, or where he was not even welcome because he was Jewish. But Lessing did not want to give up his friendship with Klages, and tried to maintain their relation. Then Klages wrote him a letter, formally terminating their friendship. Lessing visited Klages, to ask for an explanation. Allegedly, Klages coldly remarked "you are a repulsive, intrusive Jew".[105] This was the end of their friendship: "I left. We never met again", Lessing wrote in his autobiography.[106] He would regret the break ever after. And although later in life Lessing would fight accusations alleging he derived most, if not all of his philosophical ideas from Klages – and, indeed, claiming that if one of them was the leading partner in developing philosophical ideas it must have been himself rather than Klages –, whenever he mentioned Klages in his writings it was always with great respect.[107] Besides this, in 1906, he used a few lines of a poem by Klages as motto in his book *Schopenhauer – Wagner – Nietzsche*. Moreover, in this book he was distinctly positive about the contribution Klages made to the development of scientific graphology.[108] Lessing always refrained from running down or insulting Klages: he remained true to the spirit of the friendship he so deeply cherished all through his teens. As he wrote in his autobiography:

> All through my life, I continued to live with my deceased, with Ludwig Klages and with Maria. There was not a single day that I did not converse with them in a hundred dialogues.[109]

But an observation Lessing makes in his *Probevorlesung* "Wissenschaft als Kraftökonomie" is revealing. In this lecture he contends, among other things, that the personal past as an individual remembers it, is not fixed at all: the

---

104 'Niemals ist es mir aus der Tiefe verständlich geworden, warum die beiden Pole meines Lebens, der Freund und die Frau, Ludwig Klages und Maria, einander abstoßen und ausschließen mußten'; o.c., 382.
105 'Du bist ein ekelhafter, zudringlicher Jude'; o.c., 382–383.
106 'Ich ging. Wir haben uns nie wieder gesehen'; o.c., 383.
107 Lessing analysed his friendship with Klages at length in his essay Theodor Lessing, 'Meine Beziehungen zu Ludwig Klages', reprinted in: *Eunw*, 413–446; for a very well documented and balanced view of the relation between Lessing and Klages, cfr. Elke-Vera Kotowski, *Feindliche Dioskuren*; and cfr. above, 40–42.
108 *S-W-N*, 192.
109 'Ich habe das ganze Leben hindurch mit meinen Toten, mit Ludwig Klages und mit Maria weiter gelebt. Es gab keinen Tag, an dem ich nicht in hundert Dialogen mich mit ihnen auseinandergesetzt hätte'; *Eunw*, 384.

remembered past changes all the time. This is, Lessing argues, nothing less but necessary and, indeed, a prerequisite for maintaining inner balance. A human being simply has to adapt his remembered past in order to keep his mental balance. Observed from the outside, this may look like forgery, or tampering with the past, but forgery is not, at least according to Lessing, what it essentially is. Essentially, it is a necessary way of handling developments and changes in one's personal life. But occasionally, the confrontation with evidence from the past may reveal how the remembered past diverges from the past as it emerges from this evidence. This may happen, for example, when one rereads letters written in one's youth:

> Does a stronger proof exist for the function of saving strength that our memory has, than reading in browned letters? The friend who only a few years ago called you his leader, now claims that you disappointed him, and would never admit that only he himself changed, that his friendship did not survive himself. The woman who only from you received her life, claims, when she starts to love someone else, explaining herself retrospectively, that she was not happy by your side.[110]

The autobiographical inspiration for this observation is all too obvious: it refers to Lessing's break with Klages, as well as to the way his marriage with Maria Stach von Goltzheim eventually ran on the rocks.[111] – Of course, the fact that this observation is autobiographically inspired does not alter its value as such; indeed, the very idea that the past is not fixed is an essential part of Lessing's thinking on history, regardless of whether it concerns the personal past of an individual, or the shared past of a community. –

Ever since his grandfather Leopold Ahrweiler failed to live up to the promise he made to Theodor Lessing, the latter's daily life was dominated by one question only: "And from this day on at the centre of all the remainder of my path of life: the daily battle for the daily bread".[112] Obviously, Lessing now felt an

---

110 'Gibt es einen krasseren Beweis für die kraftökonomische Funktion der Erinnerung, als das Lesen in vergilbten Briefen? Der Freund, der dich vor wenig Jahren seinen Führer nannte, erklärt heute, daß du ihn enttäuscht habest und würde nicht zugeben, daß nur er selbst sich verändert, daß seine Freundschaft nicht vor sich selber bestanden habe. Die Frau, die ihr Leben erst durch Dich empfing, erklärt, wenn sie einen andern zu lieben beginnt, nachträglich sich selbst entschuldigend, daß sie an deiner Seite nicht glücklich gewesen sei.'; Theodor Lessing, "Wissenschaft als Kraftökonomie", in: *PaT*, 49.

111 For the marital problems and, eventually, the divorce of Theodor and Maria Lessing, see below, 56.

112 'Und von nun ab: Mittelpunkt des ganzen ferneren Lebensweges: der tägliche Kampf um das tägliche Brot'; *Eunw*, 371.

urgent need to complete his education and to find a job with a regular income. In 1899, he resumed his studies in Erlangen, where he attended lectures by the philosophers Gustav Class (1836–1908) and Richard Falckenberg (1851–1920). Class was strongly influenced by Kant whose ideas he tried to exceed without, however, falling back on Hegel, while Falckenberg focused his attention almost entirely on the history of philosophy, on which he wrote several at his time quite well-known books. In his dissertation, Lessing refers both to lectures by Class, and to Falckenberg's *Geschichte der neueren Philosophie von Nikolaus von Kues bis zur Gegenwart*.[113] In Erlangen, the governors of the university agreed to accept Lessing's incomplete medical education as of the same value as a schooling in philosophy; as a result, in July 1899 Lessing could take his doctor's degree in philosophy with a dissertation on the Russian Neo-Kantian philosopher Afrikan Spir (1837–1890). His erstwhile Munich teacher Theodor Lipps had published on Spir as well[114], so it is not unlikely Lipps had some influence on the choice of the subject of the dissertation. A year later, it was published. In 1900 Lessing continued his studies in philosophy and medicine in Munich and Gießen; at the latter university, he tried to complete his medical education after all, but he failed to pass the state examination, and finally gave up on a career in medicine.

Theodor Lessing and Maria Stach von Goltzheim married on January 30th, 1900, even though the material prospects for their immediate future were far from promising. Lessing tried to earn an income by his publications, and by working as a wandering teacher and lecturer, traversing Germany, and discussing all kinds of subjects. With only a tiny and irregular income, life was harsh for Theodor and Maria Lessing. But then help was at hand: first, the philosopher and psychologist Theodor Lipps, whose lectures Lessing had attended in the second half of the 1890's, not seldom in the company of Ludwig Klages, presented Lessing with a scholarship to study psychology. However, Lessing never completed his studies in psychology no more as his studies in medicine, as in 1901 he was offered a job as a teacher at the country boarding school Haubinda by his friend Hermann Lietz. Meanwhile, in rapid succession, two children were born from his marriage with Maria Stach von Goltzheim: Judith, born on January 11th, 1901, and Miriam, born on June 27th, 1902. Although Lessing did enjoy teaching at Haubinda, his career ended prematurely in 1903 with the row over the question whether pupils of Jewish descent would be allowed to attend Haubinda in years to come.[115] At about the same time as this row came about,

---

113 *Spir*, 37, for the reference to Class; and 25 and 74 for the reference to Falckenberg.
114 Theodor Lipps, 'Rezension von Afrikan Spir, *Denken und Wirklichkeit*', in: *Philosophische Monatshefte* 14 (1878), 352–361.
115 Cfr. above, 32.

Lessing suffered another tragedy. His wife Maria started an affair with one of his pupils, Bruno Frank (1887–1945), who in later years would earn some fame for himself as a novelist, and became friends with Thomas Mann. Lessing tolerated the affair for some time, hoping he might eventually save his marriage. But this affair was virtually the end of Theodor and Maria Lessing's marriage: they separated in 1904, even though it would last until 1907 before a formal divorce was eventually pronounced. Still, for Lessing even this formal divorce was not a final rift: for instance, he dedicated his book *Madonna Sixtina* (1908) to Maria, "in everlasting gratitude and reverence". For Lessing, only in 1912 the separation between Maria and himself would be complete and final.

So Lessing was on his own again: separated from his wife and his daughters, and without a job. But he managed to find a job similar to the one he had had at Haubinda, now at a country boarding school in Laubegast, close to Dresden. In a sense, the school in Laubegast was even more progressive in its approach than Haubinda: Laubegast was attended by both girls and boys, which was quite exceptional at the time. Next to his work at Laubegast, Lessing engaged himself in various social activities. He became, for instance, a spokesman in the fight for the abolition of legal prostitution, an early sign of his lifelong commitment for the emancipation of women – and a quite remarkable contrast with the jocularity of his booklet *Weiber!* from 1897. However, he had been occupied with the position of women in Western society for quite some time already, had published a couple of essays on the subject, and paid some attention to it in his introduction to contemporary German philosophy *Schopenhauer – Wagner – Nietzsche*.[116] He even had started writing a book on the subject already in his days in Munich. Eventually, it would be published as *Weib – Frau – Dame* ('Woman-Wife-Lady') in 1910.[117] His commitment to this cause appears, moreover, from stray remarks throughout his writings, for instance when he observes that one will never know how Arthur Schopenhauer's sister Adele could have developed "had the conditions for development of women been different. Had they not been, like they still are today as well".[118] In 1923, Lessing looked back on his involvement in the movement for the emancipation of women with gentle ironic mockery – and self mockery – in a column in the *Prager Tagblatt*, 'Die schönen Sünderinnen' ('The beautiful sinners'), remarking: "I spoke out in many women's societies in favour of equal rights for women, but the ladies who applauded me richly always already knew

---

116   Cfr. *S-W-N*, 329 *ff*.
117   Marwedel, o.c., 80.
118   'wenn die Entwicklungsbedingungen für Frauen andere gewesen wären. Wenn sie nicht gewesen wären, wie sie auch heute noch sind'; Theodor Lessing, o.c., 7.

everything, and the beauties whom I could have told something new preferred to play tennis".[119] And this held for his social commitment in general: he was usually preaching to the converted, and did not manage to reach those who needed to be converted.

Moreover, whilst teaching in Laubegast, Lessing started lecturing for an audience of workers from Dresden and neighbouring places, in a hall in Dresden Central Station, teaching for example an introductory course in contemporary German philosophy. One of the results of these lectures was the book *Schopenhauer – Wagner – Nietzsche* that Lessing published in 1906. Again, these lectures in Dresden were the start of a lifelong commitment. Especially after the First World War, Lessing would devote himself with great dedication to teaching the workers of Hanover in the *Volkshochschule Hannover*, of which he was, together with his second wife Ada, the driving force – she as an organizer and director, he as a teacher. This *Volkshochschule* still exists, and since 2006 bears their name: the *Ada und Theodor Lessing Volkshochschule Hannover*, in fully deserved recognition of all the work they did in between 1919 and 1933 – in the latter year National-Socialists took control of the school, and Ada Lessing was dismissed, whereas Theodor Lessing already had fled Germany.[120]

As much as Lessing enjoyed teaching his pupils at Laubegast, he did not see it as a job he would want to do for ever, and for this reason he decided to move on. He went to Göttingen, where he found a job as a theatre critic with the local newspaper, the *Göttinger Zeitung*.[121] At the time, the theatre was very important for Lessing, as he himself indicated:

> [...] those eventful years of wandering, during which I took nothing as seriously as tragedy and theatre. And I do not want to forget that my writings on theatre aesthetics and my connections with the theatre, both as dramatist and critic, gave me the richest fullness of experience and many full hours and many good friendships. The children of the moment, of momentary dreams and plays, were the one I always understood best.[122]

---

119 'Ich habe in viele Frauenverbänden für die Gleichberechtigung der Frauen gekämpft; aber die Damen, die mir reichen Beifall zollten, haben immer alles schon gewußt und die Schönen, denen ich etwas Neues hätte sagen können, zogen es vor, Tennis zu spielen'; Theodor Lessing, 'Die schönen Sünderinnen', in: *Prager Tagblatt*, October 28th, 1923.
120 See chapter one, above, 15–16, 24.
121 His criticisms now are collected in Theodor Lessing, *Nachtkritiken. Kleine Schriften 1906–1907*, edited by Rainer Marwedel (Göttingen 2006).
122 '[...] jene bewegten Wanderjahre, in denen ich nichts so ernst nahm, wie das Drama und das Theater. Und ich will nicht vergessen, daß die theater-ästhetischen Schriften und die Verbindungen mit dem Theater, als Dramaturg wie als Kritiker, mir die reichste

The great value Lessing attached to theatre fits well into a larger pattern. In late nineteenth and early twentieth century German culture, the theatre played a prominent part. As the historian Walter Laqueur puts it in his well-known study of Weimar culture: "Of all the muses Thalia was closest to the heart of Weimar; the theatre expressed most faithfully the *Zeitgeist*, the stage became almost a national institution".[123] According to Laqueur, "'Weimar Culture' antedates the Weimar Republic by at least a decade",[124] and he emphasizes that "[t]he beginnings of the golden age of German drama go back to the 1890's."[125] Characteristic for this golden age of German drama was that producing plays became an art, whereas it always had been a trade. Laqueur even claims that "Berlin was the theatre capital of the world"[126] at the time. Hence, the great importance Theodor Lessing attached to theatre was no coincidence.

Moreover, from his youth onwards, Theodor Lessing had had all kinds of connections with the world of the theatre. His father Sigmund had been a passionate amateur actor in his college days; in his autobiography, Theodor Lessing reminisces a story that as a student his father played so convincingly in a student production of *Wallenstein* by Schiller (1759–1805) that the *Hoftheater* in Kassel offered to sign him. He preferred to continue his medical studies,[127] however, but in later years would often recite verses by Schiller, and according to his son all in all had a theatrical personality.[128] As a doctor in Hanover, Sigmund Lessing also was the regular doctor of the local theatre, and did often seek the company of actors performing there.[129] Besides, Grete Ehrenbaum, who regularly took care of Theodor Lessing in his teens, was a professional actress, who, of course, had all kinds of connections in the world of theatre. She introduced him to several playwrights and actors, and encouraged his interest in theatre.[130] In his autobiography, Lessing even does not want to rule out the possibility that she quietly hoped he would have chosen a career in the theatre, but that did not happen.

Erfahrungsfülle gebracht haben und manche randvolle Stunde und manche gute Freundschaft. Kinder des Augenblicks, des vergänglichen Traums und Spiels, verstand ich wohl immer am besten.'; Theodor Lessing, 'Gerichtstag über mich selbst', 403.
123   Walter Laqueur, *Weimar. A Cultural History 1918–1933* (London 1974) 140.
124   O.c., 'Preface' (without page numbers).
125   O.c., 140.
126   Loc.cit.
127   *Eunw*, 42.
128   O.c., 63.
129   O.c., 54.
130   O.c., 159.

Nevertheless, when Lessing was living in Munich in the second half of the 1890's, being deeply involved in all kinds of literary activities, he published several plays: *Christus und Venus* ('Christ and Venus'), *Im Vorfrühling* ('In Early Spring'), *Die Nationen* ('The Nations'), and *Das Recht des Lebens* ('The Right to Live'). So when Lessing started working as a theatre critic in Göttingen, he had an intimate knowledge of the stage. He did not confine himself to writing reviews of the plays he saw in Göttingen, however, but also published widely on various aspects of the theatre, for example in a series of articles in the journal *Die Schaubühne* ('The Stage'), and he continued to do so even after he left Göttingen for a job at the *Technische Hochschule* of his native Hanover. He collected his writings on the theatre in two books, *Theater-Seele* ('The Soul of the Theatre';1907) and *Der fröhliche Eselsquell* ('The Merry Donkey Well'; 1912). In both books he expresses his views on the aesthetics of the theatre.

Apart from working as a theatre critic in Göttingen, Lessing matriculated into the local university, to study with the philosopher Edmund Husserl (1859–1938). Doing so, he followed the example of a group of students of his former teacher Theodor Lipps, who in 1905 all went to Göttingen to study with Husserl, after a visit Husserl had paid to Lipps and his students in Munich in 1904.[131] The reason they preferred to continue their studies with Husserl was, so it seems, that the latter was generally seen as the herald of a new approach in philosophy, fighting the "psychologism" that under the influence of Neo-Kantianism had been so strong in German philosophy in the second half of the nineteenth century – and that Husserl himself had favoured for quite some time. Likewise, Theodor Lipps had been a spokesman for this "psychologism" in his early publications, but developed in another direction too. Unlike Husserl, however, in historiography Lipps usually still is associated with the "psychologism" he had left behind. But to a large extent, Lipps and Husserl were thinking along the same lines – even though they initially did develop their ideas independently from each other. In fact, the German philosopher Reinhold N. Smid even claims the change in approach by Lipps preceded the change in Husserl's philosophy.[132] Be that as it may, it is beyond doubt that in the second half of the 1890's, a circle of philosophers and psychologists in Munich, of which Lipps was the central figure, developed a kind of phenomenology independently of the one Husserl

---

131 Marwedel, o.c., 88.
132 Reinhold Nikolaus Smid, '"Münchener Phänomenologie" – Zur Frühgeschichte des Begriffs', in: H. Spiegelberg and E. Avé-Lallemant (ed.), *Pfänder-Studien* (The Hague 1982), 109–153, especially 116–113; and see Theodor Lessing, 'Theodor Lipps', in: *PaT*, 253–262. For a comprehensive overview of Munich phenomenology, see the well-known study by Herbert Spiegelberg, *The Phenomenological Movement. A Historical Introduction* (third and enlarged edition, The Hague etc. 1982), 166–267. See also §2.3, below.

around the same time developed, first in Halle and from 1901 in Göttingen. Shortly after the turn of the century, there were all kinds of contacts between the group in Munich and Husserl. Hence, it is hardly a coincidence that the first members of the phenomenological movement were found both at the universities of Munich, where Lipps was teaching, and Göttingen, where from 1901 Husserl was teaching. As in historiography the publication of Husserl's influential study *Logische Untersuchungen* ('Logical Investigations'; two volumes, 1900 and 1901) habitually is seen as the origin of the phenomenological movement in philosophy, these were the very early days of this movement that proved to be so influential in twentieth century philosophy.

Although Lessing never questioned the philosophical teachings of Husserl himself, he could not take completely seriously the way others ran off with this philosopher's ideas and tried to put them into practice and popularize them. Looking back in 1924 he, quite characteristically, mocked this tendency in a witty column in the *Prager Tagblatt*:

> "Phenomenology", just like morphology or characterology, nowadays is a very popular name; on the other hand, for instance sociology has become already somewhat unfashionable; however, new scientific terms are good, like for example geopolitical, psychogeographical, psychosocial, sociopsychic. These words are hard to pronounce, and for this reason alone already very distinguished. The word "phenomenological", made fashionable by E. Husserl, can be used confidently everywhere, as long as one uses it for a) always something trivial and self-evident b) never connects it with something sensual (so nothing visible, or something that can be smelled or tasted). If one fulfils these conditions, than one is ready to qualify for a PhD.[133]

Lessing's ultimate object when starting to study with Husserl was to habilitate as a university teacher, either in Göttingen or somewhere else. In 1907, he tried

---

133 '"Phänomenologie" ähnlich auch Morpho- und Charakterologie ist eine gegenwärtig sehr beliebte Bezeichnung; dagegen ist z.B. Soziologie schon wieder etwas unmodern geworden: gut hingegen sind neue wissenschaftliche Worte, wie z.B. geopolitisch, psychogeographisch, psychosozial, soziopsychisch. Diese Worte sind schwer auszusprechen und schon darum vornehm. Das Wort phänomenologisch, durch E. Husserl „modern" geworden, kann man getrost überall anwenden, wenn man sich nur vornimmt a) immer etwas Triviales und Selbstverständliches, b) niemals etwas Sinnenfälliges (also nichts Sichtbares, Riechbares, Schmeckbares) damit zu verbinden. Erfüllt man diese beiden Bedingungen, so ist man auch befähigt, den philosophischen Doktortitel zu bekommen.'; Theodor Lessing, 'Wie werde ich gebildet?', in: *Prager Tagblatt*, January 20th, 1924.

to habilitate in Dresden, but he was rejected, allegedly because of his affiliations with the SPD (*Sozialdemokratische Partei Deutschlands*, the German Social Democratic Party) and with several trade unions. However, in 1907, with a recommendation by Theodor Lipps, Lessing was accepted for habilitation at the *Technische Hochschule* of his native Hanover. So, he returned to the city of his youth, as an external university lecturer in philosophy: "Thus, in this way I became a philosopher in Hanover, and remained it for eighteen years".[134] It was an unsalaried post: he was not paid by the *Hochschule*, but by the students he taught; as Lessing wrote in his partly autobiographical 'Leibniz in Hannover', he worked at a "polytechnic for mechanical engineers [...] where I do the work of three ordinary professors for free and in vain".[135] Hence, he had to eke out his meagre wages by continuing his activities as a wandering lecturer, and as a writer in newspapers, journals and magazines.

Although Lessing only reluctantly returned to his hometown – after all the place where he spent his youth in "two hells" – settling in Hanover brought him great happiness.[136] First of all, his daughters joined him – in between his separation from Maria and his move to Hanover, the two girls had lived in a country boarding school. Moreover, in Hanover he met Ada Grothe-Abbenthern (1883–1953), who was to become his second wife. They first met around the turn of the year 1908–1909; similar to Theodor Lessing, Ada Abbenthern lived separated from her husband – her first marriage with Ernst Grothe, an elderly tenant from Bemerode, close to Hanover, did not even last for two years. As she chose to remain silent on the matter, it is not known why Ada Abbenthern married Ernst Grothe in the first place, when she was only nineteen years old, nor why the marriage broke down so quickly. Trained as a midwife, she worked in a children's home in the vicinity of Cottbus. Her work aroused an interest in ideas on the reform of education, and this interest brought her in contact with Lessing, who, after all, published and lectured on the subject. He stimulated her interest in educational reform even more, and eventually she changed jobs and started working for the magazine *Die Schönheit* ('Beauty'); she started publishing herself on educational ideas. Moreover, she engaged in the fight against prostitution, and became a champion of women's suffrage. Only in 1912, the divorce between Ernst Grothe and Ada Abbenthern was formally pronounced.

---

134 'So bin ich denn also Philosoph in Hannover geworden und bin es durch achtzehn Jahre geblieben'; Theodor Lessing, 'Gerichtstag über mich selbst', 402.

135 'eine Hochschule für Maschinenbauer [...], an welcher ich die Arbeit dreier ordentlichen Professoren gratis und frustra verrichte'; Theodor Lessing, 'Leibniz in Hannover', in: *PaT*, 459.

136 Theodor Lessing, 'Gerichtstag über mich selbst', 402.

On July 27th of the same year, she and Theodor Lessing married. In the months before their marriage they caused a minor scandal in Hanover, as they were living together without being married.[137] On February 8th 1913, Theodor Lessing's forty-first birthday, their daughter Ruth was born.

Yet another social activity Lessing took up in these years was his involvement in the battle against noise. Inspired by the example of Mrs. Isaac L. Rice (1860–1929) in the United States, who from 1905 in New York had launched a quite successful campaign against unnecessary noise, in 1908 Lessing founded the German *Anti-Lärm Verein* ('Anti-Noise League'). This was preceded by a little booklet he published the same year, *Der Lärm* ('Noise').[138] Lessing's approach to the problem of noise in everyday life differed considerably from hers, however. Mrs. Rice was very practical, aiming for limited goals, like introducing quiet zones around hospitals; for Lessing, the battle against noise was part of his criticism of Western culture at large, and he was aiming for far bigger goals, like changes in German society as a whole, and major changes in German law. Not surprisingly, this holistic approach meant he achieved far less than Mrs. Rice in the United States. German newspapers did pay attention to Lessing's crusade for quiet, but more often than not he was poked fun at, because of his evidently over-sensitive nature. Nevertheless, his anti-noise league prospered: its membership grew steadily, and in 1911 the league demanded so much time that Lessing saw himself forced to chose between his work as a philosopher and his commitment to the anti-noise league. He preferred to continue his work as philosopher, firmly resolving to work out and publish the philosophical system of his own that was taking shape in his thinking. He handed over the responsibilities for the anti-noise league to others, but without his involvement it rapidly fell apart, and silently disappeared.

Early in 1906, in between his formal leave of his work in Laubegast and his move to Göttingen, Lessing had paid a visit to Galicia, a region that now partly is in Poland, partly in Ukraine. He wanted to get an impression of Jewish life and culture: "I travelled Galicia with the intention to get acquainted with the physical and moral need of the Jews", he wrote.[139] Jews represented the third

---

137   For Ada Lessing, see Jörg Wollenberg, '"14 Jahre Volkshochschularbeit… das lasse ich nicht aus der Geschichte Hannovers löschen". Ada Lessing als geschäftsführende Leiterin der Volkshochschule Hannover von 1919–1933', in: Paul Ciupke and Karin Derichs-Kunstmann (ed.), *Zwischen Emanzipation und 'besonderer Kulturaufgabe der Frau'. Frauenbildung in der Geschichte der Erwachsenenbildung* (Essen 2001), 133–148; and Jörg Wollenberg, 'Ada und Theodor Lessing: Rückkehr unerwünscht', *Sozial. Geschichte* 21 (2006), nr. 2, 52–66.

138   Wiesbaden 1908.

139   'Ich bereiste Galizien mit der Absicht, die physische und moralische Not der Juden kennen zu lernen'; Theodor Lessing, 'Galizien. Zur Abwehr', in: *Allgemeinen Zeitung des*

largest group of the population in the region; moreover, Galicia was the source of Hasidism, a branch of Orthodox Judaism reputed for its spiritual interpretation of Jewish religion. In December 1909, Lessing published a travel report on his visit to Galicia in a series of articles in the *Allgemeinen Zeitung des Judentums* ('General Newspaper of Judaism'), based in Berlin. Apparently, Lessing was not fully aware of what he himself had written only a few years before on the impressions travelling offers:

> Because the awful truth holds that, admittedly, everything is beautiful to see, but terrible to be. This is a great truth, which clarifies why with an observing attitude to life we experience so little of life, why, for example, when travelling, when we believe to experience most, we never have an adequate impression of human life.[140]

At the time, the *Allgemeinen Zeitung des Judentums* was an important publication, indeed one of the leading publications for German speaking assimilated Jews. It paid attention to all things Jewish – politics, culture, sports – from a liberal point of view. Lessing's travel report fitted well into the general orientation of the *Allgemeinen Zeitung des Judentums*: he himself was, after all, an assimilated Jew with an interest in Jewish culture, both in general and, more specifically, in Galicia. Or, in the terminology that was often used at the time, he was a *Westjud* (Jew from the West, i.e. an assimilated Jew from Western Europe) interested in the life and culture of the *Ostjuden* (Jews from the East, i.e. non-assimilated Orthodox Jews living in Eastern Europe). Because of his travel report, Lessing was vehemently attacked, both in the *Allgemeinen Zeitung des Judentums* itself and in other newspapers, and in a lampoon by Binjamin Segel (1866–1931), *Die Entdeckungsreise des Herrn Dr. Theodor Lessing zu den Ostjuden* ('The voyage of discovery of mister Dr. Theodor Lessing to the Jews from the East').[141] Segel himself was an author from Galicia, who tried to bridge the cultural gap between the *Westjuden* and the *Ostjuden*, attempting to reconcile the modern values of the *Westjuden* with the traditional spirituality of the *Ostjuden*. In the various reactions to his travel report, Lessing was

---

    Judentums, Heft 7, (1910), reprinted in: Theodor Lessing, *Eindrücke aus Galizien*, edited by Wolgang Eggersdorfer (Hanover 2014), 40–45, there 43.

140   'Dann gilt die furchtbare Wahrheit, daß alles zwar schön zu sehen, aber entsetzlich zu sein ist. Dieses ist eine große Wahrheit, die uns klar macht, warum wir in betrachtender Stellung zum Leben so wenig vom Leben erfahren, warum z.B. auf Reisen, wo wir doch am meisten zu erleben glauben, wir niemals einen adäquaten Eindruck vom Menschenleben erhalten...'; *S-W-N*, 137.

141   Lemberg 1910.

accused of a general lack of knowledge of Jewish culture and religion, resulting in a lack of understanding of what he had observed. Moreover, according to his critics his travel report was full of prejudices and hasty generalizations. Some of his critics even accused him of downright anti-Semitism. In a short reply to his critics, 'Galizien. Zur Abwehr' ('Galicia. In Defence'),[142] Lessing tried to defend himself, claiming that his observations eventually were nothing but the result of a genuine interest in, and a real concern for, the Jewish people from Galicia. Moreover, he accused his critics of a misplaced sense of solidarity: instead of instinctively closing the ranks because of his at times indeed critical remarks, they should take his criticisms to heart and try to improve the life of the *Ostjuden*.

The controversy over his travel report had hardly passed when Lessing, in 1910, was the central figure of a literary scandal, when he published a satirical portrait of the literary critic Samuel Lublinski.[143] Again, Lessing was accused of anti-Semitism, for instance because he describes Lublinski as "a greasy little synagogue".[144] In a balanced analysis of the Lublinski affair, Lessing's biographer Rainer Marwedel quite convincingly argues, however, that the accusation of anti-Semitism is the result of a malicious interpretation of Lessing's satire. It is not anti-Semitic, but directed against those assimilated Jews who internalised West European culture that much that they completely identified with it, and tended to forget, if not to deny willingly that they were related to the *Ostjuden*. For Lessing, Lublinski was a typical example of an assimilated Jew who identified completely with especially West European literature, and who ignored his roots and the tradition he emanated from. Lessing's criticisms were directed against this tendency, seeing Lublinski as an archetype, but not against Lublinski as an individual.[145] Indeed, in a sense the satirical portrait of Lublinski was a warning Lessing directed at himself, the warning that he, Lessing, should not ignore his cultural ties with the *Ostjuden*, and that for this very reason he should not identify completely with German culture. Be that as it may, the Lublinski portrait can nevertheless hardly be considered a demonstration of good taste, especially when Lessing addresses Lublinski's physical appearance to criticise his ways of thinking. Yet, Thomas Mann's defence of Lublinski is even far more deplorable: it is downright anti-Semitic, and was,

---

142 Theodor Lessing, 'Galizien. Zur Abwehr', *passim*.
143 See above, Chapter One, 6–7.
144 Theodor Lessing, 'Samuel zieht die Bilanz', in: *Die Schaubühne* 6, 1 (1910), 65–73; reprinted in: Theodor Lessing, *Samuel zieht die Bilanz und Tomi melkt die Moralkuh oder Zweier Könige Sturze. Eine Warnung für Deutsche, Satiren zu schreiben* (Hannover 1910), 17–27; there 17.
145 Marwedel, o.c., 134–142.

at least in part, induced by withheld motives of a personal nature. – There were several links between Lessing and Mann's family; when he lived in Göttingen, for instance, Lessing had been a quite close friend of Mann's sister Carla Mann (1881–1910), who worked as an actress there. Lessing himself refers to his companionship with Carla Mann in his essay "Ein Buchhandler" ('A bookseller'), describing how a group of people, amongst whom both Carla Mann and himself, regularly met in "Café Hapke" in Göttingen, to discuss all kinds of things.[146] They kept in touch after she left Göttingen for Mülhausen (at present Mulhouse) in the Alsace.[147] It is not at all unlikely that the shrill tone of Mann's defence of Lublinski was at least in part the result of these withheld motives – . Years later, Lessing would take some kind of revenge on Mann, in a satirical portrait in the title story of his collection of satires and stories *Feind im Land* (1923; 'Enemy within the country'), in which he for instance characterizes Mann as "the Shakespeare of the luxury sanatoria".[148]

In 1912, Lessing suffered the deepest tragedy of his life. Whilst he was travelling Italy, news reached him that at home his beloved daughter Miriam had suddenly fallen ill. She died within four days.[149] In 1925, Lessing hinted at the impact of her death on him:

> But once more something terrible happened, the most terrible: unexpected, sudden death. The death of Miriam, my most lovely, most beloved child, ten years old. To leave her a worthy memorial [...], since Good Friday 1912, when we buried her, this is the only ambition in my life.[150]

Of course, Miriam's mother, Maria Stach von Goltzheim, attended the funeral. She behaved quite coldly towards Theodor Lessing, and did not even try to make a conciliatory gesture. For Lessing, this was the very moment he finally gave up on her. After Miriam's death, Lessing was, understandably, devastated

---

146 Theodor Lessing, 'Ein Buchhandler', in: *Prager Tagblatt*, March 17th, 1931; reprinted in: *IFEG*, 395.
147 Cfr. Willi Jasper, 'Die verlorene Ehre der Carla Mann. Wurde die Schwester von Thomas Mann Opfer seiner Fehde mit dem Philosophen Theodor Lessing?', in: *Die Welt*, December 6th, 2012. Willi Jasper is Carla Mann's biographer.
148 'der Shakespeare der Luxussanatorien'; Theodor Lessing, *Feind im Land. Satiren und Novellen* (Hanover 1923), 17.
149 Marwedel, o.c., 79; Theodor Lessing, 'Moralische Noten', in *PaT*, 110.
150 'Aber noch einmal kam etwas Furchtbares, das Furchtbarste: jäher, unerwarteter Tod. Der Tod Miriams, meines herrlichsten, geliebtesten Kindes, zehn Jahre alt. Ihr ein würdiges Denkmal zu hinterlassen [...], das ist seit dem Karfreitag 1912, wo wir sie begruben, meines Lebens einziger Ehrgeiz'; Theodor Lessing, 'Gerichtstag', 402. Good Friday was April 5th, 1912.

and suffered from severe mental problems and sleeplessness, "this most horrible of all sufferings".[151] It took him some time to pick up the pieces of his life and get going again. Ada Abbenthern gave him all the support she could; later the same year, the two of them married.

In 1912, Lessing was once more at the centre of a minor literary scandal, this time over a publication in *Die Schaubühne*. For some years, Lessing regularly contributed to this journal. But now, however, its editor Siegfried Jacobsohn allegedly published a contribution that Lessing never intended to publish: a note on a new play by the at the time quite popular author and playwright Hermann Sudermann (1857–1928). Lessing had sent the note to Jacobsohn with the remark that one day he might write a piece on this play, but Jacobsohn simply published the note as such.[152] Although all in all it was a rather hazy affair, Jacobsohn and Lessing had an argument over it, did not manage to reconcile, and even ended up in court. For one thing, it meant *Die Schaubühne* never published a contribution by Lessing again. Another result of this very scandal was that the governors of the *Technische Hochschule* in Hanover started to doubt Lessing's integrity. In the 1920's, when Lessing was involved again in scandals about his publications, – this time on the serial killer Fritz Haarmann and on Paul von Hindenburg as a presidential candidate in the elections of 1925 – [153] this would do him no good.

These, then, were Lessing's "stirring wandering years", in between the time he "chased poetic dreams" and the time he developed into an "abstract philosopher".[154] As noted above, Lessing considered his philosophical system, in a sense, nothing but a reflection on his own experiences – the experiences he lived through in his childhood and his wandering years. Starting point of this system was the realization that the human condition is to be in need. Given Lessing's experiences of life up to the outbreak of the First World War, this is a quite understandable starting point: he had certainly known happiness, but his childhood and wandering years were characterised by far more than a fair share of need."Who has the right parents, the right teachers, the right youth, the right wife?", Lessing lamented in 1913, in a text on Carl Gustav Carus – an observation that is hard to read as not autobiographically inspired.[155] The

---

151   'dieses grauenhafteste aller Leiden'; Theodor Lessing, 'Eduard Pflüger. Erinnerungen', in: *PaT*, 224.
152   Theodor Lessing, 'Der neue Sudermann' , in: *Die Schaubühne* 8,2 (1912), 691–692.
153   See Chapter one, above, 7–9.
154   'jene bewegten Wanderjahre'; 'den dichterischen Träumen'; 'abstrakten Philosophen'; Theodor Lessing, 'Gerichtstag', 403.
155   'Wer hat die rechten Eltern, die rechten Lehrer, die rechte Jugend, die rechte Frau? '; Theodor Lessing, 'Carl Gustav Carus. Gedenkblatt', in: *PaT*, 210.

realization that the human condition is to be in need determines all of Lessing's philosophy: his ethics, his epistemology, his philosophy of science, and his philosophy of history.

3   Turning for Philosophy

"Only in the year 1908 my philosophical writings started", Lessing wrote in 1925 in his autobiographical 'Gerichtstag über mich selbst'.[156] Yet by that time he had already published a philosophical dissertation, and an introduction to contemporary German philosophy. His interest in philosophy was even older, indeed going back to his days at secondary school. At first, however, philosophy was only one amongst the broad variety of his interests – whereas only from 1908 Lessing saw himself first and foremost as a philosopher. Originally, his interest in literature was of more importance to him, and he had high hopes for a literary career. Initially, his interest in philosophy just showed in some of the books he read and discussed with Ludwig Klages when they were schoolboys. It was only at the *Städtisches Gymnasium* in Hameln that Lessing's interest in philosophy really developed. At this school one of his teachers was the classicist and philosopher Max Schneidewin (1843–1931), the author of a number of books, for example *Über die Keime erkenntnistheoretischer und ethischer Philosopheme bei den vorsokratischen Denkern* ('On the seeds of epistemological and ethical philosophemes with pre-Socratic thinkers'; 1868), *Die homerische Naivetät* ('Homeric naivety'; 1878), and *Drei populär-philosophische Essays* ('Three popularizing philosophical essays'; 1883). Schneidewin taught all his working life in Hameln, although he would probably have belonged better as a university teacher. Schneidewin lent Lessing books by classical poets and philosophers, and introduced him to the philosophy of Arthur Schopenhauer. The contemporary philosopher Eduard von Hartmann was a friend of his – so Schneidewin introduced Lessing to Hartmann's ideas as well. Indeed, Lessing himself does describe Schneidewin as a "Hartmannianer".[157] Hartmann's ideas were kindred to Schopenhauer's, even so much that he is quite often described as his follower; but at certain points he criticised Schopenhauer and tried to correct him. In later years, Lessing was not very positive about Hartmann, and in his discussion of his ideas in his book *Schopenhauer-Wagner-Nietzsche*, he

---

156   'Erst mit dem Jahre 1908 beginnt meine philosophische Schriftstellerei'; Theodor Lessing, 'Gerichtstag', 402–403.
157   Theodor Lessing, 'Vita', in: *Spir*, 117.

was indeed very critical.[158] Guided by Schneidewin, Lessing developed a lifelong affection for classical antiquity, and in particular pre-Socratic philosophy. With this teacher, Lessing had his first true philosophical conversations, and, moreover, Schneidewin took Lessing's first efforts in philosophical writing most seriously. All in all, Schneidewin treated Lessing as an equal partner in philosophical dialogue, and this was exactly the kind of encouragement Lessing needed. As a result, a lifelong friendship between the two developed, even though their political and philosophical ideas differed considerably. In spite of their differences in political views, Schneidewin was one of the few who publicly supported Lessing in the Hindenburg affair. And Lessing spoke a *laudatio* when Schneidewin celebrated his eightieth birthday.[159]

When he moved to Freiburg to continue his education at university, Lessing again showed his interest in philosophy. Although matriculated as a student of medicine, Lessing participated in a seminar on the English philosopher John Locke (1632–1704) that was taught by the Austrian philosopher Alois Riehl (1844–1924). Riehl was a Neo-Kantian, who in Freiburg had succeeded Wilhelm Windelband (1848–1915) as ordinary professor in philosophy; Windelband was generally considered one of the leading thinkers in Neo-Kantianism.

Neo-Kantianism more or less dominated German philosophy between 1870 and 1920. As a term it is, however, somewhat misleading. Of course, Neo-Kantian philosophers all had some characteristics in common, notably the idea that true philosophy should be "scientific", and that philosophy could only be scientific if it returns to the approach and especially the method of Immanuel Kant. Hence, "Back to Kant!" was the slogan of Neo-Kantianism, first brought forward by the German philosopher Otto Liebmann (1840–1912) in his book *Kant und die Epigonen* ('Kant and his followers'; 1865). The importance Neo-Kantianism assigned to the "scientific" character of philosophy implied a strong refutation of irrationalism, and in particular of speculative metaphysics. But apart from these common characteristics, Neo-Kantianism was deeply divided into different schools with their own leaders, doctrines and journals. And these schools were fighting each other about the right interpretation of Kant like Christian denominations do as regards the right interpretation of the Bible. Members of one school saw members of other schools as heretics, whose careers needed to be blocked by, among other things, not appointing them at certain posts or by not publishing their articles. When someone occasionally

---

158 In his dissertation, Lessing refers to both Schneidewin and Von Hartmann; cfr. o.c., 45–46. And see *S-W-N*, 181–189.
159 See Theodor Lessing, 'Gerichtstag', 394; and Theodor Lessing, 'Ein deutscher Gelehrter', in: *Prager Tagblatt*, February 15th, 1927.

left one school for another, it was almost seen as a religious conversion. Up to seven different schools within Neo-Kantianism have been identified by historians of philosophy,[160] of which the Marburg School, the Göttingen School, and the Heidelberg (or Baden) School are usually seen as the most important (these various schools are named after the university where they originated).

In at least two respects, early Neo-Kantianism was most important for its development in subsequent years. First of all, early Neo-Kantianism focused its attention almost entirely on Kant's *Kritik der reinen Vernunft* ('Critique of Pure Reason'; 1781), ignoring his other writings, in particular his *Kritik der praktischen Vernunft* ('Critique of Practical Reason'; 1788) more or less completely. So its interest in Kant was almost exclusively epistemological, focusing on the question of the foundation of human knowledge. Secondly, early Neo-Kantianism gave a quite idiosyncratic interpretation of Kant's epistemology, especially as regards his notion of *a priori* categories, claiming these categories were psychologically based. That is, early Neo-Kantianism involved the position that the *a priori* elements of human knowledge are not part of human thinking, but of the human psyche. Both elements – the emphasis on epistemological questions, and the psychological interpretation of Kant's categories – proved to be influential in the later development of Neo-Kantian philosophy.[161]

Alois Riehl followed the lead of early Neo-Kantianism in at least this respect that he, too, opposed irrationalism and speculative metaphysics, and favoured a "scientific" philosophy. His own approach of Kant was more or less historical: according to Riehl it was only through studying Kant's evolution over the years that the latter's philosophy could be understood properly. Riehl undertook this task in his *Der philosophische Kritizismus* ('Philosophical Criticism'; three volumes, 1876–1887), in which he, moreover, tries to bring Kant's philosophy up-to-date by, for instance, trying to assess what, if anything, Charles Darwin's discoveries implied with respect to Kantian thought. Still, in the end, according to the German philosopher Michael Heidelberger, in Riehl "the Kantian element is comparatively limited and [...] his treatment of Kant is very idiosyncratic and inventive"; his work is "a peculiar and at times highly original blend of English empiricism (especially in the spirit of John Locke), contemporary

---

160   Cfr. Klaus Christian Köhnke, *The rise of neo-Kantianism: German academic philosophy between idealism and Positivism* (Cambridge 1991) 200.
161   For an overview, see Andrew Bowie, *Introduction to German Philosophy: From Kant to Habermas* (Cambridge 2003); Anthony O'Hear (ed.), *German Philosophy Since Kant* (Cambridge 1999); Köhnke, *The rise of neo-Kantianism*; and Lewis White Beck, 'Neo-Kantianism', in: Donald M. Borchert (ed. in chief), *Encyclopedia of Philosophy* (Second Edition, Detroit 2006), vol. 6, 539–545.

sensory physiology with a heavy Darwinian bias, and German positivism".[162] As Heidelberger observes,

> If Riehl's work is dealt with at all in the historiography of philosophy, he is usually accorded just a few words after treatment of the Marburg and the South-West German Schools of neo-Kantianism. He is usually described as a "realist" interpreter of Kant's philosophy.[163]

As Neo-Kantianism, however, underwent an idealist turn around 1880, Riehl's position was never popular. Still, he was more important than often thought, especially because he influenced neo-empiricist thinking, in particular the physicist and philosopher Moritz Schlick (1882–1936) who himself was one of the founding fathers of the Vienna Circle.[164] In his Freiburg years – Riehl taught in Freiburg from 1882 until 1895, when he left for Kiel –, so at the time when Theodor Lessing participated in Riehl's seminar on John Locke, Riehl, if only somewhat hesitantly, started to broaden his reading of Kant, paying attention to the latter's ethics and aesthetics as well.

Apart from the seminar by Riehl, Lessing attended some other philosophical lectures as well, for instance by Heinrich Rickert (1863–1936), a well-known and very influential Neo-Kantian philosopher, who in 1891 had habilitated with Riehl, and at the time worked as an external university lecturer at Freiburg university. When teaching in Freiburg, Rickert was developing his ideas on the difference in approach between the natural sciences on the one hand, and the historical sciences on the other. According to Rickert, the natural sciences aim for generalisations, whereas the historical sciences aim for individualisation; this distinction is, according to Rickert, however, not so much a matter of principle as a matter of emphasis. Still, it was only after his years in Freiburg that Rickert would become both well-known and, indeed, very influential within the Neo-Kantian tradition of philosophy.

As the presuppositions of medical thinking he was taught in his study of medicine differed considerably from the teachings of Riehl and other philosophers, this was rather confusing for Lessing .[165] But it is probable that, insofar Lessing was influenced by any of the philosophical teachings he experienced

---

162 Michael Heidelberger, 'Kantianism and Realism: Alois Riehl (and Moritz Schlick)', in: Michael Friedman and Alfred Nordmann (eds.), *The Kantian Legacy in Nineteenth-Century Science* (Cambridge, Mass. and London 2006), 227–247, there 233–234.
163 O.c., 233.
164 O.c, *passim*.
165 *Eunw*, 263–265.

in Freiburg, this influence was of a Neo-Kantian nature. Besides his lectures in philosophy, Lessing attended in Freiburg lectures by the renowned August Weissmann (1834-1914), one of the most important evolutionary biologists of his time, and by some even considered the most important one of the nineteenth century, apart from Charles Darwin.[166] In his autobiography, Lessing describes how he was deeply impressed by Weissmann's lectures on the theory of descent, and that he preferred his mechanistic view of life over the vitalism that was more influential at the time. Moreover, Weissmann was empirically oriented, an attitude Lessing highly respected.[167]

After his move to Bonn, Lessing, disappointed about the lack of response to his debut novel, concentrated on his study of medicine. But in addition to his medical studies he attended lectures by J.B. Meyer (1829-1897), yet another philosopher who was influenced by Kant, and who is usually seen as an early representative of Neo-Kantianism. Another philosopher whose lectures Lessing attended in Bonn was C.M.W. Schaarschmidt (1822-1909), who published on philosophers like Descartes, Spinoza and Leibniz. Finally, during his year in Bonn Lessing attended lectures by Wilhelm Bender (1845-1901), a theologian who from 1876 taught at Bonn, at first in theology, but from 1888 in philosophy. He lectured on the history of various world views, hence his approach was more that of an historian of ideas than that of a systematic philosopher. But the lectures of these professors hardly made a lasting impression on Lessing. As he writes in *Einmal und nie wieder*: "after every trip into the humanities I returned merrier to the laboratories".[168]

Once Lessing had moved to Munich, he again showed his interest in philosophy. He attended lectures by Georg Freiherr von Hertling (1843-1919), who was mainly teaching political philosophy, and history of philosophy. Besides this, Von Hertling was active in the organisation of catholic education in Germany, and in politics. He was twice a member of the *Reichstag*, and from November 1st 1917 until September 30th 1918 he even served as Chancellor of the German Empire. But especially important for Lessing's development was Theodor Lipps, whose lectures he attended, sometimes accompanied by Ludwig Klages. Although Lipps did have a different background – he first studied theology,

---

166   Ernst Mayr, *The Growth of Biological Thought: Diversity, Evolution, and Inheritance* (Cambridge, Mass. 1982) 698.
167   Theodor Lessing, o.c., 259-260. In his *Schopenhauer-Wagner-Nietzsche*, Lessing refers to Weissmann's "brilliant doctrine of continuity" ('die geniale Kontinuitätslehre'), which in his opinion makes out a convincing case for mechanicism in the philosophy of nature. Cfr. *S-W-N*, 458.
168   'nach jedem Ausflug in die Geisteswissenschaft ging ich froher in die Laboratorien'; o.c., 278. Cfr. Theodor Lessing, 'Eduard Pflüger. Erinnerungen', in: *PaT*, 229-230.

then shifted to natural sciences and philosophy – he took up the study of philosophy in the early 1870's in Utrecht, the Netherlands, where Neo-Kantianism at the time was not yet influential. He did share with early Neo-Kantianism the idea that there is a close link between philosophy and psychology. He developed his view on philosophy in his book *Grundtatsachen des Seelenlebens* ('Basic Facts of Mental Life'; 1883). In the 'Preface' of this book he pays tribute to the writings of the philosopher Hermann Lotze (1817–1881), the scientist and philosopher Hermann von Helmholtz (1821–1894), and the philosopher Wilhelm Wundt (1832–1920), all three of whom are seen as important predecessors of Neo-Kantianism. In the introductory chapter of his *Grundtatsachen des Seelenlebens*, Lipps states that philosophy in his time faces a question the answer to which one should expect all philosophers to agree upon, but over which they are in fact deeply divided: the question what the specific task of philosophy is. The underlying reason for this discord is, he argues, that philosophy has lost its traditional task, due to the rise of modern natural sciences. Lipps acknowledges the importance of the natural sciences, defining them as the sciences of outer experience. On the other hand, Lipps claims, philosophy is the general term for the sciences of inner experience, or the *Geisteswissenschaften* (humanities). Psychology, logic, aesthetics, ethics, and all related disciplines, are based on inner experience; their objects are ideas, experiences, acts of will, which all differ from the object of the natural sciences. Eventually, Lipps maintains, there are but two general sciences, different in approach but equally important: natural science and philosophy. And as much as the approach of philosophy is not suitable for understanding outer experience, he argues, the approach of natural science is not suitable for understanding inner experience. Of the various disciplines within philosophy, according to Lipps, psychology is the most basic: it is the ground for all other philosophical sciences, as psychology studies inner experience at the most basic level.[169] In Theodor Lessing's publications, the influence of Lipps's idea of philosophy is manifest, for instance, in his book *Schopenhauer – Wagner – Nietzsche*, when he contends that "[p]hilosophy is psychology. But psychology is a science that deals with the world as the contents of consciousness".[170]

According to Lipps's line of thinking, the one and only instrument for philosophical inquiry is introspection – in the end, philosophy is self-observation, reflection by man on the inner experience of man. Even logic can only be understood through introspection, for logical reasoning is an inner experience

---

169 Theodor Lipps, *Grundtatsachen des Seelenlebens* (Bonn 1883) 1–6.
170 'Philosophie ist Psychologie. Psychologie aber ist Wissenschaft, welche sich mit der Welt als Bewußtseinsinhalt befaßt'; *S-W-N*, 25.

that eventually can only be understood by psychology as the most basic of the philosophical sciences. This is the so-called "psychologism" that Edmund Husserl once favoured, but started to challenge in the 1890's, with his *Logische Untersuchungen* as a result. But Lipps as well renounced this psychologism in the second half of the 1890's: "from the standard bearer of 'psychologism' he had for a long time already become its destroyer".[171] Theodor Lessing describes how he attended the very same course on logic by Lipps in two successive winters. He notes that at the start of the series of lectures he attended the second time, Lipps simply said:

> "There are some gentlemen present who have heard my lectures on logic before. I have to ask them to forget everything they have heard from me before. Because only now I can give them the right thread".[172]

The new approach Lipps started to develop was similar to the ideas Edmund Husserl was thinking out at about the same time. As Husserl's approach came to be known as phenomenology, the new ideas formulated by the Munich circle of psychologists and philosophers round Lipps are sometimes referred to as 'Munich phenomenology', both in order to distinguish it from Husserl's approach, and to refer to the similarities between these two developments.[173] In other words, Theodor Lessing was himself witness to the change of Lipps's position – he was his student when Lipps started to develop, and discussed with his students, ideas similar to the ones Husserl developed and eventually published in his *Logische Untersuchungen*. Lessing described Lipps's development as the change from "a psychological geneticist to a noölogical phenomenologist".[174] Husserl himself noticed and appreciated the change of Lipps's thinking, and saw him as an intellectual ally, as he acknowledges in his *Ideen zu einer reinen Phänomenologie und phänomenologische Philosophie* ('Ideas Pertaining to a

---

171 'Aus dem Bannerträger des "Psychologismus" war längst der Zermalmer dieser Richtung geworden'; Theodor Lessing, 'Theodor Lipps', 256–257.

172 '"Es sind einige Herrn anwesend, die schon früher meine Vorlesungen über Logik gehört haben. Diese muß ich bitten, Alles zu vergessen, was sie früher von mir hörten. Denn ich kann ihnen erst jetzt die richtigen Fäden geben"'; o.c., 257.

173 Cfr. Smid, o.c.; sometimes the term 'Munich phenomenology' is used to describe the rise of similar ideas after the First World War, developed by for example the philosophers Alexander Pfänder (1870–1941), Moritz Geiger (1880–1937), and others. For their ideas, cfr. H. Kuhn et al. (eds.), *Die Münchener Phänomenologie* (The Hague 1975). But Smid conclusively proves that 'Munich phenomenology' is older than that, and in fact originated before the turn of the century.

174 'war aus dem psychologischen Genetiker ein noologischer Phänomenolog geworden'; Theodor Lessing, o.c., 260.

Pure Phenomenology and to a Phenomenological Philosophy';1913).[175] Herbert Spiegelberg confirm's Lessing's report on the development of Lipps. According to Spiegelberg, "Lipps himself abandoned and rejected this "psychologism" as early 1903".[176] Lessing greatly admired Lipps – as a thinker, but even more so as a teacher. In fact, Lessing wrote in a tribute to Lipps that, of all the great minds in German culture, "this man is the one and only whose hand I would like to kiss out of reverence".[177] Lessing even dedicated the 1914 edition of his *Studien zur Wertaxiomatik* to Lipps, "in grateful veneration" ('in dankbarer Verehrung'). Moreover, Lipps had been instrumental in Lessing's decision to finally take his leave from medicine: "the ever recurring thought to catch up with the exams in medicine after all and start a medical practice was finally given up when I got acquainted with Theodor Lipps in Munich".[178] Most probably, this observation refers to the grant Lipps offered Lessing to study psychology, not to their very first acquaintance, when Lessing attended lectures by Lipps, shortly after his arrival in Munich.

So when Lessing, in 1906, moved to Göttingen to study with Edmund Husserl he was, in a sense, on familiar ground. Having studied with Lipps shortly before the turn of the century, he knew the kind of problems Husserl was considering and how he approached them, and he knew the results of this new approach as published by Husserl in his *Logische Untersuchungen*.

In the two volumes of this book, the result of a process of thinking that started as early as 1891, one of the things Husserl tries to show is why the "psychologism" that he himself once adhered to is wrong – that is, why psychology cannot understand logic by treating it as an expression of inner experience. Although Husserl's argument is quite lengthy, detailed, and, at times, complicated, the general principles of his approach, to which he refers time and

175 Lawrence Baron, 'Discipleship and Dissent', 36; cfr. Edmund Husserl, *Ideen zu einer reinen Phänomenologie und phänomenologische Philosophie* I, ed. by W. Biemel (The Hague 1950) 185 *ff* and 232.
176 Spiegelberg, o.c., 258. Spiegelberg claims that this change of mind in Lipps is apparent from his publications from his treatise *Inhalt und Gegenstand. Psychologie und Logik* (1905) onwards. Personal relations between Husserl and Lipps warmed up since then, Spiegelberg maintains, and an interchange of ideas between the two of them arose. Lessing seems to date the change of mind in Lipps earlier – around the time he attended lectures by Lipps. As Lessing left Munich in 1901 for a job as a teacher in Haubinda, this must have been prior to 1901. But Lessing is not very precise on when this occurred.
177 'Dieser Mann ist der einzige, dem ich in Ehrfurcht die Hand küssen möchte.'; Theodor Lessing, o.c., 262.
178 'Der immer wiederkehrende Gedanke, das medizinische Staatsexamen nachzuholen und dann eine Praxis zu gründen, wurde aufgegeben als ich in München Theodor Lipps kennen lernte'; Theodor Lessing, 'Gerichtstag', 401.

again, are quite clear, and can be summarised as follows.[179] Psychology, as an empirical science, deals with facts. But thus far, it never produced any precise scientific laws, only vague generalisations. On the other hand, the rules of logic are very precise and exact. Hence, Husserl concludes that the generalisations of psychology cannot be identified with, nor derived from the rules of logic. Secondly, the empirical generalisations of psychology are at best probable, but in principle it is always possible that one day they will be refuted. But on the other hand, the truths of logic are necessary truths. In other words, the empirical generalisations of psychology are the result of an inductive process of reasoning, whereas logical truths are not. Yet another difference between empirical generalisations and the rules of logic is that empirical generalisations describe a relation between events, whereas the rules of logic do not. An empirical generalisation in psychology can, for instance, state that people who stop smoking tend to eat more than before – that is, it relates 'stopping with smoking' with 'eating more than before'. The rules of logic, however, do not relate events. Finally, empirical generalisations imply, one way or another, matters of fact, whereas the rules of logic do not. All this brings Husserl to the conclusion that there is a difference in kind between the empirical generalisations of psychology on the one hand, and the rules of logic on the other hand. And this implies that psychology, being the empirical science it claims to be and, indeed, is, cannot be suitable to understand logic which, after all, is independent of empirical reality. This, again, leads to the conclusion that, in general, one has to distinguish between two kinds of statements: empirical, and non-empirical statements. Because psychology only deals with empirical statements, it cannot understand logic; and this implies it cannot be the most basic discipline in philosophy that, for instance, Theodor Lipps in *Grundtatsachen des Seelenlebens*, but also numerous Neo-Kantian philosophers, thought it was.

For this reason, Husserl introduced phenomenology as an alternative to psychology as the most basic discipline in philosophy, or, indeed, as the only proper way to philosophize. According to Husserl, phenomenology is the science of reality as such, that is, the descriptive science of things as they are. This terminology may be somewhat confusing – but in this context "things as they are" means "our conscious ideas of things". So when Husserl speaks about "die Sachen selbst", the things themselves, he refers to things as they appear in our consciousness. In other words, this descriptive science of things as they are is

---

179 I follow the excellent entry on phenomenology by Richard Schmitt, 'Phenomenology', in: Donald M. Borchert (ed. in chief), *Encyclopedia of Philosophy* (Second Edition, Detroit 2006), vol. 7, 278–299.

not, according to Husserl, an empirical science, but the science of phenomenological description. That is to say, phenomenology is not dependent on observation by the senses – but, as phenomenological descriptions neither are analytic statements in the traditional sense of the word, that is, clarifications of the (implied) meaning of a concept, the question arises what they are. This question was, and even still is, hotly disputed within the phenomenological tradition, and still more so outside of it. Husserl developed a method which would enable the philosopher to describe things as they appear in our consciousness – reducing the merely empirical to the essential, the merely contingent to the necessarily true. The guiding principle in this approach is a special kind of intuition, the intuition of essences (*Wesensschau* in German). Initially, Husserl tended to identify the things as they are thus perceived in our consciousness with the Kantian *Dinge an sich* (*noumena*, or things-in-themselves), but later he changed his position on this. These were the sort of questions Husserl tried to solve when he was teaching in Göttingen, with his *Ideen zu einer reinen Phänomenologie und phänomenologischen Philosophie* as a result. In this respect, it is important to keep in mind that Husserl continued thinking about these problems even after he had published his initial views, and often changed his mind, either by refining or by retracting earlier positions. So, at the time Theodor Lessing was studying with Husserl in Göttingen, these were the kind of problems Husserl was dealing with.

To sum up, then, these were the main influences on Theodor Lessing's philosophical development up to 1908, that is, up to the moment he started to consider himself primarily a philosopher. First of all, he had a general, not very specific interest in philosophy, it initially being no more than one among many others. Under the guidance of his teacher Max Schneidewin at the *Gymnasium* in Hameln, Lessing developed some familiarity with pre-Socratic philosophy and with the work of both Arthur Schopenhauer and Eduard von Hartmann. In Freiburg he was introduced to the somewhat idiosyncratic Neo-Kantianism of Alois Riehl, and to the ideas of Heinrich Rickert. During his years in Munich, he studied with Theodor Lipps, who at that time dissociated himself from his early "psychologism" and started to develop a kind of phenomenology of his own, similar to but different from the ideas Edmund Husserl was developing about the same time. Husserl was the last teacher with whom Lessing formally studied, when he was preparing to habilitate, which would enable him to teach at university. Apart from all this, his friend Omar al Raschid Bey introduced him to the tradition of Asian wisdom in the late 1890's.

Even if Theodor Lessing claims his philosophical writings started only in 1908, by then he had already published two philosophical books: his dissertation, on the epistemology of Afrikan Spir, and an introduction to contemporary German philosophy, *Schopenhauer – Wagner – Nietzsche*.

Looking back in the 1920's, Lessing himself was not very positive on his dissertation *Afrikan Spirs Erkenntnislehre*: he called it "a truly bad work".[180] In this dissertation, his very first publication in philosophy, Lessing first and foremost tries "to restrict himself to clarifying the main theoretical idea, that is the thread, in all of Spir's writings, to be able to contribute as a result to a better understanding of this often paradoxical independent thinker".[181] His starting point was "merely the subjective feeling to help an unknown thinker to his justice".[182] Only in the third and final part of the book, Lessing declares, he will attempt to complete his study of Spir with his own critical analysis and comments. In other words, his main aim is to offer an overview of Spir's most important ideas, involving topics related to epistemology. Thus, he hopes to avoid the mistake that dissertations in his opinion often exhibit, namely to criticise the ideas of a philosopher without first giving a clear exposition of what these ideas involve. According to Lessing, this all too often is characteristic for German philosophical dissertations.[183] Nevertheless, as Rainer Marwedel notes, "one can read Lessing's dissertation as a first draft for a philosophical autobiography".[184] Indeed, Lessing does not always manage to restrict himself to the task he set himself, that is, presenting Spir's ideas as neutral as possible, without including his own comments. At times, he does include his own ideas, although Marwedel's observation rather seems to be an overstatement.

The tendency to include his own views in the discussion of the ones of other philosophers is even stronger in Lessing's second philosophical book, *Schopenhauer – Wagner – Nietzsche*. In his introduction, Lessing explains what he aims for with this book, and what its background is. He notices that he does not want to reiterate the ideas of the philosophers he discusses, nor to replicate their arguments,

---

180 'eine wirklich schlechte Arbeit'; Theodor Lessing, o.c., 401. In his book *Schopenhauer-Wagner-Nietzsche*, Lessing was somewhat less negative about his dissertation, qualifying it as 'unripe' ('unreif'); see *S-W-N*, 190. In a later essay on Spir, Lessing qualified his own dissertation as a typical record of youth, overloaded, and too ambitious; see Theodor Lessing, 'Afrikan Spir', in: *PaT*, 357.
181 'zu beschränken [...] den theoretischen Hauptgedanken, der als roter Faden durch alle Spir'schen Schriften läuft, klarer zu entwickeln, um durch seine Darlegung zum besseren Verständnis dieses oftmals paradoxalen Selbstdenkers beizutragen'; *Spir*, 23.
182 'lediglich ein subjektives Pathos, einem unbekannten Denker zu seinem Recht zu helfen'; Theodor Lessing, 'Afrikan Spir', in: *PaT*, l.c..
183 *Spir*, 23-24.
184 'Man kann Lessings Dissertation lesen als einen ersten Entwurf zu einer philosophischen Autobiographie'; Rainer Marwedel, o.c., 55.

but on the one hand to explain their philosophy psychologically and make it understandable, and on the other to attempt to isolate the main problems, in order to raise the philosophical content of their ideas once again to be the subject of philosophising.[185]

This, again, should help him to rise above these philosophers and to develop a philosophical system of his own – even if Lessing states that he realises all too well that his own ideas are still under construction, and that his system is far from complete. Be that as it may, in the preliminary remarks to *Schopenhauer – Wagner – Nietzsche* Lessing does indeed hint at a philosophical system of his own. So even if Lessing claims his philosophical writings started only in 1908, the first preparatory remarks for this philosophical system of his own might well date from before 1908 and, indeed, be found in *Schopenhauer – Wagner – Nietzsche*, or even in *Afrikan Spirs Erkenntnislehre*. Indeed, in his dissertation Lessing does in passing refer to "my own doctrine"[186] and to "my worldview",[187] which at least suggests that his ideas on his own philosophical system do indeed originate from well before 1908.

Having studied in Göttingen with Edmund Husserl for a year, Theodor Lessing, though reluctantly, returned to Hanover, where on November 19th 1907 he delivered his *Probevorlesung* "Wissenschaft als Kraftökonomie";[188] an enlarged version of the text he later included in his collection of essays *Philosophie als Tat* (1914). The very same day, Lessing was accepted for *Habilitation*. His essay *Der Bruch in der Ethik Kants* ('The Break in Kant's Ethics', 1907) was accepted as his *Habilitation*-thesis. In December 1907 Lessing delivered his *Philosophisches Antrittskolleg* 'Philosophie als Tat', which he would include as well in his 1914 collection of essays. Indeed, he used the title of this essay as the title for the book, "in order that the reader knows, what he has to see as guiding ideas".[189] In Lessing's view, this involves the idea that philosophy differs from all (other) sciences in that it does not only describe or explain things as they are: philosophy judges as well, philosophy is normative and sets the norms. Ever since his appointment in Hanover, Lessing saw himself first and foremost as a

---

185 'Sondern ihre Philosophie einerseits psychologisch zu erklären und verständlich zu machen, andererseits die Kernprobleme zu isolieren versuchen, um den philosophischen Gehalt ihrer Gedanken abermals zum Gegenstand des Philosophierens zu erheben'; *S-W-N*, 2.
186 'nach meiner eigenen Lehre'; *Spir*, 57.
187 'in meiner Weltanschauung'; o.c., 91.
188 For a discussion, see Chapter one above, 21–22.
189 'damit der Leser wisse, was er als Leitgedanken zu betrachten habe'; Theodor Lessing, 'Vorbemerkung zum ersten Buche,' in: *PaT*, xv.

philosopher. A philosopher, though, with an idea of philosophy of his own: he did not want to be, nor was, a philosopher in an ivory tower. On the contrary, his idea of philosophy demanded a continuous analysis of the social and political reality surrounding him, starting from the realisation that to be human is to be in need, and that for this very reason the maxim of life should be the question "where am I needed?", that is, "where can I help to lessen the need of others?". Hence, Lessing, in addition to his work as a philosopher at the *Technische Hochschule* in Hanover, involved himself in all kinds of social activities, it being his contribution to the effort of lessening the human need in the world.[190]

In between 1908 and 1914, that is from the time Lessing saw himself first and foremost as a philosopher until the outbreak of the First World War, Lessing published extensively – both in philosophy and in other fields. Closely related to his *Der Bruch in der Ethik Kants* are his *Studien zur Wertaxiomatik* ('Studies in Value Axiomatics'), first published in two parts in the *Archiv für systematische Philosophie* ('Archives for systematic Philosophy'), in 1914 brought together in a book.[191] Originally these studies formed a whole with *Der Bruch in der Ethik Kants*. Besides this, Lessing published a number of essays that, for the greater part, he later collected in *Philosophie als Tat*. In the 'Preface' of this compilation, he explicitly claims the essays collected in the book are meant to be

> nothing but an elucidation and a portal to the principal work "Philosophie der Not" (Philosophy of Need) that is in the course of preparation since early youth. The basic ideas of my world system are alive here, like the forms of a musical drama are alive in the overture; serving for the composer as a surmounting flower, for the listener as introduction to the creation.[192]

Lessing invites his readers to relive the basic ideas of his world system, like they experience a work of art – not to enlarge their factual knowledge, not as getting acquainted with the results of an inquiry, but as despatches and occurrences from life. Moreover, in an enumeration he indicates what these basic ideas involve:

---

190 Cfr. Chapter one, above, 22–26.
191 Theodor Lessing, 'Studien zur Wertaxiomatik', in: *Archiv für systematische Philosophie*, Neue Folge, 14 (1908), 58–93 and 226–257; and *SzW*.
192 'Es soll nichts sein als Erläuterung und Vorhalle zu dem seit früher Jugend vorbereiteten Hauptwerk "Philosophie der Not". Die Grundgedanken meines Weltsystems sind hier lebendig, wie die Gestalten eines musikalischen Dramas in seiner Ouvertüre lebendig sind; dem Tondichter als Gipfelblume, dem Hörenden als Einführung in die Schöpfung dienend'; *PaT*, ix.

> The final abandoning of the belief in development, the new psychology of mimesis,[193] the theories of surrogate ecstasy and logification post festum, the final cut between utilisation and overpowering, styling and orientation of life (philosophy and science); the unexpected distinction between reality and its normative spheres (powers and values of life). Further: the theory of entropy in consciousness and the law of "intellectualisation of mental energy"; in particular, however, the theory of need as bearer of consciousness...[194]

When in 1914 the First World War broke out, Theodor Lessing was ready – or at least he claimed he was – to put down his own philosophical system on paper. In a sense, Lessing maintains, philosophy is nothing but the reflection on his own life by the philosopher concerned. This brought him the very starting point of his philosophical system: to be human is to be in need. His education made him familiar with the philosophies of Schopenhauer and Hartmann, with the Neo-Kantianism of Riehl and Rickert, and with the phenomenology of Lipps and Husserl. Lessing articulated the basic ideas of his range of thought in the philosophical texts he wrote between 1899 and 1914, and especially between 1908 and 1914 – after all, only from 1908 he saw himself first and foremost as a philosopher. What, then, did this philosophical system of his own involve? This is the question that will be addressed in the next paragraph.

4 Philosophy of Need: Notes towards a Reconstruction

As Theodor Lessing never published an elaboration of his philosophical system, its substance has to be reconstructed from, on the one hand, the publications in which he expressed what it was meant to be, and, on the other hand, his later publications in which it is presupposed. Most likely, the closest Lessing came to publishing his system as such is to be found in the summary he wrote in his

---

193   The German "Ahmung" is most difficult to translate. Literally, it means "calibrating", but I would like to suggest "cathartic understanding" as a probably more fitting translation. See §2.4, below.

194   'Die endgültige Brachlegung des Entwicklungsglaubens, die neue Ahmungspsychologie, die Lehre der Rauschsurrogate und der Logifizierung post festum, der endgültige Schnitt zwischen Auswertung und Übermachtigung, Gestaltung und Orientierung des Lebens (Philosophie und Wissenschaft); die ungeahnte Trennungslinie zwischen der Wirklichkeit und ihrer normativen Sphäre (Mächten und Werten des Lebens). Ferner: die Lehre der Entropie in Bewußtsein und das Gesetz der "Intellektualisierung seelischer Energie"; zumal aber die Lehre von Not als Träger von Bewußtsein...'; o.c., x.

study *Die Prinzipien der Charakterologie* ('The Principles of Characterology'; 1926).[195] Hence, in this paragraph I will attempt to reconstruct Lessing's philosophical system, by discussing its basic ideas in their interdependence, using his "preliminary" philosophical writings, and scattered remarks in other writings – both his later philosophical writings, and his writings in other domains. As I will try to reconstruct his philosophical ideas prior to 1914, I only use his own summarised version of his system in *Die Prinzipien der Charakterologie* to check on the validity of this reconstruction. Given Lessing's idea that, in a sense, philosophy is nothing but a reflection on the life of the philosopher concerned, his philosophical ideas should continually be read in the light of both his personal experiences up to 1914, which he retrospectively described in *Einmal und nie wieder* and which have been sketched in § 2.1 and § 2.2 above, and his formal and informal education in philosophy, as discussed in § 2.3 above.

In the enumeration of the basic ideas in the philosophical system of his own quoted above, Theodor Lessing emphasizes the importance of his theory of need as the bearer of consciousness. Hence, a discussion of this theory may be considered a proper starting point for a discussion of Lessing's philosophical system. Moreover, even in his dissertation on Afrikan Spir of 1899 Lessing already hints at this very idea. As regards Spir – that is, as Lessing presents Spir's ideas – in his view the task of philosophy is to strive after absolutely true knowledge. In doing so, philosophy has one premiss: the principle of identity ("A = A"), which is, as Spir puts it, the supreme law of thought. Spir tries to prove what he calls the objective validity of this principle of identity in three different ways. In his dissertation, Lessing mentions two of these only in passing, whereas he singles out the third for a lengthier discussion, because in his eyes it is the most interesting and fruitful. Not surprisingly, this third proof in a sense foreshadows ideas Lessing himself would later put forward, and it indeed does fit in well with his own philosophy of need. This third proof of the principle of identity regards (physical) pain. In Spir's view, as interpreted by Lessing,

> Pain is a condition which cannot remain identical with itself, which includes the desire or inner necessity to change into another (painless) condition. Every displeasure includes the tendency to nullify and destroy itself.[196]

---

195 Halle 1926.
196 'Der Schmerz ist ein Zustand, der sich selbst nicht gleich bleiben kann, der das Verlangen oder die innere Notwendigkeit enthält, in einen anderen (schmerzlosen) Zustand

This inner necessity of this condition of pain to destroy itself proves, on the one hand, that this condition lacks inner harmony or is, in other words, not identical with itself: a condition that is identical with itself logically cannot imply the tendency to destroy itself. On the other hand, it proves that the condition is anomalous: it condemns itself by this very tendency for self-destruction. Consequently, pain is in the realm of feelings what contradiction or untruth is in the realm of thinking. And contradiction or untruth likewise includes the inner necessity for change, i.e., for correction. But the very nature of pain on the one hand proves that it is the expression of an abnormal condition, and, on the other hand, it proves the existence of a normal, better condition: "precisely pain gives us the feeling that we would deserve a better condition".[197]

It is revealing that this is the very place in Lessing's dissertation where he passes on from discussing Spir's ideas to expounding his own views, as he explicitly indicates: "the following digressions are not by Spir, but the result of deliberations of my own".[198] Following up Spir's argument, Lessing asks the question – "a very deep question that never has been raised thus far"[199] – what the relation between pain and conscious life is. It is common knowledge, he claims, that pain raises our consciousness – when we are in pain we are more alert, and our intellectual capacities are stimulated; whereas lust diminishes our consciousness, that is, when having pleasure we are less alert, and our intellectual capacities are not triggered off. This observation is the stepping stone to a rhetorical question, which foreshadows some main themes of Lessing's philosophy: "Now what if all consciousness generally is the result of restraints of primary, instinctive life; if the capacities of mind and reason are indissolubly connected with the struggle for life (not with existence as such)?"[200] Lessing argues that this would imply that the human "I" (i.e., the individual consciousness of a human being) and all the contents of what it experiences should be considered an abnormity. In other words, reality as we experience it is actually a defect. But in a sense, humans have always known this: the

---

überzugehen. In jeder Unlust liegt die Tendenz, sich selbst aufzuheben und zu vernichten'; *Spir*, 49.

197 'gerade der Schmerz giebt uns das Gefühl, dass wir eines besseren Zustandes würdig seien'; o.c., 50.
198 'Die folgenden Ausführungen sind nicht von Spir, sondern Resultate eigener Erwägung'; l.c, footnote.
199 'ein sehr tiefer und bisher noch nie aufgeworfenes Problem'; loc.cit..
200 'Wie, wenn nun alles Bewusstsein überhaupt ein Resultat von Hemmungen des ursprünglichen, instinktiven Lebens wäre; wenn die Vermögen des Verstandes und der Vernunft untrennbar mit dem Daseinskampf (nicht mit dem Sein an sich) verbunden wären?'; o.c., 50–51.

realization that reality differs from what it should be underlies, according to Lessing, all philosophical, ethical, religious, and artistic pursuits. In philosophy and religion, this very realization is often phrased in questions like "why does evil exist?", or "why do righteous men and women have to suffer?". Such questions are the intuitive expression of the insight which Lessing reached through philosophical reasoning: reality fundamentally is an abnormity.[201] In a later essay on Spir, written in 1911, Lessing sums up some conclusions to which Spir's philosophy, as he understands it, leads:

> Life is not logical. Life is not ethical. Nature is not God. Values and ideals cannot be experienced. They hover before us in impassable inaccessibility, as the timeless-unconditional. An unreachable star, from which shines the light of life.[202]

Suchlike statements are quite congenial to ideas Lessing himself would later express.

In *Schopenhauer – Wagner – Nietzsche*, Lessing again discusses the relation between need and consciousness, drawing attention to the "the fact that suffering, pain, restraint only is a different definition for the fact itself of being awake, self-consciousness, and remembering".[203] Or, again, "knowledge, consciousness, rationality, all of it is tied to the presence of contradiction and restraint".[204] In his "Moralische Noten" ('Ethical Jottings'), written between 1900 and 1913, Lessing similarly contends:

> Never can something arise either in the sphere of thinking or in the sphere of experiencing without need. – The world is my need! It starts on the very spot where suffering, that is resistance starts. All consciousness is a split in I and other, and this split is where – need is.[205]

---

201   O.c., 51–52.
202   'Das Leben ist nicht logisch. Das Leben ist nicht moralisch. Die Natur ist nicht Gott. Wert und Ideal können nicht erfahren werden. Sie schweben uns vor in wegloser Unnahbarkeit, als das Zeitlos-Unbedingte. Ein unerreichbarer Stern, von dem das Licht des Lebens kommt'; Theodor Lessing, 'Afrikan Spir', in: *PaT*, 362.
203   'dem Faktum, daß Leiden, Schmerz, Hemmung nur eine andere Bezeichnung ist für die Tatsache des Wachsein, Selbstbewußtseins und Sicherinnerns selbst'; *S-W-N*, 86.
204   'Erkennen, Bewußtsein, Rationalität ist allemal geknüpft an das Vorhandensein von Gegensatz und Hemmung'; o.c. 152. Or again, " restraint is the starting point of all consciousness as well as creation" ('die Hemmung ist der Ausgangspunkt alles Bewußtseins wie alles Schaffens'), o.c. 204.
205   'Nie kann weder in der Sphäre des Denkens noch der des Erfahrens etwas ohne Not auftreten. – Die Welt ist meine Not! Sie beginnt an der Stelle, wo das Leiden, d.h. das Sich-

But in *Schopenhauer – Wagner – Nietzsche* Lessing adds that "self-consciousness has the function to assimilate victoriously an emerging restraint in inner life".[206] This very act of assimilation is painful in itself. According to Lessing, all feelings of happiness and cults of lust have to do with the unconscious, whereas all feelings of pain and suffering have to do with consciousness. Indeed, he argues,

> It is only a congested life and, so to speak, a life that is driven into a corner that rises into consciousness, like the water in a fountain that rises the higher, the stronger the pressure is that compresses it.[207]

And because human life at present mainly is conscious life, it knows more feelings of pain than feelings of joy. In individual lives as well, feelings of pain outnumber feelings of lust. For individuals, sleep helps to regain the balance of inner life – without recovery through sleep, humans would perish due to pain and suffering. Likewise, for a culture, art, especially music, has this very same narcotic function: it helps to overcome pain and suffering, it helps to forget. The very same holds for religion – and even for alcoholics and noise: they help to make life bearable.[208] This is because, according to Lessing

> Everywhere it is longing and displeasure with reality, with what is given, which invites people to come to comfort and refuge in their hopes and dreams, in a realm that is not of this world.[209]

This implies that

> Man filtered art out of the imperfections of life, in order that it gilds life and shows how it could be or should be. In ideals, it anticipates as realised, what in customary reality is potentially given, but what the

---

wehren beginnt. Jedes Bewußtsein ist ein Zerspalten in Ich und das Andere und diese Spaltung liegt dort, wo – die Not liegt'; Theodor Lessing, 'Moralische Noten', in: *PaT*, 100.
206 'das Selbstbewußtsein die Funktion hat, eine auftauchende Hemmung des seelischen Lebens siegreich zu assimilieren'; *S-W-N*, 87.
207 'Es ist nur ein aufgestautes und gleichsam in die Enge gepresstes Leben, das ins Bewußtsein steigt, wie die Wasser des Springbrunnens, die um so höher dringen, je mächtiger der Druck ist, der sie zusammenpreßt'; l.c..
208 O.c., 88–89.
209 'Überall ist es die Sehnsucht und das Ungenügen am Wirklichen, Gegebenen, was die Menschen nötigt, in einem Reich, das nicht von dieser Welt ist, in ihren Hoffnungen und Träumen sich Trost und Zuflucht zu erholen'; o.c., 129.

empirical world, once it has seen it, has to want and slowly complete and fulfil, as it imagines in the forms of beauty the dreamed life and slowly builds it out of itself.[210]

According to Lessing, this implies that art – and the very same holds for science – is nothing but "the synthetic styling of lived life, a soothing distantiation and rounding off of our experiences by our soul, until eventually they face us as independent, objective creatures without contradictions".[211] The result of all this is – and this is very important indeed in Lessing's philosophy –

that the non-existent realm of ideas and ideals that humanity lifted, projected, externalised out of its sensual and inner life, eventually became an objective realm of its own, the realm of ideas and pure forms, where "the lamentations of the troubled stream murmur no more". The realm of Plato, the sphere of ideal abstractions that now, prior to all experience, floats ahead as loadstar and indicator for the world of historical occurrences.[212]

In other words, Lessing argues, man transforms experiences of life as it is lived into ideals – in art, in philosophy, in political visions. In the course of time, these ideals gain an independent status in a realm of their own; and as such, they serve as indicators of the direction our life should take. In his *Studien zur Wertaxiomatik*, Lessing refers to this realm of ideals as "that 'third reich', that topos ouranios of pure substance opposite the world of the factual".[213] This is

---

210 'Der Mensch hat die Kunst, aus den Unvollkommenheiten des Lebens gefiltert, damit sie ihm das Leben vergolde und zeige, wie es sein könnte oder sollte. Sie nimmt in Idealen als verwirklicht vorweg, was in der gemeinen Wirklichkeit etwa der Anlage nach gegeben ist, aber was diese empirische Welt, wenn es erst einmal geschaut ist, wollen und langsam vollenden und erfüllen muß, indem sie in Gestalten der Schönheit des erträumte Leben sich vorausstellt und langsam an sich auferbaut'; o.c., 133.
211 'als synthetische Gestaltung gelebten Lebens, ein beruhigendes Distanzieren und Abstellen unserer Erlebnisse von unserer Seele, bis sie uns schließlich wie selbständige, objektive, widerspruchslose Gebilde gegenübertreten.'; o.c., 141.
212 'Und so ist das wesenlose Reich der Gedanken und Ideale, welche das Menschengeschlecht aus seinem Sinnen- und Seelenleben herausgehoben, projiziert, externalisiert hat, schließlich zu einem objektiven Reiche für sich geworden, dem Reiche der Ideen und reinen Formen, wo des "Jammers trüber Strom nicht mehr rauscht". Das Reich Platos, die Sphäre ideeller Abstraktionen, die nun vor aller Erfahrung als bestimmte Leitsterne und Richtungsweiser der Welt historischen Geschehens voranschweben.'; l.c..
213 'jenes'dritte Reich', jenes topos ouranios reiner Inhalte gegenüber der Welt des Faktischen'; *SzW*, 72; 'topos ouranios' means 'heavenly place'.

remarkably similar to the way the philosopher K.R. Popper (1902–1994) used the notion "Third World" to refer to a realm of objective ideas.[214]

This transformation of experience into ideals is the very reason, Lessing maintains, that "world's work is done by its invalids" – a favourite expression of his –. For it is not suffering as such, but the victory over suffering that made Michelangelo into a great artist, or Homer, Dante, and Petrarch into great poets. Out of their suffering, or better: overcoming their suffering, great artists and poets create another world in which longing for love is answered, in which illness is healed, and so on; another world which we, inspired by their visions, try to realise. As Lessing puts it:

> But it may be a comfort for us that the defeats and disappointments that an individual man suffers in his life do ultimately benefit the objective, creative person, the artist and the thinker, if they do not strangle and kill him. A true poet makes poetry out of all misery.[215]

This independent realm of ideals that thus is formed, serves as loadstar in the doings of man: it is what man tries to realise. In his essay on his friend Omar al Raschid Bey, written in 1912, Lessing explains the implications of the existence of this independent realm of ideas for man's relation with nature:

> Man who planted value, ideal, norm, as "the true essence" above empirical existence, who constructed the inborn self of consciousness out of the native I of the soul, that man has stopped living as a natural being like animals and plants. This is the only difference between man and natural life: man has values, that is, he lives in a dualism of soul and consciousness, he lifted himself out of nature, in so far as he is a thinking, valuing, consciously wanting, judging being.[216]

---

214 Cfr. K.R. Popper, *Three Worlds. The Tanner Lecture on Human Values, Delivered at the University of Michigan, April 7, 1978*, for the original statement by Popper.

215 'Aber es mag uns Trost sein, daß Niederlagen und Enttäuschungen, die der persönliche Mensch am Leben erleidet, dem objektiven, schaffenden Menschen, dem Künstler und Denker, wenn sie ihn nicht ersticken und umbringen, schließlich wohl zugute kommen. Ein echter Dichter schlägt aus jedem Elend Poesie […]'; o.c., 288.

216 'Der Mensch, der den Wert, das Ideal, die Norm, als "das wahre Sein" über dem empirischen Dasein aufpflanzte, der aus dem angeborenen Ich der Seele das eingeborene Selbst des Geistes herausstellte, der hat aufgehört wie Tier und Pflanze als Naturwesen zu leben. Dieses ist der einzige Unterschied des Menschen gegen das natürliche Leben: der Mensch hat Werte; das heißt er lebt in einem Dualismus von Seele und Geist, er hat sich aus der Natur herausgehoben, ebensoweit als er denkendes, wertendes, bewußt wollendes, beurteilendes Wesen ist.'; Theodor Lessing, 'Omar al Raschid Bey', in: *PaT*, 385.

This clearly foreshadows ideas Lessing would later express with regard to his philosophy of need, especially his theory of three spheres. Even if this independent realm of ideals is never complete, in the sense that man continuously adds new ideals for realisation, according to Lessing the most influential contributions to this realm were made long ago, by Socrates, Buddha and Christ. They exhorted man how life should be, how life should ideally be lived.

Lessing's ideas on this independent realm of ideals are closely connected to his idea of culture. In *Schopenhauer – Wagner – Nietzsche*, this idea of culture is not yet fully developed nor underpinned, as Lessing himself indicates.[217] However, he does make some preliminary observations on what culture in his view is. As Lessing maintains:

> All culture is a process of logisation, that is of the logical binding of life! All logisation a result of necessity, that is, intended to repel a need.[218]

Lessing claims that culture by definition exhausts life, that is, the development of culture is realized at the expense of life. This implies that the idea "that especially intellectualising, socialising, and culturation would be nothing but biological decline, eventually leads to the certainty of finiteness and, generally, the end, to the fact of death that is everywhere certain".[219] This is not, however, a reason for pessimism: it is a matter of fact that simply has to be accepted, like death in the life of man is a matter of fact that has to be accepted but no reason for pessimism. Moreover, life essentially is nothing but overcoming, phrasing, relieving, discharging or undoing of obstructing need. In fact, man needs this need – man needs conflicts, problems, disturbances, contradictions, and duality to stay alive: "Beyond our lives there are no more questions, but neither is any life left!..."[220]

In a discussion of Charles Darwin's principle of selection, written in 1909, Lessing expounds his idea of culture as the logical binding of life:

> Because man is, if not the goal of nature, at least the one who decides what these goals are. For him, the possibilities of artificial selection

---

217 Cfr. *S-W-N*, 323, where Lessing explicitly claims he still has to work out his theory of culture.
218 'Alle Kultur ist ein Prozeß der Logisierung, d.h. der logischen Bindung des Lebens! Alle Logisierung ein Product der Notwendigkeit, d.h., bestimmt , eine Not zu wenden'; o.c., 323. Lessing's wordplay with 'need' and 'necessary' ('Not' and 'notwendig' in German) is untranslatable in English. It is, however, a trademark of his philosophy.
219 'daß insbesondere Intellektualisierung, Sozialisierung, Kulturation ein biologischer Niedergang sei, kommt auf die Gewißheit der Endlichkeit und des Endes überhaupt hinaus, auf die Tatsache des Todes, die überall gewiß ist'; o.c., 343–344.
220 'Jenseits unseres Lebens gibt es keine Rätsel, aber damit auch kein Leben mehr!...'; o.c., 345.

are quite unlimited (cultivated plants, cereals, fruit trees, domesticated animals, the dog, the pigeon, the horse, and so on show, that purposive sexual selection can intervene by transforming).[221]

Lessing claims this even includes the possibility of the perfection of man through purposive sexual selection. But the various views on this possibility are strangely confused, Lessing observes, and, moreover, the ethical quality of these views should not be rated very highly. And after all, one loves a person for the sake of who he or she is, not for the sake of the possibilities he or she offers for improving the offspring.[222] So even if Lessing does indeed hint at the possibility of improving man through purposive sexual selection, it can hardly be maintained that he was truly favouring it.

Similar observations on need as bearer of consciousness or on what culture essentially is foreshadow elementary ideas of Lessing's philosophy of need. In Lessing's philosophical system, for instance, the insight that pain alerts human conscious capacities is phrased more distinctly as the idea that conscious life as such is the result of experiencing pain, of suffering, or of being in need: the *Geist* is born out of *Not*. And this very idea is indissolubly connected with Lessing's theory of different spheres.

Even if he is not yet employing the terminology that he would later use when describing this theory in later publications, in his 'Note über Religion' ('Jottings on religion'), written in 1912, Lessing clearly hints at what this theory of different spheres would imply:

> Naive, full, abundant life knows no end, because it is an end in itself, at all times. But the diminishing flush of life needs or allows substitutes. The spiritual world, the realm of ideas, of values, of meaning begins. Every gap of life is filled with an idea. And the strength to develop ideas, to believe in ideas, is the healing, redeeming strength of life itself. Life that is weakened and broken (life as consciousness) makes its own resources. Indeed consciousness itself is a resource of life. Ends, values, ideas are said to be the crutches of consciousness. Life exhausts itself in the function of

---

221 'Denn der Mensch ist, wenn auch nicht das Ziel so doch der Zielsetzer der Natur. Die Möglichkeiten künstlicher Auslese sind für ihn ganz unbegrenzt (Kulturpflanzen, Getreidearten, Obstbäume, Haustiere, Hund, Taube, Pferd usw. zeigen, daß bewußte Sexualauslese verändernd eingreifen kann).'; Theodor Lessing, 'Darwin. Kritik des Entwicklungs-Glaubens', in: *PaT*, 185–186.
222 O.c., 186.

making flush substitutes, consciousness. To live is said to be to be still able to believe. The brokenness of life is the means to its own self-conquest. Conscious life is a disease, and like every disease: remedy for life.²²³

So what did Lessing's theory of different spheres eventually imply? According to Lessing, once – "in the beginning" – there was nothing but primary, instinctive life, that is, life as a unity of all living creatures: man lived with nature, following the rhythms of nature. Man, indeed, was one with nature, like animals and plants are one with nature, or like a rare tribe in, say, the Amazon region that never had any contact with the outside world still is one with nature. This changed, however, when man got into need – in his 1921 lecture *Die verfluchte Kultur* ('Damned culture') Lessing hints at "terrible prehistoric fights over food"²²⁴ as a possible explanation of what happened. When man got into need, he became conscious of the state he was in – in fact, in Lessing's philosophy, these are two different phrasings of the very same process. In other words, "in the beginning" man was one with nature, but whilst getting in need he became conscious of the state he was in, and started to distinguish himself from nature, that is, started to see himself as different from and outside of nature, or even as being opposite to it. Or, to use Lessing's terminology, "out of need man broke out of nature", which is the very same thing as the birth of consciousness. Lessing avers that one may roughly indicate when this process of breaking out of nature started. In Western civilisation, it coincided with the rise of pre-Socratic philosophy, or rather: the rise of pre-Socratic philosophy is an indicator of the start of the process of breaking out of nature. The culmination of this process was the appearance of Socrates, Buddha and Christ, that is, with their appearance the process was complete. This process exemplifies how consciousness is born from need, the latter being the bearer of the former.

---

223 'Das naive, volle, überreiche Leben kennt kein Ziel, denn es ist Ziel, in jedem Augenblick. Aber der absinkende Lebensrausch benötigt oder gestattet Surrogate. Die Geisterwelt, das Reich der Ideen, des Werts, des Sinns setzt ein. Jede Lebenslücke stopft sich mit einer Idee. Und die Kraft Ideen zu schaffen, zu glauben ist die ausheilende, sich erlösende Kraft des Lebens selbst. Das geschwächte, gebrochene Leben (das Leben als Bewußtsein) schafft sich Ressourcen. Ja das Bewußtsein selber ist Ressource des Lebens. Ziele, Werte, Ideen nennen sich die Krücken des Bewußtseins. In dieser Funktion, Rauschsurrogate, Bewußtsein zu schaffen erschöpft sich das Leben. Leben heißt Noch-Glauben-können. Die Gebrochenheit des Lebens ist das Mittel ihrer eigenen Überwindung. Der Geist ist die Krankheit und wie alle Krankheit: Gesundungsmittel des Lebens.'; Theodor Lessing, 'Note über Religion', in: *PaT*, 125.
224 'Gräßliche Vorzeitkämpfe um Nahrung'; *DvK*, 10.

In Lessing's view, the consequence of this development was that, once man had broken out of nature, a distinction had to be made between two spheres: on the one hand the original state in which man had once been one with nature, on the other hand conscious man shaping a world of his own, being the result of his breakout from nature. Once man has broken out of nature, human consciousness imposes its own order on nature: the order of temporality, of spatiality, of causality, and so on. Lessing was not the first to develop this notion of different spheres, of course. It reminds, for example, of Kant's well-known distinction between the noumenal and the phenomenal world, and more specifically of the interpretation Arthur Schopenhauer gave to Kant's philosophy. Indeed, Lessing saw Schopenhauer as the philosopher who had "completed" Kant.[225] Lessing calls the sphere of the original state in which man was one with nature *vitalité*, and this sphere is indeed reminiscent of the sphere Schopenhauer in his philosophy referred to as "blind Will". The sphere that is shaped by human consciousness Lessing calls *réalité*; it being similar to what Kant called the phenomenal world. Lessing maintains, however, that apart from *vitalité* and *réalité*, still a third sphere should be identified. For man, *réalité* is the outer world as it is consciously perceived; but this *réalité* falls short of human wants: it is imperfect. Or, as we have seen, reality fundamentally is an abnormity. For this reason, man invents a third sphere, *verité*, which is an imagined, or rather thought out version of *réalité*: it is *réalité* as man imagines it would be if it is perfect. So, in a sense, *verité* is a replication or duplication of *réalité*: *verité* is *réalité*, but an ideal version of it, a timeless and perfect version of *réalité*. According to Lessing, the tragedy of human existence – or the human condition – is that man is aware of the existence of these three different spheres and, moreover, involved in a perpetual struggle to reunite them. In other words, man is aware of this dividedness in three spheres, but senses this is an imperfection which should be overcome. That is, man tries to heal the imperfections of *réalité* by trying to implement the ideals from *verité*, which implies imposing them on *vitalité*. This, then, is the structure of Lessing's "theory of three spheres" – the very theory he called the primordial idea of his philosophy, the idea that occurred to him in a flash when he was only seventeen. It is also the theory that is presupposed in his well-known post-1914 books like *Europa und Asien* and *Geschichte als Sinngebung des Sinnlosen*.

In the 'Preface' of the fourth, completely revised edition of *Geschichte als Sinngebung des Sinnlosen*, Lessing discusses the origins of his theory of three

---

225   See *S-W-N*, chapter two: "Schopenhauer als Vollender Kants", 51–83; and Theodor Lessing, 'Schopenhauer gegen Kant', in: *Jahrbuch der Schopenhauergesellschaft* 12 (1923–1925), 3–25.

spheres. It is the result, he claims, of his years-long wrestling with the teachings of both Theodor Lipps and Edmund Husserl, his guides in the years before he found his own way as a philosopher. Lipps taught him to distinguish primordial life and reality as given in consciousness, or, in Lessing's terminology, *vitalité* and *réalité*. Husserl, on the other hand, taught him to distinguish reality as given in consciousness and the realm of timeless truth, or, in Lessing's terminology, *réalité* and *vérité*.[226] Thus, Lessing's theory of three spheres originates in the context of early phenomenology – I would even be inclined to conclude it is Lessing's own variant of phenomenology. With his own alternative, he tried to correct what he at the time thought faulty in Lipps and in Husserl.

In later years, Lessing would gradually distance himself somewhat more from his teachers. But is no exaggeration to claim that after his move to Munich in 1895, Lessing as a philosopher developed in the context of early phenomenology, and that he even was part of the tradition of phenomenology. This shows expressly from books like *Studien zur Wertaxiomatik* and *Der Bruch in der Ethik Kants*, but holds as well, if less expressly, for his publications written during the First World War: the series of articles "Europa und Asien" in *Die Aktion* and the first edition of *Geschichte als Sinngebung des Sinnlosen*. But in fact, Lessing's perception of for instance Husserl's attitude during this war – Lessing blamed him for searching for timeless truths behind closed windows when the world was on fire[227] – might well have been one of the reasons Lessing started to distance himself from phenomenology.

All this might seem quite an abstract line of thought, but for Lessing this philosophical analysis could be observed in everyday life, as an example may illustrate. In réalité, man, say, experiences that harvests do not always bring as much food as necessary to meet all the needs of a community. Hence, man imagines plants with a richer harvest that do bring enough food: in *vérité*, man assumes the existence of plants that do bring a richer harvest, that do bring enough to satisfy the needs of the community. Now man connects this ideal from *vérité* with *réalité*, that is, he tries to realise the ideal in everyday life, by improving plants. But plants can only be improved by infringing on nature as it is: by trying to improve plants we do not accept them as we find them in nature, but impose our ideal on them. In Lessing's terminology, in *réalité* we try to realise *vérité* by infringing on *vitalité*: guided by our ideal, in our everyday world we change nature as we find it. Lessing avers that this is exactly what

---

226   GSS4, 8–10.
227   Cfr. *EuA*, 52. Husserl allegedly said: 'Die Philosophie ist reine Wissenschaft und hat als solche gar nichts mit allgemeiner Kultur zu tun.' ('philosophy is a pure science and thus as such has nothing to do with general culture.').

culture is, that is, culture by definition is restraining nature under the guidance of an ideal. But this very process by definition is at the expense of nature as it is: consequently, culture endangers nature, *vérité* endangering likewise *vitalité*. For this very reason, Lessing warns against the "decline of earth due to the spirit" ('der Untergang der Erde am Geist'), that is the ruin of *vitalité* by imposing *vérité* on it in *réalité*. To return to the example: a continuous effort to improve a plant might result in the extinction of the original plant. In general terms, culture might kill nature – but, of course, the risk is that if culture kills nature, culture will die with nature. This is the very risk Lessing warns against.

Even if Lessing argues that imposing *vérité* on *vitalité* always goes at the expense of *vitalité*, this does not imply – as one probably might expect – that his judgment on this process is unambiguously negative. That is, the fact that consciousness broke out of nature not only is the cause of problems, but conscious mind can be the answer to these very same problems as well. Lessing compares consciousness with the lance of Achilles, one of the heroes of Greek mythology. With his lance, Achilles could inflict injuries, but with this very same lance he could heal injuries as well. The same holds for consciousness: it is Janus-faced – it infringes nature, but it is able to save nature as well. In fact, if there is a way out of the crisis into which the birth of consciousness out of need eventually plunged mankind, only consciousness can find, and show, this way out of the crisis. Hence, the question whether Theodor Lessing is pessimistic with regard to the future of Western civilisation or not, cannot be answered unambiguously. Now he is pessimistic, emphasizing that the infringement of consciousness on nature will inevitably lead to the fall of civilisation, now he is less pessimistic, emphasizing the healing powers of consciousness. What is certain, however, is that all of this is an irreversible process: consciousness cannot lead mankind back to nature, back to *vitalité* – by definition, it leads further away from *vitalité*. The open question thus is, whether eventually this leads to the fall of civilisation or not. All of this might seem to be a quite abstract line of thought, but according to Lessing it is a process which may be observed in everyday life. The example of contemporary mobility probably can clarify the argument. Mankind is fully aware that the way transport is currently organised goes at the expense of nature and cannot go on forever: on the hand the exhaustion of natural resources threatens, on the other hand pollution is a huge problem. This is a fitting example of how products of consciousness infringe nature. Man cannot, however, go back to a world without cars, trains, and aeroplanes. What man can do, is to develop cars, trains, and aeroplanes which do not exhaust natural resources and which do not pollute – which are more economical in their use of natural resources, or use resources that are inexhaustible, like solar energy or wind energy. Indeed, if we compare cars, trains, and aeroplanes of today with those of, say, fifty years ago, they already are more economical and they pollute less. But suchlike inventions, of course, are products of the very same consciousness that was at the root of the problem... This, then, is the paradox of consciousness in Lessing's philosophy: it is Janus-faced, and sometimes Lessing emphasizes the one side, then the other – sometimes he is distinctly pessimistic with regard to the future of Western civilisation, sometimes less so. – Optimistic would be an overstatement, however: after all, mankind faces huge problems. The question is whether these problems will prove too much for mankind, or not. – One may safely conclude from all this, however, that Theodor Lessing did not give up on rationality, that he did not yield himself to irrationality. If there is hope for civilisation, this hope rests with the abilities of conscious mind to find solutions for the very problems its birth generated.

Both these theories – the theory of need as the bearer of consciousness, and the theory of three spheres – are the most fundamental ideas of Theodor Lessing's philosophical system. Indeed, other important ideas within his philosophy can only be understood in the light of these two basic ideas. This applies to, for instance, his repudiation of the idea of progress that dominated most of Western philosophy of his time and, moreover, scientific thinking of his days; or to his idea of preconscious understanding or *Ahmung*; or to his idea that man retrospectively gives meaning to (historical) occurrences, called by him *logificatio post festum*. And the same holds for other positions Lessing adhered to, for example his view on the nature of science, or his theory of truth: in cases like these, Lessing's particular position should be seen in the light of the two basic ideas that make up the foundation of his philosophical system.

Of the many ideas Lessing developed in relation to the fundamentals of his philosophy of need, I will select only two for further discussion: his idea of *Ahmung*, and his idea of *logificatio post festum*. The idea of *Ahmung* is one Lessing highly valued – he was inclined to see it as his single most important contribution to philosophy, even though it did not get the recognition he expected and which it, in his view, deserved. The notion of *logificatio post festum* is pivotal in Lessing's philosophy of history, and consequently of particular importance for the argument that will be developed in this study.

The idea of *Ahmung* is the theme of an essay Lessing wrote in 1908, which he included in his 1914 collection *Philosophie als Tat*: "Psychologie der Ahmung".[228]

---

[228] Theodor Lessing, 'Psychologie der Ahmung', in: *Archiv für systematische Philosophie*, Neue Folge XVIII (1912), Heft 2, 209–223; reprinted in *PaT*, 127–151. Lessing indicates the essay was written in 1908 in *PaT*, 127, even if it was only published in 1912.

However, he does hint at this idea several times in his 1906 book *Schopenhauer – Wagner – Nietzsche*,[229] which is the reflection of lectures he gave in 1904. So one may assume that he had been thinking about this idea for quite some time already when he published this essay. In this essay, Lessing develops his argument more or less in dialogue with publications by Theodor Lipps relating to this issue, it being plausible, therefore, that he started to reflect on this topic already around the turn of the century. What, then, does Lessing's idea of *Ahmung* imply? And how does it relate to his philosophy of need?

Lessing borrowed the term *Ahmung* from, as he puts it, "one of the most beautiful places of the old Nibelungenlied",[230] where Hagen uses the word "ahmenswert" ('worth *ahmen*'). The word *Ahmung* fell out of use in everyday German, however. Its stem can be found in the verb "nachahmen", to imitate, that still is in use in contemporary German. The literal meaning of the verb "ahmen" is "to calibrate",[231] but Lessing uses *Ahmung* as an alternative to the term *Einfühlung*, empathy, because he objects to the way the term *Einfühlung* is being used in German philosophy of his times, amongst others by his revered teacher Theodor Lipps.

What, then, are Lessing's objections to the term *Einfühlung* as it was used by Lipps and others? And how does his idea of *Ahmung* differ from the commonly used *Einfühlung*? In his 1908 essay, Lessing points out that *Einfühlung* has become a highly fashionable term, bandied about all the time. It refers to a number of different mental phenomena, however, without making proper distinctions between them."We suspect that in that big container empathy is piled up what has no more in common than precisely that it concerns processes about which – psychologists know nothing", Lessing claims.[232] It is clear, however, that the term always refers to a condition of unconsciousness "in which, be it consciousness and object or be it I and you, stay together undivided".[233] Hence, in Lessing's view, instead of *Einfühlung*, alternatives like *Ineinsfühlen* (feeling together) or *Einsfühlen* (feeling one) would be preferable: after all, these expressions suggest the sense of oneness Lessing has in mind.

---

229   S-W-N, for example 121–122, 147–148, 170–171, 210–212.
230   'einer der schönsten Stellen des alten Nibelungenliedes'; o.c., 'Psychologie der Ahmung', in: *PaT*, 127.
231   Communication by the late prof. J.A. Huisman, professor in old Germanic languages, at Utrecht University, in a letter to the present author.
232   'Wir argwöhnen, daß in den großen Einheitstopf Einfühlung zusammengeworfen ward, was nicht mehr miteinander gemein hat, als eben dies, daß es sich um Vorgänge handelt, von denen – die Psychologen nichts wissen'; Lessing, o.c., 132.
233   'in welchem, sei es Bewußtsein und Gegenstand oder sei es Ich und Du, ungeschieden ineinander bleiben'; o.c., 133.

This sense of oneness is something we experience, for example, when we are confronted with an overwhelmingly impressive work of art:

> Immediately, in one and the same act, I experience through the object of the experience – myself. It is not like, here is my I and there, opposite the I, the perceived object. But I experience this I only through the object. The object serves as transparent for my I. I myself am the object, that is, I live in the line of march that is dictated by the object.[234]

It is this very category of experiences that Lessing refers to with the terms *ahmen* and *Ahmung*:

> thus I call every mental activity, in which my I functions in a restrained line of march, according to necessities of an outer world. I say necessities, to emphasize expressly the contrast with the character of demands that this outer world only acquires from the very moment it is an outer world, that is, it opposes the I that *ahms* in it.[235]

In other words, *Ahmung* is a process that occurs before human consciousness makes a distinction between either I and object or I and you; in this process, experience and (self) understanding form a whole. Within this process, Lessing distinguishes between different kinds of *Ahmung*: one can sense some kind of preconscious attraction to others or to the outer world, which Lessing calls *Mitahmung*; or one can sense some kind of preconscious aversion to others or to the outer world, which he calls *Gegenahmung*. Yet another kind of *Ahmung* is *Aufahmung*: this is the kind of *Ahmung* that is characteristic of religion and art. To explain this, Lessing compares it with erotic attraction: the image we form of the person we feel attracted to does not correspond with reality, as we tend to idealise this person. That is, the image we form of the person we feel

---

234 'Unmittelbar, in ein und dem selben Akt erlebe ich durch den Gegenstand des Erlebnisses hindurch – mich selber. Es verhält sich nicht so, daß hier mein Ich ist und dort, dem Ich gegenüber der ästhetische Gegenstand. Sondern ich erlebe dies Ich nur durch den Gegenstand hindurch. Der Gegenstand dient meinem Ich als Transparent. Ich selber bin der Gegenstand, d.h. ich lebe in der von dem Gegenstande vorgeschriebenen Marschroute'; o.c., 135.

235 'so nenne ich jede seelische Aktivität, in welcher mein Ich in gebundener Marschroute funktioniert, gemäß Nötigungen einer Außenwelt. Nötigungen sage ich, um ausdrücklich einen Gegensatz zu betonen zu dem Forderungscharakter, den diese Außenwelt erst von dem Zeitpunkt an gewinnt, wo sie Außenwelt wird, das heißt dem in ihr ahmenden Ich gegenübertritt'; o.c., 137.

attracted to in a sense raises this person above reality. In Lessing's view, this is similar to what happens in *Aufahmung*: we sense idealised potentialities, and thus raise the object above reality.

Summing up, Lessing objects to the idea of *Einfühlung* for two reasons. One is that, at least according to Lessing, *Einfühlung* presupposes a distinction between subject and object, regardless whether this object is another person or a thing. In contrast, Lessing's idea of *Ahmung* presupposes a fundamental oneness in the process, prior to any distinction being made between subject and object by human consciousness. The second reason is that *Einfühlung* is too general a term: it lumps together different phenomena which according to Lessing should be distinguished. As he puts it himself: "I see in my notions of *Mit-*, *Gegen-* and *Aufahmung* three descriptions of preconscious processes, which in contrast to the old psychology of *Einfühlung* allow to raise a whole fullness of precise mental gradations into the light of consciousness".[236]

In the light of all this, I would suggest that a proper English translation of *Ahmung* could be "cathartic understanding", where catharsis is used in the sense as used by Aristotle in his *Poetics*. In Aristotle's view, a spectator in the theatre identifies so much with the play he or she is watching that no distinction is made between the "world" of the stage and his or her I opposite it ; hence, he or she can truly experience the play, and this results in a kind of (self) understanding that is more intuitive than rational. Similarly, *Ahmung* is a kind of preconscious (self)understanding, resulting from a confrontation with the outer world, in which human consciousness does not make a distinction between I and the outer world.

How does this idea of *Ahmung* relate to Lessing's philosophy of need? As we have seen, one of the fundamental ideas of Lessing's philosophy of need is his theory of three spheres: *vitalité*, *réalité*, and *vérité*. *Vitalité* is the sphere of primordial life, that is, the sphere that originally existed before consciousness was born out of need. Once consciousness awakes, it makes a distinction between the 'I' and 'the outer world' opposing it. The theory of three spheres is based on this distinction, and accordingly the result of the distinction between the 'I' and the outer world opposing it.[237] In this connection, *Ahmung* is the way of (self)understanding associated with the sphere of *vitalité*, where a distinction between the subject and the surrounding world does not (yet) exist. Lessing means by this that some of our experiences may be so overwhelming

---

236 'Ich sehe in meinen Begriffen Mit-, Gegen- und Aufahmung drei Charakteristika für vorbewußte Vorgänge, welche gegenüber der alten Einfühlungspsychologie eine ganze Fülle seelischer Feinheiten ins Licht des Bewußtseins emporzuheben verstatten.'; o.c., 151.
237 Cfr. above, 89 *ff*.

that we sense the original oneness as it existed before consciousness made a distinction between three different spheres. If this happens, one understands by experiencing this sense of oneness – that is, by *Ahmung*.

Another subject that deserves special attention in Lessing's philosophy is his notion of *logificatio post festum*. As we have seen when discussing Lessing's break with Ludwig Klages,[238] according to Lessing the personal, i.e. the remembered past of an individual should not be conceived as being fixed. For in order to keep our inner balance, we continuously adapt our remembered past, in order to bring it in line with our present-day situation. There is no forgery involved with this, however, but only a way to deal with changes and developments in our personal lives and circumstances: it is actually simply the way how we preserve our mental health. This idea foreshadows what philosophers later in the twentieth century – for example the French philosopher Paul Ricoeur (1913–2005) – have written about the notion of narrative identity. In studies like *Temps et Récit* and *Soi-même comme un autre*,[239] Ricoeur emphasizes that our personal identity is essentially a narrative one, that is, our personal identity is formed by the story we tell about our past; and this story is not fixed, but changes continuously in the light of our present.

Lessing discusses his notion of *logificatio post festum* at length in his *Studien zur Wertaxiomatik*.[240] This notion as well should be understood in the light of his theory of three spheres. As we have seen, when consciousness is born out of need – or when, to use Lessing's terminology, *Geist* is born out of *Not* – consciousness orders primordial life, using categories like temporality, spatiality, and causality. According to Lessing, many of the notions we use in ethics – like guilt, virtue, sin, destiny, duty, penance, and aim – are similar to these categories, that is, they as well are categories we use to order primordial life. If we contemplate an act, in a sense all of reality, including the entire past, has made this act possible: the act would not have occurred exactly as it did if only one aspect of (past) reality had been different. As Lessing puts it: had the position of the stars been different, had the weather been different, had the physical condition of the persons concerned been different, the act would have been different. But we use notions like guilt, virtue, sin, duty, etc., in order to single out a specific factor, which we accordingly call "the" cause.

---

238 Cfr. above, 52–54.
239 Paul Ricoeur, *Temps et récit* (three volumes, Paris 1983–1995) and *Soi-même comme un autre* (Paris 1990).
240 *SzW*, 89–95.

In other words, consciousness builds reality, the latter being a construction of the first. This is a process that is necessary, born out of need: if man does not invent reality, he faces an unbearable chaos, and sheer madness. Hence, it is a logical-psychological necessity for man to shape reality, and as this necessity operates retrospectively, Lessing calls it *logificatio post festum*. This is a phenomenon everyday life constantly bears witness of. If someone falls ill with a cough, one looks for a specific aspect that may be singled out and accordingly called "the" cause; if a crime is committed, we look for someone we can point to as "the" culprit, even though we know multiple factors should be taken into account, knowing, for instance, that usually society at large is at least partially responsible.[241] Lessing points out that it is telling that the Greek αἰτία and the Latin *causa* both mean "cause" as well as "guilt". In Lessing's view, we judge reality ultimately from an ethical point of view, and not, like the Greeks and the Romans, as a chain of causes and events. So where for the Greeks and Romans one word sufficed, we need two – guilt and cause – in order to express the difference as it exists for us.[242] As Lessing points out:

> Now this is the mental occurrence that we can witness everywhere where "guilt" is invented and decreed."Guilt" is an invention through which man keeps disturbing emotions at length [...] we have to want and value. Not fact, existence, nature, objectivity, only ethics and value is the human domain. Man is "the valuing animal".[243]

In other words, "the chaos of life is subjected to consciousness",[244] and as a result we believe that

> [o]ur cosmos is the product of our mind. Our reason has built it. So we think it is reasonable.[245]

---

241 This is exactly what Lessing in the 1920's pointed out in his book on Haarmann, as we have seen in Chapter one above, 8.
242 O.c., 92.
243 'Dies nun ist der Seelenvorgang, der überall zu beobachten ist, wo eine 'Schuld' herausgefunden und dekretiert wird. Die 'Schuld' ist eine Erfindung, mittels deren der Mensch sich störende Emotion vom Leibe hält [...] wir müssen Sollen und Werten. Nicht Tatsache, Dasein, Natur, Objektivität, einzig Ethik und Wert ist menschliche Domäne. Der Mensch ist 'das auswertende Tier'.'; o.c., 93.
244 'Das Chaos des Lebens dem Geiste zu unterwerfen.'; loc. cit..
245 'Unser Kosmos ist Produkt unseres Geistes. Unsere Vernunft hat es gebaut. Also finden wir es vernünftig.'; o.c., 94.

Lessing briefly hints at the importance this way of thinking has for our interpretation of history:

> Behind blindly reigning destinies we look for the clairvoyance of a "providence". And we logificate life just as long as it lasts until it seems to be born out of "world reason".[246]

This line of argument would indeed play a pivotal part in Lessing's analysis of historical thinking in years to come.

These, then, are some of the central thoughts of Lessing's philosophy of need – a philosophical system of his own that he intended to elaborate in a book which was to be entitled *Philosophie der Not* ('The Philosophy of Need'), a book he considered his major and most personal contribution to the tradition of philosophy. *Philosophie der Not* was never written, however. It was the outbreak of the First World War that prevented him from writing it down. In the first place, Lessing had more urgent problems in his daily life to deal with, like surviving the war with his wife and children. Secondly, he felt a moral obligation to give priority to his reflections on the war as a philosopher, instead of elaborating a philosophical system of his own. After all, he had written in his "Philosophie als Tat" that it was nothing less than a crime if an individual dedicated himself to a life of passivity and meditation when life was miserable for large groups of the population.[247] In these times of war, the need was indeed very urgent for large groups of the population. Hence, in his philosophical activities – both as a public lecturer and a writer – Lessing concentrated on clarifying questions with regard to the war, questions which, in accordance with his idea of philosophy, were now far more urgent than the elaboration of his system.

In this connection, the question of Lessing's views on the outbreak of the war arises. Did he consider it a just war? Did he share the views of his contemporaries, or did he rather disagree with their positions? In trying to answer these questions one has to make a distinction between Lessing's spontaneous and immediate reaction to the outbreak of the war, and his intellectual, more distant response. Evidence for his immediate reaction may be found in his

---

246 'Hinter blind verwaltenden Schicksalen suchen wir die Hellsicht einer 'Vorsehung'. Und wir logisieren so lange am Leben herum, bis es uns aus 'Weltvernunft' geboren scheint.'; loc. cit.. Of course, 'Weltvernunft' is an allusion to the philosophy of history of G.W.F. Hegel.
247 Cfr. Chapter One above, 22.

diaries and notes of 1914, in the texts of public lectures he gave in the autumn of this year, and in stray remarks in later publications. His intellectual response to the war was his book *Geschichte als Sinngebung des Sinnlosen* ('History as giving Sense to the Senseless'; 1919), written during the war but published only afterwards. In the next chapter, Lessing's immediate reaction to the war will be addressed, while in chapter four his intellectual reaction in *Geschichte als Sinngebung des Sinnlosen* will be dealt with.

The *Prager Tagblatt* reporting on Lessing's murder on September 1st, 1933

CHAPTER 3

'Et Si Omnes, Non Ego'

Theodor Lessing and the First World War

On August 1st, 1914, after weeks of growing tension and diplomatic crisis following the murder in Sarajevo, on June 28th, of the Austrian Archduke Franz Ferdinand and his wife Sophie, Duchess of Hohenberg, Germany declared war on Russia. As a reaction, France, being an ally of Russia, promptly decided to mobilize. In reply, on the very same day, Germany occupied Luxemburg; the next day, Germany demanded from the Belgian government a free passage through Belgium for its army. The Belgian government refused this demand, which induced Germany to declare war on Belgium as well. On August 3rd, Germany declared war on France too. The next day, German troops invaded Belgium, which prompted Great Britain to declare war on Germany on the very same day. With this the devastating confrontation started that at present is known as the First World War.[1]

On August 4th, the German Emperor Wilhelm II addressed representatives of all political parties in the *Reichstag*, the German parliament. The closing words of his speech ran as follows:

> Here I repeat: I no longer know any parties, I only know Germans. In token of the fact that you are firmly resolved, without keeping up a distinction between parties, without a distinction between clans, without a distinction between religious communities, with me through thick and thin, through distress and death, I summon the leaders of the different parties in this House to come forward and to vow this in my hand.[2]

---

1   The literature on the subject is overwhelming. See for example Niall Ferguson, *The Pity of War. Explaining World War One* (London 1998); Hew Strachan, *The First World War: A New History* (London 2003); and David Stevenson, *1914–1918: The History of the First World War* (London 2004).
2   'Hier wiederhole Ich: Ich kenne keine Parteien mehr, Ich kenne nur Deutsche. Zum Zeichen dessen, daß Sie fest entschlossen sind, ohne Parteiunterschiede, ohne Stammesunterschiede, ohne Konfessionsunterschiede durchzuhalten mit Mir durch dick und dünn, durch Not und Tod, fordere Ich die Vorstände der Parteien auf, vorzutreten und Mir das in die Hand zu geloben.', in: 'Verhandlungen des Reichstags. Dreizehnte Legislaturperiode. Zweite Session. 1914. Eröffnungssitzung im Weißen Saale des Königlichen Schlosses zu Berlin am Dienstag den 4. August 1914', in: *Verhandlungen des Reichstags, Stenographische Berichte, 1914/16*, Bd. 306, 1–2.

© HERMAN SIMISSEN, 2021 | DOI:10.1163/9789004464773_004

With these words, drafted by Chancellor Theobald von Bethmann-Hollweg (1856–1921), the Emperor proclaimed the so-called *Burgfrieden*, a truce between the political parties represented in the *Reichstag*, in which they agreed to abandon party politics for the duration of the war, in order to maintain national unity. Likewise, the trade unions agreed to abandon social conflicts and strikes. Or, in the words of the politician and banker Johannes Kaempf (1842–1918), president of the *Reichstag*: "United in all parties, united in all classes!".[3] Both political parties and trade unions saw this *Burgfrieden* as their patriotic duty, now that the country was at war. This *Burgfrieden* was generally received with enthusiasm, even by the socialist SPD, although only a few days before, between July 25th and 30th, it had organised large peace demonstrations in several big cities. All in all, over half a million people had joined in these demonstrations. But at August 4th the SPD accepted the *Burgfrieden* and, moreover, later that very same day it supported a bill to make so-called *Kriegskredite* available for the government, that is, a special budget to pay for the costs of war. Only two members of the SPD parliamentary party did not support this bill, and abstained from voting. Thus, the vast majority of the SPD joined in with the other political parties in support of the war – in glaring contrast to the line it had followed before August 1914. After all, ever since its formation, international solidarity between workers of all nations had been one of the main ideas in the ideology of the SPD, and in 1912 the German SPD had even been one of the driving forces at the international socialist conference in Basel, Switzerland, in phrasing an appeal to all workers of Europe to resist war.

The *Burgfrieden* would not exist for a long time: a first omen was that Karl Liebknecht (1871–1919), Member of Parliament for the SPD, already on December 2nd 1914 voted against making even more extra funds available for warfare. – Liebknecht's attitude towards the policy of the SPD concerning the war was most critical ever since, and eventually he would even be expelled from this party just because of his opposition to the *Burgfrieden*. Afterwards, he was involved in the foundation of the German communist party, the KPD, but Liebknecht was killed during the Spartacist uprising of 1919 in Berlin. – In 1915, the *Burgfrieden* started to show more cracks. As the war continued, and the expected easy victory failed to materialize, the first protest demonstrations and strikes started to occur. Moreover, in 1916, political debates arose on the goal that was strived after with this war, in this way party politics returning again in the German political arena.

---

3 'Einig in allen Parteien, einig in allen Ständen!'; Dr. Kaempf, Untitled contribution, in: Georg Gellert (ed.), *Das eiserne Buch. Die führenden Männer und Frauen zum Weltkrieg 1914/15* (Hamburg 1915), 139.

Although the *Burgfrieden* only lasted for a short time, it would play an important part in German politics, not only during the war, but especially afterwards. The national unity and harmony as experienced in August 1914, was generally referred to as "the spirit of 1914". This "spirit of 1914" had given the German people strength and zest, it was said. In the course of the war, this spirit was transformed into a set of related ideas, referred to as "the ideas of 1914" – thoughts about national unity, fellowship, self-sacrifice, and the unique identity of German national culture. These thoughts were contrasted with "the ideas of 1789": the universal ideals of liberty, equality, and fraternity that had inspired the French Revolution. Similar to the way "the ideas of 1789" had inspired so many people in France and beyond, "the ideas of 1914" would inspire future generations of Germans, and prove to be of lasting importance for the German people, it was claimed. Indeed, the glaring contrast "the ideas of 1789" and "the ideas of 1914" boiled down to this: the former laid claim to universal validity, whereas the latter only addressed the German people. In short, it is the opposition between the universalism that is characteristic of the Enlightenment and the particularism being characteristic of Romanticism. Ever since 1915, it was common practice in political debates in Germany to refer to "the ideas of 1914", usually to justify particular political opinions, though sometimes in a rather critical sense. As such, both notions – "the spirit of 1914" and "the ideas of 1914" – would be used up to well after the First World War, both during the Weimar Republic and the Third Reich.[4]

1 "The Spirit of 1914"

How did the German people react to the outbreak of war in August 1914? By tradition, the declaration of war was greeted with great, even exuberant enthusiasm all over the country: troops leaving for the front were cheered, volunteers presented themselves in great numbers – even more than the army could admit –, and the German people stood united behind its Emperor, its government, and its army. A telling description of the atmosphere that had developed was given for instance by the writer and poet Ernst Toller (1893–1939) in his

---

4   Again, the literature on the subject is overwhelming. See for example Steffen Bruendel, *Volksgemeinschaft oder Volksstaat. Die „Ideen von 1914" und die Neuordnung Deutschlands im Ersten Weltkrieg* (Berlin 2003); Helmut Fries, *Die große Katharsis. Der Erste Weltkrieg in der Sicht deutscher Dichter und Gelehrter*, 2 vols., (Konstanz 1994–1995); Hermann Lübbe, *Politische Philosophie in Deutschland. Studien zu ihrer Geschichte* (München 1974 [first edition: Basel 1963]), part 4, Die philosophischen Ideen von 1914, 171–235; and Hans Maier, 'Ideen von 1914 - Ideen von 1939? Zweierlei Kriegsanfänge', in: *Vierteljahrshefte für Zeitgeschichte* 38 (1990), nr. 4, 525–542.

autobiographical book *Eine Jugend in Deutschland* (1933; 'A Youth in Germany') – but it would be easy to give other examples; a well-known case in point is the description by Stefan Zweig (1881–1942) in his *Die Welt von Gestern* (1942; 'The World of Yesterday') –. At the time the war broke out, Toller lived as a student in Grenoble, France. He managed to return to Germany only after considerable difficulties. Toller writes about his return to home soil:

> I can still hear the voices of people yelling that France had been attacked, and now I read in German papers that Germany is being attacked, and I do believe it. French aeroplanes, the Chancellor said, threw bombs on Bavarian territory, Germany was assaulted, I do believe it.
>
> At stations we are given cards with the portrait of the emperor, with the caption: 'I no longer know political parties'.
>
> The emperor no longer knows political parties, here it is written in black and white, the country no longer knows races, everyone speaks one language now, everyone defends one mother: Germany.[5]

Toller volunteered, and after only a short basic military training his unit left for the front: "In mid-August we leave Munich, decorated with flowers, accompanied by women and children".[6] When his unit crosses the Rhine, one of the recruits struck up the song *Die Wacht am Rhein* ('The Guard at the Rhine'), with its refrain "Dear fatherland rest assured, dear fatherland rest assured: the guard stands firm and faithful, the guard at the Rhine! The guard stands firm and faithful, the guard at the Rhine!".[7] Other recruits join in. Toller concludes:

---

5 'Ich habe die Stimmen der Menschen noch im Ohr, die schrien, daß Frankreich angegriffen sei, jetzt lese ich in deutschen Zeitungen, daß Deutschland angegriffen wird, und ich glaube es. Französische Flieger, sagte der Reichskanzler, haben Bomben auf bayerisches Land geworfen, Deutschland wurde überfallen, ich glaube es.
An den Bahnhöfen schenkt man uns Karten mit dem Bild des Kaisers und der Unterschrift: »Ich kenne keine Parteien mehr.«
Der Kaiser kennt keine Parteien mehr, hier steht es schwarz auf weiß, das Land keine Rassen mehr, alle sprechen eine Sprache, alle verteidigen eine Mutter, Deutschland.'; Ernst Toller, *Eine Jugend in Deutschland* (first edition Amsterdam 1933; I used the Rowohlt edition [Reinbek bei Hamburg 1984]), 38–39.
6 'Mitte August verlassen wir, blumengeschmückt, von Frauen und Kindern begleitet, München.'; o.c., 40.
7 'Lieb Vaterland magst ruhig sein, lieb Vaterland magst ruhig sein: Fest steht und treu die Wacht, die Wacht am Rhein! Fest steht und treu die Wacht, die Wacht am Rhein!'. The text of the song was written in 1840, the melody in 1854. From 1870, it served as an unofficial national anthem in the German Empire. It was quite popular during both the Franco-Prussian War of 1870–1871 and the First World War.

Indeed, we live in a whirl of excited feelings. The words Germany, fatherland, war have a magic power, when we say them they do not evaporate, they float in the air, they circle around themselves, they ignite themselves and us.[8]

Toller, for that matter, would change his mind quite strikingly, for during the war he developed into a pacifist with leftist, socialist ideas. At the end of the war, he was one of the leaders of the Bavarian Council Republic, which was established when the November Revolution spread to the Bavarian capital. But in May 1919, the Council Republic was overthrown. Because of his involvement, Toller was sentenced to five years imprisonment. After he was released, he lived in Berlin until 1933. After the National-Socialists took power, Toller emigrated; on May 22nd 1939, he committed suicide in New York, suffering from major psychic problems in his exile.[9] In a preceding chapter of his book, Toller writes about the possible background of the enthusiasm about the outbreak of the war. He was still at secondary school, when in 1911 a disagreement on colonial interests led to the Morocco Crisis. A German warship appeared before the harbour of Agadir, and, he writes,

> Everyone speaks about a war between France and Germany. The teachers at school warn us confidentially for the French teacher, who teaches languages as an exchange teacher, all French people are spies, the innocent are the smartest, we should not let ourselves be questioned, Monsieur reports every fart to Paris.
>
> We boys want the war to come, peace is an idle and war a great time, the teachers say, we long for adventure, perhaps we will be exempted from the last school years, and we will be in uniform tomorrow, that will be a life.[10]

---

8   'Ja, wir leben in einem Rausch des Gefühls. Die Worte Deutschland, Vaterland, Krieg haben magische Kraft, wenn wir sie aussprechen, verflüchtigen sie sich nicht, sie schweben in der Luft, kreisen um sich selbst, entzünden sich und uns.'; Toller, o.c., 41.

9   For an overview of his life, see for example Richard Dove, *He was a German: A Biography of Ernst Toller* (London 1990) or in German, Richard Dove, *Ernst Toller. Ein Leben in Deutschland* (Munich 1993).

10 'Alle reden vom Krieg zwischen Frankreich und Deutschland. Die Professoren der Schule warnen uns vertraulich vor dem französischen Lektor, der als Austauschlehrer Sprachunterricht erteilt, alle Franzosen seien Spione, die harmlosen seien am gerissensten, wir sollten uns nicht ausfragen lassen, Monsieur melde jeden Furz nach Paris.
    Wir Jungen wünschen den Krieg herbei, der Friede ist eine faule und der Krieg eine große Zeit, sagen die Professoren, wir sehnen uns nach Abenteuern, vielleicht werden uns die letzten Schuljahre erlassen, und wir sind morgen in Uniform, das wird ein Leben.'; Toller, o.c., 28.

The mood Toller describes in this passage may partially explain the enthusiasm with which quite a number of people greeted the war: some people were simply bored with life as it was, and believed war would bring renewal – a political and social renewal, spiritual renewal, and a cultural one. The idea that any kind of restoration would be better than continuing the status quo, even if a war was necessary to bring this about, was quite widespread at the time, not only in Germany, but in many European countries, especially among intellectuals.[11]

Recent historical research, however, seriously questions the traditional picture that Toller so aptly describes in *Eine Jugend in Deutschland*. Was the war indeed greeted all over Germany with such a general and great enthusiasm as we are supposed to believe, or is this rather an image that has been created at the very moment, in August 1914, by a governmental propaganda campaign? In a groundbreaking study, *The Spirit of 1914*, using contemporary evidence like local and regional newspapers, the American historian Jeffrey Verhey demonstrated quite convincingly that the enthusiasm about the outbreak of the war was not as widespread a phenomenon as is generally assumed. It mainly occurred in the big cities of Germany, especially in the capital Berlin. Throughout the country, however, people were hardly enthusiastic about the war, feelings of uncertainty, anxiety, and even fear being dominant. Moreover, even in the big cities the enthusiasm was restricted to particular classes, especially the upper and middle ones. But among the working classes, the enthusiasm for the war was far less widespread. So all in all, the idea that almost all of the German people was enthusiastic about the war is, in Verhey's view, historically inaccurate: in fact, the reactions were far more mixed. So how did the idea arise that a vast majority, if not all of the German people enthusiastically supported the war? In this respect, according to Verhey, two factors are relevant. On the one hand, at the time government propaganda had every reason to spread the idea that the war was enthusiastically supported: it was a way to ensure the government of wide support, and to nip political opposition to the war in the bud. And on the other hand, one group in society that by and large indeed did enthusiastically support the war proved to be very influential: intellectuals. They had every opportunity to make themselves heard in public debates – and so they did: by means of speeches, newspaper articles and all kinds of other publications. Thus, they contributed to both creating and spreading the idea

---

11   For an overview of this widespread feeling, all over Europe, that some kind of renewal was absolutely necessary, and of the reactions to the war related to this feeling, cfr. for instance a recent study by the Dutch historian Ewout Kieft, *Oorlogsenthousiasme. Europa 1900–1918* (Amsterdam 2015).

that the war was indeed generally enthusiastically supported by the majority of the German people.[12]

2 German Intellectuals and the "Spirit of 1914"

One section of the people that indeed did greet the war with great enthusiasm was that of the intellectuals. – This is not the place to dwell on the question how the notion "intellectuals" should be defined. I refer, quite pragmatically, to those German academics, literary figures, journalists and so on, who joined in public debates on the war, either by public speeches or in writing, in roughly the first year of the First World War.[13] – Numerous writers, journalists, philosophers, historians, theologians, and economists wrote passionate arguments, in which they discussed the war, defending it in large numbers, and the German foreign policy in general as well. In the words of the German philosopher Kurt Flasch: "Many intellectuals gladly undertook this task as their patriotic duty".[14] The bibliography of books, essays, articles, and speeches listing contemporary discussions of the war – excluding factual reports on the course of battle – compiled by Flasch contains over 13.000 items, which shows how widespread indeed the enthusiasm was with which the war was welcomed by intellectuals.[15] Not infrequently the authors not only had a high reputation in their own days, but are still renowned in our time. To mention but a few examples, it concerns literary authors like Thomas Mann, Gerhard Hauptmann (1862–1946)

12 Jeffrey Verhey, *The Spirit of 1914: Militarism, Myth, and Mobilization in Germany* (Cambridge 2000), *passim*.
13 For a careful consideration of the notion "intellectuals", see for instance Stefan Collini, *Absent Minds: Intellectuals in Britain* (Oxford 2006), especially part one, 15–68. In 1927, Theodor Lessing himself characterized the intellectuals quite cynically: "That is a big number of people who sit down and write: newspapers, journals, thick books. Well! In our youth we all did write poetry at one time. But these people continue to write poetry, on and on. And why? […] These people suffer from an unstoppable want to waffle. […] This is a disease, out of which all kinds of things can be made: politics, literature, science. " ('Das sind eine Unzahl Leute, die dasitzen und schreiben: Zeitungen, Zeitschriften, dicke Bücher. Nun ja! In unserer Jugend haben wir ja alle mal gedichtet. Aber diese Leute dichten nun immer so weiter, immer weiter. Und warum? […] Die Leute leiden an unhemmbaren Bedürfnis zu schwatzen. […] Das ist eine Erkrankung, aus der sich allerlei machen läßt: Politik, Literatur, Wissenschaft'; Theodor Lessing, 'Schmerzensruf einer Normalen', in: *Prager Tagblatt*, December 20th, 1927; reprinted in *IWFG*, 199.
14 'Viele Intellektuelle ergriffen freudig diese Aufgabe als ihre vaterländische Pflicht'; Kurt Flasch, *Die geistige Mobilmachung. Die deutschen Intellektuellen und der Erste Weltkrieg* (Berlin 2000), 373.
15 O.c., 11.

and Ernst Jünger (1895–1998); historians like Friedrich Meinecke (1862–1954) and Hans Delbrück (1848–1929); philosophers like Rudolf Eucken (1846–1926), Ernst Troeltsch (1865–1923) and Hermann Cohen (1842–1918); theologians like Adolf von Harnack (1851–1930) and Adolf Deißmann (1866–1937); economists like Adolph Wagner (1835–1917), Lujo Brentano (1844–1931) and Gustav Schmoller (1838–1917); and the biologist Ernst Haeckel (1834–1919).

But a small number of intellectuals opposed this strong support for the war, however, they sometimes being highly reputed as well, like the literary authors Karl Kraus (1874–1936) and Heinrich Mann (1871–1950), the elder brother of Thomas Mann; a philosopher like Ernst Bloch (1885–1977); and the scientist Albert Einstein (1879–1955). They condemned the war, sometimes on principle out of a convinced pacifism, sometimes only out of opposition against this war in particular.

The German philosopher Hermann Lübbe emphasizes, however, that for a proper understanding of the reaction of German intellectuals to the war, in particular philosophers, one should keep in mind that in nineteenth and early twentieth century Europe it was generally considered self-evident that in case of war philosophers should put themselves at the service of their nation, endeavouring to justify the position and conduct of their country. In this respect, German philosophers were not exceptional, for English and French philosophers behaved likewise. According to Lübbe, the "scholarly chauvinism" and the passionate tone of the arguments in Germany were hardly different from those elsewhere in Europe.[16]

A typical example of the mood dominating the vast majority of German intellectuals, is this fragment from a speech by the German-Austrian writer Hermann Bahr (1863–1934), delivered on August 12th, 1914:

> Even if I will live up to a hundred years, I will never forget these days. It is the most magnificent that we ever experienced. We did not know that something as magnificent as this may be experienced. Only three weeks ago, we would not even have been capable of imagining it. This feeling, to have experienced something that we cannot yet even put into words, overwhelms all of us. Everyone can see it in the other, and feels it with the pressure of his determined hand. Speaking has become useless, everyone knows silently what everyone feels. Nothing lives in us but that one, enormous thing: to us appeared the essence of Germany.

---

16   H. Lübbe, o.c., 171.

At long last we looked at each other. Now, for the first time we know, how we really are. That is the indescribable gift of these great times. Because of this in this difficult hour all hearts beat so fast. We have never been so serious, but neither so cheerful as well. We stand together in a confident cheerfulness that we have never known before. Because the essence of Germany has appeared to us.[17]

One year after the war broke out, the German jurist and historian of law Otto von Gierke (1841–1921) gave a long speech, in which he looked back on the first days of the war. His enthusiasm was hardly less than Bahr's at the outbreak of the war:

> Truly! It were not only imagined dangers that threatened our inner unity, our national strength and our moral spirit. And that is why just now I thought we should welcome it gratefully as a divine order that this terrible struggle for life was forced upon us.
> Because now, like a wonderful miracle, came that mighty revival of the soul of the German people that exceeded all inkling and hope. Now the German people found itself again in sudden self-reflection. All discord, all party quarrels, all petty selfishness, all unpatriotic behaviour was as blown away by the breath of history. Every single individual only felt as part of the whole, and forgot his personal fortunes in this one thought: what matters is the fatherland! With a bright eye and superior mind our emperor took the lead, called the people to arms, and spoke the fine word, he would henceforth know no parties anymore, he would only know Germans. [...] Never before a people has felt so at one with its state, never dedicated itself with such loyalty, never trusted its monarch, its army command, its government so firmly – like this people of almost

---

17 'Und wenn ich hundert Jahre würde, diese Tage werde ich nie vergessen! Es ist das Größte, was wir erlebt haben. Wir wussten nicht, dass so Großes erlebt werden kann. Noch vor drei Wochen wären wir unfähig gewesen, es uns auch nur vorzustellen. Dieses Gefühl, etwas erlebt zu haben, was wir selber noch gar nicht aussprechen können, überwältigt alle. Jeder sieht's dem anderen an und fühlt am Drucke seiner entschlossenen Hand. Reden ist unnütz geworden, jeder weiß stumm, was jeder fühlt. Nichts lebt in uns als das Eine, das Ungeheurere: uns ist das deutsche Wesen erschienen.

Wir haben einander endlich erblickt. Wir wissen jetzt zum erstenmal, wie wir wirklich sind. Das ist das unbeschreibliche Geschenk dieser großen Zeit. Davon schlagen in dieser schweren Stunde die Herzen alle so hoch. Niemals sind wir ernster gewesen, aber auch nie so froh. In einer gläubigen Freudigkeit stehen wir beisammen, die wir niemals kannten. Denn uns ist das deutsche Wesen erschienen.'; Hermann Bahr, 'Das deutsche Wesen ist uns erschienen!, Bayreuth, 12 August 1914', quoted from Georg Gellert (ed.), o.c., 73.

70 million heads. There was no distinction between classes, not between upper-class and humble, rich or poor, learned or unlearned, employer or worker, elderly or youth. The conscripts jubilantly followed the banners, with passionate impatience those who were not conscripted pushed forward to volunteer for the army that could not absorb the superior number of the applicants – one speaks of two million.[18]

Both, admittedly long, but revealing quotations describe how, according to a vast majority of intellectuals, the German people allegedly experienced the outbreak as well as the first weeks of the First World War.

In several writings, published during the war, the German sociologist and political scientist Johann Plenge (1874–1963) discussed the significance of the war within the context of German history in general. In one of these, his *1789 und 1914. Die symbolischen Jahre in der Geschichte des politischen Geistes* ('1789 and 1914. The Symbolic Years in the History of Political Consciousness'), published in 1916, Plenge wrote:

> It is a basic fact that in 1914, at the beginning of the war, an entire people instantly had changed its inner mental attitude and its way of cooperation, and that it subsequently became a goal of life to secure this inner

---

[18] 'Wahrlich! Es waren nicht bloß eingebildete Gefahren, die unsere innere Einheit, unsere nationale Kraft und unseren sittlichen Geist bedrohten. Und darum meinte ich vorhin, wir müssten es dankbar als eine göttliche Fügung begrüßen, dass dieser furchtbare Daseinskampf uns aufgezwungen wurde.
Denn nun kam gleich einem herrlichen Wunder der über alles Ahnen und Hoffen großartige Aufschwung der deutschen Volksseele. Nun fand das deutsche Volk in plötzlicher Selbstbesinnung sich selbst wieder. Wie weggeblasen vom Hauche der Weltgeschichte war alle Entzweiung, aller Parteihader, alle kleinliche Selbstsucht, alles unpatriotische Gebaren. Jeder einzelne fühlte sich nur noch als Glied des Ganzen und vergaß sein persönliches Wohl und Wehe in dem einen Gedanken: es geht ums Vaterland! Mit leuchtendem Auge und hohem Sinn ergriff unser Kaiser die Führung, rief das Volk zu den Waffen und sprach das schöne Wort, er kenne fortan keine Parteien mehr, er kenne nur noch Deutsche. [...] Nie zuvor hat ein Volk sich so eins mit seinem Staate gefühlt, nie sich ihm mit solcher Treue hingegeben, nie seinen Fürsten, seiner Heeresleitung und seiner Verwaltung so felsenfest vertraut – wie jetzt dieses Volk von fast 70 Millionen Köpfen! Da war kein Unterschied der Stände, keiner zwischen Vornehm und Gering, Reich oder Arm, Gelehrt oder Ungelehrt, Unternehmer oder Arbeiter, Alter oder Jugend. Jubelnd folgten die zum Heere Einberufenen den Fahnen, mit stürmischer Ungeduld drängten sich die Nichtberufenen freiwillig zum Eintritt ins Heer, das die Überzahl der sich Meldenden – man spricht von zwei Millionen – nicht fassen konnte.'; Otto von Gierke, 'Krieg und Kultur, 1915', quoted from Klaus Böhme (ed.), *Aufrufe und Reden deutscher Professoren im Ersten Weltkrieg* (Stuttgart 1975), 70–71.

attitude and this way of cooperation permanently, beyond the time of the great patriotic upsurge. What first became reality, [now] has to become an idea, the true situation of a great time [has to become] the inner example for future life. The entire people thus has revealed the spirit, which afterwards the idea has to hold on to.

For this reason, at present no one has the task to proclaim, as a prophet, a new idea to the German people which it does not yet know, and which he, in his mind, came up with as the first. But the task is and was merely to raise into an idea what was accomplished by an entire people in the hour of historical need.[19]

In comparison with the observations by Bahr and von Gierke, Plenge definitely strikes a less euphoric tone, his argument being more detached. But Plenge tries to transform the euphoria of August 1914 into a lasting political idea – and in this sense, his analysis marks the transformation from "the spirit of 1914" into "the ideas of 1914". This approach is characteristic of a great number of speeches, articles, essays and booklets by literary authors, theologians, philosophers, historians, and others, in which – from about two years after the war broke out onwards – they tried to keep "the spirit of 1914" alive, and to use it as a lasting inspiration for German politics. After the end of the *Burgfriede*, when political conflict cropped up again in politics, especially parties and groupings from the right appealed to "the spirit of 1914" to justify their ideals and approach. Parties and groupings from the left, on the other hand, usually fell back on the terminology as used by the socialist party in the years preceding the war.

In political debates after the First World War, the reference to "the ideas of 1914" still played a part as well. It is, for instance, quite prominent in the work of the author Oswald Spengler (1880–1936), renowned in his lifetime and currently especially known for his book *Der Untergang des Abendlades* ('The

---

19 'Es ist die Grundtatsache, dass 1914 beim Kriegsbeginn ein ganzes Volk seine innere geistige Haltung und die Weise seines Zusammenarbeitens wie mit einem Schlage geändert hat und dass es daraufhin zum Lebensziel wurde, diese innere Haltung und diese Weise des Zusammenarbeitens über die Zeit der großen vaterländischen Aufwallung hinaus dauernd zu sichern. Was zuerst Realität wurde, soll Idee werden, der wirkliche Zustand einer großen Zeit zum inneren Vorbild künftigen Lebens. Das ganze Volk hat demnach den Geist offenbart, den der Gedanke nachträglich festhalten soll.

Darum hat auch niemand die Aufgabe, in dieser Zeit dem deutschen Volk als Prophet eine neue Idee zu verkünden, die es noch nicht kennt, und die er als einzelner in seinem Kopf gefunden haben will. Sondern die Aufgabe besteht und bestand nur darin, das von einem ganzen Volk in der Stunde der geschichtlichen Not in ganzer Hingabe Vollbrachte in die Idee zu erheben.'; Johann Plenge, *1789 und 1914. Die symbolischen Jahre in der Geschichte des politischen Geistes* (Berlin 1916), 85–86.

Decline of the West'; two volumes, 1918–1922). Spengler is considered one of the leaders of the so-called "conservative revolution", a group of conservative intellectuals in the Weimar Republic that is often seen as an ideological precursor of National-Socialism. Spengler was very outspoken in his rejection of the November Revolution of 1918, which resulted in the replacement of the German Empire by the Weimar Republic. About this revolution he observed:

> Once more, it was not the people, not even the mass schooled in socialism; it was the scum lead by the literary rabble that came into action. The true socialism stood in the last struggle at the front or was laying in the mass graves of half of Europe, that [socialism] which had arisen in August 1914 and which one betrayed here.[20]

Spengler condemns the November Revolution: although it was claimed as a revolution on behalf of socialism, this was not the case, he maintains. For true socialism, according to Spengler, were the feelings of unity as experienced by the German people at the outbreak of the war:

> But a true revolution is only the one of an entire people, an outcry, an iron grasp, a fury, a target.
> And that, this German socialist revolution, occurred in 1914. It took place in legitimate and military shapes. It will, in its significance that on average will hardly be understood, slowly overcome the horrors of 1918 and integrate them as factor in its progressing development.[21]

Similar ideas were expressed by the National-Socialist *Führer* Adolf Hitler, for instance in *Mein Kampf*: Hitler as well condemned the November Revolution, and like Spengler he rejected Marxist socialism, and contrasted it with "the spirit of 1914", that is, with the "real German socialism" that existed in the early

---

20   'Es war wieder nicht das Volk, nicht einmal die sozialistisch geschulte Masse; es war das Pack mit dem Literatengeschmeiß an der Spitze, das in Aktion trat. Der echte Sozialismus stand im letzten Ringen an der Front oder lag in den Massengräbern von halb Europa, der, welcher im August 1914 aufgestanden war und den man hier verriet.'; Oswald Spengler, *Preußentum und Sozialismus* (Munich 1920), 9.

21   'Aber eine echte Revolution ist nur die eines ganzen Volkes, ein Aufschrei, ein eherner Griff, ein Zorn, ein Ziel.
   Und das, diese deutsche sozialistische Revolution, fand 1914 statt. Sie vollzog sich in legitimen und militärischen Formen. Sie wird, in ihrer dem Durchschnitt kaum verständlichen Bedeutung, die Widerlichkeiten von 1918 langsam überwinden und als Faktor ihrer fortschreitenden Entwicklung einordnen.'; o.c., 12.

months of the war in August 1914.[22] This view on the early days of the war grew more and more influential in political debates in the time of the Weimar Republic, and was indeed dominant in the Third Reich.

Of course, there were different views on the August experience as well, albeit these were by far in the minority. An example is the German writer Kurt Tucholsky (1890–1935), who wrote a very critical article on the commemorative ceremonies in August 1924, ten years after the war broke out. Tucholsky turned against the glorification of both the war itself and the mood in August 1914:

> But that now, ten years afterwards, adult German people gather and speak otherwise about the poor, pointlessly killed victims of the massacre than merely with the ardent wish: "how do we avoid it next time? How? How?"; that not a single one, without exception, of the authoritative German men summons up the moral courage to dissociate himself from this advertising for war; that not a single one can speak otherwise about the war than by announcing a more or less dexterously concealed cry for revenge in favour of another bloodbath – that this is possible, that I am at liberty to call a disgrace.[23]

But Tucholsky's view was not widely shared: the opposite view, which glorified the feeling of unity that Germans allegedly experienced during the first weeks of the war, was dominant by far.

Even after the Second World War, the historian Friedrich Meinecke (1862–1954) looked back with a certain nostalgia on the experiences in August 1914. At the time, Meinecke was considered the grand old man of German historiography, someone, moreover, whose behaviour during the Third Reich was above suspicion. Meinecke was the first German historian who, after 1945, made an effort to understand what had happened in Germany during the interwar period to bring about the catastrophic turn German history had taken with

---

22 Cfr. Adolf Hitler, *Mein Kampf. Zwei Bände in einem Band. Ungekürzte Ausgabe* (Munich 1943 [originally 1925, 1927]), 184–185.

23 'Aber dass heute, nach diesen zehn Jahren, erwachsene deutsche Menschen zusammentreten und von den armen, nutzlos getöteten Opfern der Schlächterei anders sprechen als mit dem heißen Wunsch: »Wie kommen wir um das nächste Mal herum? Wie? Wie?«; dass keiner, ausnahmslos keiner der deutschen maßgebenden Männer den moralischen Mut aufbringt, von dieser Kriegsreklame abzurücken; dass nicht ein einziger anders über den Krieg reden kann, als mehr oder weniger geschickt verhüllt seinen Racheschrei für ein neues Gemetzel kundzutun – dass das möglich ist, das darf mir doch wohl unverwehrt sein eine Schande zu nennen.'; Kurt Tucholsky, 'Der Geist von 1914', in: *Die Weltbühne*, August 7th, 1924, Nr. 32, 204.

National-Socialism. The result of this effort is his book *Die deutsche Katastrophe*, published in 1946. In this book, Meinecke wrote about "the spirit of 1914":

> The exaltation of the days of August 1914 belongs for all those who experienced it to the indelible memories of the highest rank, – despite its ephemeral character. All ruptures that had existed within the German people until then, within the bourgeoisie as well as between the bourgeoisie and the workers, suddenly were covered up by the danger that had happened to us and that tore us out the safety of material prosperity we enjoyed hitherto. Moreover, one sensed thereby indeed in all camps that this was more than simply the unity of an association with a common aim, [and] that an internal restoration of the entire state and culture was necessary. One often even fancied that it had begun already and would continue in the common experience of the war that was conceived as a war of resistance and defence. With our hopes we foisted a lovely delusion. Already within a year, the unity was broken, the German people again split up into different ways. Was the upsurge of August 1914 in the end only a last flare-up of former ideals, of older forces of development, now coming to an end?[24]

Even though Meinecke admits that eventually the euphoria of August 1914 mainly was a delusion, the tone of his description nevertheless shows nostalgic feelings: he remembers August 1914 with mixed feelings, and not merely with disapproval.

---

24 'Die Erhebung der Augusttage 1914 gehört für alle, die sie mit erlebt haben, zu den unverlierbaren Erinnerungswerten höchster Art, — trotz ihres ephemeren Charakters. Alle Risse, die im deutschen Menschentum sowohl innerhalb des Bürgertums wie zwischen Bürgertum und Arbeiterschaft bisher bestanden hatten, überwölbten sich plötzlich durch die gemeinsame Gefahr, die über uns gekommen war und uns aus der bisher genossenen Sekurität materiellen Gedeihens herausriß. Und mehr als das, man spürte dabei wohl in allen Lagern, daß es mit der bloßen Einigkeit eines Zweckverbandes nicht getan sei, daß eine innerliche Erneuerung für das Ganze von Staat und Kultur Not tue. Man glaubte sogar vielfach, daß sie jetzt schon begonnen habe und weitergehen werde in dem gemeinsamen Erlebnis des Krieges, den man als einen Abwehr- und Verteidigungskrieg empfand. Wir unterlagen mit unseren Hoffnungen einer holden Täuschung. Schon ein Jahr später war die Einigkeit in die Brüche gegangen, spaltete sich das deutsche Menschentum wieder auf verschiedenen Wegen. War der Aufschwung vom August 1914 am Ende nur ein letztes Aufflackern früherer Ideale, älterer, jetzt zu Ende gehender Entwicklungskräfte?'; Friedrich Meinecke, *Die deutsche Katastrophe: Betrachtungen und Erinnerungen* (Wiesbaden 1947 [first edition 1946]), 43–45.

So, from August 1915 onwards, the notion of "the spirit of 1914" developed into a powerful political myth in German politics – a myth, to which regularly reference was made in political debates both during and after the First World War. After August 1914, this spirit had gradually disappeared, but it was generally put forward that only a revival of this very spirit could bring Germany a victory in the war. After the war, both during the Weimar Republic and the Third Reich, in political debates the "spirit of 1914" was regularly referred to, usually with a certain nostalgia by parties and right-wing groupings, which saw in a revival of this spirit the remedy for most, if not all problems Germany faced both in national and international politics. Thus, the notion of the "spirit of 1914" developed into a powerful political myth, comparable with the myth of the "Stab-in-the-back", claiming that Germany was not defeated on the battlefield in the First World War, but by a stab-in-the-back by those civilians of the home front, who were responsible for the overthrow of the monarchy in November 1918 and subsequently signed the Armistice of November 11th. This myth of the stab-in-the-back became part of the "official" interpretation of history during the Third Reich, but the same holds for the myth of the "spirit of 1914". In other words, the interpretation of what happened in August 1914 has been of major importance in German politics.

3 Justifying the War Historically

In their reactions to the outbreak of the war, a vast majority of German intellectuals expressed their enthusiasm about it and, especially, about the newly discovered sense of national unity. Moreover they tried to justify the war as well, using all kinds of arguments to defend the German position. Quite regularly, in defending the German stand, they appealed to history to support their claims. In this connection, a number of recurrent topics may be distinguished, even in a provisional exploration that does neither aim for nor claim completeness[25] – topics that are interrelated and not infrequently part of the very same argument.

A first recurrent topic in the appeals to history regards an interpretation of European history leading up to the war. Sometimes these interpretations only

---

25   In his study *Die geistige Mobilmachung*, the German philosopher Kurt Flasch emphasizes that the overwhelming number of writings and speeches by German intellectuals on the First World War makes it almost impossible to draw more than provisional conclusions on the subject. The mere number of titles – more than 13.000 – makes it unfeasible to get an overall picture. Cfr. K. Flasch, o.c., 228–229.

concern the months or even weeks immediately preceding the outbreak of the war, but more often they deal with a longer period of time, for instance the years following the Franco-Prussian war of 1870–1871. An example in question is the "Aufruf Bonner Historiker" ('Appeal by historians from Bonn') of September 1st, 1914. Though it must be admitted that it will take many years to ascertain what exactly has happened prior to this war, these historians argue, some questions may already be answered with near certainty. For instance, it is beyond reasonable doubt that with respect to Germany the war that broke out in 1914 is a defensive war. After all, the main goal of countries like France, Russia and England is to destroy the position of power that Germany managed to attain after the war of 1870–1871 and forty years of hard work in times of peace. For this reason, before the war of 1914 they surrounded Germany diplomatically. This means that Germany not only is forced to fight for its existence as a state, but for "the most precious properties of European culture"[26] as well. These properties are betrayed by France, Russia and England, especially by English commercialism, the historians' Appeal argues. A similar line of argument is pivotal in the "Aufruf an die Kulturwelt" ('Appeal to the civilized world') of October 1914, also known as the "Manifest der 93" ('Manifesto of the Ninety-Three'). This appeal was drafted by the playwright Ludwig Fulda (1862–1939), and co-signed by ninety-two often renowned German scientists, artists and writers. Like in the "Aufruf Bonner Historiker", in this manifesto as well it is claimed that for Germany the 1914 conflict is a defensive war, and that Germany had indeed done everything in its power to prevent it. After all, "in the 26 years of his reign, Wilhelm II has often enough proved himself as patron of world peace",[27] even to the extent that he was mocked in the foreign press for his efforts with respect to this. Germany is accordingly not to blame for this war, nor are the allegations valid that Germany violated Belgian neutrality: France and England were determined to violate Belgian neutrality, and Germany simply had to act to prevent its own destruction. Likewise, accusations of German atrocities are simply lies, according to this appeal: Germany fights this war as a civilized nation, for which the heritage of Goethe, Beethoven and Kant is as sacred as its hearth and home. In response to the manifesto *Why we are at war*[28] by members of the Oxford faculty of modern history, in their "Erklärung gegen die Oxforder Hochschulen" ('Statement against the Oxford colleges'), a number of German

---

26 'die edelsten Güter europäischer Kultur'; 'Aufruf Bonner Historiker', in Klaus Böhme (ed.), o.c., 50.
27 'Oft genug hat Wilhem II. in den 26 Jahren seiner Regierung sich als Schirmherr des Weltfriedens erwiesen'; 'Aufruf an die Kulturwelt', in: o.c., 47.
28 Ernest Barker et al., *Why we are at war. Great Britain's case* (Oxford 1914).

historians denied that their country had any responsibility for the current war, and claimed that this conflict was forced upon them by other countries, especially England. This in spite of the fact that Germany never had shown any animosity towards England, and indeed had only strived for honest friendship with this country. So why was this war forced upon them, they wonder; moreover,

> Can you tell us with what right England has subjected India, occupied Egypt, brought the Boer states under the yoke? Why England up until very recently has opposed commitment to international law, by substituting governmental instructions, that is to say English interest-driven policies, for international laws?[29]

For many, many years now, in international politics England has always only followed its own interests, the historians argue, the current war eventually being the result of this very policy.

In his long address on "Krieg und Kultur", mentioned above,[30] the Berlin jurist Otto von Gierke emphasized that from the very beginning of human history, war had decided the fate of nations and states. War should, however, not so much be seen as a test for the military strength of a nation, but rather as a bringing to the proof of its spiritual strength. In a war, everything that lacks inner strength will simply disappear, but what is strong enough will survive and eventually blossom – this simply is how history always progresses. The older generations of Germans, to which von Gierke himself belonged, had experienced this in the 1870–1871 war – this war, he says, which

> with all its sacrifices of blood and goods for our people [was] a gift of divine grace! Where would we be without it? We owe to this war that we have forever overcome that disastrous disunity for centuries into an unbreakable unity [...] By means of this, Germany moreover acquired the capability to rise to [the status of] world power, with the creation of a powerful navy to regain the lost prestigiousness at sea and with the acquisition of colonies to get a foothold in other parts of the world.[31]

---

29 'Können sie uns sagen, mit welchem Recht England Indien unterworfen, Ägypten besetzt, die Burenstaaten unterjocht hat? Warum England bis in die jüngste Zeit hinein sich gegen völkerrechtliche Bindung gesträubt hat, indem es gouvernementale Instruktionen, das heißt englische Interessenpolitik, an die Stelle der Völkerrechte setzte?'; 'Erklärung gegen die Oxforder Hochschulen', in: Klaus Böhme (ed.), o.c., 55.

30 Cfr. above, 111.

31 'So war der Krieg von 1870 mit allen seinen Opfer an Blut und Gut für unser Volk ein göttliches Gnadengeschenk! Was wären wir ohne ihn? Ihm verdanken wir, daß wir die unselige

Moreover, in Germany itself this war had brought rejuvenation in all respects, which showed especially in an unequalled economic growth. As a result, Germany became rich and Berlin, for example, changed into a true metropolis. However, the German nation did not manage to maintain the unity the 1870–1871 war had brought about – it was threatened by political and economic competition, von Gierke argues. He blamed in particular the Social Democrats for this loss of national unity, on the one hand because of their internationalism, on the other hand because of their rejection of the monarchy. Internationalism and cosmopolitan tendencies in general started to threaten German national unity again, von Gierke complains, in particular the ideals of the French Revolution being involved. Moreover, a general slackening weakened Germany: in the years since the 1870–1871 war, the proverbial German idealism gradually gave way to materialism, that is, to an overrating of material wealth and possessions. Thus, greed became a dominant force in all classes in society. For this very reason, von Gierke argues, the German nation should be glad that the 1914 war was forced upon it: after all, it offers almost unprecedented opportunities for spiritual revival, and the chance to recover the true nature of the German people. Considering its inner strength, it may be expected that Germany eventually will win this war, and consequently German culture will become dominant after the war, von Gierke claims. But already now one may conclude that the newly regained national unity of the German people will never again be broken, even if party politics will be resumed after the war. The German people will cling to the virtues that from early days have been characteristic of it: loyalty, a strong sense of duty, seriousness, etc. With God's help, after this war Germany will only be stronger, von Gierke concludes.

Like von Gierke, the Swedish political scientist and politician Rudolf Kjellén (1864–1922), who unconditionally took the German side in the 1914–1918 war, in several writings interpreted the 1914 war in the light of the French Revolution of 1789, comparable to the analyses by Johann Plenge.[32] In fact, he argued, this war was a struggle between 1789 and 1914, France and England representing 1789, and Germany 1914. It was the fight between on the one hand unrestrained, even degenerated freedom, and on the other hand order. The organic order that according to Kjellén was characteristic of Germany since the outbreak of

---

Zerklüftung von Jahrhunderten in unzerreißbarer Einigkeit für immer überwunden haben. [...] Durch ihn erlangte Deutschland darüber hinaus die Fähigkeit, zur Weltmacht emporzusteigen, mit der Schaffung einer seegewaltigen Flotte die verlorene Geltung auf den Meeren zurückzugewinnen und mit dem Erwerbe von Kolonien in anderen Erdteilen Fuß zu fassen.'; Otto von Gierke, o.c., 67.

32   See above, 111.

the war, was an entirely new phenomenon in world history – and a new ideal that put the outdated ideals of the French Revolution entirely into the shade.[33]

On October 13th, 1914, the Munich historian Erich Marcks (1861–1938) delivered a public speech in his hometown, in which he tried to analyse the 1914 war in its historical and cultural context. According to Marcks, in a sense in the present situation actually nothing new is involved: ever since 1500, competition for power has been typical of European history, with now one country, than again another one being dominant. Likewise, within living memory war has been typical of European history. It is accordingly hardly surprising that almost all major changes in European history originate from war. A sequence of major conflicts has passed through European history in between 1500 and 1800 – as the result of clashes of forces in economy, society, and culture, or as the result of the rise of one country or another. In the nineteenth century this tendency even strengthened, as European countries developed into true world powers – but this was nothing but the natural consequence of ongoing processes. Thus, "the earth became a unity – a unity of contrasts".[34] But this does not imply a change in history: it only is a natural development, Marcks argues. Over the last thirty years, the contrasts between various European cultures deepened. Germany, as a young nation, has a special position in this constellation. In three stages, Germany had to establish itself: first in 1866 as a new national state, next in 1870–1871 as a new European power, and now, in 1914, as a world power. The main enemies that now confront Germany are France, which first and foremost wants revenge for the defeat in 1870–1871; Russia, which feels threatened by the new position of Germany as a world power, and in particular fears losing influence in the Balkans; and England that wants to maintain its dominance as colonial superpower and ruler of the waves, feeling challenged by Germany. According to Marcks, it is no exaggeration to claim that ever since 1904 the main aim of English foreign policy has been to block a further increase of German international and economic power. For this very reason, England allied with France and Russia, which traditionally had been its enemies. Hence, in this war "England truly is our mortal enemy".[35] England accordingly is the most important enemy Germany has to beat in this war – not only for its own sake, but on behalf of all young, upcoming nations of the world. – Some ten years later, Theodor Lessing would mock Marcks in his

---

33 H. Lübbe, o.c., 209–210.
34 'die Erde wurde eine Einheit – eine Einheit von Gegensätzen.'; Erich Marcks, 'Wo stehen wir? Die politischen, sittlichen und kulturellen Zusammenhänge unseres Krieges', in: Klaus Böhme (ed.), o.c., 82.
35 'England ist unser wahrer Todfeind.'; o.c., 88.

collection of satires and stories *Feind im Land*, claiming that as world history was far too complicated for him, he turned to Marcks for clarification, and "the incomparable acuteness of our German school of historians then has supplied me too with an Ariadne's thread through the labyrinth".[36] –

An opinion similar to the one of Marcks is offered by the Berlin theologian Adolf von Harnack (1851–1930) in an address entitled "Was wir schon gewonnen haben und was wir noch gewinnen müssen" ('What we have won already and what we still have to win'): England "wages the horrible world fight out of a mean rival envy and it fights it like a pirate".[37] Like Marcks, Harnack emphasizes that ever since the 1870–1871 war, German national unity gradually weakened and, moreover, that the idea of "fatherland" gradually developed into an abstract notion. But as a result of the outbreak of war in August 1914, the true meaning of the idea of "fatherland" was rediscovered, and the national unity was truly experienced in an unprecedented way in the first days and weeks of the war. In this sense, "the war came at the right moment", because it did "spark the holy flame of the fatherland again".[38] Does this imply that Germany dismisses ideals like liberty, equality, and brotherhood? Not at all, according to Harnack: liberty first and foremost implies that Germany never will be the servant of any foreign country anymore. Equality is distinctly characteristic of the German army, in which every single individual fights for all, and all fight for one: the camaraderie in the German army transcends all ranks. Finally, brotherhood is what the German people experienced in August 1914 – a brotherhood which expressed itself for instance in an unequalled spirit of self-sacrifice.

Rudolf Eucken, bestselling philosopher at the turn of the century and winner of the Nobel Prize for Literature in 1908, criticized the development of Germany since 1870–1871 already in the years before the war. According to Eucken, these were years of material prosperity, the result of hard work by a most diligent people, but this prosperity was a shallow success. The German people lacked the idealism that was so vitally important in the process of the country's unification earlier in the nineteenth century. Hence, Eucken emphasized the necessity of a new idealism, and the importance of a spiritual revival of the German nation. – His characterisation of Germany in the

---

36 'der unvergleichliche Scharfsinn unserer deutschen Historikerschule hat mir denn auch einen Ariadnefaden durch das Labyrinth in die Hand gegeben.'; Theodor Lessing, *Feind im Land. Satiren und Novellen* (Hanover 1923), 111.
37 'es leitet den ungeheuren Weltkampf aus gemeinen Konkurrenzneid und es führt ihn als Pirat.'; Adolf von Harnack, 'Was wir schon gewonnen haben und was wir noch gewinnen müssen', in: Klaus Böhme (ed.), o.c., 89.
38 'der Krieg [ist] zur rechten Zeit gekommen'; 'die heilige Flamme des Vaterlandes wieder entfacht'; o.c., 93–94.

years after the Franco-Prussian War inadvertently reminds of the notorious description of the German *Wirtschaftswunder* in the 1950's by the literary and cultural critic George Steiner: "a hollow miracle".[39] – As a result of this striving after material prosperity, the true nature and even the unity of the German nation was threatened, Eucken argued. For example, from the capital Berlin a superficial attitude to the problems of life gradually spread all over the country, a phenomenon he called "Berlinismus".[40] Thus, Germany ran the risk of losing its specific character. Not surprisingly, Eucken perceived the 1914 conflict as an opportunity for the spiritual revival and reunification that he had already promoted in the years preceding the war and that in his eyes was pivotal for the future of Germany. For Eucken, the war was in essence a test for the inner life of the German nation: if it can manage to preserve its most inner spiritual health, it will eventually win this war. And he was convinced it would indeed manage: "as surely we are thus confident that world history has a sense, so surely we may also be confident that the German kind is indispensable, and that it will assert itself victoriously against all hostile attacks".[41] Germany has to stand by its own true nature, and then it will eventually win this war, Eucken concludes.[42]

The Heidelberg historian Hermann Oncken (1869–1945) tried to place the 1914 war in its historical context. From this perspective, the war is both the inner and the outer completion of German fate, he argues. He briefly discusses German history up to the unification in the nineteenth century, to conclude that this process was only finally completed in 1914, when, at long last, all inner contradictions within the nation were overcome: only now one may safely say "that the whole world of these historical contradictions truly belongs to the past".[43] For Germany, this process of unification was exceptionally difficult, Oncken claims, because it coincided with major social changes stemming from the process of industrialization: unlike other European countries like England and France, Germany at once had to accomplish both a national and a social

---

39 George Steiner, 'The Hollow Miracle', in: George Steiner, *Language and Silence. Essays 1958–1966* (Harmondsworth 1979 [first edition 1967]), 136–151.
40 Rudolf Eucken, *Die Sinn und Wert des Lebens* (Leipzig 1908), 165, quoted from H. Lübbe, o.c., 180.
41 'So sicher wir daher überzeugt sind, daß die Weltgeschichte einen Sinn hat, so sicher dürfen wir auch überzeugt sein, daß die deutsche Art unentbehrlich ist, und daß sie sich gegen alle feindlichen Angriffe siegreich behaupten wird.'; Rudolf Eucken, *Die weltgeschichtliche Bedeutung des deutschen Geistes* (Stuttgart and Berlin 1914), 23.
42 For an analysis of Eucken's writings from a broader perspective, cfr. K. Flasch, o.c., 17–35.
43 'daß die ganze Welt dieser historischen Gegensätze wirklich der Vergangenheit angehört.'; Hermann Oncken, 'Die Deutschen auf dem Wege zur einigen und freien Nation', in: Klaus Böhme (ed.), o.c., 103.

mission. This explains why "millions of German citizens stood in an inwardly dismissive and unfriendly relationship with the state in general, and with the nation-state that enclosed them".[44] The 1914 war helped the Germans to overcome this problem: the "criminal attack"[45] on their nation unified all Germans, including the Social Democrats who unconditionally and loyally supported the government. Now, the most important aim of the war is to keep up this unity forever, which implies the ultimate integration of the former opponents of the German state within the nation. According to Oncken, some of the ideas of the Social Democratic leader Ferdinand Lassalle involve the possibility to realize exactly this: they may help the Social Democrats to address the problems relating to the future of Germany, rather than the problems of labourers worldwide. But one should not forget that the Social Democrats already contributed to German culture, Oncken argues. For instance, the way Germans currently organize is part of a long tradition to which historical figures as diverse as king Friedrich Wilhelm I (1688–1740) and Karl Marx contributed, but to which the German trade unions belong as well. In short, Oncken claims, eventually the various aspects of the German past form a whole, and should be experienced as such; and this holds true for all groups within the German nation. However, for their part the Social Democrats should realize that the power of the German labourer is restricted to the German state. That is, only a German victory in the current war can, and will, secure the material future of the German labourers. This victory can only be achieved if the cultural values of all classes in German society will be shared by all Germans, and thus will be dissolved into a new whole: a nation that is unified in each and every respect. Only then the future German state will be able to fulfil its world historical mission: the education of mankind towards freedom. Thus, the current war may eventually create new life, Oncken concludes.

The constitutional jurist Gerhard Anschütz (1867–1949) develops a similar argument, claiming the current war will eventually increase German national unity:

> Then the war that now is imposed upon us will in our history gain the significance of a new great war of unification, on a par with its predecessors, the wars of 1866 and 1870–1871, which have given us the foundations and

---

44 'daß Millionen deutschen Staatsbürger in einen innerlich abgeneigten und unfreundlichen Verhältnis zum Staate überhaupt und zu dem Nationalstaat, der sie umschloß, standen.'; o.c., 104.
45 'frevelhafter Angriff'; o.c., 105.

the constitutional form of our national unity. What those [wars] accomplished, this one will complete.⁴⁶

Over the last decades, there was no major progress in inner politics in Germany, Anschütz argues – implying, though not saying so expressly, that this war came at the right time. At present, the major task facing the German nation is to uphold the independence and strength of its country in order to maintain its reputation and importance in the world: "The fatherland above all".⁴⁷ All German politicians should keep this in mind – it is the one aim of both domestic and foreign German politics, Anschütz concludes.

It would be easy to give many more examples of public addresses, speeches, appeals, essays and articles by German intellectuals, delivered or published in the first year of the First World War, which correspond with the examples discussed: interpretations of European and German history from the Franco-Prussian War of 1870–1871 onwards, which come to the conclusion that the 1914 war was forced upon Germany, with this implying that Germany was not to blame for this war. Even the more moderate interpretations, in which it is admitted that Germany played a part in starting the war, nevertheless emphasize that Germany was forced into this conflict, as its very existence was threatened by England, France, and Russia. Thus, time and again history is appealed to in efforts to justify the war: according to these German intellectuals, history "proves" that Germany was justified in almost everything it had done in the summer of 1914.

A second recurrent topic in arguments by German intellectuals is an appeal to the "natural", "normal", or "logical" course of history. That is, it is suggested that the rise of Germany as an international power should be seen as a development being the natural outcome of history. Hence, the current war should be seen as an effort by France, Russia and, in particular, England to infringe on the "natural" or "normal" course of history. In Thomas Mann's words: it is an effort by "those who want to exclude a great people from participating in the rule of the world in proportion to its late discovered capability".⁴⁸

---

46 'Dann wird der jetzt über uns verhängte Krieg in unserer Geschichte die Bedeutung eines neuen großen Einheitskrieges gewinnen, ebenbürtig seinen Vorgängern, den Kriegen von 1866 und 1870–1871, die uns die Grundlagen und die verfassungsrechtliche Gestalt unserer nationalen Einheit gegeben haben. Was jene schufen, wird er vollenden.'; Gerhard Anschütz, 'Gedanken über künftige Staatsreformen', in: o.c., 114.
47 'Das Vaterland über alles.'; o.c., 115.
48 'diejenigen, die einem großen Volke wehren wollen, an der Verwaltung der Erde nach dem Maße seiner spät entdeckte Tüchtigkeit teilzunehmen.'; Thomas Mann, Untitled contribution, in: Georg Gellert (ed.), o.c., 41.

The economist and sociologist Werner Sombart (1863–1941) argues likewise, maintaining that world history shows a continuous succession of nations that rise, rule and fade away: "the single peoples grow, blossom and fade away like flowers in God's garden: only this we can consider as the sense of development of mankind".[49] And now it is Germany's turn: "[...] the chosen people of these centuries is the German people"[50] – other European countries should acknowledge this, instead of trying to exclude Germany from a place it is entitled to. Crown prince Friedrich Wilhelm (1882–1951), again, uses this very same argument, claiming that "only thus, leaning on the good sword, we can obtain the place in the sun that is our due, but is not acknowledged voluntarily".[51] Friedrich Wilhelm adds that over the last decades, people all over the world have dreamt about perpetual peace on earth, but he flatly rejects this cosmopolitan dream: it is "undeutsch" ('atypical German'), and, indeed, every German who truly loves his country has to be on his guard against "the peace lullaby of the utopians".[52] After all, riffling through the pages of history shows that the military capacities of a people are a necessity: a nation, even if it is very strong indeed, cannot do without a strong army, Friedrich Wilhelm argues. Ultimately, "until the end of the world, the sword will eventually always be and remain the decisive factor".[53] Chancellor von Bethmann-Hollweg uses a similar argument, claiming that "a people of the greatness and capability like the German [people], does not allow to be constricted in the free development of its strength."[54]

Closely related to both recurrent topics mentioned – interpretations of European and German history since roughly 1870, and claims that the "natural" course of history and in particular the "natural" development of Germany is infringed upon by this war that Germany never wanted – is yet a third one: interpretations of English history, and especially English foreign and imperial

---

49   'Die einzelnen Völker wachsen, blühen und welken wie Blumen im Garten Gottes: das allein vermögen wir als den Sinn der Menschheitsentwicklung zu erkennen.'; Werner Sombart, 'Die andern und wir', in: Georg Gellert (ed.), o.c., 96–97.
50   '[...] das auserwählte Volk dieser Jahrhunderte ist das deutsche Volk.'; o.c., 97.
51   'Nur so, auf das gute Schwert gestützt, können wir den Platz an der Sonne erhalten, die uns zusteht, aber nicht freiwillig eingeräumt wird.'; Friedrich Wilhelm, Kronprinz des Deutschen Reiches, 'Deutschland in Waffen', in: o.c., 101.
52   'dem Friedenswiegenlied der Utopisten'; o.c., 102.
53   'so wird das Schwert bis zum Untergang der Erde immer der letzten Endes ausschlaggebende Faktor sein und bleiben'; o.c., 107.
54   'Ein Volk von der Größe und Tüchtigkeit des deutschen, läßt sich in der freien Entfaltung seiner Kräfte nicht einschnüren.'; Reichskanzler Von Bethmann-Hollweg, Untitled contribution, in: o.c., 131.

policy, aimed at proving that England is mainly responsible for the 1914 war, France and Russia being only too happy to support England.

The renowned scientist Ernst Haeckel, for instance, contended that for four centuries England has been aimed, with iron consistency and great success, at maritime world dominion, using its privileged geographical position as an island, its enormous wealth, and its mighty fleet to support this policy. But eventually, the driving force is "the conceit that England would be the chosen people, selected by Divine Providence, to bring true culture to all other nations".[55] One of the means England successfully put on was setting nations on the European continent against each other – always to the advantage of its own power and wealth. Of course, the current war should be seen as another example of this policy. England fights this war, because it is aimed at destroying Germany as a free and independent world power, and as a rising, dangerous rival on the world market, Haeckel argues.

Chancellor von Bethmann-Hollweg argues in the same vein, claiming that England's foreign policy is exclusively guided by one indisputable dogma: England is the arbitrator of the world, and it can keep up this position on the one hand due to its uncontested dominion of the seas, and on the other hand by subtly orchestrating a balance of power on the European continent. England is not willing, however, to accept that this dogma is outdated, because of the increasing strength and power of Germany. But England should have adapted to the new situation, and accordingly should have tried to come to terms with Germany. Instead, it preferred to go to war: "England wants to fight until Germany is forced to its knees economically and militarily".[56] Pan-Slavic forces applaud these English efforts, whilst France sees them as a unique opportunity to revenge the defeat of 1870–1871.

Not surprisingly, as he formed part of the same government as von Bethmann-Hollweg – in which, for that matter, he was quite moderate, having strived for friendly relations between Germany and England in pre-war years –, Secretary of State Gottlieb von Jagow (1863–1935) argued almost identically:

> History has shown that it is not easy to strike down the German people. Thousands of lives will be sacrificed, much blood will be shed, and all of this due to the fact that Germany dared to become strong and

---

55 'der Einbildung, daß England das auserwählte Volk sei, von der göttlichen Vorsehung auserlesen, allen anderen Nationen die wahre Kultur zu bringen.'; Ernst Haeckel, 'Weltkrieg und Naturgeschichte', in: o.c., 56–57.

56 'England will kämpfen bis Deutschland wirtschaftlich und militärisch niedergezwungen ist.'; Reichskanzler Von Bethmann-Hollweg, o.c., 132.

mighty alongside England, [and] due to the fact that England believed its unconditional dominion of the seas being challenged, its trade monopoly threatened, its domination of the world challenged by a progressing nation. Only this is the origin of the war.[57]

Moreover, von Jagow adds,

> Does anyone who knows England's history believe, even just for a single moment that England fights for unselfish purposes? England with its love of one's neighbor and humaneness, which sets itself up as champion of those who suffer, whilst it starved thousands of women and children in order to expand its domination over the free Boers [...][58]

In the end, England simply did not want any rivals on the seas – this is the origin of this war: "despite all twaddle and repudiations, history and facts show that England demands unconditional political dictatorship of the world", Jagow claims.[59]

According to the economist and politician Hermann Paasche (1851–1925), vice-president of the *Reichstag*, the 1914 conflict in the last resort is a "Freiheitskampf" ('struggle for freedom') by the German people against English domination of the world: "we fight for the freedom of the seas, and our development and that of others".[60] Germany does not want an empire of its own, to replace the English one, but it wants freedom for itself and for other rising nations – this is what this war ultimately is about, Paasche argues.

---

57 'Die Geschichte hat gezeigt, daß das deutsche Volk nicht leicht niederzuschlagen ist. Tausende von Menschenleben werden geopfert werden, viel Blut wird noch fließen, und alles, weil Deutschland gewagt hat, neben England stark und mächtig zu werden, weil England seine unbedingte Seeherrschaft in Frage gestellt, sein Handelsmonopol gefährdet, seine Weltbeherrschung durch eine fortschreitende Nation in Frage gestellt glaubte. Dies allein ist der Ursprung des Krieges [...].'; Staatsekretär von Jagow, 'Über den Krieg mit England', in: o.c., 154.

58 'Glaubt den jemand, der Englands Geschichte kennt, auch nur einen Augenblick, daß England für selbstlose Ziele kämpft? England mit seiner Nächstenliebe und Menschlichkeit, das sich zum Vorkämpfer der Leidenden aufwirft, während es Tausende von Frauen und Kindern hungern ließ, um die britische Herrschaft über die freien Buren auszudehnen [...].'; o.c., 155.

59 'Trotz allem Gerede und allen Ableugnungen zeigen Geschichte und Tatsachen, daß England die unbedingte politische Diktatur in der Welt verlangt [...].'; o.c., 156.

60 'Wir kämpfen für die Freiheit der Meere und die Entwicklung für uns und die anderen.'; Geheimrat Paasche, 'Englands Weltherrschaft und der Krieg', in: o.c., 173.

To sum up: an important argument in many justifications of German foreign policy in the summer of 1914, including the war, by a great number of German intellectuals, is an appeal to history. History is being referred to in order to "prove" that Germany never wanted the 1914 war at all and that this war was indeed forced upon Germany; moreover, history was referred to in order to "prove" that England was basically to blame for the war, rather than France and Russia. These appeals to history mostly implied interpretations of European and German history since 1870; or interpretations of the "natural" course of history that was infringed upon by the English and adjusted by the war; or interpretations of English history, in particular English foreign and colonial policy over the last couple of centuries.

4 Theodor Lessing on the Great War

This, then, is the historical context of Theodor Lessing's response to the outbreak of the First World War. An overwhelming majority of German intellectuals – literary authors, philosophers, historians, economists, journalists, and so on – reacted enthusiastically to the outbreak of the war. They used all kinds of different arguments to justify the war, and often referred to history to underpin their claims. Moreover, they were instrumental in spreading the idea that virtually all of the German people enthusiastically supported the war. Only a small number of intellectuals opposed the war – and this opposition provoked the animosity, and even hatred of right wing nationalist parties and movements, not only in 1914, but in the years to come as well. This continued well into the 1920's and 1930's, during the Weimar Republic and the Third Reich. Those who had opposed the war were referred to as unpatriotic or even "volksfeindlich" ('hostile to the people'), and they regularly fell victim to persecutions by political opponents. After all, it was claimed, by breaking the national unity they had considerably weakened German political and military strength, and thus they were at least partially to blame for the eventual defeat in the war. During the Third Reich, a number of them was captured and murdered.

Among those who opposed the war from the very beginning was Theodor Lessing. It seems quite likely that there is a linkage between his stand against the war and the fact that some years later his satire on the then presidential candidate Paul von Hindenburg incited such vehement protests that he eventually was forced to resign as lecturer at the *Technische Hochschule* in Hanover.[61] But

---

61   Cfr. chapter one above, 8–9.

most likely, this has also been the reason that he was ultimately murdered by the nazi-regime in 1933. After all, ever since 1914 Lessing was considered unpatriotic, and even an internal enemy of the German people, by all right wing and nationalist circles, someone, moreover, who refused to be silenced and continued his outspoken criticism of the political developments of his time and especially of National-Socialism, even after his flight to Czechoslovakia.

Lessing's prompt reaction to the outbreak of the war may be found in his diaries, some occasional jottings, a number of public speeches he gave in the autumn of 1914 in Hanover, and some stray remarks in later publications, in particular his autobiography *Einmal und nie wieder*. The entries in Lessing's diary from August 1914 – which he would later work up in a small but most interesting and revealing article, "Ausflug nach Goslar" ('A Trip to Goslar'), published in the *Prager Tagblatt* in December 1925 – show how widely spread the confusion was in Germany in the days before and after the outbreak of the war. A warning issued by the government resulted in German people all over the country looking for secret French gold transports on their way to Russia. Moreover, one was in search of foreign secret agents all over the place: the fear of foreign spies was widespread. Theodor Lessing himself was arrested in Goslar station, in the Harz, where he went for a short stay in a sanatorium, because he was close to a nervous breakdown. Locals took him for a Russian spy – not very surprising, as he writes with subtle self-mockery, because he wore a full beard and, moreover, "Anyhow, someone with black hair is a virtual Russian".[62] He was surrounded by a number of people, and in a trice soldiers with fixed bayonets arrived. Lessing was led away to the local barracks, where his identity was quickly established, however, whereupon he could continue on his way undisturbed – he fared far better than several others, who were picked up and molested by a hysterical crowd."I did not yet know that just in these days, when all felt for one and one for all, every random bum had the right to have anyone arrested for the fatherland whom he deemed worthy of being arrested", Lessing wrote.[63] But after this incident, Lessing preferred to return home, realizing a stay in Goslar would not bring him the rest he needed, now that the country was at war. Once home, he decided to enlist in the medical corps, using his abandoned medical training as qualification for this job. This enlistment gave him the opportunity to relieve some suffering, without actually being in

---

62 'ein Schwarzhaariger ist ohnehin so gut wie ein Russe'; Theodor Lessing, 'Ausflug nach Goslar', in: *Prager Tagblatt*, December 6th, 1925.
63 'Ich wußte es noch nicht, daß just in diesen Tagen, wo alle für einen und einer für alle fühlten, jeder beliebige Strolch das Recht hatte, fürs Vaterland verhaften zu lassen, wen immer er für verhaftungswürdig hielt.'; loc.cit..

combat. He started working in a provisional hospital in the former Military Academy of the Kingdom Hanover, in the city of Hanover itself, where he was involved with the care of prisoners of war. Afterwards, Lessing would publish a series of articles on his experiences in this hospital, entitled "Das Lazarett" ('The military hospital').[64] At the time, in 1914, Lessing had for more than three years been writing a philosophical work, he maintains – his "Philosophie der Not" – but he felt as if, under the circumstances, he was completely estranged from his own project."I could no longer reflect on anything; all thoughts were nonsense, thinking itself was indeed nonsense", Lessing observes.[65] Yet finishing the book that he expected to be his major contribution to philosophy was what kept him going: "I hardly know, whether I may wish myself a longer life – what keeps me on my feet is only the thought that I have to complete the 'Philosophy of Need'", Lessing wrote in his diary.[66] – The tone of his diaries is understandably far more emotional, and even desperate, than that of the 1925 article in the *Prager Tagblatt*, but both deal with the same events, the article being based on the diary. – In those days, he lived in a village close to Hanover, in a house with a view on the railway line between Berlin and Cologne; during the first week of the war, trains passed by all day, carrying troops to the German border with Belgium and France. Lessing's mind was fully occupied with the noise of the passing trains, and the enthusiasm with which the leaving troops were seen off by cheering crowds.

> The German people was incomprehensibly cheerful-rapturous. For the children the waving from both sides and the passing by of constantly new soldiers was a continuous feast. At every railway station, big or small, were laughing women and embellished girls, greeting, cheering those who set out, giving them roses, kisses, sandwiches […] Surely, that there could be a war once again was something I had indeed believed, but [I had] not anticipated that people would indulge as they did.[67]

---

64   Theodor Lessing, 'Das Lazarett', in: *Prager Tagblatt*, 10.2.1929; 17.2.1929; 2.3.1929; 7.3.1929; 23.3.1929; 6.4.1929; 19.4.1929; reprinted in: *IFEG*, 354–386.
65   'Ich konnte mich auf nichts mehr besinnen; die Gedanken waren Unsinn, das Denken selbst war ja Unsinn'; Lessing, 'Ausflug nach Goslar', loc.cit..
66   'Ich weiß kaum, ob ich mir noch längeres Leben wünschen darf. – Mich hält einzig der Gedanke, daß ich die "Philosophie der Not" vollenden muß.'; Theodor Lessing, 'An den Nerven krank und dem Zusammenbruch nahe – Tagebuchnotizen August 1914', in: *Wmnm!*, 21.
67   'Unbegreiflich fröhlich-glückselig war das deutsche Volk. Den Kindern war das hinüber- und herüberwinken und das Vorüberziehen immer neuer Soldaten ein dauerndes Fest. An allen Bahnstationen, großen und kleinen, standen lachende Frauen und geschmückte

Did all of them go out of their mind, Lessing wondered, or did he himself go mad and were they right after all? This question occupied his mind all the time – the reaction to the outbreak of the war by the various political parties, by so many intellectuals, and so many compatriots in general, took him completely by surprise. That war was still possible in twentieth century Europe did not surprise him, but the reactions to the war indeed did, as they differed completely from what he had expected:

> If war comes (so I believed) two powers have become strong, because of which every mass murder of people will fail: the great International of the exploited and that of the mothers, who are born to love together, not to hate together. But now it was just the social democracy, which after all on principle refuses all means to the army, which behaved most foolishly on behalf of patriotic enthusiasm, and the women all seemed to be mothers of Spartans, who hand the shield to their son with the words: "Return with it or on it; not without it."[68]

So in particular the groups Lessing put his hope in, disappointed him deeply, since they supported the war without reserve:

> The proletariat, the International, the women, even the communists and pacifists could no longer to be counted on; they all gave in; I saw it; but in Germany there were, however, indeed a couple of hundred enlightened minds. These were the poets and thinkers who had educated me and in whom I believed. I relied on these for my plan. At night by the rolling of restless dull wheels, at night I drafted an "Appeal to Europe's Foremost Minds".[69]

Mädchen, grüßten, bejubelten die hinausziehenden, schenkten ihnen Rosen, Küsse und Butterbrote. Gewiß, daß noch einmal Krieg kommen könne, hätte ich wohl geglaubt, aber nicht erwartet, daß die Menschen dann sich so darleben würden wie sie es taten'; Theodor Lessing, 'Ausflug nach Goslar'.

68 'Kommt Krieg (so hatte ich geglaubt) dann sind zwei Mächte stark geworden, an denen alles Massenmorden der Völker scheitert: die große Internationale der Ausgebeuteten und die der Mütter, welche geboren sind, um mitzulieben, nicht mitzuhassen. Und nun gebärdete sich gerade die Sozialdemokratie, die doch grundsätßlich [sic!, HS] alle Mittel zur Wehrmacht verweigert, ganz toll vor vaterländischer Begeisterung, und die Frauen schienen alle Spartanermütter zu sein, die dem Sohn den Schild reichen mit den Worten: "Kehre mit ihm oder auf ihm; nicht ohne ihn".'; loc.cit..

69 'Mit dem Proletariat, mit der Internationale, mit den Frauen, selbst mit Kommunisten und Pazifisten war nicht mehr zu rechnen; sie alle fielen um; ich sah; aber es gab ja doch in Deutschland ein paar hundert leuchtende Geister. Das waren jene Dichter und Denker,

He did not even complete the draft of this appeal, let alone distribute it. But he did hold on to his rejection of the war, a topic he regularly addressed in his writings, when looking back on August 1914 in later years. Thus, in his *Der jüdische Selbsthaß* (1930) he repeated more extensively what he had written in 'Ausflug nach Goslar', again emphasizing that before 1914 he had counted on the proletariat and the women to prevent a war:

> The solidarity with the need, with the poor and those who suffer in all countries will turn out to be stronger than the greed for expansion and pillage of the agencies and the capital. No socialist will ever allow credits for war. And without social democracy no battle can be fought. [...] It will be impossible that women and girls change into hyenas.[70]

Moreover, in contrast to his 'Ausflug nach Goslar', he mentioned yet another group of which he had hoped at the time that it could have prevented a war: the Jews – quite appropriate in a book – *Der jüdische Selbsthaß* – that, after all, deals with the issue of Jewish-German identity. As the Jews were spread over numerous countries, Lessing had hoped they might be able to build bridges between the peoples of these countries.

> It seemed hardly likely to me that a group of people, of which it is said everywhere that it is only tolerated and not being associated, would change into rude "patriots" and [...] fall upon one another in the service of their oppressors.[71]

But in this respect he proved to be wrong as well: like the socialists and women, the Jews reacted in a way that he failed to anticipate. For also the majority of the Jewish community in Germany did support the war enthusiastically: "The socialists betrayed poverty; the mothers love; the Jews their meaningful

---

die mich erzogen hatten und an die ich glaubte. Auf diese baute ich meinen Plan. Nachts beim Rollen der rastlos dumpfen Räder, nachts entwarf ich einen "Aufruf an Europas führende Geister".'; loc.cit..

70 'Die Solidarität der Not, der Armen und Leidenden in allen Ländern, wird sich stärker erweisen als die Erweiterungs- und Beutegierden der Ämter und des Kapitals. Kein Sozialist wird jemals Kriegskredite bewilligen. Und ohne die Sozialdemokratie kann keine Schlacht geschlagen werden.[...] Es wird unmöglich sein, daß Mütter und Mädchen sich in Hyänen wandeln'; *DjS*, 192.

71 'Daß eine Menschengruppe, der überall gesagt wird, sie sei nur geduldet und nicht mit zugehörig, sich in wüste "Patrioten" verwandeln und [...] übereinander herfallen würde im Dienste ihrer Bedrücker, das schien mir wenig wahrscheinlich zu sein.'; loc.cit..

vocation".[72] The impact it had on Lessing was profound and indelible, judging by what he wrote in *Der jüdische Selbsthaß*:

> Until my death, I will not think back to the days of August 1914 otherwise than as the clearest revelation that ever fell to me about the lovely delusional ideas of mankind. Ideals are crutches. Progress is only a delusion. History: a lie.[73]

Lessing intermingles these observations with some personal memories of the first weeks of the First World War, when it seemed that almost all people were possessed by one fear only: to miss the "great moment".

> It was the end of individual freedom. There was no conscience, no evaluation, no examination of the heart. Out of lust for a fight, haughtiness, stupidity, pursuit of profit, cowardice, herd bliss, lust for adventure, credulity, in short out of all that is good and all that is bad in human nature the fate of nations piled up. Everyone felt like his neighbour. Everyone did what his neighbour did. And if it were the common *fashion* to die, then everyone died. The leader was the one who said what everyone wanted to hear at this time. What everyone needed to hear. Everyone wanted to be a leader. Everyone thought, at long last his moment had come, and the world had only waited for him.[74]

Again, he mentions his idea of drafting a plea for peace, an appeal to the foremost minds of Europe – the appeal he never completed drafting, let alone distributed –, this time including the names of some persons he had had in mind: in Germany itself Stefan George, Gerhart Hauptmann (1862–1946), and Richard Dehmel (1863–1920); in France Anatole France (1844–1924), Romain

---

72   'Die Sozialisten verrieten die Armut; die Mütter die Liebe; die Juden ihre sinnvolle Sendung.'; loc.cit..
73   'An die Tage des August 1914 werde ich bis zum Tode nie anders zurückdenken, als an die klarste Offenbarung, die mir je zuteil ward über die schönen menschheitlichen Wahnideen. Ideale sind Krücken. Fortschritt ist nur ein Trug. Geschichte: Lüge.'; o.c., 192–193.
74   'Da war zu Ende die Freiheit des Einzelnen. Da gab es kein Gewissen, kein Auswerten, keine Herzensprüfung. Da ballte sich aus Rauflust, Hochherzigkeit, Dummheit, Gewinnsucht, Feigheit, Herdenseligkeit, Abenteurergier, Gläubigkeit, kurz aus allem Guten und allem Schlimmen der Menschennatur: das Völkerschicksal. Jeder fühlte wie sein Nachbar. Jeder tat, was sein Nachbar tat. Und ward es zur allgemeinen *Mode* zu sterben, dann starb ein Jeder. Führer war, wer das sagte, was zu dieser Stunde alle hören wollten. Alle zu hören nötig hatten. Führer wollte jeder sein. Jeder wähnte, nun endlich sei seine Stunde gekommen, und die Welt habe nur auf ihn gewartet.'; o.c., 193.

Rolland (1866–1944), and Henri Bergson (1859–1941); in England G.B. Shaw (1856–1950), John Galsworthy (1867–1933), and H.G. Wells (1866–1946); and in Russia Nikolai Mynski (1855–1937), Leonid Andrejev (1871–1919), and Valery Bryusov (1873–1924). But Lessing's comment on this initiative is telling:

> This delusion of me. – Waking up was terrible. Precisely those men, in whom I had believed, as examples and educators on my path, changed into raging madmen.[75]

To give but one example: Henri Bergson wrote a pamphlet entitled *La signification de la guerre* (1915; 'The meaning of the war') in which he accused Germany of an unprecedented barbarism, a "barbarism that strengthened itself by capturing the forces of civilization".[76] Germany did not even respect martial law: the German army took to arson, rape, attacking women and children, and destroying monuments, Bergson claimed. So, even the great European minds in whom Lessing placed his trust tended to support their own country unconditionally, and even if he had managed to complete his appeal and to distribute it, it would not have found receptive ground. Of course, there were exceptions like the English philosopher Bertrand Russell (1872–1970) and the French writer Romain Rolland, both of whom like Lessing opposed the war; but like Lessing they were solitary figures who could not start off internationally organised resistance to the war.

Already in the autumn of 1914, Lessing publicly expressed his aversion to the war in a number of speeches. On October 14th, in the little auditorium of the *Technische Hochschule*, he delivered an address entitled *Et si omnes ego non*. Lessing voiced his astonishment, and even bewilderment with regard to the reactions the outbreak of the war induced:

> The famous authorities of socialism, of ethics, of religion renounced within an hour everything they had instructed all of their lives. That mixture of worry about property and power and the will to power and property that arises whenever there is sudden danger for a country, did wash away in a single orgiastic moment all bounds of reason, and united all

---

75   'Dies mein Wahn. - Das Erwachen war schrecklich. Gerade diejenigen Männer, an die ich geglaubt hatte, als an Vorbilder und Erzieher auf meinem Wege, verwandelten sich in Rasende.'; loc.cit..
76   'barbarie qui s'est renforcée elle-même en captant les forces de la civilisation.'; Henri Bergson, *La signification de la guerre* (Paris 1915), 19.

German people in a delightful illusion, all those who never let themselves be united for a true idea. The shared worry made them into brothers. The shared hate into lovers.[77]

In his collection of short stories *Feind im Land* (1923), Lessing summed up the events in the summer of 1914 in only two sentences:

> In August 1789, people decided to become cosmopolitans. In August 1914, they decided the opposite.[78]

This observation echoes what Lessing had written in *Geschichte als Sinngebung des Sinnlosen*:

> The finest moment in European history (August 4th, 1789) was followed by its most infamous (August 4th, 1914). Then, machine revolted against machine. Man became a filling without a will of his own. Sixty million, everyone is guilty to everyone, did unto each other what no-one wanted. The mere fact that we outlive this age makes even the most innocent answerable for an indelible burning shame.[79]

With these and similar observations in his speech *Et si omnes ego non*, Lessing, of course, explicitly turned against the ideas of 1914. As the very title of his speech shows – which he borrowed from the Gospel of St. Matthew, and may be translated as "even if all others, not I" – he was fully aware that he took up a minority position.

---

[77] 'Die berühmten Autoritäten des Sozialismus, der Ethik, der Religion verleugneten binnen einer Stunde alles, was sie ein Leben lang gelehrt hatten. Jenes Gemisch von Sorge um Besitz und Macht und Wille zu Macht und Besitz, das bei jeder plötzlichen Landesgefahr entsteht, hatte in einer einzigen orgiastischen Stunde alle Schranken der Vernunft hinweggespühlt und alle deutschen Menschen in einer herrlichen Illusion geeint, alle welche niemals um einer echten Idee willen sich vereinigen ließen. Die gemeinsame Sorge machte sie zu Brüdern. Der gemeinsame Haß zu Liebenden.'; Theodor Lessing, 'Et si omnes ego non', in: *Wmnm.*, 38.

[78] 'Im August 1789 beschlossen die Menschen, Weltbürger zu werden. Im August 1914 beschlossen sie das Gegenteil.'; Theodor Lessing, *Feind im Land*, o.c., 106.

[79] 'Dem schönsten Augenblick der europäische Geschichte (4. August 1789) folgte ihr ruchlosester (4. August 1914). Da empörte sich Maschine gegen Maschine. Der Mensch wurde willenloses Füllsel! Sechzig Millionen, jeder schuldig an jedem, taten einander, was keiner wollte. Die bloße Tatsache, daß wir dieses Zeitalter überdauern, behaftet auch den Schuldlosesten mit unaustilgbar brennender Scham.'; GSS, 165.

As Lessing would later write in his autobiography *Einmal und nie wieder*, for him the position someone took up with regard to the outbreak of the war became his criterion for judging people, "the standard I used to measure authenticity and falseness, truth of life and self-deceit with all those people I felt a spiritual bond with until then".[80] He broke with those who had enthusiastically supported the war, or who had tried to justify the German role in the outbreak of the war. This was the case, for instance, with the philosopher Max Scheler, a friend of Lessing's, knowing him and moving in the same circles since the days both of them studied in Munich in the second half of the 1890's. Ever since, they were friends, even though their relation was not without tensions. But Scheler's attitude with respect to the war resulted in Lessing feeling compelled to end this friendship:

> But Scheler got lost. Like everyone, he was sparked off at the vast flaming ecstasy of the fatherland. He did not want to miss the great moment. He wrote a blood-dripping book, which justifies the world historical bloodbath dialectically and which seemed to me worse than a murder. At that time only we split up once and for all.[81]

The book Lessing refers to is Scheler's *Der Genius des Krieges und der Deutsche Krieg* ('The Genius of War and the German War'), written immediately after the outbreak of the war, and published in January 1915. This was not the only book in which Scheler discussed the war. In 1916 he published *Krieg und Aufbau* ('War and Reconstruction'),[82] a collection of essays on the war mainly written in the second half of 1915. In this collection he emphasized the importance of the unity that the German nation allegedly experienced in the first phase of the war. All Germans had the same experience of the war, that is, they shared the same hopes, the same fears, the same dangers, the same suffering, day in, day out – and this is what made the Germans into a tightknit society. In fact, Scheler argues, this is the main difference between war and peace: in times of war nations share their experiences like being an enlarged person, while in times of peace individuals just have their own particular experiences. Hence,

---

80   'der Maßstab wurde, nach dem ich Echtheit und Unechtheit, Lebenswahrheit und Lebenslüge abmaß an all den Menschen, denen bis dahin ich mich geistig verbunden fühlte.'; *Eunw*, 344.

81   'Scheler aber entfiel. Er erbrannte wie alle am großen Flammenrausch des Vaterlandes. Er wollte die große Stunde nicht verpassen. Er schrieb ein bluttriefendes Buch, das die weltgeschichtliche Metzelei dialektisch rechtfertigt und mir schlimmer schien als ein Mord. Damals erst gingen wird endgültig auseinander.'; loc. cit..

82   Leipzig 1916.

in times of war a new mode of knowing arises: the way a nation knows as a "collective person" ("Gesamtperson" is the word Scheler uses in German). The experience of being incorporated into a collective person in a sense even reconciles man with death: it makes one realize that the value of individual life is usually overestimated, while what really matters is the collective person of the nation, not the individual person. The war accordingly unveils the true nature of both the nation and the individual.[83] After the war, in 1927, Scheler once more discussed the subject of war in a speech entitled *Die Idee des Friedens und der Pazifismus* ('The Idea of Peace and Pacifism'),[84] which was posthumously published in 1931. But the book Lessing refers to in his autobiography is the notorious *Der Genius des Krieges und der Deutsche Krieg*. In this book, Scheler defined war as an essential aspect of life, which for this reason alone should be embraced by everyone. Moreover, he claimed that war was an appeal for the spiritual renewal of mankind, it being an additional reason to cherish this particular war. Furthermore, Scheler was convinced the war would bring out the very best with the German people.[85] Scheler, of course, is a notorious example of a public figure who was of the opinion that war would be most rewarding for the German people, but he was hardly an exception.

Hans Graf von Schwerin-Löwitz (1847–1918), the then president of the Prussian House of Representatives, claimed as well that the war would heal the German people both physically and spiritually. After the war, he argued, Germany would be stronger militarily, more independent economically, and in general would have a stronger international position. Moreover, the German nation would be less divided, and more unanimous and idealistic."Thus, the purifying fervor of this global conflagration will – so help us God – recover our people", he concluded.[86] Similar ideas were expressed by field marshal Colmar Freiherr von der Goltz (1843–1916): he maintained that as a result of the war the German people would "gain in inner strength, reject the inclination toward materialism that started to proliferate alarmingly, and become more united and stronger, and thus to secure a duration of centuries more in world history.[87] Theodor Lessing detested ideas like these from the very bottom of his heart.

---

83   K. Flasch, o.c., 130–131.
84   Max Scheler, *Die Idee des Friedens und der Pazifismus*, ed. by Maria Scheler (Berlin 1931).
85   For a thorough analysis of Scheler's war time writings, cfr. K. Flasch, o.c., 103–146.
86   'So wird die Läuterungsglut dieses Weltenbrandes – mit Gottes Hilfe – unser Volk gesunden.'; Graf von Schwerin-Löwitz, Untitled contribution, in: Georg Gellert (ed.), o.c., 10.
87   'an innerer Kraft gewinnen, den Hang zum Materialismus, der erschreckend zu wuchern begann, von sich weisen, einiger und stärker werden, um sich so eine um Jahrhunderte

Besides the reactions of all too many German intellectuals and other public figures to the outbreak of the war, Lessing criticized the character of the war as well. Already in the autumn of 1914, in his address *Et si omnes ego non*, he observed:

> In this war butchering and slaughtering techniques have come into the world, in comparison with which all murders of people of the primeval world shamefacedly pale. Bombs thrown out of airships on innocent cities [...] Machine guns, mechanically killing hundreds of people. Handgrenades, to tear the enemy into a hundred pieces. [...] Everywhere: murder, maliciousness, violence! No international law, and any means allowed.[88]

All this was condoned and even welcomed by the German press, which, moreover, day in day out poisoned the public opinion with awful lies. But even worse than the press were the intellectuals, Lessing maintains:

> There they sit, the ones who stayed behind at their desks, and give a superior sense to the bloody chaos. There stands the patriot on duty in the illuminated ballroom, there stands "the famous novelist" and "the distinguished naturalist", "the well-known economist" and "the profound thinker". And each one tells what everyone wants to hear now. Thus, they all make their virtues of necessity. But still more unscrupulous, more awful are those highly gifted who indulge in "the great metaphysical experience". Those most sophisticated, most deformed, for whom the awful statement by Flaubert holds: "tout est matière pour nous". What compels them to talk and to write the ineffable to death?[89]

---

längere Dauer in der Weltgeschichte zu sichern.'; Freiherr von der Goltz, Untitled contribution, in: o.c., 13.

88 'In diesem Kriege sind Metzger- und Abschlachtetechniken zur Welt geboren, gegen die alles Menschenmorden der Vorwelt schamhaft verblaßt. Bomben aus Luftschiffen auf ahnungslose Städte niedergeschleudert. [...] Maschinegewehre, mechanisch Hunderte tötend. Handgranaten, um den Gegner in hundert Stücke zu zerreißen. [...] Überall: Mord, Heimtücke, Gewalt! Kein Völkerrecht und jedes Mittel erlaubt.'; Theodor Lessing, 'Et si omnes ego non', 40.

89 'Da sitzen sie, an ihren Schreibtischen zurückgeblieben, und geben dem Blutchaos einen erhabenen Sinn. Da steht der Konzertpatriot im erleuchteten Festsaal, da steht "der berühmte Romancier" und "der bedeutende Naturforscher", der "bekannte Nationalökonom" und der "tiefsinnige Denker". Und ein jeder redet das, was ein jeder jetzt hören will. So machen sie alle aus der Not ihre Tugenden. Ruchloser aber noch, furchtbarer sind jene Hochbegabten, welche "das große metaphysische Erlebnis" genießen. Jene Gebildetsten, Verbildetsten, für die Flauberts furchtbares Wort gilt: "tout est matière pour nous".

Of course, Max Scheler's *Der Genius des Krieges und der Deutsche Krieg* is an outstanding example of this way of thinking about the war, but the same holds true for "the ideas of 1914" in general.

Lessing's analysis of the war, and especially of the role of the press and the Socialist Party in it, is in sharp contrast with that by Werner Sombart.[90] Sombart explicitly opposed the idea of brotherhood between nations which, he claimed, was still influential at international socialist conferences:

> That the international tendency of the proletariat is, from the perspective of the viewpoints represented here, only a great evil, I don't have to say explicitly. To which extent our labourers, returning home from the trenches, will be cured from this illness, we will have to wait and see. And whether they – which would be desirable – will be strong enough to liberate themselves from that clique of international editors that until now has put the heavy yoke of internationalism on them. It is to be hoped that our German social democracy, which despite all speaking otherwise, always has been the most patriotic-minded – to the annoyance of the radical internationalists at various congresses [...] – now will just properly emphasize again the national needs of the labour movement.[91]

Sombart's statement expresses what so many German intellectuals thought about the war – his views were therefore not at all exceptional, but rather

---

Was zwingt sie das Unsägliche zu zerreden und zu zerschreiben?'; o.c., 43–44. Without referring to Flaubert, Lessing quotes the same expression, "tout est matière pour nous" ('for us, everything is material'), in his 'Tomi melkt der Moralkuh', reprinted in: Theodor Lessing, *Theater-Seele und Tomi melkt die Moralkuh. Schriften zu Theater und Literatur*, ed. by Jörg Wollenberg (*Ausgewählte Schriften*, vol. 3, Bremen 2003), 277–314, there at 314. I did not manage to track the quote of Flaubert. In his *Médaillons et camées* (Paris 1885), the French writer and journalist Charles Buet (1846–1897), in the text 'Emile Zola – Du naturalisme', uses almost the same expression: 'Tout est matière pour vous [...]' ('for you, everything is material'; 224).

90 Cfr. the discussion of Sombart above, 125.

91 'daß die internationale Tendenz des Proletariats vom Standpunkte der hier vertretenen Anschauungen nur ein schweres Übel ist, brauche ich nicht ausdrücklich auszusprechen. Wie weit unsere Arbeiterschaft, die aus den Schützengräben heimkehrt, von dieser Krankheit geheilt sein wird, muß abgewartet werden. Und ob sie – was zu wünschen wäre – stark genug sein wird, sich von jener Clique internationaler Redakteure frei zu machen, die ihnen bis jetzt das schwere Joch des Internationalismus aufgelegt hat. Zu hoffen ist, daß unsere deutsche Sozialdemokratie, die trotz allem Andersreden, doch immer die patriotischest gesinnte gewesen ist, - zum Ärger der radikalen Internationalisten auf den verschiedenen Kongressen [...] – nun erst recht die nationale Note der Arbeiterbewegung wieder betonen wird.'; Werner Sombart, o.c., 88.

expressed the position of the majority. This indicates not only how much Lessing's position differed from most of his contemporaries, but also explains why he was so much hated by right wing parties and groups in the years after the war.

As early as the autumn of 1914, Lessing did not have any faith in the eventual outcome of the war:

> No clairvoyant or sage can at this moment predict how this war will end, and which effects it will have, but one really has to be neither a clairvoyant nor a sage to foresee that this end will have nothing to do with reason nor with righteousness and justice, and that it will carry the germ of new wars and embroilments.[92]

And he added:

> I have no words to describe the shame at the sight of this time. How shall I bear the profound, unforgettable disappointment that alienated me from so many in whose inalienable vocation in life, in whose tragic greatness I have believed so innocently. Should I seek expression for the deep disgust at all this shameless abuse of language? At the phrase of heroism that reigns widely? At the lack of loyalty towards the most idiosyncratic past or nature?[93]

Closely related to considerations like these is a scepticism with respect to history, which is not prominent in Lessing's lecture, but may be discerned in some passages of the text. Lessing argues, for instance, that "I only have a dispute with those who have provided the 'logificatio post festum' of this hideous present, the theory of justification, the poetic glorification of the need of the masses".[94] For Lessing, arguments like these are redundant, as they represent

---

92 'Wie dieser Krieg ausgeht, welche Folgen er hat, das kann in diesem Augenblick kein Seher und kein Weiser sagen, aber um vorauszusehen, daß dieses Ende nichts mit Vernunft, nichts mit Gerechtigkeit und Recht zu tun haben wird und den Keim zu neuen Kriegen und Verwicklungen verbergen wird, dazu braucht man wirklich weder ein Weiser noch ein Seher zu sein.'; Theodor Lessing, 'Et si omnes ego non', 37.

93 'Ich besitze keine Worte, um die Scham beim Anblick der Zeit zu bezeichnen. Wie soll ich die tiefe, nie mehr vergeßliche Enttäuschung ertragen, die mich so vielen entfremdet, an deren unverlierbare Lebenssendung, an deren tragische Größe ich arglos geglaubt habe. Soll ich Ausdruck suchen für den Tiefen Ekel vor all diesem schamlosen Mißbrauch der Sprache? Vor der allgeläufigen Phrase des Heroismus? Vor dem Mangel an Treue gegen die eigenste Vergangenheit oder Eigenart?'; o.c., 43.

94 'Mit denen allein rechte ich, die die "logificatio post festum" dieser gräßlichen Gegenwart zu besorgen haben, die Rechtfertigungstheorie, die dichterische Verklärung der Massennot.'; loc. cit..

convictions that simply reflect the present viewpoints of their authors, and the society they belong to. After all, in twenty years' time or so, the situation will be completely different, Lessing argues, enemies turning into friends, and friends into enemies, as a result convictions changing accordingly. In case of defeat, people will dispute exactly those political ideas which they enthusiastically supported when their country was victorious. These convictions therefore do not represent enduring values: eventually, it is chance that determines the fate of world views and political ideas, as it determines the process of history itself, Lessing claims.

Apart from the public address *Et si omnes ego non*, in the autumn of 1914 Lessing gave a speech on "Europa und Asien" as well, which, likewise, was prompted by the outbreak of the war. He elaborated this address into a book with the same title, *Europa und Asien*, which was eventually published in 1918. Parts of the text of this book were prepublished in 1917 in the weekly *Die Aktion* ('Action'). *Die Aktion* was a literary and political magazine, edited by the journalist, literary critic and editor Franz Pfemfert (1879–1954); the journal promoted literary expressionism and left-wing politics, without having affiliations with a political party, however. During the First World War, Pfemfert presented *Die Aktion* as if it was a purely literary magazine, in order to escape a ban on publication; nevertheless, he published quite outspoken criticisms of the war, all be it in a somewhat concealed manner. Remarkably enough, *Die Aktion* was published all through the war.

In "Europa und Asien", Lessing relates the outbreak of the war to the significant population growth in Europe. From a nationalist position this is used by arguing that people can only gain victory in the struggle for power, when they pursue a policy that manages "to put the greatest number of sons on the world, to establish the greatest number of colonies, and with its language, its national traditions, its breed of people, to appropriate and overwhelm the largest part of the world".[95] But, Lessing asks, is it really true that the dominance of what Europeans call culture is "the purpose of history, be it natural, be it required by reason"?[96] As a result of this kind of thinking, the world is at war: each and every country tries to conquer as much land as possible, while blaming other countries for the war, "and tries to denounce them for the great fabulous

---

95 'die meisten Söhne in die Welt setzt, die meisten Kolonien begründet und mit seiner Sprache, seinen Landessitten, seiner Menschenart den größten Teil der Erdoberfläche an sich reißt und übermächtigt.'; Theodor Lessing, 'Europa und Asien', in: *Die Aktion* 7 (1917), column 318.
96 'das Ziel, sei es das natürliche, sei es das vernunftgebotene Ziel der Geschichte.'; loc.cit..

history".⁹⁷ Only exhaustion or chance – "that chance which we retrospectively call 'historical destiny'"⁹⁸ – can bring an end to this war. One of the implications of the war might well be, Lessing claims, a rise of Asia. But Europeans hardly know Asia, let alone understand it. In order to understand Asia, Europeans first and foremost have to realize that their own way of life is not the only possible one, and their culture not the only culture; and that, indeed, it is not at all necessary that Europeans teach their logic, their politics, their science and their revered art to those 900 million people who are completely different, and whose thoughts and feelings are closer to life than that of Europeans.

This, then, is the starting-point of Lessing's discussion of Asia as compared to Europe, which will not be discussed here in detail, but only insofar as it relates to his perception of the First World War. Having published a first edition of *Europa und Asien* in book form in 1918, Lessing published four more editions afterwards.⁹⁹ From the second, much enlarged edition onwards, Lessing used his comparison of Europe and Asia to expound his own philosophical views. In these editions, Europe and Asia are actually not discussed as geographical entities, but rather in the context of expounding a dimension of his theory of spheres. In this connection, "Europe" refers to *vitalité*, and "Asia" to *vérité*, while *réalité*, that is the world of which we are conscious, lies in between the "poles" of *vitalité* and *vérité*. – To recapitulate what has been explained above: the world of which we are conscious is by definition dependent on consciousness, which came into being as a result of need that forced man to break out of nature. Hence, consciousness may be described as a moving away from *vitalité*, that is, the sphere of the original state in which man was one with nature. *Vérité*, on the other hand, is the sphere of ideals that direct human actions, functioning as a lodestar; hence, humans try to move towards *vérité*. *Réalité* accordingly lies in between the poles of *vitalité* and *vérité*. For this reason, the history of mankind, being part of the sphere of *réalité*, may be described as a permanent movement away from *vitalité* towards *vérité*, which is epitomized by a movement from "Europe" towards "Asia".¹⁰⁰ – The series of articles in *Die Aktion* and the first edition of *Europa und Asien* are, however, not so much

---

97 'und vor der großen Fabelerzählerin Geschichte auszuschwärzen versucht.'; o.c., column 319.
98 'Jenes Zufall, den wir von nachhinein "historisches Fatum" nennen.'; loc.cit..
99 Four or three: it is not clear whether the fourth edition of the book, which was announced by the publisher, was actually published.
100 The contrast with Hegel's philosophy of history is noteworthy: according to Hegel, history moved from the East to the West, culminating in Europe in his own day and age. The difference in appreciation of Europe is, of course, telling: Lessing was, after all, most critical of the development of European culture.

focused on Lessing's philosophy, but should rather be seen as being part of his reaction to the outbreak of the war in 1914 and were also mainly written in that year.

Comparing Europe and Asia, Lessing observes that one of the notable differences between the two relate to religion: Christianity is a religion that articulates norms and ideals for mankind as regards the way it should live. This implies that Christianity judges life ethically as it is lived. Asian religion, in contrast – though Lessing points out that one should actually differentiate between the various Asian religions – does not articulate norms and ideals, but is, in a profound sense, one with life. The activist attitude, however, which in Lessing's view is characteristic of European culture, is indissolubly connected with Christianity. In contrast with the Asian attitude to life, the one of Europeans is dominated by the slogan "Progress or development!", Lessing maintains. The notions of progress and development are pivotal with both Hegel and Darwin, but, Lessing argues, by this both actually mix fact and value, reality and ideal. This even has become a dominant feature of Western thinking, and of Western civilization in general. And now, Lessing wrote in 1914, we witness the appalling result:

> "Historical necessity" has become the magic word of contemporary Europe.
> Even the senseless, preposterous infamous begins to hold as logically sanctioned and ethically justified for millions [of people], provided that it is only talked into them as "historically necessary", that is, genetically substantiated. And especially Europe's clear-headed minds [...] pay tribute to this historicism and at one stroke capitulate to "history" and "necessity".[101]

Lessing would elaborate these observations on history at length in *Geschichte als Sinngebung des Sinnlosen*, his analysis of historical thinking incited by the outbreak of the war in 1914, and in particular by the way German intellectuals tried to explain and justify this war historically. – It is remarkable indeed that Lessing managed to publish comments like these in 1917, when censorship in

---

101 "'Geschichtliche Notwendigkeit" ist der Zauberwort des gegenwärtige Europa geworden. Selbst das Sinnlose, Widersinnige, Verruchte, beginnt für Millionen als logisch sanktioniert und ethisch gerechtfertigt zu gelten, wofern es ihnen nur als "geschichtliche notwendig", das heißt als genetisch begründet eingeredet wird. Und gerade Europas denkenden Seelen [...] huldigen diesem Historismus und kapitulieren mit einem Schlage vor "Geschichte" und "Notwendigkeit" [...]'; Theodor Lessing, o.c., column 450.

Germany was quite strict. Even though Franz Pfemfert presented *Die Aktion* as a purely literary magazine to evade censorship, the political implications of Lessing's argument are unmistakable. –

People do not even apologize for the way they try to justify the war, forgoing philosophical insights for history, Lessing observes. On the contrary, they see it as their patriotic duty: one should not look for something more elevated or profound behind political history than "either eat or be eaten", he claims. In Europe, people use words like "Weltgeist"('world spirit'), "Weltwille" ('world will') and "Weltbewußtsein" ('world consciousness'), but these expressions eventually are nothing but reflections of the European activistic attitude towards life. The Asian attitude is completely different, however: it acquiesces in life as it is, and contemplates it as such. Hence the worship of the symbols of procreation, birth, fertility, life, and death in Asian religion, which is alien and even incomprehensible to Europeans. But Lessing does not deny the achievements of European culture: European technology, for instance, indeed is truly impressive, it being able to build airplanes and submarines. But these are used to spread their inhumanity into the skies and underwater. – Again, it is remarkable that an allusion to the war like this was published in 1917. – European culture thus proceeds at the expense of the beauty and sanctity of life. And now, in the age of the masses and the great numbers, even more so, Lessing argues. And this destructive culture spread all over the world, Europeans shattering "the heaven of innocence".[102] At the same time, millions of Asians pray each and every day: may all creatures be free from pain today...

In the first edition of the book *Europa and Asia*, the argument of the series of articles in *Die Aktion* is repeated in more detail. The opening passages of the book are literally identical, but hereafter Lessing distinguishes in the book at length between the various Asian religions, which for the sake of brevity he could not do in the series of articles.[103] The thrust of the argument is the same, however. Like in *Et si omnes non ego*, Lessing plainly expresses his despair over the outbreak of the war, in a telling passage which was, understandably, not included in the series of articles:

> Where then are the heroes of European progress at this time, in the autumn of 1914? Where Europe's socialists? The thinkers and poets who are called to preserve the inter-national? The women born for pure humanity? Where? – O, be comforted! All of them: socialists, women,

---

102   'den Himmel der Unschuld'; o.c., column 550.
103   Cfr. Theodor Lessing, *Europa und Asien* (Berlin 1918), 17–24.

thinkers and poets, all, all of them will tomorrow or the day after tomorrow furnish the markets again with progress, evolution, morality and humanity, when there is no more danger to get rounded up when selling morality, when trading humanity, and to be executed.[104]

But Lessing does not have any faith in the thinkers and artists of his day: "When the guns roar they become martial, and when the bells ring devout".[105] But when it really matters, at the decisive moment, like in August 1914, the ideals and values of these thinkers and artists prove to be nothing but a "wardrobe of masks".[106] If Europeans really took seriously their own religious ideals – loving one's neighbour, the spirit of self-sacrifice, helpfulness, veracity –, or if Europeans truly lived in accordance with Kant's categorical imperative, of course their rule of the world will instantly cease, Lessing argues. It is only because it is a habit of Europeans strictly to maintain disestablishment that they can preach and not put into practice what they preach: ideals are proper to the pulpit – but politics is politics, trade is trade, and never the twain shall meet. Politicians who mix up ideals and politics will eventually ruin even the strongest state.

But the most unprecedented presumption of the European mind, Lessing claims, is that "the history of the earth is directed towards mankind, in particular towards European man as the 'crown of creation'; – that history therefore does not advance almost blindly before us and only retrospectively is related to, geared to and adjusted for human sense and human purposes, no!, that it would a priori incorporate human sense and 'reasonable world order', approximately the purpose of the 'perfect constitutional order.'"[107] This presumption Lessing would discuss at length in his *Geschichte als Sinngebung des Sinnlosen*.

---

104 'Wo denn sind gegenwärtig, Herbst 1914, die Heroën europäischen Fortschritts? Wo Europas Sozialisten? Die zur Wahrung des Zwischenvölkischen berufenen Denker und Dichter? Die zu reinerer Menschlichkeit geborenen Frauen? Wo? – O, getrost! Alle: Sozialisten, Frauen, Denker und Dichter, alle alle werden morgen oder übermorgen wieder die Märkte mit Fortschritt, Entwicklung, Sittlichkeit und Humanität versorgen, wenn kein Gefahr dabei besteht beim Verkauf von Sittlichkeit, beim Handel mit Humanität erwischt und füsiliert zu werden.'; o.c., 29–30.
105 'Wenn Kanonen brüllen werden sie martialisch und wenn die Glocken läuten fromm.'; o.c., 40.
106 'Maskengarderobe'; o.c., 53.
107 'daß die Geschichte der Erde auf den Menschen, insbesondere auf den europäischen Menschen als auf die "Krone der Schöpfung" hinziele; – daß also Geschichte nicht etwa blind an uns vorgehe und dann von nach hinein auf Menschensinn und Menschenzwecke bezogen, zugeschnitten, zurecht gelegt werde, nein!, daß sie a priori menschheitlichen Sinn und "vernünftige Weltordnung", etwa den Zweck der "vollkommenen Staatsordnung", in sich berge.'; o.c., 74.

Lessing concludes this first edition of the book *Europa und Asien* with a prospect, which implies a devastating criticism of Europe:

> In August 1914, a veil tore. Behind the mask of culture, the beast appears. The smart, capable of everything, knowing everything, achieving everything, the beast Europa overpowering the world. Europe, its Christianity, its heroic morality, its ethics of development, its progress and its happiness, now stands naked for all to see.[108]

Lessing adds to this that all people of Europe plunged into the destructive machinery of war, with millions of dead and wounded as a result. No one knows whether he will survive. This doesn't apply, however, to "the big men", who will survive – that is, everyone who speeches and writes, feeling most important. But tomorrow they will have forgotten what they say and write today, tomorrow they will have new ideals, and the day after tomorrow yet again – and they will be applauded because they always tell what people like to hear.

On March 18th, 1921, Lessing was invited to address the *Verein der Freunde Indischer Weisheit* ('Society of Friends of Indian Wisdom'); he elaborated this speech, entitled *Die verfluchte Kultur* ('The damned culture'), into a booklet with the same title.[109] In his 'Preface', Lessing explains that the booklet may be considered an introduction to the ideas he had expounded in (the first edition of) his *Geschichte als Sinngebung des Sinnlosen*. Though Lessing does not mention it, its contents have much in common with his *Europa und Asien* as well.

The main argument of *Die verfluchte Kultur* is that culture by definition goes at the expense of nature, which conforms to the ideas Lessing developed in the years before the First World War. Lessing puts himself explicitly in the tradition of the French philosopher Jean-Jeacques Rousseau (1712–1778), who likewise had claimed that culture by definition infringes on natural development. Again, the comparison between Europe and Asia is pivotal in Lessing's argument, as culture is nowhere as extremely developed as in Europe. – Just for clarity: Lessing does not refer to Europe in the geographical sense, but as a cultural entity. For him, Europe includes the United States and Australia,

---

108   'August 1914 riß ein Schleier. Hinter der Kulturmaske zeigt sich die Bestie. Die kluge, alles könnende, alles wissende, alles leistende, die Erde übermächtigende Bestie Europa. Europa, sein Christentum, seine Heldenmoral, seine Entwicklungsethik, sein Fortschritt und sein Glück steht jetzt nackend vor aller Augen.'; o.c., 126.

109   Theodor Lessing, *Die verfluchte Kultur. Gedanken über den Gegensatz von Leben und Geist* (Munich 1921); the booklet was reissued in 1981 (Munich 1981); I quote from this reprint.

both of which he considers offspring of Europe, in essence corresponding with it. – Orienting his text towards his specific audience, Lessing intersperses his argument with references to Indian philosophy, in particular the Vedas. Again, Lessing's criticisms of European culture are devastating, for instance when he points out the huge number of animals that have become extinct as a direct result of European culture.[110] "In view of this immeasurable ossuary of culture", Lessing wonders, "what does that tiny copping-stone that we have recently witnessed, our so-called world war, matter?"[111] It brought death and destruction, but eventually it was nothing but business as usual. According to Lessing, no single word does characterize European civilization better than the title of Karl Marx's best-known book: *Das Kapital* ('Capital'), even though he saw Marx as one of the main jack-o'-lanterns of Western thought. Implied in these observations is the conclusion that the First World War was neither an excess nor an exception: it was just a demasqué of Western civilization, showing what it truly and essentially is. Hence, Lessing claims, it is both telling and symbolic that when in 1914 a town in northern France was completely destroyed during an attack, just one building remained erect: a big stores.[112]

In the post-war years, Lessing would every now and then return to the First World War in his writings. Thus, in the title story of his collection of satires and stories *Feind im Land* – a satire on a political crisis over the occupation of the Rhineland after the war – he frequently alludes to this war. Lessing mockingly refers, for instance, to "the spirit of 1914": "we stir a fatherland-psychosis spreading all over the country".[113] Of course, with comments like this, Lessing will only have antagonized more the right wing and nationalist factions that saw him as a "Volksfeind" ('enemy of the people') ever since he opposed the war from August 1914 onwards. Included in the collection is also "Kamerad Levi" ('Comrade Levi'), a story about a shrewdly calculating soldier who manages to muddle through the war – until he cannot stand the cries of a dying horse in agony, goes out at the risk of his own life and gets killed after having given the horse the coup de grâce, thus dying "so senseless a death".[114] The story "Episode", too, takes place in the First World War – a story about a French

---

110   O.c., 16–20.
111   'Angesichts dieser unermeßlichen Leichenfelder der Bildung, was kümmert uns jener winzige Schlußstück, welcher wir jüngst vor Augen hatten, unser sogenannter Weltkrieg?'; o.c., 20.
112   O.c., 42.
113   'Wir erregen ein durch das ganze Land sich verbreitende Vaterlandspsychose'; Theodor Lessing, *Feind im Land*, o.c., 23.
114   'einen so sinnlosen Tod'; o.c., 171.

soldier who at great risk for himself saves a heavily wounded German soldier, with a spontaneous, if only temporary cease-fire as a result.[115]

In his regular contributions to the *Prager Tagblatt*, Lessing frequently refers to the First World War as well, sometimes discussing the war or some aspects of it, or occasionally mentioning it only in passing when writing on a different topic. On the occasion of Christmas 1923, for example, Lessing wrote a delicate elegy entitled "Erinnere Dich..." ('Remember...'), about recollections that forced themselves upon him, for instance of those he had known and were killed in action: "That is you, Erni Herzfeld, little pale lancer, poor grief-stricken child's face, astonished eyes not at all realizing what happened here to you, child, just so carried away, until near Verdun the redemptive bullet found you". And when he remembers one of the fallen, the recollection of yet another one follows, "...and on Christmas Eve, many mothers light their little candle and think of the one whom only they knew, only they amongst all others, and who meant everything to her, and who now is already lost for so many years".[116] And Lessing remembers how on Christmas Day the soldiers were given a honey cake on behalf of Hindenburg, after all so kind-hearted a man, before he marched them off to the front, never to return...

In 1929, Lessing published his recollections of his days spent in a field hospital for prisoners of war, with some hundred German malingerers suffering from venereal disease, in a series of articles in the *Prager Tagblatt*.[117] He had volunteered for the job, and was accepted because of his medical training, even though it was incomplete. Every now and then, Lessing inserts a personal opinion in these recollections, for instance:

> In this war, what a twaddle about "national characteristics". In a field hospital, however, amongst the dying, one senses that ultimately we all are completely equal, and yet again individually everybody unique.[118]

---

115   O.c., 173–186.
116   'Das bist Du, Erni Herzfeld, kleiner blasser Ulan, armes vergrämtes Kindergesicht, verwunderten Auges gar nicht erfassend, was mit Dir Kinde hier geschah, nur so mitgestoßen, bis die erlösende Kugel vor Verdun dich fand.'; '... und am Weihnachtsabend zünden viele Mütter ihr Lichtlein an und denken an Einen, den nur sie kannten, sie ganz allein unter allen, und der ihr alles war und nun schon so viele Jahre dahin.'; Theodor Lessing, "Erinnere Dich...", in: *Prager Tagblatt*, December 25th 1923, reprinted in: *IFEGt*, 352.
117   Theodor Lessing, 'Das Lazarett', o.c..
118   'In diesem Kriege, welch Geschwätz über "Nationalcharaktere". In einem Lazarett aber, unter Sterbenden, fühlt man, daß im Letzten wir alle völlig gleich sind und im Einzelnen doch wieder jeder unverwechselbar.'; o.c., 360.

It so happened that one of the patients in the field hospital turned out to be a serial killer, who poisoned a number of his fellow patients. Why? Lessing claims he might know the answer:

> This cheerful ignorant boy did, what the years of war did with everyone. He worked on human material, and in doing so possibly was no less heartless than the big generals, who send ten thousand into death and write warm-hearted family letters. After all, they are just in power. And only one thing on earth is evil and definitely worth fighting for: the power of a person over other people.[119]

In an essay on German students around 1925 – in the background of this text lurk the problems Lessing was confronted with because of his notorious essay on Hindenburg[120] –, Lessing begins his argument with a sketch of the circumstances in which these students started their studies:

> A new world consciousness had implanted world war and revolution in Europe's youth. Blindly, it tumbled into this terrific slaughtering of nations. The most gifted, the most promising, the blossom of every nation, were sacrificed. But those who came out of this mass insanity again, emerged as changed men. [...] Many ideals were shattered, many illusions buried.[121]

Lessing makes a similar observation in the essay "Irrende Helden" ('Errant Heroes'): "When on November 8th, 1918, the Revolution broke out, it found the

---

119   'Dieser frischfröhliche unwissende Junge tat, was die Kriegsjahre mit allen taten. Er operierte am Menschenmaterial und war dabei vielleicht nicht weniger gemütlos wie die großen Feldherren, die zehntausend in den Tod schicken und warmherzige Familienbriefe schreiben. Sie haben ja eben die Macht. Und nur Eins auf Erden ist böse und schlechthin bekämpfenswert: die Macht einen Menschen über andere Menschen.'; o.c. 371.
120   Cfr. chapter one, above, 8–9.
121   'Ein neues Weltbewußtsein hatte Weltkrieg und Revolution in die Jugend Europas gepflanzt. Blindlings war sie hineingetaumelt in das ungeheure Morden der Völker. Die begabtesten, hoffnungsvollsten, die Blüte jeder Nation, wurden zum Opfer. Diejenigen aber, die aus dem Massenirrsinn wieder heraus kamen, kamen als Gewandelte heraus. [...] Viele Ideale waren zertrümmert, viele Illusionen begraben.'; Theodor Lessing, 'Deutsche Studentenschaft um 1925', in: *Die neue Erziehung* 7 (1925), 637–643; reprinted in: *IFEG*, 75.

bourgeois youth completely disorientated."[122] In both last-mentioned texts, Lessing tries to explain the confused political situation in the Weimar Republic resulting from the Great War. In an essay on "Der Tag der Tiere" ('World Animals Day'), Lessing expresses his mixed feelings with respect to this day. On the one hand, he is, of course, all in favour of treating animals well; but on the other hand, he emphasizes that doing so deserves our attention each and every day and not just this day in particular. Lessing compares the celebration of World Animals Day with the temporary cease-fire at Christmas 1914. The next day, the killing continued – like, as from tomorrow, we will continue to treat our animals as usual, not paying them the attention they deserve.[123] In the late 1920's and early 1930's, warning against the rise of National-Socialism became an important theme in Lessing's essays: he published a number of outspoken criticisms of the NSDAP and its leaders. In one of these, "Wie es kommen wird" ('As it will turn up'), Lessing observes: "In August 1914, a people was drummed into death; nowadays there is again a drumming into death".[124]

On January 31st, 1933, the day after Adolf Hitler was appointed as chancellor and some other members of the NSDAP at high-ranking cabinet posts, which implied that the National-Socialists actually had seized power, Lessing published the essay "Nein!" ('No!'), presumably his last publication in Germany. It embraced a passionate appeal against war, and in particular against the use of poison gas. In 1918, at the end of the world war, eight different sorts of poison gas existed, Lessing claims, but now there are more than 800. He emphasizes that he does not want to scare his readers, but cannot stress enough that a gas attack is by far worse than anything they may imagine – worse than they read in books or see in films. As compared to the 1914–1918 war, the Franco-Prussian War of 1870–1871 was only a "light opera-war"; but as general Erich Ludendorff (1865–1937) pointed out, the Great War was nothing but a house fire as compared to the coming war, Lessing maintains. For one reason or another, however, humans always tend to think that they themselves will escape disaster – calamities will always strike anybody but themselves. Hence, they continue to do what they always did. Wrongly so, Lessing argues:

---

122 'Als am 8. November 1918 die Revolution ausbrach, fand sie die bürgerliche Jugend völlig desorientier.'; Theodor Lessing, 'Irrende Helden', in: *Prager Tagblatt*, November 27th, 1930; reprinted in: *IFEG*, 83.

123 Theodor Lessing, 'Der Tag der Tiere', in: *Prager Tagblatt*, October 2nd, 1930; reprinted in: *IFEG*, 275–277.

124 'August 1914 wurde ein Volk in den Tod getrommelt; heute wird wieder in den Tod getrommelt.'; Theodor Lessing, 'Wie es kommen wird', in: *General-Anzeiger für Dortmund*, June 19th, 1932; reprinted in: *IFEG*, 111.

Mankind has once had a Middle Ages. At that time, the burning of heretics and the persecution of witches raged. Today we say: "That was madness!". We think to have advanced. Our delusion is greater.[125]

Lessing cannot be optimistic about the effect of his appeal: "Let us not think, however, that with our biting protest against gas warfare anything has been achieved".[126] Still, Lessing urges an immediate and complete change in attitude towards gas warfare.

Even in one of his very last publications, "Deutschland" ('Germany'), Lessing refers to the early days of August 1914, when almost all of Europe seemed overwhelmed by madness,

> there was a small group of solitary people, all hated – Ghandi and Romain Rolland, Rilke and Karl Spitteler, Galsworthy and Minski, Bertrand Russell and Albert Einstein. They knew: love is more triumphant than hatred. He has no love, who when he talks of "brotherhood" and "comradeship" gets angry eyes. Who loves only *the likes of him*, loves no one. And who foams at the mouth at the word fatherland, disgraces his fatherland.[127]

Thus, Lessing uses his recollections of the outbreak of the war to unmask the nationalism that increasingly dominated post-war politics in Germany, and in particular the ideology of National-Socialism.

It is safe to conclude that these examples of recurrent references to the First World War in Lessing's writings – the preceding overview neither is, nor meant to be exhaustive – indicate that this war has been one of the most decisive experiences of his life. The war shaped his thinking, though not in the sense that he changed his philosophical ideas. On the contrary, he actually considered these

---

125 'Die Menschheit hat einst ein Mittelalter gehabt. Damals wütete Ketzerbrand und Hexenverfolgung. Wir sagen heute: "Das war Wahnsinn!". Wir glauben weitergekommen zu sein. Unser Wahn ist größer.'; Theodor Lessing, 'Nein!', in: *Volkswille*, January 31st, 1933; reprinted in: *WeU*, 349.
126 'Wähnen wir doch nicht, daß mit unserem bißen Protest gegen Giftkämpfe irgendetwas getan ist.'; loc.cit..
127 'da gab es eine kleine Schar ganz einsamer, allen verhaßte – Ghandi und Romain Rolland, Rilke und Karl Spitteler, Galsworthy und Minski, Bertrand Russell und Albert Einstein. Sie wußten: die Liebe ist siegreicher als der Haß. Der hat keine Liebe, der, wenn er von "Brüderlichkeit" und "Kameradschaft" redet, böse Augen bekommt. Der liebt niemandem, der nur *seinesgleichen* liebt. Und der schändet sein Vaterland, dem beim Worte Vaterland der Schaum vom Munde tropft.'; Theodor Lessing, 'Deutschland', in: *Aufruf. Streitschrift für Menschenrechte* 3 (1933), Special issue, 'Judenverfolgung', March 1933, Heft 6; reprinted in: *WeU*, 357.

ideas rather being corroborated by his wartime experiences. It was therefore the war that encouraged Lessing to bring his views more vigorously to the fore. This holds true in particular for his analysis of historical thought: historical thought was, after all, used by many of his contemporaries to justify the very war that Lessing whole-heartedly rejected. His analysis of historical thought in his *Geschichte als Sinngebung des Sinnlosen* is the subject of the next chapter.

CHAPTER 4

'Aber Wir Benötigen Geschichte, Um Geschichte Zu Machen'

Lessing's Reflections on History

∵

In chapter three, we discussed Theodor Lessing's immediate reaction to the outbreak of the First World War, and to the enthusiasm this war was greeted with by most of his contemporaries.[1] As we have seen, Lessing opposed the war from the very beginning – "with every drop of blood disgusted by the awful barbarism of the age"[2] –, and he was disappointed in, and even appalled by, the enthusiasm of especially a number of German intellectuals, who by all means tried to justify the war. As a result, Lessing broke with some of his friends who supported the war, for example the philosopher Max Scheler, whose book *Der Genius des Kriegs und der Deutsche Krieg* (1915) truly repelled Lessing. But the outbreak of the war induced Lessing to a more distant, intellectual reaction as well: an analysis of historical thinking. For many of the intellectuals who tried to justify the war appealed to history to substantiate their point. They claimed that in the light of recent history, Germany had every reason to defend itself – even by a pre-emptive strike – because the young German nation was in danger of being hampered in its natural development, or because German culture was in imminent danger of being crushed by European civilisation.[3] Precisely this instrumental use, or rather abuse, of history induced Lessing to his "Kritik der historischen Vernunft" ('Critique of Historical Reason'), resulting in the book *Geschichte als Sinngebung des Sinnlosen*. As Lessing puts it himself in his autobiographical essay "Gerichtstag über mich selbst" (1925): "How I experienced it [i.e., the war], that can be read in *Geschichte als Sinngebung des Sinnlosen*, a book written during the war, which brought me my first success".[4]

---

1 A translation of the chapter title is, 'But we need history, in order to make history'.
2 'mit jedem Blutstropfen angewidert von der gräßlichen Barbarei des Zeitalters'; Theodor Lessing, 'Gerichtstag über mich selbst', in: *Eunw*, 404.
3 Cfr. chapter three above, 116–127, for examples.
4 'Wie ich ihn erlebte [...], das steht zu lesen in *Geschichte als Sinngebung des Sinnlosen*, einem im Kriege niedergeschriebenen Buch, das mir den ersten Erfolg brachte'; Theodor Lessing, loc.cit..

© HERMAN SIMISSEN, 2021 | DOI:10.1163/9789004464773_005

1   Preliminary Observations on History

Although *Geschichte als Sinngebung des Sinnlosen* was Lessing's first lengthy contribution to philosophy of history, he had an interest in the subject already for some time. This is evidenced by stray remarks in his publications ever since 1895, when he published his lampoon in defence of the playwright Oskar Panizza.[5] In his defence of Panizza, Lessing observed:

> And the uncalled cause of all quarrels of so-called mankind?
> Basically – of course in the year 70 as well – private worries, private disagreements between a few, most likely completely uninteresting, indifferent human beings, who are completely remote of all those who give up their life for them, who are damned little concerned with their well-being and sorrows – because that all of so-called world history basically is the family chronicle of nobility and the private experience of the courts, that every war between two civilised nations in the last resort was the war between their governments, that only deliberately blind forging of history can want to deny.[6]

This criticism of the subject of history as a discipline, showing only interest in nobility, might well be inspired by the example of Johannes Scherr, the Swiss historian who was one of Lessing's favourite authors in his youth, as we have seen. Moreover, it fits well with Lessing's leftish political views.

Even in such an unlikely place as his volume of light verse *Weiber!*, his sighs on the fair sex, Lessing included a critical observation on history:

---

5 Cfr. Chapter one above, 6.
6 'Und die Gelegenheitsursache aller Kämpfe der sogenannten Menschheit? Im Grunde genommen – Anno 70 natürlich auch – Privatsorgen, Privatdifferenzen von ein paar vielleicht ganz uninteressanten, gleichgültigen Menschenkinder, die all denen, die für die in den Tod gehen, völlig ferne stehen, ihr Lebenswohl und –wehe verdammt wenig tangieren – denn daß die ganze sogenannte Weltgeschichte, bei Lichte besehen, die Familienchronik des Junkerstandes und das Privaterlebnis der Höfe ist, daß jeder Krieg zweier Kulturnationen in letzter Instanz der Krieg ihrer Kabinette war, das kann nur absichtlich blinde Geschichtsfälschung leugnen wollen'; Theodor Lessing, *Der Fall Panizza. Eine kritische Betrachtung über 'Gotteslasterung' und künstlerische Dinge vor Schwurgerichten* (Munich 1895), 33.'In the year 70' refers to the Franco-Prussian War of 1870–1871.

Had Helena, when Paris first of her caught sight
Been troubled by a cold,
Today Troy would still be upright
And no pupil read the Iliad.

The nose of Cleopatra
Was guilty of Rome's decline
The dimple in the chin of Aspasia
Changes the world.

Every wise man, every loony
Turns on a pivot
And all of world history
Follows ex utero. – [7]

Here, he claims that history as a process usually is the result of chance, and that history does not show any logic of its own.

In his *Schopenhauer-Wagner-Nietzsche*, Lessing again questioned the discipline of history, especially its claims of being a science. According to Lessing, the history of philosophy eventually is nothing but "a pragmatic enumeration of deceased systems of thought and biographical occurrences".[8] As such, the history of philosophy is as little a science in the true sense of the word as the history of culture, the history of literature, or the history of art. This is

---

[7] 'Wär Helena als die der Paris gesehen
Mit einem Schnupfen behaftet gewesen
So würde heute noch Troja stehen
Und kein Primaner die Ilias lesen.

Die Nase der Kleopatra
Ward Schuld an Roms Zerfall.
Das Grübchen im Kinn der Aspasia
Verändert den Erdenball.

Um ein Mittelachse dreht
Sich jeder Weise, jeder Thor.
Und alle Weltgeschichte geht
Ex utero hervor. –'
Theodor Lessing, *Weiber! 301 Stoßseufzer über das 'schönere' Geschlecht* (Berlin 1897), 58.

[8] 'pragmatische Aufzählung abgestorbener Gedankensysteme und biografischer Ereignisse'; *S-W-N*, 180.

"[b]ecause not facts, but laws are science!".[9] For this very reason, according to Lessing the history of thought should be placed at the lowest step of the ladder of scientific disciplines.

Discussing the personality and philosophy of Friedrich Nietzsche, Lessing almost in passing makes an observation that is quite telling for the ideas he would later elaborate with regard to history:

> Perhaps we know only a little about the soul of the ancient Germans, Athenians, Spartans, mediaeval crusaders. For our characterisations of historical personalities, we always depend on sympathies and antipathies. But we need history in order to make history. And a past paradise, a golden age that we mourn as being lost, is the mirror image of what we do not befit to expect from our future. But every belief is certain of what it believes. And as soon as we are only impressed with the past, we are already on our way to incorporate it as present.[10]

This passage, concise as it may be, foreshadows ideas Lessing later would develop in his publications on history: scepticism with regard to what we really can know about the past, the involvement in or presence of the historian in the image he sketches of the past, and, finally, the importance of an image of the past in all cultures, serving as a lodestar in the present.

According to Lessing, Nietzsche's *Über den Nutzen und Nachteilen der Historie für das Leben* ('On the Use and Abuse of History for Life'), one of his *Unzeitgemäßen Betrachtungen* ('Untimely Meditations'), probably was the most important publication in this phase of Nietzsche's life. Lessing reports at length how Nietzsche argues that too much history can paralyze a culture: "the constructive power of a people can only bear a certain quantity of past".[11] In general, the inclination towards history is a disease, he argues, but there are three forms of history that may be meaningful for a culture: monumental

---

9   'Denn nicht Tatsachen sondern Gesetze sind Wissenschaft! '; loc.cit..
10 'Wir wissen vielleicht wenig von der Seele des alten Germanen, des Atheners, des Spartiaten, des mittelalterlichen Kreuzritters. Wir sind mit unserer Charakteristik historischer Menschen immer auf Sympathieen [sic!] und Antipathieen [sic!] angewiesen. Aber wir benötigen Geschichte, um Geschichte zu machen. Und ein gewesenes Paradies, ein goldenes Zeitalter, das wir als verloren betrauern, ist Spiegelbild dessen, was wir von unserer Zukunft zu erwarten nicht anstehen. Jedem Glauben aber ist sein Geglaubtes gewiß. Und sobald wir daher von historischer Vergangenheit nur durchdrungen sind, sind wir schon auf dem Wege, sie als Gegenwart zu verleiblichen.'; o.c., 263–264.
11 'Die plastische Kraft eines Volkes kann nur ein bestimmtes Quantum Vergangenheit vertragen.'; o.c., 270.

history, which records great actions, heroes and ideals; antiquarian history, which lovingly records out of reverence; and critical history, which discriminates between what is obsolete and what is eternal and still fruitful. Nietzsche's treatise on history would prove to be an inspiration for Lessing, especially when he tried to show how history may be meaningful for a culture, even though what we can truly know about the past is very limited indeed.

Even though Lessing fully admits the importance of Nietzsche, he thinks it is rather enigmatic that Nietzsche is so very famous, whereas so many of his contemporaries – who were accomplished philosophers and authors as well – are completely forgotten:

> Because everything historical is unpredictable and coincidental. And everything that we call genius, heroism, importance, and immortality, and which indeed it is, are glittering drops, flung to the highest top by an unforeseeable vis a tergo.[12]

Again, Lessing emphasizes that history is a blind process, the outcome of which is completely unpredictable.

In his *Probevorlesung* "Wissenschaft als Kraftökonomie", Lessing discusses the history of the natural sciences in a way that almost seems to announce Thomas Kuhn's *The Structure of Scientific Revolutions* (1962). According to Lessing, for quite a long time, the community of scientists tries to resist new insights into the working of nature, but once it cannot but accept them it retrospectively tries to give the impression that the new theory mainly confirms what was known all along: "the long period of not seeing, persecuting, misjudging suddenly is forgotten, and even the opponents or deniers of the new suddenly discover that they did recognise it all along".[13] Like Kuhn would do in 1962, Lessing underlines that the development of scientific theory is a process taking place amongst scientists as well as a purely intellectual undertaking. But then Lessing adds:

> According to this energy saving principle of separation and overlooking, of ignoring and straightening, of re-melting and lying, all in accordance

---

12   'Denn alles historische ist unberechenbar und zufällig. Und alles, was wir Genie, Heldentum, Größe und Unsterblichkeit nennen, und was es auch ist, das sind schillernde Tropfen, die eine unvorhersehbare vis a tergo auf die höchste Spitze geschleudert hat.'; o.c., 418. In this context, 'vis a tergo' can be roughly translated as driving force.
13   'Die langen Zeiten des Nichtsehns, Verfolgens, Verkennens sind plötzlich vergessen, und selbst die Gegner oder Ableugner des Neuen entdecken plötzlich, daß sie es ja schon immer "anerkannt" haben.'; Theodor Lessing, 'Wissenschaft als Kraftökonomie', in: *PaT*, 53.

with the necessities of life, vital interests, values and points of view, eventually that most scandalous, through and through accidental fable convenue comes about that humankind calls its world history! [...] No domain is more remote from truth, freedom and value than the domain of so-called "historical reality".[14]

In other words, the story told about the past in historiography is mainly a function of present needs, and thus not at all a true story about past reality resulting from scientific inquiry. Hence, historiography first and foremost reflects the (psychic) necessities of a society, not past reality.

In a footnote to this passage, Lessing refers to the ongoing debate in his time about the status of the historical sciences, in which philosophers like Heinrich Rickert (1863–1936) and Wilhelm Windelband (1848–1915) played an important part. They maintained that the historical sciences indeed are sciences, all be it sciences of a different kind in comparison with the natural sciences. In contrast to the natural sciences, they argued, historical sciences are not aimed at formulating laws, but at describing individual processes. Without expanding on this matter, Lessing observes that history is not, nor can be, the science of past reality, because "the stuff of history already passed through the general forms of human consciousness before the historian encounters it".[15] Moreover,

> all specific categories of history (the historical individual, historical success, historical causality, historical connection) definitely are subtractive hotchpotches. They are in a completely different and incomparably deeper sense unreal than whichever abstraction of the knowledge of nature. Nothing, too, can be more incorrect than the idea that empirical historical research could serve as a world court. Indeed, the so-called historical sense (that our German professors are in charge of) is nothing but their lack of sense of value.[16]

---

14 'Nach diesem kraftsparenden Prinzip des Sekretierens und Übersehens, des Totschweigens und Zurechtebiegens, des Umschelzens und Umlügens, je nach den Lebensbedürfnissen, vitalen Interessen, Werten und Standpunkten kommt zuletzt jene urinfame, durch und durch zufällige fable convenue zustande, welche die Menschheit ihre Weltgeschichte nennt! [...] Und kein Bereich liegt soweit ab von Wahrheit, Freiheit und Wert als das Reich der sogenannten "historischen Wirklichkeit."; loc.cit.. The *dictum* 'l'histoire est une fable convenue' (history is a fable upon which we agree) is attributed to Napoleon.

15 'der Stoff der Geschichte schon durch die allgemeinen Formen menschlichen Bewußtseins hindurchging, ehevor der Historiker ihn vorfand'; o.c., footnote, 53–54.

16 'alle spezifischen Kategorieen [sic!] der Geschichte (das historische Individuum, der historische Erfolg, die historische Kausalität, der historische Zusammenhang) sind durchaus substruktive Klitterungen. Sie sind in ganz andern und ungleich tieferem Sinne unwirklich, als irgendwelche Abstraktion des Naturwissens. Nichts auch kann unrichtiger

But for Lessing, in 1907, when he delivered his *Probevorlesung*, there was no need to discuss "the complex and subtle problems of philosophy of history"[17] – at least, not yet... Again, Lessing demonstrates his scepticism with regard to the discipline of history, especially in relation to its claims of having true knowledge of the real past.

In a discussion of the ideas of Charles Darwin, Lessing, again, makes a critical observation on the subject matter of history: "It is a prejudice of man that the history of the earth has to relate to him and to his desires to development".[18] In his reminiscences of the writer Helene von Dönniges (1843–1911), once the lover of the politician Ferdinand Lasalle (1825–1864)[19], Lessing again discusses the discipline of history, claiming that historical facts eventually are nothing but the twisting of real occurrences – it could be simply demonstrated by studying the obituaries in remembrance of von Dönniges.[20] In a footnote, Lessing explains his view:

> O history, history! If only the times came when the overpowering of reality, which man proudly calls "world history", will become the concern of the most gifted novelists. What, after all, is reality? Who, after all, did really live? Imagine Plato or Paul together with the man who writes thick volumes on them! The real Plato would not understand the historical Plato. The real Paul would not have a single idea in common with the followers of the historical one. All speeches, documents, anecdotes of humans of a thousand years ago are an invention."Historical personality" – that is a human being who induces the fantasy of his heirs (mostly through death, madness, accident, power, noise, accidental success) to fabricate the only real, empirical into history and truth.[21]

---

      sein, als die Meinung, daß die empirische Geschichtsforschung ein Weltgericht zu prästieren vermöchte. Ja der sogenannte historische Sinn, (den unsre deutschen Professoren in Pacht haben) ist nichts als ihr Mangel an Sinn für Wert'; loc.cit.. In this passage, Lessing hints at the famous *dictum* by Friedrich von Schiller: 'die Weltgeschichte ist das Weltgericht' – world history is the world court.

17   'die komplexen und subtilen Probleme der Geschichtsphilosophie'; o.c., 54.
18   'Es ist das Vorurteil des Menschen, daß die Geschichte der Erde sich durchaus auf ihn und auf seine Entwicklungswünsche beziehen muß'; Theodor Lessing, 'Charles Darwin', in: *PaT*, 172.
19   In fact, Lasalle died as result of a duel over von Dönniges: he was mortally wounded by her fiancée.
20   Theodor Lessing, 'Ferdinand Lasalle', in: *PaT*, 398.
21   'O Geschichte, Geschichte! Käme doch erst die Zeit, wo die Wirklichkeitsübermächtigung, die die Menschen stolz "Weltgeschichte" nennen, zur Sache der begabtesten Romanschriftsteller würde. Was ist denn Wirklichkeit? Wer hat denn wirklich gelebt? Man denke Plato oder Paulus mit den Menschen zusammen, welche dicke Bücher über

In his *Studien zur Wertaxiomatik*, Lessing criticizes the discipline of history again, for yet another reason: this time for its inclination merely to concentrate on the peaks and lows, and thus to ignore the average. As a result, all what remains of a person who was important in his own time usually is no more than a single trait or a single anecdote.[22]

In his *Der Bruch in der Ethik Kants*, Lessing emphasizes that man, being the "valuing animal"[23] that he is, ceaselessly tries to interpret the facts of power and chance as rational, ethical phenomena. Even chaos will be interpreted as meaningful. Because only when it is interpreted as meaningful, man can accept the (as such) irrational facts of power and chance. These relations surface especially in the philosophy of history, Lessing argues – indeed, in his *Geschichte als Sinngebung des Sinnlosen* it is one of the themes he would discuss at greater length. For instance, when someone is in power, almost immediately some great minds will turn up who prove that it is both right and rational that this person is in power. It is a quite remarkable paradox, Lessing claims that generally one tends to see the historical as the expression of what is rational, whereas great historical figures like for instance Napoleon acknowledged the fortuity of their power. Be that as it may, eventually, "the interpretation of history makes facts of right out of facts of power, and makes coincidental facts 'meaningful'."[24]

If we try to assess, then, what Lessing's views on history prior to the publication of *Geschichte als Sinngebung des Sinnlosen* imply, we can conclude that he was indeed very critical about history. His criticisms are of two kinds, one which one could call metaphysical, the other one epistemological. The metaphysical criticism implies – contrary to, for instance, the well-known and influential philosophies of history of G.W.F. Hegel or Karl Marx – that the process of history is completely determined by blind chance, or, in other words that there is no inner logic whatsoever underlying the outcome of history. The

---

sie schreiben! Der wirkliche Plato verstünde den historischen nicht. Der wirkliche Paulus hätte keinen Gedanken mit den Anhängern des historischen gemeinsam. Alle Reden, Dokumenten, Anekdoten von Menschen vor tausend Jahren sind Erfindung. "Historische Persönlichkeit" – das ist ein Mensch, der (meistens durch Tod, Wahnsinn, Unglück, Macht, Lärm, Erfolgszufälle) die Phantasie der Nachfolgenden dazu anregt, das bloß Wirkliche, Empirische in Geschichte und Wahrheit umzudichten'; o.c., footnote, 398–399.

22 *SzW*, 67.
23 'das auswertende Tier'; *BEK* (quoted from the reprint Leipzig 2012), 204.
24 'Die Geschichtsbetrachtung schafft aus Machtstatsachen Rechtstatsachen und macht zufällige Fakten "sinnvoll".'; o.c., 205.

epistemological criticism implies that the discipline of history does not offer – indeed, cannot offer – any true knowledge of past reality. Instead, it offers an overpowered version of the past, a fabrication that is primarily the result of present needs, interests, wishes, and ideals. More often than not, these are not the ideals Lessing himself shared... Nevertheless, Lessing did admit that history often plays an important part within a culture, in the sense that the images of the past it sketches may serve as a lodestar in the present. Induced by the outbreak of the First World War, Lessing would develop at length similar thoughts about history in his *Geschichte als Sinngebung des Sinnlosen*.

2 Lessing's Critique of Historical Reason

In 1919 Lessing published his book *Geschichte als Sinngebung des Sinnlosen*, his reflections on historical thinking, induced by the First World War and, in fact, written during the war. It is his main contribution to the philosophy of history, together with the fourth edition of the book that he published in 1927. This fourth edition contains so many changes and alterations that it is, though bearing the same title, almost another book. In chapter five, the fourth edition of *Geschichte als Sinngebung des Sinnlosen* will be discussed, while in this chapter the first edition will be dealt with.

The 1919 edition of *Geschichte als Sinngebung des Sinnlosen* consists of two main parts, the first one discussing "Geschichte als Wirklichkeit" ('History as Reality'), and the second "Geschichte als Ideal" ('History as an Ideal'). In general, one could maintain that the first part is mainly a critique of historical thinking as it is, whereas the second part deals with the issue what function history might have in a culture or society. For even if Lessing is critical, sometimes even extremely, about the claims historians themselves make with regard to their discipline, in particular the claim of offering true knowledge of the past, he does not deny the importance history may have within a culture or society. Or, in the terminology of the English philosopher Francis Bacon (1561–1626), an author Lessing highly appreciated, the book has a destructive part and a constructive one. These observations on the plan of *Geschichte als Sinngebung des Sinnlosen* should, however, not leave the impression that the book is rigidly organised. On the contrary: in writing, Lessing tended to follow his associations quite freely; as a result, at times one comes upon arguments in the first, "destructive" part of the book that one would expect in the second part, or just the other way round.

Even when discussing in the first part of *Geschichte als Sinngebung des Sinnlosen* historical thinking as it is, Lessing hardly mentions contemporary historians, nor does he quote contemporary history books. He is sometimes criticised for this. Though the observation that Lessing hardly refers to historians or history books of his own time is certainly justified, as a criticism it is, I think, misplaced, for it shows a lack of understanding what Lessing's approach is aimed at. After all, Lessing definitely did not undertake an empirical study into the practice of writing history, that is, his question is not: how do historians in actual practice proceed when they write history? This raises the question what his approach actually was.

To answer this question we should, in my opinion, consider Lessing's development in the years preceding the First World War. As we have seen in chapter two, in his youth Lessing had strong literary ambitions; pressured by his father, however, he started reading medicine. But both during his last years at secondary school and his medical studies, he exhibited his interest in philosophy. When living in Munich, he made a turn for philosophy, mainly under the influence of the philosopher and psychologist Theodor Lipps. At the time, Lipps himself was moving away from his original philosophical position – which was not Neo-Kantian, though it resembled Neo-Kantianism in several respects – towards a kind of phenomenology of his own. On the advice of Lipps, in 1906 Lessing – like several other students of Lipps before him – switched to Göttingen, to continue his studies with Edmund Husserl. At that time, Husserl was developing his phenomenology. When, in 1907, Lessing was admitted as *Privatdozent* at the *Technische Hochschule* of his native Hanover, the main influence on his philosophical thinking definitely was phenomenological – both the phenomenology of Lipps and that of Husserl –, even if earlier influences on his thinking had been Neo-Kantian. Of course, this is not to say that Lessing was an obedient follower of either Lipps or Husserl – he was far too opinionated to be simply a follower. This is plainly manifest, for instance, in his *Antrittskolleg* "Philosophie als Tat", in which he develops the idea that philosophy should eventually contribute to the lessening of the need in the world. Thus, in Lessing's thinking the (political and social) activism is far more prominent than in the philosophy of either Lipps or Husserl. Nevertheless, Lessing's philosophical writings published between 1908 and 1914 – *Der Bruch in der Ethik Kants*, *Studien zur Wertaxiomatik*, the essays collected in *Philosophie als Tat* – clearly show the influence of both Lipps and Husserl. I would therefore argue that it is no overstatement to claim that these books should be classified within the phenomenological tradition.

In his *Studien zur Wertaxiomatik*, Lessing explicitly expounds what phenomenology implies:

> By phenomenology we mean every analytical and abstracting investigation of immediate data of inner perception [...] without mingling

epistemological clarification with the question for existence, that is, without concerning ourselves about whether these phenomena are given in a consciousness, within my 'I' or other 'I's', whether somewhere in time or reality as empirical facts and in an empirical connection.[25]

In conformity with the ideas Husserl expressed at the time, Lessing pointed out that the findings of phenomenology resemble "pure thought" in the sense that they are "intuitively and not demonstrably certain".[26] Lessing adds that

> Phenomenological analyses of ideas are not "sciences", like psychology or natural sciences are "sciences" with their particular objects and methods [...] Phenomenology is epistemology, that is retracing from elementary notions to the immanent perception of data that are immediately given in it. Thus, the phenomenologist does not assume anything "known", neither objects nor an I, neither something objective or something subjective; he does not explain, but elucidate, that is, he investigates everything that for example science achieves, eventually "means".[27]

Hence, the phenomenologist does not deny or contest the findings of the sciences – his questions relate to what these findings imply, how science is possible, and what the meaning of its findings is. Phenomenology

> takes the phenomenon as it finds it, without asking how it can be explained; it is not causal "thinking" [...] but retracing to what is intended in thinking in notions.[28]

---

25 'Unter Phänomenologie aber verstehen wir jede analytische und abstraktive Erforschung unmittelbarer Gegebenheiten innerer Wahrnehmung [...] ohne die erkenntniskritische Klärung mit der Frage nach Existenz zu vermengen, d.h. ohne uns zu kümmern, ob diese Phänomene in einem Bewußtsein, innerhalb meines Ichs oder anderer Iche, ob sie irgendwo zeitlich oder realiter als empirische Fakte und in empirischen Zusammenhängen gegeben sind'; *SzW*, 6.
26 'intuitiv und nicht demonstrativ gewiß'; o.c., 8.
27 'Phänomenologische Begriffsanalysen sind keine "Wissenschaft", so wie Psychologie oder Physik "Wissenschaften" sind mit speziellen natürlichen Gegenständen und Methoden. [...] Phänomenologie ist Erkenntnistheorie, d.h. ein Rückgang von den Elementarbegriffen auf immanente Anschauung des in ihnen unmittelbar Gegebenen. Der Phänomenologe setzt somit nichts "Gewußtes" voraus, weder Gegenstände noch ein Ich, weder Objektives noch Subjektives; er erklärt nicht, sondern klärt auf, d.h. er forscht, was alle das, was Wissenschaft etwa leistet, zuguterletzt zu "bedeuten" habe'; o.c., 9.
28 'nimmt das Phänomen so wie sie es vorfindet, ohne zu fragen, wie es denn etwa zu erklären sei; sie ist kein kausales "Denken" [...] sondern ein Zurückgehen auf das im begrifflichen Denken Intendierte.'; o.c., 10.

In this respect, phenomenology differs from all sciences.

Even if Lessing's rendering of phenomenology clearly shows the influence of Lipps and especially Husserl, when he describes it as analytical and abstractive investigations without assumptions as regards the existence of its data, he is far from uncritically accepting everything that is claimed in the name of phenomenology. "To us it seems inconsequent that recently the so-called phenomenology keeps being more strongly defined as downright science, even as 'knowing or philosophy as such'", Lessing observes.[29] But although Lessing showed some reserve with regard to what was maintained in the name of phenomenology, I think one may conclude that his approach to philosophical problems in the years preceding the First World War may be qualified as phenomenological. He might not have been the most obedient follower of the tradition of phenomenology, he might have taken some liberties in developing his own ideas, but in these years the main influence on his thinking definitely was phenomenology.

In *Geschichte als Sinngebung des Sinnlosen* as well, his approach is phenomenological, I think. The book is certainly not an analysis of the writings of historians or an empirical study of the discipline of history. It actually is, I would argue, an analytical and abstracting investigation into historical thinking as, in Lessing's view, it is immediately given in consciousness. In other words, the book is Lessing's *Wesensschau* of historical thinking; hence, he only sporadically refers to history books or historians: he tries to uncover what historical thinking essentially is, apart from actual examples from historiography.

As noted above, *Geschichte als Sinngebung des Sinnlosen* consists of two parts, one dedicated to "History as Reality" and the other to "History as an Ideal". The first part is subdivided into "two books", the first one on "the epistemology of history", the second book on "the psychology of history". The second part consists of one book only, entitled "History as an Ideal". The two books of part one are preceded by an introduction, in which Lessing expounds his premises. In this portal, he discusses, on the one hand, the commonly made distinction between nature and history, and, on the other hand, his own theory of three spheres.

In his discussion of the distinction between nature and history, Lessing goes back to the argument he already discussed in his *Probevorlesung* "Wissenschaft als Kraftökonomie".

---

29 'Es erscheint uns inkosequent, daß neuerdings immer überschärfter die sogen. Phänomenologie als die Wissenschaft schlechthin, ja als "Erkennen oder Philosophie überhaupt" definiert wird.'; o.c., 9, footnote.

Generally, it is assumed that the natural sciences deal with invented, fictional reality: the reality of atoms, monads, and forces, whereas history deals with (past) reality. The reality of the natural sciences thus is the result of human thinking, but the reality of historiography the result of mirroring "the one, true, real, proper, immediately given reality".[30] Countless great minds adhered to this distinction, which Lessing, however, dismisses as a "delusion".[31] Paradoxically enough, historians readily admit that their approach is more subjective than that of the natural sciences – it would not make sense to write a "Prussian, catholic or Buddhist zoology"[32], but it is completely acceptable for historians to have such a priori sense giving values for a starting-point.[33] Nevertheless, historians claim as well to give a description of (past) reality as such, "immediately and without fuss".[34] Lessing, however, thinks history is neither reality nor science – he intends to demonstrate this by discussing questions like "What do reality, progress, development, sense, reason mean in history?".[35] In this way, he wants to develop a theory of historical categories.

Next, Lessing places history within his own theory of three spheres. Obviously, history does not belong to the sphere of *vitalité*, of original primordial life: after all, history presents "the contents of human consciousness that is called reality",[36] and consciousness only came into existence by breaking out of *vitalité*, incited by need. On the other hand, history does not belong to the sphere of *verité* either: history does not present timeless truths like logic or mathematics, nor eternally valid ideals. So, history does belong to the sphere of *réalité*: "indeed, history is only about reality".[37] Hence, history can never be true: truth, in Lessing's view, is reserved for the sphere of *verité*. This brings Lessing to an interim conclusion:

---

30 'die eine, die wahre, echte, eigentliche, unmittelbar gegebene Wirklichkeit'; GSS, 12.
31 'Wahn'; loc.cit..
32 'Preußische, katholische oder buddhistische Zoologie'; o.c., 13.
33 Lessing writes 'a priori Sinn gebender Willenschaften', which brings us to the question of how to translate so pivotal a term in his thinking as 'Sinn'. The German 'Sinn' can be translated in several different ways, of which two are important in this respect: 'sense' and 'meaning'. Both are more or less adequate, but I think 'sense' is preferable. In 'sense', the connotation with ideology is stronger than in 'meaning', and thus 'sense' corresponds more with what Lessing had in mind.'Willenschaften' is, of course, an untranslatable pun, an allusion to the German 'Wissenschaften' (sciences), that can be roughly translated as 'strivings'.
34 'unmittelbar und ohne Umschweif'; loc.cit..
35 'Was bedeutet Wirklichkeit, Fortschritt, Entwicklung, Sinn, Vernunft in der Geschichte?'; o.c., 14.
36 'den Wirklichkeit genannten Inhalt menschlichen Bewußtseins'; loc.cit..
37 'Geschichte hat in der Tat nur mit Wirklichkeit zu tun'; loc.cit..

> History is temporal reality, and like all contents of consciousness actively shaped by those categories without which the contents of consciousness would not even exist at all: by the forms of connectedness in time, progress, movement, in which an "historical subject" as the bearer of history exists, preserves itself, and endures. In no way, however, does history reveal a hidden sense, a causal connection, a development in time as such; but history is writing histories, that is, founding this sense, providing this causal connection, inventing this development. It does not find the sense of the world; it gives it.[38]

In the main argument of his book, Lessing aims at the underpinning and demonstration of the validity of this preliminary conclusion.

3 Epistemological Questions

In the first book of part one of *Geschichte als Sinngebung des Sinnlosen*, Lessing discusses questions concerning the epistemology of history. Under this heading, he addresses three topics: identity, or the question for the historical subject; causality in history; and the teleology of history. The overall leading question in this first part of book one is, whether the historian can truly know what happened in the past: is it possible to know the past as it actually happened? Like in the portal to the first part of *Geschichte als Sinngebung des Sinnlosen*, Lessing starts with some general questions, which mainly serve as an opportunity to explain more specifically the purposes he has in mind with this book.

At the outset, Lessing resumes the question which he already addressed in the portal to the first part of the book, to wit, whether history simply mirrors (past) reality as such. Not surprisingly, again he argues against this idea. In his argument, he refers to the distinction made by Kant in his *Kritik der reinen Vernunft* between *Wahrnehmungsurteile* ('judgments of perception') and

---

38 'Geschichte ist zeitliche Wirklichkeit und wie jeglicher Bewußtseinsinhalt eben auch aktiv gestaltet durch jene Kategorien, ohne die Bewußtseinsinhalt überhaupt nicht da wäre: durch die Formen des Zusammenhangs in der Zeit, des Fortschreitens, der Bewegung, worin ein "historisches Subjekt" als Träger der Geschichte sich selber hat, hält und erhält. Keineswegs aber wird durch Geschichte ein verborgener Sinn, ein Kausalzusammenhang, eine Entwicklung in der Zeit per se offenbar; sondern Geschichte ist Geschichteschreibung, das heißt die Stiftung dieses Sinnes, die Setzung dieses Kausalzusammenhanges, die Erfindung dieser Entwicklung. Sie vorfindet nicht den Sinn der Welt; sie gibt ihn.'; o.c., 15.

Erfahrungsurteile ('judgments of experience'). Kant's own example, Lessing rightly claims, is illuminating. If I notice that the sun shines, and that a rock is warm, this is a judgment of perception. But if I observe that the rock is warm *because* it is heated by the sun, this is a judgment of experience. According to Kant, a judgment of perception is not science: science only starts with judgments of experience. Lessing claims exactly the same holds true for history:

> Mere ascertainment of occurrences in time never is history [...] History only arises, when the occurrence gets the character of an event within a chronology that is arranged according to a viewpoint of evaluation.[39]

In other words, history does not mirror (past) reality, history orders (past) reality; and it orders (past) reality by means of a pre-existing frame: a viewpoint of evaluation. The confusion over this question stems, Lessing claims, from the very fact that the meaning of the word "history" is ambiguous: it may mean "the writing of history", "what happened in the past", or "the contents of what happened in the past". In everyday language, these various meanings are not kept apart; as a result, characteristics of history in one sense of the word are unthinkingly attributed to history in another sense of the word. Notions like unity, progress, development, and so on, belong to the domain of "writing history", but quite often they are unthinkingly attributed to "what happened in the past". But, Lessing maintains, "the unity of history does not exist but in the act of unification"[40] by the historian, that is, in the writing of history. The writing of history, however, is driven by the "desire and will, want and aim"[41] of mankind. Lessing intends to demonstrate irrefutably how "the contents of consciousness or object of history" is linked with "the preoccupations, that is, the prejudices and pre-valuations of the historian".[42] All this implies that the "sense of history is merely the sense that I give myself and historical development is the

---

39   'Die bloße Feststellung individueller Geschehnisse in der Zeit ist niemals Geschichte [...] Geschichte wird erst dann, wenn in einer nach einem Wertgesichtpunkt geordneten Zeitreihe das Geschehnis den Charakter des Ereignisses erhält.'; o.c., 17.
40   'Einheit der Geschichte [besteht] nirgendwo, wenn nicht in dem Akte der Vereinheitlichung'; o.c., 19.
41   'Wunsch und Wille, Bedürfnis und Absicht'; loc.cit..
42   'Bewußtseinsinhaltes oder Gegenstandes Geschichte'; 'Präokkupationen, d.h. zu den Vorurteilen und Vorwertungen der Geschichteschreiber'; loc.cit.. Lessing's use of 'Bewußtseinsinhaltes' in this respect supports, I think, my claim that his approach in *Geschichte als Sinngebung des Sinnlosen* is in accordance with the tradition of phenomenology.

development from me and towards me."[43] Lessing wants to demonstrate for history what Kant had done for the world of objects: "to understand, not human affairs out of reality, but reality out of consciousness."[44] In other words, Lessing tries to show how human consciousness transforms mere occurrences in the past into history. The result of this transformation is by definition not "true" – truth, after all, never is, nor can be, dependent of the wants of mankind.

Lessing claims that any science is either descriptive or explanatory. Botany and zoology are examples of purely descriptive and classificatory sciences. But in this sense, history is not, nor can it be, a purely descriptive science, Lessing argues. History, after all, describes events by placing them in the course of time – but time, like space and causality, is generated with, and by, human consciousness. That is, as Lessing contends in his theory of three spheres, ever since consciousness was born out of need, it orders reality which it is conscious off by using categories like time, space, and causality. In other words, time did not nor does exist in *vitalité*: "historical time comes into existence with the clock and the law that measures time".[45] This implies, Lessing maintains, that history and historical thinking are characteristic of the Western world: history, in the sense of world history or the history of art and so on, did not exist in antiquity, nor does it exist in the Orient.[46] This indicates that people in antiquity were, and in the Orient are "closer" to *vitalité* than people in the Western world: in the Western world the process of disassociation of *vitalité* is much more advanced than in either antiquity or in the Orient.

Lessing subsequently discusses the subject of history. If we write the history of, say, Europe, or the history of a political party, we simply assume that Europe or this political party exist. We do not come upon Europe or this political party when we are writing history, that is, they are not the result of historical thinking – we assume that they exist before we start writing their history. Thus, they are, as Lessing calls it, the "bearing I" of history, "that historical subject, to which we relate all history as its history".[47] In other words, if we write the history of Europe, "Europe" is the "bearing I" of history, to which we relate all of history

---

43   'Sinn von Geschichte ist allein jener Sinn, den ich mir selber gebe, und geschichtliche Entwicklung ist die Entwicklung von Mir aus und zu Mir hin'; loc.cit..
44   'Nicht die menschlichen Angelegenheiten aus Wirklichkeit, sondern Wirklichkeit aus Bewußtsein zu begreifen'; loc.cit..
45   'die historische Zeit entsteht mit der Uhr und dem zeitmessenden Gesetz.'; o.c., 21.
46   O.c., 30.
47   'jenes geschichtliche Subjekt, auf welches wir alle Geschichte beziehn, als seine Geschichte'; o.c., 22.

– we see all of history in the light of the history of Europe. What more can we say about the subject of history? "What else is this historical subject striding through history, what else can it be, but a self-concerned reflection of our own image?", Lessing claims, what else but "a kind of idol-human with all the interests, needs for happiness and strivings for self-preservation of our species?"[48] So, in Lessing's view, whether we write the history of Europe, or the history of a political party, or the history of whichever phenomenon, eventually the subject of history is nothing but the mirror image of the knowing subject, that is, of the historian – not so much as an individual, but as a representative of his or her time, nation, class, and so on. But this mirror-image, this idol-human, is a kind of abstraction, an imaginary construction stripped of all specific individual characteristics – eventually being nothing but a completely empty form. An empty form, however, which can be filled with all kinds of wants, sufferings, needs, love, and hate:

> Because without this engagement either in favour or against, everything historical would be completely dead, and a matter of indifference. However, by imparting evaluative emphasis to occurrences that are insignificant, incalculable, or endless as such, depending on whether we find ourselves and our individual or shared prejudices confirmed or rejected by them, we reach the so-called historical connection.[49]

In other words, what we call historical connections are nothing but webs of which the historian him- or herself is both the centre and the origin. This implies that

> We consider even the most senseless historical reality, like the blood shedding acts and atrocities of, say, Timur, historically inevitable and necessary, because without Timur's appearance in history, currently Turks

---

48 'Was aber ist dieses durch Geschichte schreitende geschichtliche Subjekt anders, was kann es anders sein als eine ichbezügliche Spiegelung unseres eigenes Bildes?'; 'eine Art Anbild-Mensch mit allen Interessen, Glücksbedürfnissen und Erhaltungsstrebungen unserer Gattung?'; o.c., 22.'Anbild' is not a common German word; it roughly means 'an image that is an example'.

49 'Denn ohne diese Teilnahme Für oder Wider wäre alles Historische völlig tot und das Eine so gut wie das Andere. Indem wir aber den an sich gleichgültigen, unübersehbaren oder uferlosen Geschehnissen Wertakzente verleihen, je nachdem wir uns selbst und unsere Einzel- oder Gruppenvorurteile durch sie bestätigt oder verworfen finden, kommen wir zum sogenannten geschichtlichen Zusammenhang.'; o.c., 23.

would rule Europe and our own highly esteemed world history would not be. Thus, a logificatio post festum, underlies all history, whatever happens in the world.[50]

Though Lessing does not explicitly draw the parallel with his own time, given the fact that he wrote *Geschichte als Sinngebung des Sinnlosen* during the war, the resemblances with the First World War are all too obvious – all senseless blood shedding, all atrocities can be considered historically, that is, they can be considered inevitably and necessary from some point of view. Whatever happens, a historian may give it sense.

What we eventually remember about history, is therefore nothing but the ghostly-abstract and worthless pushing back and forth of nations on maps – that is, what we actually call world history. Everything truly human about it has been forgotten for a long time. Forgotten are – here Lessing explicitly refers to the First World War – the flowers that were crushed when Liège was occupied, forgotten are the skies over Belgrade, forgotten the animals that were burned when Louvain was on fire – forgotten everyone and everything that did not immediately contribute to what we call our world history. In this sense, history is similar to the natural sciences. For the reality of the natural sciences is an abstraction from the concrete world as well: atoms, monads, molecules are as much fiction as the abstractions of history are fiction, Lessing claims.

But if we try to consider history apart from the ideologically charged abstractions by historians, what, eventually, is it? "Senseless tragedies of life of an anthill, which, driven by hunger, oestrum, vanity, lives on until it will perish without a trace [...] like everything perished."[51] After all, Lessing claims, "one can never find reason and ethics in history itself."[52] And if the definition of history by the German philosopher Wilhelm Dilthey (1833–1911) is valid, claiming that man can only come to self-knowledge through history, man can learn nothing else, Lessing says, but that he is a mixture of a fool and a brute.[53] Moreover, one should never forget, Lessing claims, "that even our most comprehensive "world history" remains the Western matter of a well-defined family and,

---

50 'Wir beurteilen sogar die unsinnigste historische Wirklichkeit, etwa die Bluttaten und Greuel eines Timur, als historisch unvermeidlich und notwendig, weil ohne Timurs geschichtliche Erscheinung heute Türken in Europa herrschen würden und unsere eigene wertgehaltene Weltgeschichte nicht vorhanden wäre. So liegt aller Geschichte eine logificatio post festum zugrunde, was auch immer auf Erden geschehen mag.'; o.c., 23–24.
51 'Sinnlose Lebenstragödien eines Ameisenhaufen, der, von Hunger, Brunst, Eitelkeit getrieben, dahinlebt, bis er [...] spurlos zugrundegehen wird, wie alles verging.'; o.c., 26.
52 'Man kann aber niemals Vernunft und Ethik in der Geschichte selber vorfinden'; o.c., 28.
53 O.c., 29.

in the not very distant hour when European civilisation perishes, will perish with it."⁵⁴

As an additional argument against the idea that history mirrors past reality as such, Lessing denies the reality of collectives as they are frequently discussed in history: collectives like religious sects, social groups, political parties, nations, cities, and so on. Such collectives merely show some continuity, Lessing claims, but they lack reality, that is, they do not really exist; and after some time the founding fathers of, say, a political party are no more than a hardly remembered name. All in all, Lessing contends, these collectives are no more than imaginary forces in history.⁵⁵ – Here, Lessing's argument foreshadows the objections the English philosopher of history R.G. Collingwood (1889–1943) would later make against what he called "substantialism" or "essentialism", i.e., the idea that if one writes the history of, say, ancient Rome, there must be some kind of substance, or essence, or unchanging kernel that is present throughout all of this history, it essentially *being* ancient Rome. Lessing claims that if a phenomenon lacks such substance or essence, it does not really exist, and thus is no more than imaginary. Collingwood opposed this substantialism as well, but unlike Lessing does not consider it an argument against the reality of these phenomena, nor against the validity of historical thinking. On the contrary, according to Collingwood historical thinking should abstain from thinking that substances or essences exist: it should recognize that historical thinking implies acknowledging that the phenomena it studies develop and change continuously, and that these phenomena never have an unchanging kernel.⁵⁶

Lessing goes on to discuss causality in history – a topic which for him is yet another argument against the idea that history mirrors past reality. Like time and space, causality is one of the categories man uses to order the reality which he is conscious off, Lessing maintains. That is, causality is one of the categories which came into being when consciousness was born out of need. Hence, causality does not exist in *vitalité*, only in *réalité*, like time and space only exist in *réalité*."After the unexpected, meaningless, absurd, abrupt suddenly broke in and became an occurrence, man will always look for reasons and always will

---

54 'daß auch unsere umfassendste "Weltgeschichte" die abendländische Angelegenheit eines eng umgrenzten Geschlechtes bleibt und in der nicht allzu fernen Stunde, wo die europäische Kultur zugrundegeht, mit zugrundegehen muß.'; o.c., 30.
55 O.c., 31–32.
56 Cfr. R.G. Collingwood, *The Idea of History*, revised edition, edited with an introduction by Jan van der Dussen (Oxford etc. 1993), 42 *ff.*

find reasons, why everything had to happen as it happened",[57] Lessing claims. In other words, causal judgments emanate from psychic needs of mankind, not from scientific research. In fact, this way of thinking in terms of causes is nothing but a basic psychic want of mankind, even a superstition. And this superstition reached a high degree of absurdity during the "current war", Lessing writes – with authors explaining that the war was inevitable and necessary because of the position of the stars, or because of the extremely low level of groundwater all over Europe, and so on. "With a similar logic, geologists 'explained' the war from changes in the earth, chemists from incidents in the circulation of matter, physiologists from processes in the nerves, psychologists from the laws of the soul; and one series of causes is as good and as reassuring as the other", Lessing observes.[58]

The peculiarity of this kind of reasoning is even more evident, according to Lessing, when historians discuss motives as causes of events. The historian, remarkably enough, does not even confine him- or herself to assigning all kinds of motives to individual persons – "he courageously lets motives being operative between peoples and groups, about which the single parts of these peoples and groups, to wit individuals, could either not learn at all, or only years later; like everyone only retrospectively learns from books, what the *Zeitgeist* or the *Volksgeist*, in general the style and character of his age was, even though he himself was part of this age."[59] Similarly, a people gets informed whether to love or to hate another people – so in 1916, the Japanese are supposed to love the Russians, Lessing observes, whereas only ten years before they were supposed to hate the very same Russians. But, Lessing maintains, whatever historians claim, peoples as such do neither love nor hate; a people quite simply has to deal with the changes of policy its government sees fit to put into effect.

But there is even a more general problem with regard to assigning motives to people, and to put forward these motives as cause for what happened in

---

57   'Nachdem das Unerwartete, Widersinnige, Absurde, Abrupte plötzlich eingebrochen und Ereignis geworden ist, wird der Mensch immer Gründe suchen und immer Gründe finden, warum alles so habe kommen müssen, wie es eben kam.'; Theodor Lessing, o.c., 38.
58   'Mit ähnlicher Logik haben Geologen aus Erdveränderungen, Chemiker aus Vorgängen des Stoffwechsels, Physiologen aus Nervenprozessen, Psychologen aus seelischen Gesetzen den Krieg verklärt; und die eine Kausalreihe ist ebenso gültig und ebenso beruhigend wie die andere.'; o.c., 39.
59   'Er läßt kühnerhand sogar zwischen Völker und Gruppen Motive walten, von denen die einzelnen Bestandteile dieser Völker und Gruppen, nämlich die Individuen, entweder gar nicht oder doch erst viele Jahre später erfahren können; so wie jedermann erst nachträglich aus Büchern erfährt, wie die Zeitgeist oder der Volksgeist, überhaupt der Stil und Charakter seiner Zeit gewesen sei, obwohl er ein Stück dieser Zeit eben selber war.'; o.c., 40.

history, Lessing claims. Even an individual cannot say with certainty what the motives for his own actions are. The stories an individual tells about the motives that underlie his actions are a typical example of *logificatio post festum*, according to Lessing: motives do not precede actions, actions precede motives. But even though it is rather problematic to assign motives to one's own actions, historians commonly without reservations do not hesitate to assign motives to collectives, and even to entire parts of the world, like Europe. But, Lessing asks,

> where exactly lie the motives of history? Who has them? Who raises them? I mean those motives, about which the historian drivels, when he writes for example: "The trade envy of England caused the 1914 war." "With noble wrath all of Germany rose." "The call for revenge shook all of France." "All of Italy was glowing with enthusiasm."[60]

Eventually, such observations are nothing but symbolic abbreviations, and it is not at all clear what they imply; moreover, every case may be different. What, for example, did really underlie the enthusiasm with which the war was greeted in Germany in August 1914,

> How much herd compulsion, psychic surprise, unhealthy anxiety, mass suggestions, will to power, lack of judgment, sense of adventure, stupidity, delusion, and so on, actually occurs, the most noble magnanimity and simplicity not less than any criminal instinct and any self-deceit.[61]

It is hardly surprising that with such critical observations on the "spirit of 1914" and the "ideas of 1914", Lessing incited the animosity, even hate, of those right wing and nationalist groups, which in the interwar period saw this very "spirit of 1914" and these very "ideas of 1914" as the spiritual foundation of a future Germany. Be that as it may, Lessing gathers some fundamental questions from these observations:

---

60 'Wo denn eigentlich liegen die Motive der Geschichte? Wer hat sie? Wer trägt sie empor? Ich meine jene Motive, von denen der Historiker faselt, indem er etwa schreibt: "Der Handelsneid Englands verschuldete den Krieg von 1914". "In edlem Zorn erhob sich das gesamte Deutschland". "Der Ruf nach Rache durchzitterte ganz Frankreich". "Ganz Italien war von Begeisterung durchglüht".'; o.c., 43.

61 'Wie viel Herdentrieb, psychische Überrumpelung, ungesunde Angstneurose, Massensuggestionen, Machtwilligkeit, Urteilslosigkeit, Abenteuerlust, Dummheit, Wahn usw. eigentlich eingeht, edelste Herzenshoheit und Einfalt nicht minder als jeglicher Verbrecherinstinkt und jegliche Selbsttäuschung'; o.c., 44.

Who, from the bottom of his heart, believes in peoples, states, groups, universalities? Who believes in historical motives?[62]

In the light of all this, it is nothing less than superstition, if one believes that history mirrors past reality, Lessing concludes: history, on the contrary, is nothing but the way to conquer irrational chaos by giving sense to occurrences that are senseless *in se*, and thus to make life bearable.

Yet another argument against assigning motives to people from the past is, according to Lessing, the fact that the human mind-set changed: humans nowadays are so very different from humans about, say, two thousand years ago that we simply do not understand what induced them to do what they did do. As a result, historians regularly assign the wrong motives to people of the past, sometimes even motives contrary to what really induced them.[63] – Lessing's argument here seems to be self-refuting: when he claims that historians assign the wrong motives to people of the past, he apparently knows what these motives actually were. This implies that there must be a way of knowing these motives after all. – Moreover, Lessing claims, "there necessarily is an injustice implied when the historian explains everything his hero did out of heroic, everything his stepchildren did out of low motives."[64] At present, Lessing maintains, czar Nicolas II gets most of the blame for causing the 1914 war, but probably the war is more of a torment for him than for any other head of state – the czar was forced into a war, for fear of losing his throne, or even his life.[65] – With this, Lessing again advances an opinion on current events which goes against the view that at the time dominated public opinion in Germany. –

All in all, Lessing claims, one simply has to conclude that in considering causes in history, the motives historians assign to people of the past are no more than simplifying fictions: this consideration therefore supports his position that the reality of history is an alleged reality that takes the place of the irrational chaos that the past actually is. Even if historians themselves seem to realize that the way they transform what happened in the past into a coherent history sometimes goes too far, they nevertheless tend to stick to it. After all, the need to give sense to the past and the related need for causality first and foremost have a function for the human psyche: they serve to give rest

---

62 'Wer glaubt denn in der Tiefe des Herzens ab Völker, Staaten, Gruppen, Genera? Wer glaubt an historische Motive?'; loc. cit..
63 O.c., 45–46.
64 'Auch liegt eine notwendige Ungerechtigkeit darin, daß der Historiker seinen Helden alles aus heldischen, seinen Stiefkindern alles aus niedrigen Motiven deutet.'; o.c., 46.
65 Loc.cit..

to the soul, they satisfy the need for mental balance in human beings. Simply explaining what happened by claiming it had to happen as it happened, usually is enough to quiet a tormented soul, Lessing maintains. In practice, this almost always implies affirming situations as they are. Even situations which are highly unfair – hunger, war, slavery – simply are accepted once they are explained historically, that is, once they are described as inevitable and necessary from a particular point of view. Thus, almost anything can be made acceptable – "if need will force to eat human flesh, then science will prove it is healthy", Lessing cynically observes.[66] But eventually, it all comes down to a tendency that all humans seem to have in common: the inclination to accept voluntarily what they have to accept anyway, because they cannot change it. Thus, we keep up the illusion of freedom, whereas in fact necessity forces us. And this implies that we retrospectively approve what happened, irrespective of we previously wanted it to happen or not. This, indeed, is what we call causal explanation, Lessing claims. Usually, this means that we retrospectively approve what was successful, and disapprove what was a failure: eventually, success is the measuring staff the historian uses when judging history. Historians adore those who succeeded, and despise those who failed – the true villain in history is the one who fails to achieve. On the other hand, even the utmost cruelties will be forgiven the one who is successful. Success in history, however, is not a personal merit, as the course of history is determined by blind chance, neither by personal qualities nor by a lack of personal qualities.[67] After all, Lessing claims, "world historical decisions which retrospectively seem meaningful and seem to reveal values, may depend on extremely trivial accidents of the nerves".[68] Had, for instance, Napoleon lost his ability to sleep at will not in 1815, but already in, say, 1797, would world history not have run a different course?

Lessing connects these criticisms of historical causality with the idea of *logificatio post festum* that he developed in several earlier publications.[69] Starting-point for his argument here is the observation that the Greek word αἰτία means both "cause" and "culpability": the ancient Greeks did not distinguish between a natural cause and a cause in the moral sense of the word. For the Greeks, Lessing maintains, "everything logical originally is of a moral

---

66 'würde Not dazu zwingen, Menschenfleisch zu essen, so würde die Wissenschaft beweisen, daß das gesund sei.'; o.c., 48.
67 O.c., 49–52.
68 'weltgeschichtliche Entscheide, die von hinterher sinnvoll und wertoffenbarend scheinen [können] von ganz banalen Zufällen der Nerven abhängen.'; o.c., 55.
69 Cfr. chapter two, above, 97–98.

character",[70] that is, trying to point out a cause really is looking for culpability – a causal judgment eventually is a moral judgment. Even though this does not seem to be realized, this very way of thinking did not disappear, but still is dominant in modern Western culture. Though we tend to distinguish "cause" and "culpability", nevertheless with a causal judgment a moral judgment is still tacitly implied. We blame a draught when we catch a cold – but this always implies a moral judgment as well as a causal judgment, Lessing claims. The moral aspect of this judgment first and foremost serves to quiet our souls: it gives us the illusion that we could have controlled the situation (by closing the window to prevent a draught, for instance) and, even more important, that we can control similar situations in future.

In Lessing's view, two different kinds of historical causality should be distinguished: the causality of the scapegoat, and the causality of sin. The causality of the scapegoat hardly needs explaining: it simply implies blaming a scapegoat for something going wrong. Under the causality of sin, however, an individual or group blames its own faults in explaining failure and suffering. This quite commonly implies explaining accidents, defeats in war, and even natural disasters as a judgment by God, following misbehaviour by an individual or group. This exactly fits the causal superstition of historical science, Lessing claims. On the other hand, success is often explained by claiming God was on the side of the winner, as could be observed following the first German military victories in August 1914. Sometimes, this line of reasoning is expressed by referring, not to God, but to the working of Reason in history, but the argument is essentially the same, Lessing maintains.[71] But eventually, this way of giving sense to history is nothing but an "emergency exit" for the tormented soul.[72] This kind of reasoning is characteristic of history – instances of this quite peculiar logic are observations like:

> The world war had to be, in order to knit humanity together for a war to end war. It was historically necessary for me to break a leg, in order that in future I would be more careful not to break a leg.[73]

---

70   'alles Logische ursprünglich von moralischer Art ist.'; Lessing, o.c., 56.
71   Of course, this is an allusion the philosophy of history of G.W.F. Hegel.
72   The German word for 'emergency exit' is 'Notausgang', yet another example of the way Lessing in his philosophy of need plays with the different meanings of the word 'Not'.
73   'Der Weltkrieg mußte sein, um die Menschheit zum Krieg gegen den Krieg zusammenzuschmieden. Es war geschichtlich nötig, daß ich mir ein Bein brach, um künftig mich besser gegen Beinbruch in acht zu nehmen.'; Lessing, o.c., 61.

This peculiar kind of logic provokes strange behaviour, Lessing claims: "When for example in June 1916 in Germany the news spread that the English Admiral of the Fleet Kitchener had died in a shipping accident, flags were put out in the streets of German cities, and from the pulpit it was preached that God had executed a judgment on England, and through this accident wanted to show his will".[74] Lessing concludes that "an unheard primitive directedness towards itself and towards its own" characterizes "the so-called science of reality, history."[75] However, because "the history of the defeated is always written by the winners, of the dead by the survivors",[76] this tendency usually will be unthinkingly accepted. This tendency implies that all history eventually is nothing but a preparatory phase for the present. Hence, it implies the ability to bear heroically "immense numbers of torments, ceaseless downfalls of others".[77] But as long as the historian and his or her ideals – or the ideals of his or her community or nation – are not threatened, seeing the past a preparatory stage for the present will be unquestionably accepted, Lessing maintains.

Of course, it is possible to distinguish between two points of view with regard to history – the point of view of those who make history, and the one of those who undergo history; that is, the point of view of the decision makers and that of the cannon fodder. Which point of view is chosen naturally makes a big difference:

> How would a history written from the position of those who got off badly change historical traditions? How could a history of Rome and the Roman Empire be written from the Punic position? How a history of Spain from the position of the Aztecs?[78]

---

74 'Als z.B. im Juni 1916 in Deutschland die Kunde sich verbreitete, daß der englische Großadmiral Kitchener bei einem Schiffsunglück ums Leben kam, wurde in den Straßen der deutschen Städte geflaggt und von den Kanzeln gepredigt, Gott habe an England ein Strafgericht vollziehen und durch den Unglücksfall seinen Willen beweisen wollen'; o.c., 62.
75 'der sogenannten Wirklichkeitswissenschaft Geschichte'; loc.cit..
76 'Immer schreiben Sieger die Geschichte von Besiegten, Lebensgebliebenen die von Toten'; o.c., 63.
77 'unermeßliche Summen von Qualen anderer, unaufhörliche Untergänge anderer'; loc.cit..
78 'Wie würde eine Geschichtsschreibung vom Standpunkt der Schlechtweggekommenen die historischen Überlieferungen ändern? Wie würde Geschichte Roms und des römischen Reiches vom punischen Standpunkt aus zu schreiben sein? Wie Geschichte Spaniens vom Standpunkt der Azteken? '; loc.cit..

What happened in history, be it the fall of the Roman Empire or the rise of the United States, is neither good nor bad, neither positive nor negative as such, Lessing maintains; whether we consider it good or bad depends on the position of the historian; and the judgment of the historian is determined by present, personal necessities. In this respect, it would for instance be interesting to study a theme like the resentment of the historian in historiography. Tacitus, for example, claimed to write history *sine ira et studio*, but he produced highly biased texts, which nevertheless even today influence our view of Roman and German history, and by some readers are considered true. The positions of historians change in course of time, Lessing observes: positions that were common coin fifty years ago are completely unacceptable now, and vice versa. If at present one disapproves of the annexation of Alsace, one is seen as a traitor of the ideals of the German nation, Lessing claims; but had one defended the annexation of Alsace fifty years ago, one would have been seen as... a traitor of the ideals of the German nation. This holds true for all ideals in history, and thus for the writing of history with these very ideals as a starting-point: they can change overnight. A typical example is, in Lessing's view, what happened in August 1914, when "European socialism, woefully characterless missed the decisive moment when its international ideas had to prove themselves and could have become true, but rethought the old international phraseology immediately, as soon as the masses wanted to hear it again".[79] Hence, it can hardly be denied that the writing of history eventually is nothing but an activity with practical goals, it accordingly being a function of present needs. History may be about the past, but present needs dictate which story will be told about the past. Lessing's position is in this respect close to that of the Italian philosopher Benedetto Croce (1866–1952) who, in his *Teoria e storia della storiografia* (1916) argues that the questions historians ask about the past by definition are questions that arise in the present. In this sense, Croce famously argues, "all veritable history is contemporary history".[80] According to Croce, this is even the fundamental difference between history proper and chronicles: chronicles are ordered in accordance with chronological sequence, whereas history proper is arranged according to questions as they arise in the present. In contrast to Lessing, however, Croce does not conclude from this that this

---

79 'oder wie der europäische Sozialismus, August 1914, den entscheidenden Augenblick, wo sein internationaler Gedanke sich erproben und zur Wahrheit werden konnte, kläglich charakterlos verpaßte, aber auf die alte internationale Phraseologie sich sofort besann, sobald die Massen sie wieder zu hören wünschten'; o.c., 68.
80 'Ogni vera storia e storia contemporanea'; Benedetto Croce, *Teoria e storia della storiografia* ('Theory and history of historiography'; quoted from the second revised edition, Bari 1920), 4.

necessarily implies that for this very reason it is impossible to know what happened in the past. Both Lessing and Croce claim that the writing of history is a function of the present; for Lessing, this implies that we ultimately cannot know the past, for Croce, it does not. This is, of course, not to say that according to Croce it is possible to know the past as it "really" happened: he is fully aware of the fact that the past as such is gone, and that the past that the historian describes is a construction based on evidence the past has left. This realization does not bring Croce to the drastic scepticism as regards our knowledge of the past, however, as put forward by Lessing.

The two different points of view from which one may consider history are exemplified by the positions of two nineteenth century German philosophers, Lessing claims: G.W.F. Hegel and Arthur Schopenhauer. Hegel is an outstanding example of a philosopher who considers history from the position of the maker of history: "Hegel always considers his very own logical I as the acting subject of history".[81] Schopenhauer, on the other hand, is an outstanding example of a philosopher who considers history from the perspective of those who endure history."Both of these thinkers represent opposite poles of conceptions of history", Lessing maintains.[82] Ordinary men usually take now the one, then the other conception of history as their starting-point, and sometimes even both at the very same time, their thinking about history usually not being very systematic. Be that as it may, eventually "views on history prove what a human being wants and needs".[83] In the end, it comes down to a very simple formula, Lessing claims: "'I want to eat' or 'I don't want to be eaten'."[84]

Next, Lessing discusses the third and last topic of his considerations on the epistemology of history: the teleology of history.

If one considers history as a development in the course of time, it by definition has to have a goal: "all development strives for a goal", Lessing maintains.[85] But the very goal of this development always is nothing but "the own living I of the thinking person!", according to Lessing.[86] In the image "of the living I, history is being thought and written. All history!".[87] Irrespective of whether it is the history of a person or a group, a political party, a city, nation, or even a part

---

81 'Immer denkt Hegel sein eigenstes logisches Ich als handelendes Subjekt der Geschichte.'; Theodor Lessing, o.c., 70.
82 'Die beiden Denker vertreten Gegenpole der Geschichtsauffassung.'; loc.cit..
83 'Geschichtliche Meinungen beweisen, was ein Mensch will und was er nötig hat.'; o.c., 71.
84 '"Ich will fressen" oder "Ich will nicht gefressen werden".'; loc.cit..
85 'alle Entwicklung ist zielstrebig.'; o.c., 76.
86 'das eigene lebendige Ich des Denkenden!'; loc.cit..
87 'des lebendigen Ich wird Geschichte gedacht und geschrieben. Jede Geschichte! '; loc.cit..

of the world like Europe – the historian inevitably puts himself or herself in the story: it is inevitable that the historian, in describing the past, "at the same time lays down his I".[88] This implies that history, as it is recorded by the historian, never is nor can be the process of life itself:

> The experience as experiencing and as ascertained experience very obviously are of two kinds. They not only can, but they should be distinguished![89]

In other words, even recording an experience transforms the experience – which, Lessing explicitly claims, implies a criticism of contemporary schools in philosophy like for instance phenomenology, which pretend that it is possible to describe experiences as they are experienced, that is, without transforming them. But then again, Lessing maintains, "the great European war most clearly showed what conceptual philosophy that speculates behind closed windows about history, logic, ethics, sense and development in the midst of war and murder, and probably at the end of the world as well, eventually is worthy of".[90] In a footnote to this passage, Lessing refers to his brief discussion of statements by the philosophers Georg Simmel, Edmund Husserl, Hermann Cohen, and Heinrich Rickert in the first edition of his *Europa und Asien*; all four claimed, judging from the citations Lessing quotes, that philosophy should not worry about contemporary events like the war, but rather focus on higher, abstract truths.[91] – Clearly, Lessing here distances himself from phenomenology where

---

88 'zugleich sein Ich niederlegt'; loc.cit..
89 'Das Erlebnis als Erleben und als konstatiertes Erleben sind ganz offenbar zweierlei. Sie können nicht nur, sondern müssen unterschieden werden!'; o.c., 77.
90 'Der große europäische Krieg hat aufs klarste bewiesen, was Begriffsphilosophie, die inmitten von Völkerbrand und Menschenmord, und wahrscheinlich auch noch beim Untergang der Erde hinter geschlossenen Fenstern über Geschichte, Logik, Ethik, Sinn und Entwicklung spekuliert, schließlich wert ist.'; o.c., 78.
91 Cfr. *EuA,* 52. The quotations in question are: 'Das menschliche Denken vollzieht sich unberührt von geschichtlicher Wirklichkeit nach seinen eigenen Gesetzen.' (Simmel; 'human thought develops untouched by historical reality along laws of ist own.'); 'Die Philosophie ist reine Wissenschaft und hat als solche gar nichts mit allgemeiner Kultur zu tun.' (Husserl; 'Philosophy is a pure science and has as such nothing to do with general culture.'); 'Das Denken macht die Welt als ein System abstrakter Symbole.' (Cohen; 'Thinking creates the world as a system of abstract symbols.'); 'Ich hoffe, daß man meinem Werk nicht anmerkt, daß Kanonendonner hineindröhnte.' (Rickert; 'I hope one cannot notice from my work that the boom of canons roared into it.'). Lessing wondered, whether philosophers who wrote sentences like these were truly alive... *Europa und Asien* originates in a series of lectures Lessing delivered in the autumn of 1914. Lessing published parts of these lectures in the journal *Die Aktion* in 1917; the first edition of this book is

it abstains from speaking about contemporary political and social problems. Nevertheless, I think that *Geschichte als Sinngebung des Sinnlosen* in its general approach belongs to the phenomenological tradition, though Lessing tries to combine phenomenology with a more activist attitude. –

Lessing claims that historiography is subject to the very same psychological laws to which the consciousness of an individual is subject when dealing with personal experiences. Similar to the consciousness of an individual, historiography readjusts experiences over and over again, for as long as necessary until they fit the connection they are supposed to fit. In case this is not feasible, the experiences in question are simply ignored; but this is exceptional. All experiences, though, that are transformed into history, are assigned a place in a particular development, and thus by definition serve a specific goal. But as historians usually simply ignore and even dissociate themselves from asking epistemological questions, they at will and light-heartedly find as much "sense, development, goal, reason, necessary epochs, times of transition, heydays, times of decline, laws of levels, rhythmic periods, simultaneities, similarities, meaningful parallels in history" as they like.[92] They simply never dwell on the question what all these notions mean, and this is the very reason they continue using these notions without any concern, Lessing argues. But according to Lessing, it always comes down to this: "a situation or substance, which according to the verdict of the historian is useful or desirable, is made into the provisional end of a chain of historical development, and thus towards this provisional end all occurrences have to be oriented and ordered".[93] But this is nothing but "enormous self-deceit of all who write history".[94] In the end, what we can learn from historiography is only what kind of a person the historian in question is, and what he or she values: the point of view of the historian determines what history is. If the historian focuses on either politics or economics or on cultural or intellectual development – then politics or economics or cultural or intellectual development is the decisive factor in history. As a result, it is all too easy to explain retrospectively what happened in history: historians

---

based on the texts in *Die Aktion*. See Theodor Lessing, 'Europa und Asien', *Die Aktion* 7 (1917), col. 317–319, 347–350, 365–370, 449–454, 506–508, and 550–551.

92 'Sinn, Entwicklung, Ziel, Vernunft, notwendige Epochen, Übergangszeiten, Blütezeiten, Verfallszeiten, Stufengesetze, rhythmische Perioden, Gleichzeitigkeiten, Korrespondenzen, sinnreiche Parallelen'; GSS, 79.

93 'ein Zustand oder Inhalt, der nach Urteil des Historikers für nützlich oder wünschenswert zu gelten hat, wird zum vorläufigen Endpunkt einer historischen Entwicklungskette gemacht, auf welchen Punkt hin man die Ereignisse daher hinorientieren und hingruppieren muß'; o.c., 80.

94 'dieser ungeheure Selbstbetrug aller Geschichteschreibenden'; loc.cit..

simply find what they look for, because they only see what they look for…. In retrospect, the storming of the Bastille started the French Revolution in 1789 – but at the time, no one really bothered, let alone saw it as the start of a revolution. So much for historical necessity: it simply is what historians themselves assign to history, Lessing claims.[95]

Ultimately, history is completely senseless, Lessing maintains, and he quotes an observation attributed to Montesquieu: "Happy the people whose history is boring". History is a "senseless hell of never wanting to end fights for a change of power, a continuous battle of all against all".[96] But man gives sense to history, indeed, man has to give sense to history, because "it would be impossible for the human mind to imagine historical realities without sense, because the reality of which we are conscious already implies being formed".[97] Hence, according to Lessing it is impossible to believe in natural development, progress, immanent order of values, God, or God guiding history: they are not history, but what historians assign to history. In short, Lessing expects "all good in future from the destruction of the delusion of history".[98]

4 Psychological Questions

Lessing opens the second book of the first part of *Geschichte als Sinngebung des Sinnlosen* with two preliminary observations. The first implies that history never rests on "sober remembrance and clinging to the past, but on an enigmatic, productive achievement of the fantasy that is inaccessible to all scientific phrasing, in which the will to survival and to recovery, to comply with wishes, desires, or hope are fulfilled."[99] Hence, the psychology underlying historiography is the theme of this part of *Geschichte als Sinngebung des Sinnlosen*. The second observation refers to the fact that this part of the book

---

95 O.c., 81–82.
96 'sinnlose Hölle nie endenwollender Machtwechselstreitigkeiten, dieser unaufhörliche Kampf aller gegen alle'; o.c., 82.
97 'daß es dem Menschengeiste unmöglich wäre, geschichtliche Wirklichkeiten ohne Sinn vorzustellen, weil Bewußtseins-Wirklichkeit schon Gestaltet-sein in sich schließt.'; o.c., 83.
98 'Alles Heil der Zukunft erwarten wir von Zertrümmerung des Geschichtswahns.'; o.c., 85.
99 'niemals das nüchterne Sicherinnern und Festhalten an Vergangenheit, sondern eine aller wissenschaftlichen Formulierung unzugängliche, geheimnisreiche, produktive Leistung der Phantasie, worin Erhaltungs- und Ausheilungswille, Wunscherfüllung, Sehnsucht oder Hoffnung sich bewähren.'; o.c., 87.

was mainly written during the first months of the great European war, that is, between July and December 1914.

Lessing first of all examines the reliability of eyewitness accounts in history. In general, eyewitnesses are not to be trusted, Lessing claims, not because they are malignant, but simply because "behind all consciousness of reality lives the unconscious satisfaction of desires, always some shifting, deceits, or reordering of facts".[100] Even more important is the craving to shape experience. This craving helps to explain why those involved in history usually are not the most reliable eyewitnesses: a soldier does not even know what happened a mile north or south of him, let alone what the overall picture was. Thus, he is not in a position to give an account of what happens, but he has, nevertheless, the inclination to shape his own personal experiences. But the resulting report can never be a reliable account of what happened: reliable history cannot be written by someone who was involved. Moreover, man, to a very high degree, is a creature of habit – his everyday habits determine what he sees and what he does not see. Almost all people are only interested in what happens in their immediate surroundings, and they do not even notice what happens outside of these surroundings. This does not add to their reliability as eyewitnesses in history.

Next, most eyewitnesses are extremely self-centred, especially the ones that were well-known in their own days. Julius Caesar is an outstanding example: his *De bello Gallico* is almost absurd in its self-centredness, Lessing maintains. As a result, it cannot be reliable. But in a sense, this self-centredness is characteristic of all history: it puts, though not like in Caesar's case involving the person of the historian, but, in a similar way, his or her group, nation, or culture at the centre of the story. And the idea that some invisible force – or, as economists often call it, an invisible hand – holds together such a group, nation, or culture, is false as well. Likewise, there was not some kind of invisible metaphysical force that united the German people in August 1914, Lessing claims. It is a simple fact – which even holds for animals! – that groups, including nations, are knitted together in time of need or war, but this can hardly be considered some kind of cosmic harmony. Moreover, political unity in times of war is something utterly different from positive love, good nature or brotherhood.

---

100   'hinter dem Wirklichkeitsbewußtsein unbewußte Wunscherfüllungen, immer aber irgendwelche Verschiebungen, Täuschungen oder Verstellungen von Tatsachen lebendig sind.'; o.c., 88.

In times of war, Lessing writes in a digression, behind the frontline a heard of hyena's waits: the "representatives of the spirit".

> They sow opinion, give away views, prefer war and the decline of masses, murder of millions, and psychic need as the stuff for their orations and poems [...]
> This, this kind of people bestows the laurels of history! These people inflict, when they want to, the civic, indeed eternal death penalty.[101]

This is the "execution tribunal of public opinion"[102] of the so-called press. But usually, the press is not well informed. Indeed, historical tradition often is the eventual result of preconceived deceit, Lessing maintains. He advances inter alia a personal experience to support this claim. In 1909, newspapers in several European countries reported on an alleged meeting in London, between representatives of anti-noise movements from the United States, Germany, and the United Kingdom, Lessing himself being the representative of the German anti-noise movement. But in fact, there never was such a meeting: there was a coincidental encounter between three people who happened to share a distaste for noise. They cleverly used the press to spread the rumour of their official meeting, and subsequently used the newspaper reports in their battle against noise. The historical tradition on this very meeting is nothing but the result of a deceit, in which Lessing himself was involved. Likewise, most of the archives that historians use are the result of similar deceit: archival materials are collected with the interest of a royal family or a nation in mind, and truth has nothing to do with it. Evidence that is negative for the reputation of the royal family or nation will simply be destroyed. Thus, all archives are systematically tampered with. And gullible historians use these very archives to tell the truth...

So, the evidence historians use to base their stories about the past on – eyewitness accounts and archives – does not at all reflect the past as such, Lessing claims. On the contrary, historians display an intentional tampering with the evidence, while the unconscious desires, wishes, and needs of those who give eyewitness accounts or collect archives are not considered. – Here, Lessing seems to underestimate the way historians deal with their evidence,

---

101 'Sie säen Meinung, verschänken Gesinnung, erwählen Völkerbrand und Massenuntergang, Millionenmord und Seelennot zum Stoff ihrer Reden und Dichtung [...]
    Diese, diese Art Menschen verleiht die Lorbeeren der Geschichte! Diese Menschen verhängen, wenn sie wollen, die Strafe bürgerlichen, ja ewigen Todes.'; o.c., 95.
102 'das Henkertribunal der öffentlichen Meinung'; loc.cit..

however. Historians, after all, do not simply retell what the evidence at their disposal dictates: they approach this evidence critically, by asking questions, and thus draw the information from their evidence that they want to have. This may even imply that they infer conclusions from the evidence at their disposal that, for instance, an eyewitness did not intend to give or, indeed, intentionally tried to hide. An outstanding example is R.G. Collingwood's discussion of Caesar's account, in *De bello Gallico*, of his invasion of Britain. Caesar mentions this invasion only in passing, without going into his motives. This is in remarkable contrast with his accounts of his other military campaigns. Another remarkable contrast is that no triumph followed Caesar's invasion of Britain. Both these contrasts possibly indicate that the invasion was considered a failure. Next, Collingwood compares Caesar's military force with the one Claudius used for his – successful! – invasion of Britain. All this leads Collingwood to the conclusion that Caesar's invasion of Britain was part of a failed attempt to conquer Britain – which explains why Caesar almost suppressed his British campaign in *De bello Gallico*. In other words, a critical analysis of the evidence at his disposal leads Collingwood to the very conclusion that Caesar wanted to conceal: his invasion of Britain was part of a failed attempt to conquer it.[103]

In contrast to Lessing's suggestion, the historian is therefore not at the mercy of his evidence: the historian is not the slave, but the master of his evidence. By critically questioning the evidence at his disposal, the historian draws the information from the evidence that he or she wants to have, which may be different from or even contrary to what an eyewitness or compiler of an archive wanted to convey. Of course, this definitely does not imply that the evidence a historian uses reflects the past as such. Nevertheless, a critical investigation of the evidence a historian has at his or her disposal can lead to conclusions about the past that are provisionally true in the light of this evidence. –

Next, Lessing discusses historical reputations. In this connection he observes that the reputation a person has in history gives no indication of his or her importance or value as a human being: "history does not reveal the value of persons, but records their historical efficacy",[104] Lessing claims. But historical efficacy is a category of its own, which needs careful analysis; this holds true for history in general, but for the history of art or the history of thought as well.

---

103   Cfr. R.G. Collingwood and J.N.L. Myres, *Roman Britain and the English Settlements*, Oxford History of England, part I (second edition, Oxford 1937), chapter 3.
104   'Geschichte sagt nichts über den Wert von Menschen, sondern verzeichnet ihre historische Wirkung'; Theodor Lessing, o.c., 104. The German 'verzeichnen' means both 'to record' and 'to distort'; there is no English translation that unites both meanings of the word, but it is not unlikely that Lessing alludes to both connotations.

Who lives on in history first and foremost depends on current needs. For this very reason, it would be

> unscrupulous to claim that world history would be the world court. If it were, its jurisdiction will be exactly as unjust and immoral as that of every other mass tribunal.[105]

Eventually, an investigation into why a particular person is considered important, while another one not, is a dead-end road, Lessing maintains. Ultimately, nothing much can be said about this question. Of course, there are some conditions that influence the reputation a person has: power and wealth strengthen the chance that someone will be remembered in historiography: "because the most insignificant word spoken from a church tower is more important and meaningful for history than the profoundest oration that fades out on a lonely heath".[106] Hence, "historical success is nothing but mere fact, and is as such beyond sense, law and justice".[107] But once someone has a historical reputation, it will not easily disappear, Lessing claims. One the one hand, the masses tend to follow success out of a human herd instinct; and on the other hand, out of envy a historical reputation will be contested – but the very fact that it is contested will keep it in the public eye.

Historical reputations do not, however, often show continuity: they can change overnight. And "the figures of Alexander, Napoleon, Caesar, Friedrich, who are essentially admired for nothing but their big success, in several ages have been the bearer of different, indeed contrary values".[108] According to Lessing, this is yet another argument to support the claim that history is inadequate as knowledge of (past) reality. Reputations in the history of art or the history of thought often change as unpredictably as reputations in general history: examples are the contemporary reviews of works by Shakespeare, Descartes and Gauguin – contemporary critics scorned their works, whereas

---

105 'ruchlos, zu behaupten, die Geschichte sei das Weltgericht. Wäre sie es, so wäre ihre Rechtsprechung genau so ungerecht und unsittlich wie die jedes anderen Massengerichtes.'; o.c., 105.

106 'Denn das unbedeutendste Wort, vom Kirchturm herabgesprochen, ist für Geschichte wichtiger und bedeutungswerter als tiefsinnigste Rede, die auf einsamer Heide verhallt.'; o.c., 107.

107 'Historischer Erfolg ist somit nichts als bloße Tatsache und steht als solche jenseits von Sinn, Recht und Gerechtigkeit.'; o.c., 108.

108 'Ebenso sind die Gestalten Alexanders, Napoleons, Cäsars, Friedrichs, an denen im Kern nichts als der große Erfolg bewundert wird, in verschiedenen Epochen die Träger verschiedener, ja einander entgegengesetzten Werte gewesen.'; o.c., 109.

currently they are ranked among the very best in their discipline, a judgement, however, that might be entirely different again in fifty or hundred years time. Moreover, Lessing maintains, quite often it is completely accidental that some work of art, literature or philosophy came down to us from the past, while others did not. And some thinkers even live on in history *because* their ideas were totally misunderstood.

A final question that has to be answered with regard to historical reputations is, whether there is a relation between historical importance and ethical value: are they compatible? As regards political and military history, the answer is all too obvious, Lessing claims: politics and war are beyond ethics. Moreover, politicians and military men embody, in a sense, a dualist nature: on the one hand, they are ordinary human beings, but on the other hand they serve as symbols. If one, say, contests the policy of a prime minister, it is not the person of the prime minister who is opposed, but his function: the person is considered the symbol of the function concerned. The historian or, for that matter, the biographer focuses mainly on the symbol, not the person, because what happens in history is admittedly done by persons but in their symbolic capacities: the individual "only is the representative of occurrences that concern his group".[109] Thus, "every crime in history (the Inquisition, St. Bartholomew's Day massacre, the Sicilian Vespers, the schisms of Islam) is just the act of individuals, but these acts are on the other hand only possible because the individual gets hold of existing desires of groups".[110] For reputations in history holds, Lessing maintains, what he put forward earlier in his book with regard to epistemological questions: ultimately, success or failure is the measuring staff of historians. This mostly implies endorsing the status quo; in this way, the actions of someone being successful are approved or applauded. But this always relates to persons in their symbolic capacities, not to the person as such: "once a human being becomes historical, his personal nature just cannot be ascertained".[111] Lessing calls the historical reputation of a person his or her "mythical afterimage in history".[112] As such, the existence of these afterimages should not be considered a problem, he avers: why would it be a problem to

---

109 'daß dabei der einzelne nur Vertreter der Vorgänge ist, welche seine Gruppe angeht.'; o.c., 115.
110 'Und so ist jedes Verbrechen der Geschichte (die Inquisition, die Bartholomäusnacht, die Sizilianische Vesper, die Spaltungen des Islam) einmal die Tat einzelner Individuen, andrerseits aber sind diese Taten nur dadurch möglich, daß der einzelne sich bestehender Gruppenwünsche bemächtigt.'; loc.cit.,
111 'Wenn ein Mensch historisch wird, so läßt sich seine Eigennatur eben nicht mehr erraten.'; o.c., 118.
112 'fabelhaftes Nachbild in der Geschichte'; o.c., 119.

call, say, Immanuel Kant helplessly middle-class as a person, whereas the historical Kant is rightly considered a genius? But historians cannot accept this dichotomy; they just want to discuss the historical Kant. Does all this, then, imply that history eventually is a lie? Lessing does not think so: truth and falsity are categories that in his view do not apply to history. History cannot tell the truth about the past, because even recording what happened is already transforming the past into history. Nevertheless, history has an inner truth, like myths have an inner truth.[113] But this is a subject Lessing only discusses at length in the third part of his book.

Having discussed historical reputations, Lessing turns his attention to historical personalities. He emphasizes that no more than general history, biographies or, for that matter, autobiographies, reflect the past as such: they are, like general history, transformations of the past. This even holds for diaries and private letters, for historians the most intimate kind of evidence they have at their disposal: even this intimate kind of evidence does not reflect the past as such, Lessing claims.[114] According to Lessing, the persons we encounter in history books are no more real than the Laura who was celebrated by Petrarch in his poetry: the main characters in history books are as imaginary as Laura is. Thus, the best-known characters in history eventually are nothing but "a façade of illusions",[115] not the "contradictory, changeable empirical human being"[116] that we meet in everyday reality. Lessing compares this transformation of the empirical man into a historical figure with the deification of, for instance, Roman emperors: these emperors as well were stripped of their ordinary human characteristics, and one or at most a few traits of character were enlarged and considered the essential characteristics of the deity. In history, this process may go "upward" or "downward", that is, sometimes positive characteristics are enlarged, but then again negative characteristics. Referring to his theory of *Ahmung*, Lessing calls the upward transformation *Aufahmung*, and the downward transformation *Abahmung*. That is, in the very process of intuitively understanding someone, this person may be "raised" to a higher level, or "pressed down" to a lower level. *Aufahmung* is what, for instance, happens in the process of falling in love as well: one idealizes the person one falls in love with, that is, all of his or her positive traits of character are enlarged, and all of his or her negative traits of character are minimized. Hence, the

---

113   O.c., 120–121.
114   O.c., 121–122.
115   'Illusionsfassade'; o.c., 122.
116   'der widerspruchsvolle, wandelbare empirische Mensch'; loc.cit..

person one falls in love with no longer is (identical with) the empirical person. In a nutshell, this is what history is about, according to Lessing. This implies, however, that everything mediocre, average, or moderate will be ignored by historians, and, thus, will eventually be forgotten. For this very reason, history always is a story of highs and lows. But this story can only be told from some distance in space and time: then, after all, empirical man can no longer be in the way of the historical figure, and nothing can obstruct the transformation of empirical man into a historical or even mythological figure. Once this transformation is complete, almost every ideological value may be assigned to this historical figure. This again raises the question, "whether the figures one has as making history, are not really, retrospectively, the products of history".[117] Thus, czar Peter is considered the creator of Russia, and Bismarck the architect of Germany – but is the historical czar not himself the product of the process that the creation of Russia was, or is the historical Bismarck not himself the product of the unification of Germany?

Lessing goes on to discuss the relation between the individual and the group again. History may be approached from both perspectives: after all, "the individual is nothing in itself, and the group is only embodied in the individual".[118] Nevertheless, there is a contrast between individual and group. In this respect, Lessing refers to Immanuel Kant's well known idea of "unsocial sociability", that is, the idea that man on the one hand needs to live in, and be part of a group, but on the other hand wants to distinguish himself from this very same group. According to Kant, this unsocial sociability is a fundamental characteristic of the human condition. Awareness of this dualism within man, Lessing maintains, raises a vital question that thus far has never been asked, let alone answered: what is the goal of history? Is it the best possible development of an exceptionally gifted individual, or the best possible development of the group? But this again raises another question: does history have a goal? And what if the alleged goal of history is negative, that is, say, the eventual fall of mankind?[119] – Oddly enough, Lessing seems to ignore Kant's philosophy of history here. In his *Idee zu einer allgemeinen Geschichte in weltbürgerlicher Absicht* ('The Idea of a Universal History on a Cosmopolitical Plan'; 1784), Kant, after all, asks the very same questions, and, moreover, answers them. According to

---

117 'ob die Gestalten, welche man Geschichte machen läßt, nicht eigentlich erst von hinterdrein Produkte der Geschichte sind'; o.c., 125.
118 'Das Individuum ist nichts aus sich selbst, und die Gruppe verkörpert sich nur im Individuum'; o.c., 126.
119 O.c., 128–130.

Kant, it is an essential characteristic of man that he can learn from the experiences of others. This implies that the goal of history is not the best possible development of an individual, but the development of mankind: history will be completed, not in the individual but in humankind. After Kant, other philosophers like for instance Karl Marx spoke out on this problem as well; given Lessing's aversion to the philosophy of Marx, it is perhaps not surprising that he does not mention him, but it is indeed surprising he does not mention Kant as well.[120] –

Lessing subsequently discusses historical development, emphasizing once again that development or growth is something the historian assigns to phenomena in history, it not being inherent to the past itself. Every single person is convinced that he or she has a personal history; this personal history is, Lessing argues, a chain of accidental occurrences, with a metaphysical essence: the self. Everything that happens relates to this self – it is the history of this particular man or woman. But the very same holds for the history of a people, a state, or community: everything that happens is the history of this people, state, or community if, and only if, it relates to this people, state, or community. Thus, this people, state, or community is the metaphysical essence of the history concerned. Intuitively, one tends to distinguish between two kinds of causality with regard to the history of a person, people, state, or community: an inner causality, and an outer causality. If someone, say, walks on a street and is hit by a loose brick that is blown away by a storm, this is considered outer causality – it interferes with the course of events that one might expect. Similarly, natural disasters (floods, earthquakes) are considered outer causality in historical developments: the growth of a nation may be influenced by such a disaster, but it is considered a force from outside. But in Lessing's view, this very distinction eventually is nothing but mysticism. For it is ultimately

---

120   I do not include G.W.F. Hegel here: according to Hegel, the present is the end of history, and it is impossible to predict what will happen in the future. Hegel's philosophy of history retrospectively considers history with the (i.e., his) present as the logical starting point of this consideration, as the present is, after all, the culmination of the process of history. In contrast to Marx, Hegel does not predict what will happen in the future: for him history does not end in the future, but in the present. In this respect, Francis Fukuyama, in his bestseller *The End of History and the Last Man* (London 1992) completely misses the point of Hegel's philosophy of history by discussing the question whether the end of history should be placed, not in Hegel's time, but later. Fukuyama justifies his approach by claiming he is not an orthodox Hegelian, but follows the lead of the Russian-French philosopher Alexandre Kojève; Kojève, however, did not seriously suggest that the end of history should be placed later, but made an ironic joke. Fukuyama seems to have missed the irony of Kojève's suggestion, however.

based on what the historian chooses as the topic of his writings and, thus, as its metaphysical essence. What in relation to one topic is outer causality, is inner causality in relation to another topic. Hence, the distinction between these two kinds of causality eventually reflects the presuppositions of the historian; for this very reason, Lessing maintains, in an inquiry like the one he himself is undertaking with *Geschichte als Sinngebung des Sinnlosen*, the focus has to be on the presuppositions of the historian.

One of these presuppositions is, Lessing contends, the idea of development, a superstition, as he calls it, that he already discussed – and claims to have refuted! – in an earlier essay on Charles Darwin. – Lessing's argument against Darwin rests on his theory of three spheres. According to Lessing, Darwin fails to distinguish between the spheres of *vitalité* and *réalité*: development in the course of time is something that is inherent to the world as it appears to our consciousness, that is, it is inherent to *réalité*. But Darwin assumes, Lessing maintains, that development is inherent to *vitalité*, that is, it is inherent to primordial life. The difference, of course, is that according to Lessing development ultimately is the product of human consciousness, whereas according to Darwin it is not.[121] – Lessing is of the opinion that Darwin's error is symptomatic for a failing in Western science and philosophy; the very same error may be found in the ideas of, amongst others, Hegel, Herder, and Comte. But, as Lessing maintains,

> If history indeed warrants progress, then any authority that came into power can quietly lay itself himself down to sleep in the belief of being the temporary summit of a necessary natural process, and thus enjoy his power as a right. Progress, culture, development of people, state, fatherland, these are the familiar manners of speaking behind which there is nothing but the self-justification of the will to power and success of the groups that rule or want to rule.[122]

Likewise, it is a misconception to consider every stage in the life of an individual a further progress towards death and eternal beatitude; every stage of a life is an end in itself. – In this respect, Lessing's argument seems to correspond

---

121 Cfr. above, 149 *ff*; and Theodor Lessing, 'Charles Darwin', in: *PaT*.
122 'Wenn nämlich Geschichte den Fortschritt verbürgt, dann kann jede zur Herrschaft gelangte Macht ruhig sich auf dem Glauben schlafen legen, zeitweiliger Gipfel eines notwendigen Naturprozesses zu sein und somit ihre Gewalt als ihr Recht genießen. Fortschritt, Kultur, Entwicklung von Volk, Staat und Vaterland, das sind die bekannten Redensarten, hinter denen gar nichts steckt, als die Selbstrechtfertigung für Macht- und Erfolgswilligkeiten herrschender oder herrschwilliger Gruppen.'; *GSS*, 134.

with Ranke's well-known observation that "every era is immediate to God",[123] which implies that considering history a continuous progress towards an ultimate end is misplaced, as it would imply that earlier generations are sacrificed for the benefit of later generations. This would be an injustice of God towards earlier generations, and for this reason this idea should be rejected, Ranke argues: in his view every era in history is an end in itself. Besides this, Lessing questions the idea that man would be the alpha and omega of history, as is presupposed by all views of history in which the idea of development is pivotal. After all, it is man himself who puts man in the centre of history... Be that as it may, historical optimism rules Western civilization, whereas down-to-earth pessimism with regard to history is considered an affection, and someone who does not share this optimism "a grudging despiser of man".[124] Still, it might well be possible that not optimism, but pessimism with regard to history is the healthier attitude, Lessing argues. After all, pessimism manifests the ability to bear life as it is, whereas historical optimism demands the sedative of desires and wishes that are ascribed to the future – and thus softens reality as it is. Eventually, historical pessimism is usually rejected, not because one disagrees with it, but because one realizes it is difficult to live with, this being the real reason it is denounced.

An argument that is regularly brought up against pessimism with regard to history is that all crimes and misery simply are necessary to enable the (cultural or other) highs that history undeniably knows as well. Lessing quotes Anatole France, who, in 1915, praised war because it enabled prosperity: like the wars in antiquity eventually enabled prosperity in the Roman Empire, similarly the current war will bring prosperity. Lessing scorns this kind of reasoning:

> It could be possible that all righteousness is nourished from the source of violence, all spirit from the power of barbarity, and the complete world of beauty and goodness from need and suffering. Does this allow for a theodicy of violence, of barbarity, or of suffering? No! It just allows for the conclusion that the summit of beauty and goodness of such a world would be that it would not exist...[125]

---

123 'jede Epoche ist unmittelbar zu Gott'; Leopold von Ranke, *Über die Epochen der neueren Geschichte* (Leipzig 1906 [first edition 1854]), 17.
124 'vergrollter Menschenverächter'; Theodor Lessing, o.c., 138.
125 'Es wäre ja möglich, daß alle Gerechtigkeit aus der Quelle Gewalt, aller Geist aus Kraft der Barbarei und die ganze Welt der Schönheit und Güte aus Not und Leiden gespeist würde. Gestattet das eine Theodize der Gewalt, der Barbarei oder des Leidens? Nein! Es gestattet nur den Schluß, daß der Gipfel der Schönheit und Güte einer solchen Welt eben ihr Nichtvorhandensein wäre...'; o.c., 140.

The very idea of progress in history is a European-American invention, Lessing claims; it fits current Western civilisation, but eventually it is nothing but a substitute for true religion, a kind of "happy-progressive hurrah Christianity"[126] that has nothing to do at all with true religiosity. But it has proven its usefulness – at least for the Western half of the world, though it also has made the other half of the world very unhappy indeed. After all, in the name of progress, half of the world was colonized, robbed, even murdered, for the benefit of the West. Nevertheless, this "barbarity of culture"[127] is still being promoted by Western man. It would be far more reasonable, however, to abandon this unjustified belief in progress, and to admit the fact that every simple life born into this world is an end in itself, Lessing concludes.

Next, Lessing discusses the idea of destiny in history. His reflections on this topic are in part prompted, as he explicitly indicates, by "two highly praised, downright criminal works: 'Der Genius des Krieges under der deutsche Krieg' by Max Scheler and 'Der Krieg und die deutsche Selbsteinkehr' by Rudolf Borchardt".[128] They, and like-minded authors, do not only quietly accept the current barbarities – which suffices to make them accessories –, but, moreover, they explain these as the result of a necessary process or necessary development, and so on. This is, however, a kind of metaphysics of history that should be strictly distinguished from history as a discipline. – Even if Lessing is very critical about history as a discipline, especially with regard to its claims of knowing past reality, this metaphysics of history is even worse, he thinks, and he apparently feels the urge to defend history against this kind of metaphysical interpretations. – According to this interpretation of history, every individual is subjected to his or her historical destiny, from which there is no escape: "Someone who is born into a historical situation can retrospectively approve it, sanctify it, give sense to it (he will perish if he does not!), but he cannot duck out of the situation of the world as it befalls him [...]".[129] Thus, man cannot freely make his own history, as he does not make all of it himself. But it still is

---

126   'eine Art Juchhechristentum, freudig-fortschrittlich'; o.c., 141.
127   'Barbarei von Kultur'; o.c., 142.
128   'Die Ausführungen [...], im Jahre 1915 geschrieben, richteten sich vornehmlich gegen zwei damals vielgerühmte, schlechthin verbrecherische Werke: 'Der Genius des Krieges und der deutsche Krieg' von Max Scheler und 'Der Krieg und die deutsche Selbsteinkehr' von Rudolf Borchardt'; the title of Scheler's book in English is 'The Genius of War and the German War', and that of Borchardt's book 'The War and German Self-Repentance' ; o.c., 144.
129   'Der in einen Geschichtszustand Hineingeborene kann ihn somit zwar von nachhinein billigen, heiligen, mit Sinn erfüllen (er geht zugrunde, wenn er das nicht tut!), aber er kann nicht dem überkommenen Weltzustand sich entziehen;'; o.c., 146.

considered *his* history, as it reveals the kind of person he is – had he been a different person, his history would have been different. Lessing rejects this kind of thinking, however: in his opinion all this rubbish about historical necessity just shows how people give a specific sense to something that is senseless *in se*:

> We have history just so far as we have a destiny. To have a history exactly means to have a predestined destination. A chaos has no history.[130]

In other words, the destiny man thinks to find as predestined in history, is the destiny man himself gives to (his) history: it is his very own interpretation of his past and his future. In the logical sense of the word, however, nothing what happens in history is necessary, Lessing claims; everything is simply accidental:

> The world as preceding fact is precisely nothing but mere material! Man could make the world into heaven just as well as he makes it into hell. He could be a creature of joy and freedom just as well, as he with all his middle-class and social virtues merely is the product of need and necessity.[131]

In other words, every appeal to historical necessity simply is nothing but an appeal to human nature: it is human nature that makes man into what he is, and makes history into what it is. But this implies, Lessing maintains, that history may never be used in justification of cruelty, despotism, slavery, war, and so on. Far from it: man should experience history as his very own, immense shortcoming. After all, history is shaped in our very own image: history reflects what man is. Man as a natural creature, i.e., biological man, has no history; historical man is the result of the very same transformation that makes history out of the past. And this transformation is carried out by man himself."Fate", then, eventually is a religious concept, expressing a deeply felt truth of life, similar to notions like original sin and grace, which are religious concepts as well, expressing truths of life. Fate eventually expresses the feeling an individual has that his life, at least in part, is shaped by a transcending force. This is not meant in a metaphysical sense, but refers to the fact that every individual is part of a group, a class, a nation, etc.; and this very fact limits the possibilities

---

130 'Wir besitzen Geschichte grade so weit als wir fatum haben. Geschichte haben besagt eben: schicksalsmäßige Besstimmung haben. Ein Chaos hat keine Geschichte.'; o.c., 147.
131 'Die Welt als vorhistorische Tatsache ist eben nichts als bloßes Material! Der Mensch könnte die Erde so gut zu Himmel machen, wie er sie zur Hölle macht. Er könnte so gut Geschöpf der Freude und Freiheit sein, wie er in allen seinen bürgerlichen und sozialen Tugenden nur das Produkt von Not und Notwendigkeit ist.'; o.c., 148.

an individual has in shaping his own life. But this feeling should not be confused with necessity in the logical sense of the word: it simply does not imply, Lessing argues, that everything that happened in history had to happen.

Lessing emphasizes that nature – i.e., flora and fauna – has no history: nature simply is. It is only man who started to distinguish himself from nature, that is, started to see himself as different from and outside of nature, or even as being opposite to it, when consciousness was born. Or, in Lessing's terminology, when "out of need man broke out of nature". Hence, it is human consciousness that places man outside of, and even opposite to nature."The fact of the matter is that history is an act of giving sense or value to the natural, it not already being given, however, with the natural itself".[132] As such, everything that happens is, in Lessing's view, the result of blind chance. If man finds sense in it, it is because he gives sense to it. Hence, ice ages, forest fires, earthquakes, and other natural disasters are the result of blind chance; they only become history when man gives sense to them – be it by describing them as divine punishments, be it by explaining them scientifically. That is, the accidental character of these disasters is reasoned away in a process of *logificatio post festum*. In other words, "nature as well only gets 'sense' insofar we give it a history."[133]

Eventually, the very idea of historical necessity is nothing but "the cheerfully ringing acceptance of that what has to be accepted not voluntarily anyway."[134] Voluntarily accepting what has to be accepted gives a feeling of liberation; this is something that can be witnessed every day in the current war, Lessing observes. Someone who actually is powerless regains his dignity by voluntarily doing what he has to do anyway, even if it leads to certain death. It is the illusion of being in control that matters. According to Lessing, this is a fundamental characteristic of the human condition: man simply has an innate urge to give sense to "all this senseless irrationality of the factor of history", it is "simply an ineradicable, indestructible need of the heart".[135]

But this urge definitely has a function: it serves to liberate man from life as such:

> If one notices how the terrible, senseless, absurd facts of life are retrospectively bent into history, and in the end can be read in the historical

---

132 'Die Sache ist eben die, daß Geschichte ein Akt der Sinn- oder Wertgebung des Natürlichen, nicht aber mit dem Natürlichen selber schon gegeben ist.'; o.c., 151.
133 'Auch die Natur erhält nur soweit "Sinn", als wir ihr eine Geschichte geben.'; loc.cit..
134 'freudig getönten Bejahung dessen, was unfreiwillig bejaht werden muß.'; o.c., 153.
135 'all die sinnlose Irrationalität des Elements von Geschichte'; 'ein unausrottbares, unvertilgbares Herzensbedürfnis'; o.c., 154.

tradition as so innocent and simple, as if all pain and all need and all the suffering of the soul is stripped away [...]; if one notices how everything that was so painful and rough to experience may retrospectively be read as a colourful, exciting novel, one could come to the idea that man with history does not aim at reporting the occurrences of his life, but exactly the opposite: his recovery and liberation from everything painful that befalls him as his lot.[136]

Thus, history is "a healing act of self-deceit",[137] it is diluting life into a sensible story. It is the way man protects and liberates himself from life as the irrational chaos it actually is.

In this sense, history is already taught at primary and secondary schools. Thus, these delusions are forced upon the helpless minds of young children, together with all kinds of prejudices about patriotic duties, discipline, self exaltation of the nation over other nations, and so on. All this implies that an "exam in history eventually is a bare test of political faith".[138]

Subsequently, Lessing discusses the relation between history and politics. Is history the school for politics, as is often said, or is politics nothing but applied history? Ideas like these fail to recognize, Lessing claims, that history deals with what once was, that is, the one-off, and not with generalities. Politics, however, deals with ideals that are supposed to be generally valid, even if politicians do not always seem to realize this. On the contrary, appealing to the notion of *Realpolitik*, they even advocate the view that politics can be made on the basis of experience and vision only, as if no ideals and principles are needed. Lessing strongly rejects this idea. Likewise, he rejects the distinction that is often made between ethics for private life and ethics for public life. This distinction mainly serves to justify acts in politics and war that are totally unacceptable in private life, and which should be unacceptable as such – it being the reason Lessing dismisses the distinction between private ethics and a so-called public

---

136 'Wenn man sieht, wie die entsetzlichen, sinnlosen, irrsinnigen Gegebenheiten des Lebens von hintennach zu Geschichte umgebogen werden und sich dann schließlich in der Geschichtsüberlieferung so harmlos und einfach lesen, als sei aller Schmerz und alle Not und das ganze Leiden der Seele davon abgestreift [...]; wenn man sieht, wie alles von nachhinein dann wie ein bunter, spannender Roman sich liest, was doch so schmerzlich und rauh zu erleben war, so könnte man auf den Gedanken kommen, daß der Mensch mit der Geschichte nicht die Wiedergabe seiner Lebensereignisse bezwecke, sondern grade das Umgekehrte: seine Ausheilung und Erlösung von allen den quälenden Begegnissen seines Geschicks.'; o.c., 156.
137 'ein heilsamer Akt der Selbsttäuschung'; loc.cit..
138 'die Schulprüfung in Geschichte zuletzt eine nackte Gesinnungsprüfung!'; o.c., 158.

ethics. In August 1914, however, this distinction was often referred to, usually relating it to the way it had been expressed by the German philosopher Johann Fichte (1762–1814). At the time, it even became part of the dominant political ideology, but in no other country political ideology was overrun with lies like in Germany, Lessing claims. But even if countries like the United Kingdom, France, and the United States claim to fight the current war in the name of democracy, their reaction to the Russian Revolution shows that they do not really want democracy all over the world, Lessing maintains. After all, it can hardly be denied that, whatever the outcome of the Revolution, it is a step toward democracy, given the autocratic character of the czarist reign. All this merely shows, Lessing argues, that whichever political system a country has in the end is completely indifferent to those in power – as long as they themselves are in power, they accept any system. If only Germany had had a democratic revolution in August 1914 instead of a war, Lessing laments. But "logic and ethics are not of this world",[139] "love, goodness, beauty"[140] have no power – only if they are promoted by some other force they can become influential. But actually they are not… After all, Lessing asks,

> Who made the era of the big murder? All those who did not resist it from the first hour (in August 1914)! All those, who deep down in their heart indeed feel the truth, but do not tell it when it is dangerous to tell the truth.[141]

But those who are chosen as political leaders are not the great minds, not the ones who tell the truth. Hence the result:

> Revolution, confusion, reaction – this is the eternal cycle of so-called world history! That is what it was, that is what it is, that is what it will be until the crash of that poor earth will save that ill-fated humanity to rest.[142]

However, what eventually matters is one thing, and one thing only: "[…] the demand: decrease suffering".[143]

---

139 'Logik und Ethik sind nicht von dieser Welt'; o.c., 176.
140 'Liebe, Güte, Schönheit'; loc.cit..
141 'Wer hat denn das Zeitalter des großen Mordens gemacht? Alle, die ihm nicht von erster Stunde an (im August 1914) widerstanden! Alle, die im tiefsten Innern die Wahrheit zwar fühlen, aber sie niemals sagen, wenn es gefährlich ist, Wahrheit zu sagen.'; o.c., 177.
142 'Revolution, Konfusion, Reaktion – das ist der ewigen Kreislauf der sogenannten Weltgeschichte! So war es, so ist es, so wird es bleiben bis zur Zusammenprall der armen Erde die unglückselige Menschheit zur Ruhe rettet.'; o.c., 179.
143 'die Forderung: Mindere das Leiden!'; o.c., 183.

By way of a conclusion to the first part of *Geschichte als Sinngebung des Sinnlosen*, Lessing tries to class his book in the tradition of historiography. He notes that the tradition his book belongs to started in 1725, when the Neapolitan philosopher Giambattista Vico (1668–1744) published his *Scienza nuova*. Ever since, two ideas have dominated all thought on history, Lessing claims: the idea that there is some necessary coherence in everything that happened in history, and the idea of progress. The latter idea totally dominated the ideology of the last generations, with, alas, disastrous results: Western man infringed upon both the non-Western world and nature, bringing about indescribable suffering of the non-Western world and an increasing exhaustion of nature. What will all this result in? "Someone who experienced the years from 1914 until 1918 with open senses, knows what he, in future years, can expect from development and progress",[144] Lessing observes.

What we need, is a new kind of history, Lessing avers, a kind of history that does not try to explain the present from the past, nor to predict the future from past and present. We need a kind of history that is nothing but everlasting present, that is, a history that can inspire the present."This history no longer flatly-confidently says 'It was like this!', but with a clear conscience and proudly demanding 'It must have been like this!'",[145] Lessing claims. What this new kind of history implies, is the question Lessing addresses in the third book of *Geschichte als Sinngebung des Sinnlosen*.

By way of recapitulation of the "destructive" part of *Geschichte als Sinngebung des Sinnlosen* – that is, the first two books, respectively on the epistemology and psychology of history – in the following some comments will be made. In this part of *Geschichte als Sinngebung des Sinnlosen*, Lessing offers a series of arguments, which eventually all are directed against the idea that history would mirror past reality. At least since Ranke, this idea dominates historiography, Lessing claims, but he thinks it is as wrong as it is naïve. History does not mirror past reality, history shapes and orders past reality: eventually, it is not the past but the (present!) historian who determines what history is. Historians, with their almost innate distaste for philosophical, i.e. epistemological questions, simply do not seem to realize what their own discipline implies. According to Lessing, the very fact that history shapes and orders past reality means that it is impossible to know the past as it has been. In other words, a

---

[144] 'Wer die Jahre 1914 bis 1918 wachen Sinnes erlebt hat, der weiß, was er künftig von Entwicklung und Fortschritt in Natur und Geschichte zu halten hat.'; o.c., 187.
[145] 'Diese Geschichtsschreibung sagt nicht mehr platt-zuversichtlich "So war es!", aber sie sagt reinen Gewissens und stolz-fordernd "So soll es gewesen sein!"'; loc.cit..

radical scepticism as regards the epistemological status of history as a discipline is perfectly justified: history cannot offer knowledge of the past as it happened. Moreover, it is not even possible to describe the past in this way, since a description of the past already implies a transformation of the experience as such, Lessing claims. In this respect, he explicitly distances himself from the phenomenology of his erstwhile teacher Edmund Husserl who, at least according to Lessing, held that it is indeed possible to describe experiences as they appear in our consciousness without at the same time transforming these experiences.

Lessing's arguments against the idea that history mirrors past reality are frequently an elaboration of the arguments advanced in earlier writings, which I qualified as epistemological and metaphysical, that is, arguments claiming respectively that it is impossible to know the past, and that history as a process is irrational, chaotic, and senseless. However, Lessing does not conclude from this that history as a discipline is futile, as one might expect: in his view, history definitely has a function within a culture, but this function is not offering true knowledge of past reality. The question what this function indeed is, Lessing tries to answer in the "constructive" part of *Geschichte als Sinngebung des Sinnlosen*, that is, in the third and last book, "History as an ideal".

5   History as an Ideal

For a start, it is appropriate to note that the second, constructive part of *Geschichte als Sinngebung des Sinnlosen* is much shorter than the first, destructive part: the first two books cover almost three quarters of the entire publication. Moreover, Lessing uses the first two – of four! – chapters of this third book partly to recapitulate ideas he discussed in earlier writings, or in the first part of *Geschichte als Sinngebung des Sinnlosen*.

Starting point for his reflections on history as an ideal is a definition of what, in his view, history as a discipline does: it "rewrites the sensory data of the world of appearances, by placing them into evaluative connections".[146] Thus, history is a "rewriting *Willenschaft*" that "weaves together the essence of appearances into a temporal connection on the basis of 'points of view'".[147] This implies that the meaning of history as an ideal is, according to Lessing, completely different

---

146 'die sinnlichen Gegebenheiten der Erscheinungswelt, sie in Wertzusammenhänge einstellend, umdichten'; o.c., 191.
147 'umdichtende Willenschaft'; 'verwebt die Inbegriffe der Erscheinungen zu zeitlichem Zusammenhang an Hand von "Gesichtspunkten".'; loc.cit..

from the meaning of history as discussed in the first two books of *Geschichte als Sinngebung des Sinnlosen*. History as an ideal is not lead by causes or motives, but by values. Even though values as such have been widely discussed in Western philosophy, the relation between values and history has been neglected, Lessing claims. But as a matter of fact, the relation between values and history reveals a form of causality of its own that has always been overlooked. Values and ideals are, Lessing maintains, "a demanding world beyond history, in the light of which, however, all reality of history is being thought and thoughtfully shaped; a silent world of the mind that nowhere firmly and factually intrudes in the activity of historically effective motivating forces, but still holds out the true example and model, the regulative, the direction, with every judgment that the mind, willing or thinking, passes on reality".[148] Or, in the terminology of Lessing's theory of the three spheres, these values and ideals belong to the realm of *vérité*: that is, the timeless and perfect version of *réalité* that man develops in his thinking. In other words, under the heading "history as an ideal" Lessing discusses history in its relation to the sphere of *vérité*. History as an ideal thus belongs to the realm of pure thought – but if man tries to realize his ideals, that is, if man tries to implement *vérité* in *réalité*, the ideal becomes a lie.[149] – Lessing's outspoken view indeed reminds of debates on socialism in the 1960's and 1970's. Some critics of the Soviet Union tried to defend the ideal of socialism by strictly distinguishing between the ideal of socialism as such and "the really existing socialism" in the Soviet Union, and claimed that the political and social system in the Soviet Union was nothing but a perversion of the ideal of socialism, sometimes even going so far as completely denying any link between the system in the Soviet Union and the ideal of socialism. Others, however, claimed that the faults of the system in the Soviet Union were inherent in the ideal of socialism itself, that is, any effort to put the ideal of socialism into practice would inevitably lead to similar abuse. – Lessing, for one, maintained that every effort to implement an ideal in practice could only lead to a perversion of the ideal, simply because the ideal belongs to the realm of *vérité*, and an effort to implement an ideal in the realm of *réalité* necessarily cannot succeed – the twain, *vérité* and *réalité*, never shall meet...[150] Since

---

148 'eine fordernde Welt über Geschichte, eine Welt, an Hand deren freilich alle Wirklichkeit der Geschichte gedacht und denkend gestaltet wird; ein stilles Geisterreich, das nirgend derb und faktisch in das Getriebe der Geschichte-wirkenden Motivkräfte eingreift, dennoch aber das eigentliche Vor- und Anbild, das Regulativ, die Richte abgibt, bei jeden Urteil, das wollend oder denkend der Geist über Wirklichkeit fällt.'; o.c., 194.
149 O.c., 195.
150 According to Lessing, the correctness of his analysis is confirmed by the status of Immanuel Kant's "categorical imperative": this notion is true in the realm of pure thought, or as

it is impossible to "transfer" an ideal from *vérité* to *réalité*, this is, indeed, the tragedy of the human condition. Man recognizes the imperfection of the dividedness between three distinct spheres and accordingly has an inborn urge to unite them, but this is by definition impossible and, hence, these efforts are bound to fail. Thus, the importance of ideals does not depend on the question whether it is possible to implement them or not, that is, on their relevance for *réalité*. What, then, is their meaning?

Lessing emphasizes that historical ideals are not something an individual can choose at will – the kind of (historical) ideals an individual has is predetermined by his or her historical context (place of birth, nationality, class, sex, and so on). Moreover, these ideals always reflect a collective or personal need. This may clearly and easily be illustrated by the example of historical materialism, Lessing claims: the ideals of historical materialism simply reflect the fact that large parts of the population in contemporary industrial societies suffer the most elementary material needs. But this principle holds in general: ideals, one way or another, reflect needs. Even if it is, according to Lessing, a truism that ideals cannot be implemented in practice, nevertheless they somehow influence reality. This implies that the relationship between *vérité* and *réalité* is not so much a direct one, but rather, disconnected: "the pole of the normative never can itself become effective and historical, but it teaches the actual world that is moved by need to judge and to assess rightly".[151] Thus, the ideals from *vérité* work more as a lodestar in *réalité*, that is, they give a general direction but not the details of a course. Or, in Kantian terminology, they are "regulative ideas": goals worth striving for, even though strict criteria to indicate when the goal is reached are lacking, and even though it is not altogether clear what has to be done to reach this goal. Humans almost all strive for justice, or for health; no clear criteria exist to indicate when the goal of justice, or of health, is reached, that is, when a society is completely righteous or a person completely healthy; nor it is clear what exactly has to be done to bring about justice, or health. Still, we believe in these goals, and we judge reality with these ideals in mind, and we realize our world is not yet righteous, or that we are not yet completely healthy. So, the very fact that an ideal exists implies that reality

---

Lessing calls it, in the sphere of *vérité*. But it is not indispensable obligating in practice, that is, in the sphere of *réalité*. Lessing claims that Kant never managed to demonstrate, even though he desperately tried, how his "categorical imperative" may be operative in practice. This is what Lessing calls the "break" in Kant's ethics, to which he dedicated his study *Der Bruch in der Ethik Kants: Wert- und willenstheoretische Prolegomena* (Bern 1908).

151 'den Pol des Normativen, welcher niemals selber tathaft und historisch werden kann, wohl aber die notbewegte Welt des Tatsächlichen richtig beurteilen und auswerten lehrt.'; o.c., 205.

will be judged in the light of this ideal; subsequently, efforts will be made to close the gap between ideal and reality, if only to some extent. Hence,

> All of the history of mankind is the result of dreams! The tapestry of occurrences is woven in accordance with a dreamed of model. By shame and longing, desire and hope, fear and encouragement, guilty conscience, by all forces of the human soul.[152]

Thus, "what history bears witness to is the desires of the heart".[153] This implies, Lessing argues, that history does not place humans in a tale of an objective, mechanistic world of causality – on the contrary, history liberates humans from a world like this.

This is, however, only possible because the story the historian tells suggests that it is not only about the occurrences discussed – there always is the suggestion that this story mysteriously reveals some eternal truth that transcends the occurrences as such:

> Because as the simple observation "This was then; there and thus" history would be the most useless burden of the mind, whereas as graphically described reality, however, it exercises the same enigmatic fascination as any work of art, which always shows something specific, though exactly through its specific characteristics showing something exemplary which holds for all life.[154]

So, history by definition is a mixture of data and dream, of fact and desire. We know this, but we do not know and, indeed, cannot know to what extent this mixture is fact and to what extent desire: though we can distinguish these elements, we cannot separate them. This is not peculiar to history, Lessing maintains, arguing that it is characteristic of all human life. This implies that all human ideals are nourished by history: "human ideals cannot be unconnected

---

152   'Die ganze Geschichte des Menschengeschlechtes ist Ergebnis von Traum! Der Teppich der Ereignisse wird nach geträumten Musterbild gewebt. Von Scham und Sehnsucht, Wunsch und Hoffnung, Angst und Ermutigung, Schuldgefühl, von allen Mächten der Menschenseele.'; o.c., 197.
153   'Was aus Geschichte spricht, sind Herzenswünsche.'; o.c., loc.cit..
154   'Denn als bloße Feststellung: "Dies war damals; dort und so" wäre Geschichte die unnützeste Belastung des Geistes, während sie doch als anschauliche Wirklichkeit den selben geheimnisvollen Zauber ausübt wie jedes Kunstwerk, welches immer etwas bestimmtes vor die Augen stellt, gleichwohl aber gerade vermittelst seiner Sonderzüge ein für alles Leben Gültiges vorbildlich schauen läßt.'; o.c., 198.

images of thought",[155] they always taking root in history, or, in other words, human ideals originate from a specific historical context and reflect that context.

Lessing observes that different kinds of historiography may be distinguished. A first step towards this distinction was made by Friedrich Nietzsche in his *Vom Nutzen und Nachteil der Historie für das Leben*. Nietzsche distinguished monumental, antiquarian, and critical history respectively: monumental history serves to encourage those who take action; antiquarian history is aimed at preserving and honouring the past; and critical history belongs to those who suffer and need to be liberated, its main criterion being whether it supports the vitality of a people. But, Lessing maintains, this classification is far from exhaustive: there are many more points of view which can, and indeed do serve as starting point for writing history. In Lessing's view, three main kinds of historiography should be distinguished: aesthetic, heroic, and logical. These three kinds of historiography correspond to the three main ways man may overcome the need of life: "shaping-beholding; judging-evaluating; classifying-orienting".[156] Likewise, one may distinguish the sensitive, the irritable, and the thoughtful historian, or "l'histoire sensitive, irritable, pensive".[157]

The most original of these main kinds of historiography is the aesthetic view of history. This is the view of history that is closest to primordial life: it just contemplates history, free of all need, almost oblivious of the distinction between the self and the outside world. It all but sees history as a pageant; there is no need at all to judge it, and thus the aesthetic view of history is not interested in questions about good or bad, or right or wrong.

In this sense, heroic history – the second main kind of historiography – is completely different: it is driven by indignation. The historian who writes this kind of history is more of a prophet, or even a judge of the world: for him or her, history is not a spectacle that may be enjoyed, on the contrary, history has to be evaluated and judged.

The third main kind of historiography is written by the thinking, logical historian, whose main inspiration is the sheer pleasure in scientific research, and who simply enjoys making historical connections and discovering historical necessities.

---

155 'Menschheitliche Idealbildungen können nicht beziehungslose Gedankenbilder sein.'; o.c., 203.
156 'gestaltend-anschauend; beurteilend-auswertend; einordnend-orientierend'; o.c., 208, footnote.
157 Loc. cit..

Subsequently, Lessing discusses ideals from a completely different perspective. Starting point for this discussion is the observation that history often is described as a process, and that it is at least possible to see the whole of history as a process. Now a process by definition has both a beginning and end, it being, according to Lessing, simply implied by the very idea of process. Moreover, a process is made possible by making use of some kind of drive. In this sense, Lessing claims that history may be defined as a process from the most basic, elementary life to complete consciousness:

> Pure element of life as beginning. Pure immateriality as end.[158]

The pure element of life precedes reality as given in consciousness, whereas pure immateriality is beyond life: it is completely static and perpetually valid. The world of which we are conscious lies in between these poles, that is, somewhere between pure element of life and pure immateriality. These poles often are described as antithetic notions, for instance as eros versus logos, will versus idea, Apollo versus Dionysus, Europe versus Asia.[159]

History, then, as a process from one pole to the other, goes at the expense of life force: in the beginning, there was nothing but life force, and in the end there will be no more life force left. In other words, according to Lessing life force is the drive of history, and history might well be described as a process of the gradual decay of life force. One may conceive of this process by comparing it to the stages of (human) life: birth, youth, maturity, old age, death – after all, (human) life as well is a process of gradual decay of life force. Moreover, likewise we do not, and, indeed, cannot know by experience our past prior to our birth, nor what death implies.

Thus, human history may be seen as a growth towards pure consciousness, originating from need. After all, Lessing claims consciousness as such was born out of need; likewise, the growth towards pure consciousness is driven by need. As we have seen, in Lessing's view, ideals express the needs of life, a particular ideal reflecting some kind of need. Efforts to realize an ideal – even if they are bound to fail, as the spheres of *vérité* and *réalité* cannot be united – by definition increase the distance from primordial life. Lessing claims this implies that ideals are an artificial substitute for life force, which by definition goes at the expense of life force. Hence, ideals have a dualist nature: "by creating values

---

158 'Reines Lebenselement als Beginn. Reine Geistigkeit als ende.'; o.c., 209.
159 Hence, Lessing's *Europa und Asien* – first published as a series of articles, later as a book that he revised several times – is an exploration of what these poles respectively imply, and not an empirical study of Europe and Asia as geographical parts of the world.

that use life, life exhausts and maintains itself".¹⁶⁰ In a sense, this is nothing but self-deceit, Lessing argues, but it enables man to continue living, at least for the moment, even though it implies gradually exhausting life force, and thus moving towards an inevitable end of life.

All this means that man does have reason to be proud of everything he created, that is, of culture in the broadest sense of the word, as long as he realizes that the development of culture by definition goes at the expense of life force. In short, the development of culture inevitably brings man closer to the end of life. But there is no alternative: history is, after all, an irreversible process – man cannot turn back, and move away from the pole of pure consciousness towards the pole of pure element of life. Hence, there is no cause for pessimism: history is a process which will come about anyway, irrespective of how man values this process. For this reason, the best thing man can do is stoically face the fact of this development towards the inevitable end of life, without either pessimism or optimism. Once we realize that consciousness stems from need and as such is a symptom of an unhealthy situation, and once we realize that consciousness by definition goes at the expense of life force, the utter senselessness of history is made understandable. All irrational, incomprehensible acts of man essentially are a revolt against reason as the force that brings man closer to the end of life. Reason never rules the world, even if man likes to imagine he is a rational being. But sensing that reason eventually is incompatible with life, man tends to cling on to life, and to reject reason: hence, "through all life of history runs the leaning towards saving on consciousness".¹⁶¹ In other words, man

> loves and admires the messenger of glad tidings, and kills those who illuminate. He deifies those who make the world stage difficult, and despises those who make it easy. He rather prefers a hundred times going into ecstasies than a judgment. Because the bright, demolishing knowledge is threatening – with death.¹⁶²

Consequently, everything that man hails as rationality, eventually is nothing but self-deceit, Lessing claims, while on the other hand, "the bright light, that

---

160 'Im Erschaffen der das Leben verbrauchenden Werte erschöpft und unterhält sich das Leben selbst.'; o.c., 211.
161 'Das gesamte Leben der Geschichte durchpulst der Hang nach Bewußtseinsersparnis.'; o.c., 213.
162 'Er liebt und bewundert den Verklärer und tötet die Aufklärer. Er vergöttert die großen Schwermacher der Weltschau und verachtet ihre Vereinfacher. Er gewinnt hundertmal lieber eine Verzückung als ein Urteil. Denn das wache, abbauende Wissen droht – den Tod.'; loc. cit..

is the enemy".¹⁶³ After all, if man is really rational, he never had indulged in a Great War which demanded so much: sacrifices, material destruction, enormous amounts of money. With this money the Sahara could have been made into a blooming garden, Lessing maintains. Moreover,

> There would be not a single miserable, not a single hungry person on earth, when all the value and strength, instead of being put at the service of a self-destruction that will have an effect for centuries to come, had been put at the service of reason. But in 1930, historians will prove that all this was "historically necessary": the great war [was necessary] for the great revolution, the great revolution for the great war; and so on, endlessly, because we humans are – "intellectual beings".¹⁶⁴

Once again, Lessing discusses historical reputations, emphasizing again – like he did in the destructive part of *Geschichte als Sinngebung des Sinnlosen* – that the reputations of historical figures eventually are nothing but the result of chance and randomness. Even if it is true that, for instance, Mozart or Nietzsche are rightly saved from oblivion, countless others are improperly forgotten.

> That history retrospectively proclaims someone a good man and his contemporaries who did not know him thickheads, will not comfort anybody. [...] The glory of history is worthless for its owners.¹⁶⁵

Subsequently, Lessing once again underlines that history never will or can be a science like the natural sciences. History, after all, does neither look for a reality beyond the world of appearances nor for causal connections, like the natural sciences. History deals with appearances themselves, and understands these as the expression of ideals that consciousness tries to realize in reality, and as reality. If we really understand history, we do not conceive it as a straight causal chain that inevitably leads to "now". Eventually, Lessing claims, there is nothing but a perpetual present, and up against this perpetual present history

---

163 'Das wache Licht, das ist der Feind.'; o.c., 214–216.
164 'Es gäbe keine elenden, keine hungrigen Menschen mehr auf Erden, wenn diese Werte und Kräfte statt in den Dienst der auf Jahrhunderte hinaus wirkenden Selbstzerstörung in den Dienst der Vernunft gestellt worden wären. Aber im Jahre 1930 werden die Historiker beweisen, daß das alles "historisch notwendig" war: der große Krieg für die große Revolution, die große Revolution für den großen Krieg; und so ins Unendliche weiter, denn wir Menschen sind – "intellektuelle Wesen".'; o.c., 216, footnote.
165 'Daß die Geschichte ihn von nachhinein für einen braven Mann erklärt und die Zeitgenossen, die ihn nicht kannten, für Dummköpfe, das tröstet niemanden. [...] Der Ruhm der Geschichte ist für seine Eigner wertlos.'; o.c., 218.

is nothing but fiction and thought: "It is giving sense retrospectively (logificatio post festum)".[166] Or, in terms of Lessing's theory of three spheres, history is not about *vitalité*, it is not about *vérité*, history is about *réalité*: "Because that which we have in mind as historical tradition, already is realization of idea and ideal on an elementary level by man".[167] But to be able to realize ideas and ideals in reality – and we have to keep in mind that these efforts are bound to fail as *vérité* is no more than a lodestar for *réalité* –, man needs inspiration. History, for one, can offer this inspiration: "History is the thought by means of which man raises himself out of nature".[168] Historical figures like Alexander the Great, Caesar, Luther, etc., live on because of the stories that are told about them. These are the kind of stories that may inspire us in our present life, and this is why we need history: we need it to be able to make history, not because of the knowledge it claims to offer us, but because we need to be inspired in order to act properly.

But are these inspiring stories true? This is the question that is always asked about history – indeed, the question that was the starting point of the destructive part of *Geschichte als Sinngebung des Sinnlosen*. What is real, Lessing maintains, is "the endless moaning wildernesses of fields with dead bodies, soldiers covered with mud, brooks of blood, charred fields of rye, burning cities".[169] But this reality is transformed into "letters and words";[170] these words will be repeated time and again, and thus our imagination will gradually shrivel up – and eventually, we can no longer imagine (past) reality. One could say, therefore, that in Lessing's view imagination is the victim of traditional history conceived as "letters and words", supposedly reproducing past reality. And because man no longer can imagine past reality, he does not learn from history: every generation has to have its own experiences."The bloody reality of yesterday degenerates already today in a titillating play in the theatre…",[171] Lessing claims – and we cannot learn from this degenerated version of reality.

In a sense, Lessing maintains, the historian is comparable to the painter: it is the painter who determines what we see on a painting, not the landscape. The painter teaches us to see the landscape, more precisely: to see the landscape like he did. This implies that afterwards we no longer see the landscape as

---

166 'Sie ist Sinngebung von nachhinein (logificatio post festum).'; o.c., 220.
167 'Denn das, was uns als geschichtliche Überlieferung vor Sinnen steht, das ist schon Verwirklichung von Idee und Ideal am Elementarischen durch den Menschen.'; o.c., 221.
168 'Geschichte ist Gedanke, mittels dessen der Mensch sich aus Natur erhebt'; o.c., 222.
169 'Die endlosen wimmernden Wüsten der Leichenfelder, die kotbedeckten Soldaten, Bäche voller Blut, verkohlte Roggenfelder, brennende Städte.'; o.c., 223.
170 'Buchstaben und Worte.'; loc.cit..
171 'Die blutige Wirklichkeit des gestrigen Tages heute schon zum kitzelnden Schauspiel der Schauhäuser entartet.'; o.c., 224.

such: we recognize, say, a Turner in the landscape we see. Historians work likewise: it is not the past, but the historian who determines what can be read in a history book. If it turns out well, the story a historian tells may change the view of an entire people as regards its own history, either by, say, drawing attention to a person or a group that until then had been neglected, or by pointing out a person or a group was not as important as always had been thought. According to Lessing, this implies that the historian does not only have the right, but even the duty to ignore what might disturb his or her story. In the end, it all comes down to "creative acts of the imagination".[172] As a result, what eventually will survive in history is what arouses the imagination, all the rest will fade away.

Hence, every historical personality is for at least a half the product of the imagination; "the retrospective investigation into what was in point of fact 'historically real' and what, transforming it, the imagination added, is as hopeless as fruitless".[173] This implies that if, for instance, we call an era "a Golden Age", the character of this era is not in the nature of things, but in the way we present it. The past as such is senseless – it is the historian who gives sense to history.

> By this, the historian becomes the healing doctor of mankind. He gives meaning to the big human anthill and, like the poet, raises the sense of life and self-confidence, by ignoring and forgetting everything indifferent, useless, disastrous, negative, and leaves as an abstract of what really was only tidings of great acts, beautiful abilities, moving fates, exemplary lives and glorious souls.[174]

This implies that history can only be written, and has to be written "cum ira et studio".[175] In other words,

---

172 'Schöpfungsaksten der Einbildung'; o.c., 224.
173 'Die nachträgliche Untersuchung, was eigentlich "historisch wirklich" was und was Einbildung umgestaltend hinzubrachte, ist so aussichtslos als unfruchtbar.'; o.c., 226.
174 'Damit wird der Geschichtsschreiber zum heilenden Arzt am Menschengeschlecht. Er gibt dem großen Menschenameisenhaufen Bedeutung und steigert gleich dem Dichter Lebensgefühl und Selbstbewußtheit, indem alles Gleichgültige, Unbrauchbare, Heillose, Verneinende übersehen und vergessen wird und als Auszug des Wirklichgewesenen nur Kunde von großen Taten, schönen Begabungen, bewegten Schicksalen, vorbildliche Lebensabläufen und herrlichen Seelen übrig bleibt.'; o.c., 227.
175 Of course, Lessing hints at the well known expression that history should be written 'sine ira et studio' – 'without anger and fondness' –, that is, the historian should (try to be) impartial with regard to his object. The expression is by Tacitus, in his *Annals*; the idea was, and is, widespread amongst historians.

When awareness and knowledge say: "Do not deceive yourself. See the world in a sober reason. There is no use. Nothing makes sense", then history comes comfortingly and with sweet hands and whispers "I know that. This is the very reason I am necessary".[176]

History, then, has to tell stories, over and over again, to make life, senseless as it as such is, bearable for man. The task of history "as guardian of glamour and noble image [is] to weigh up the unholy, disenchanting knowledge of our awareness".[177] The more humanity knows, the harder it is necessary that history spins its web of progress and connections. As a result, history shows a terseness and a beauty which the past as such does not have. According to Lessing, the correctness of this analysis is confirmed by everyday experience: what an individual in his personal life experiences as chance and senselessness, becomes necessary and sensible once it is incorporated in the story the historian tells. Thus, acts, occurrences, and individuals are lifted out of the reality of the past "into the paradise and hereafter of history".[178]

6   Conclusion

Lessing completes *Geschichte als Sinngebung des Sinnlosen* with what he calls "the dome" ("die Kuppel") – an overview of the implications the argument of his book has from his personal perspective.

In Lessing's view, there are eventually two different attitudes to life a man may adhere to as the solution for the perplexities of life. One is the attitude of Epicurus, the other one the attitude of Buddha. Epicurus' outlook is to enjoy life as it comes, that is, to give oneself up to life as it appears, whereas it is Buddha's attitude to respond to the call of need, that is, to try to diminish the need in the world. These two attitudes to life contradict each other – a contradiction that according to Lessing is inherent to human consciousness. In a nutshell, this contradiction may be phrased as two alternative possibilities: "rather a slave than dead" or "rather dead than a slave".[179] Both alternatives can

---

176 'Wenn Erkenntnis und Wissen sprechen: "Mache dir nichts vor. Sieh die Welt nüchtern. Es ist alles unnütz. Nichts hat Sinn!", dann kommt tröstend und mit linder Hand die Geschichte und flüstert: "Das weiß ich. Und grade darum bin ich notwendig".'; o.c., 228.
177 'als Hüterin des schönen Scheins und edlen Bildes die unheilige ernüchternde Erkenntnis unsres Wissens aufzuwägen.'; o.c., 229.
178 'in das Paradies und die Nachwelt der Geschichte'; o.c., 230.
179 O.c., 247, footnote.

be supported by convincing arguments – there is no conclusive argument in support of either the one or the other.

But, Lessing claims, there are three possible ways to reconcile both attitudes. First, one might try to interpret Buddha's attitude as the ultimate consequence of Epicurus' attitude, that is, to see Buddha's attitude as, in a sense, an extension of the one of Epicurus.

Secondly, one might conceive of a kind of peaceful coexistence between both attitudes, that is, adhere to the one while at the same time acknowledging the validity of the other.

Thirdly, Lessing suggests the possibility that an individual manages to reconcile both attitudes in his own soul, gradually blotting out the contradictions between the two. This would be the supreme solution, Lessing claims, actually being an amalgamation of both poles.

Geschichte als Sinngebung des Sinnlosen ultimately aims at liberating man from history, Lessing maintains, in particular in times when history vigorously forces itself upon mankind, this being, of course, an allusion to the First World War. Admittedly, Lessing avers, the book bears the marks of the era in which it was written, with all the drawbacks of its time. But he considers it a message-in-a-bottle in the hope of presenting a key to the verve of history for future friends who are as yet unknown.

Hence, *Geschichte als Sinngebung des Sinnlosen* is Theodor Lessing's reflection on history, urged by the outbreak of the First World War. He was utterly horrified both by the war itself and by the way a great number of his contemporaries reacted to the outbreak of the war. All too many German intellectuals greeted the war with euphoric enthusiasm and, moreover, tried to justify it, obviously, of course, from the German stand. These attempts to justify the war often included an appeal to historical arguments, they frequently being based on a specific historical interpretation. In Lessing's view, historical reasoning indeed appeared to be capable of justifying almost any evil. For him, this was the very reason to consider historical thinking, and the notion of history in general. These reflections on history brought him to several related conclusions. First of all, he arrived at the position that the process of history as such is senseless and chaotic, a rationality underlying history accordingly being absent. Moreover, there is also no end history would lead to. The stories historians tell about the past do not, however, reflect the senseless and chaotic character of history, but try to show, on the contrary, both its sense and order. This implies, on the one hand, that the stories historians tell do not reflect past reality, and, on the other hand, that the sense and order that these stories display are assigned to the past by historians themselves. They do this, because they value the past from their own specific point of view, reflecting their ideals. These ideals, for their part, reflect the (sometimes individual, but usually collective) needs of the time of the historian. Thus the writing of history eventually is a function of the present. All this implies that the stories historians tell about the past are not, and indeed cannot be true, for truth cannot be dependent on the needs of mankind. For this reason, a radical scepticism with respect to history is fully justified: history cannot offer true knowledge of past reality, Lessing claims.

However, this does not imply that writing history has no use. On the contrary, history is essential to a culture – but not because it offers knowledge of the past. It is essential because it tells stories about the past. In these stories, values and ideals are involved – and these stories accordingly serve to impress these ideals on, say, a society, a nation, a political party. As such, they serve as an inspiration: they inspire the people who have to act. In short, Lessing claims history is indispensable in Western culture, but for a quite different reason than usually thought. The misconception of the main characteristics of history eventually is the result of the fact that historians in general don't show any interest in philosophical questions. In consequence, they do not realize what their very own discipline implies: they think they (have to) offer true knowledge of the past, whereas in fact they have to tell appealing stories about the past in order to inspire people in the present.

CHAPTER 5

'Den Früheren Auflagen Gegenüber Ein Völlig Neues Werk'

The Fourth Edition of Geschichte als Sinngebung des Sinnlosen

For Theodor Lessing, *Geschichte als Sinngebung des Sinnlosen* was the book "which brought me my first success".[1,2] It was rapidly reprinted twice, without alterations, both reprints being published in 1921. Moreover, in 1921 Lessing was awarded the *Strindberg Preis* for the book. This Strindberg Prize was an initiative of Erich Schering (1873–1951), a German man of letters, well known at the time, not only for his own publications but even more so for his translation of the complete works of the Swedish author August Strindberg (1849–1912), in an edition of 47 volumes. Moreover, Schering promoted Strindberg's work continuously with publishers and stage directors. Part of this campaign to promote Strindberg was the establishment of the Strindberg Prize. In a prospectus, the underlying idea was explained:

> The catastrophe of the World War induced Strindberg's children, Strindberg's translators and Strindberg's publishers in 1920, to establish a prize of 3000 Mark annually, for the best poem or writing in German language which promotes the reconciliation between nations; it will be awarded every year on Strindberg's birthday (January 22nd).[3]

Originally, professor Carl Ludwig Schleich (1859–1922), a surgeon and amateur philosopher who, as a personal friend of the Swedish playwright had been active in promoting Strindberg's works as well, was invited to award the prize. When he declined because he was overburdened with work, Schering undertook to do the job himself. The prize was awarded only twice: due to inflation, the deposit vanished almost overnight, and thus the initiative ended. – Yet another token of recognition of *Geschichte als Sinngebung des Sinnlosen*

---

1 A translation of the chapter title is, 'a completely new work as compared to earlier editions'.
2 'das mir den ersten Erfolg brachte'; Theodor Lessing, 'Gerichtstag über mich selbst', in: *Eunw*, 404.
3 'die Katastrophe des Weltkriegs [hat] Strindbergs Kinder, Strindbergs Übersetzer und Strindbergs Verleger im Jahre 1920 veranlaßt [...], für die beste Dichtung oder Schrift in deutscher Sprache, welche die Versöhnung der Völker fördert, einen Preis von dreitausend Mark jährlich zu stiften, der jedes Jahr an Strindbergs Geburtstag (22. Januar) verliehen wird'; quoted from *Die Fackel* 23 (1921), R 568–571, May 1921, 45.

© HERMAN SIMISSEN, 2021 | DOI:10.1163/9789004464773_006

was that Lessing was invited to address the *Internationale Geschichtstagung* (The International Historical Conference) that was organised by the *Bund Entschiedener Schulreformer* (The League of Determined School Reformers) in the first week of October 1924. Lessing himself was a member of this League.[4] Due to illness, Lessing could not deliver his speech, entitled "Was ist Geschichte?" ('What is history?'). The text was included, however, in the proceedings of the conference.[5]

1   What Is History?

The argument of Lessing's "Was ist Geschichte?" generally corresponds with the argument of *Geschichte als Sinngebung des Sinnlosen*. Of course, the address is only a short text, not a full-length book. Still, some differences are noticeable. First of all, Lessing's tone in "Was ist Geschichte?" is far more balanced and terse: he presents himself as a philosopher bringing out an argument for an audience of academics. In his book, in contrast, he had regularly allowed himself, among other things, emotional outbursts and cynical comments. Moreover, *Geschichte als Sinngebung des Sinnlosen* includes many a reference to contemporary occurrences – after all, the World War was what Lessing induced to contemplate history and to write the book in the first place –, whereas in "Was ist Geschichte?" he refrains from suchlike references, confining himself to developing his argument.

Lessing opens his address with a general observation on his approach. He emphasizes that philosophy is not a science amongst all the other sciences: "[philosophy] is the study of the meaning of knowledge itself, a critique of knowing, equally remote from doubt as from dogma".[6] In his *Studien zur Wertaxiomatik*, Lessing had used almost exactly the same words to characterize phenomenology.[7] This shows that even though he was a self-willed pupil of Lipps and Husserl, Lessing was indeed influenced by phenomenology. Now, as a philosopher, Lessing asks the fundamental question what history means – what is history?

According to Lessing, history as an intellectual activity has a number of characteristics. First of all, history deals with occurrences in time, in chronological

---

4   Cfr. Chapter two, above, 33.
5   Theodor Lessing, 'Was ist Geschichte?', in: *Die ewige Revolution, Ergebnisse der Internationalen Geschichtstagung, 2.-4.x.1924*, ed. by Siegfried Kawerau (Berlin 1925), 17–34; reprinted in: *WeU*, 229–248.
6   '[Philosophie] ist Bedeutungslehre des Wissens selbst, eine von Zweifel und Dogma gleich weit entfernte Kritik unsres Erkennens'; o.c., quoted from *WeU*, 229.
7   Cfr. Chapter four, above, 163.

order. Secondly, these occurrences are real, not fictional. Thirdly, these occurrences are one-off, that is, they do not happen twice in exactly the same way. Lastly, ascertaining what happened only precedes history proper – it is not yet history. For the most essential characteristic of history is that it makes events out of occurrences. That is, the historian, by an act of the mind, adds something to the mere occurrences – and it is exactly this fourth characteristic that distinguishes history from all the other sciences. What does this particular activity of the historian imply? It is, Lessing argues, ordering occurrences from a specific evaluative viewpoint, saying:

> The reality of the knowing consciousness is the springboard that man needs and uses for an [...] activity completely different from knowing. To wit, to realize with this certain projections of desires to the reality of his consciousness. Through continuously *projecting* hopes and desires, aims and expectations on "what happened in time" [...] out of the dead world of dead occurrences he forms a big human work of art and dreams: a meaningful world *above* the reality of occurrences.[8]

But once the historian has completed his or her work, it is not possible to distinguish what the contribution of the historian was, Lessing claims:

> However, once we have the historical world lying in front of us like a landscape that gradually gets clearer, it has become impossible to distinguish retrospectively to what extent it is "real" and to what extent "*realized*", to what extent mechanically thought and to what extent *made* meaningful. It suffices to know that in history what was experienced and what was dreamed of, element and idea, are lumped together inseparably, and can only be distinguished conceptually and artificially.[9]

---

8 'die Wirklichkeit des erkennenden Bewußtseins ist das Sprungbrett, welches der Mensch benötigt und benützt zu einer ganz anderen als erkennenden [...] Tätigkeit. Nämlich dazu, daß er an dieser seiner Bewußtseinswirklichkeit bestimmte Wunscheinblendungen verwirklicht. Dadurch, daß er beständig Hoffnungen und Sehnsüchte, Absichten und Erwartungen in [...] "Geschehen in der Zeit" *hineinblendet*, formt er aus toter Welt toter Geschehnisse ein großes menschheitliches Kunst- und Traumwerk: eine sinnvolle Welt *über*wirkliches Ereignens.'; o.c., 234. The italics are Lessing's.
9 'Haben wir nun aber diese geschichtliche Welt wie eine mählich klar werdende Landschaft vor uns liegen, so ist es unmöglich geworden, nachträglich an ihr zu scheiden, wieviel daran "wirklich", wieviel *ver*wirklicht, was an ihr mechanisch gedacht und was an ihr sinngebend *gemacht* ist. Genug, wenn wir wissen, daß Erlebtes und Erträumtes, Element und Idee als Geschichte untrennbar zusammengewirkt sind und nur begrifflich und künstlich auseinandergehalten werden können.'; o.c., 234–235. The italics are Lessing's.

All this implies, according to Lessing, that history is driven by utopia, in a double sense. On the one hand, utopia motivates those who make history: they are lead by ideals which they try to realize. On the other hand, utopia is the norm according to which historians – and, in fact, all people – judge what happens in history. As a consequence, history can never be true. One can imagine that this conclusion was rather surprising for those who read this address without any prior knowledge of Lessing's philosophy. In the light of what he had written in *Geschichte als Sinngebung des Sinnlosen* the conclusion is rather obvious, however: history deals with reality, but truth belongs to another realm: the sphere of *vérité*. What Lessing in his address calls utopia corresponds with what he calls ideal in the book. Hence, utopia can be true, but history cannot. His explanation in "Was ist Geschichte?" is so very succinct that it may have been confusing for at least some of his readers.

Next, Lessing discusses the historical object, say – the examples are his – the history of an infantry regiment, of chemistry, of Europe, of England, or of the reform of education. It is evident, Lessing claims, that an infantry regiment, or chemistry, or Europe is not real in the same sense that a tree or a cat is real. Other than a tree or a cat, an infantry regiment, or chemistry, or Europe is real as an idea. Likewise, a category like causality is proper to consciousness and does not exist prior to consciousness. Again, this is evident, Lessing maintains: it needs no argumentation. Because causality is always a connection that we (as humans) establish ourselves, a causal connection is never certain – in fact, we may connect everything with almost everything else. Apart from this, it would be a mistake to think that history has to discuss causes: even if it is customary, it is not at all essential for history to ask for causes. According to Lessing, one would in fact ignore some very interesting contributions to historiography if one confines history to studies that focus on causal connections. Moreover, the confusion concerning "historical causality" is widespread: several different notions are mixed up: "motivation, psychic causality, mechanical causality, and cause in the sense of norm of what happens".[10] Lessing maintains he has to leave the details of this problem aside, and, moreover, that he cannot go into the details of similarly problematic notions like progress, development, culture, cultural development, and so on, either: it does not fit within the scope of his address. Instead, his focus will be on one topic only: "the idea of history as a linear continuum in time",[11] or "history as a chain of generations in time".[12]

---

10 'Motivation, psychische Kausalität, mechanische Ursächlichkeit und Ursache im Sinne von Norm des Geschehens'; o.c., 237–238.
11 'Der Gedanke einer Geschichte als eines linearen Kontinuum in der Zeit'; loc.cit.. o.c., 239.
12 'Geschichte als einer Generationenkette in der Zeit'; loc.cit..

For Western man in the twentieth century, this idea of history is more or less self-evident, even to the degree that he can hardly imagine it is merely a specific idea of history, other ideas of history being conceivable as well. This dominant idea of history is one-dimensional (history seen as exhibiting a line in time); but one could imagine a two-dimensional or a three-dimensional idea of history as well. The one-dimensional idea of history is the one we are used to in modern Western culture, however, and for this reason Lessing focuses on this notion. He explicitly denies that this linear idea of history necessarily implies the idea of continuous progress: on the contrary, in Lessing's view history does not show continuous progress, there being relapse and dying out as well, and even those who adhere to the linear idea of history should acknowledge this. The most distinct feature of the linear view on history is that it meets deeply felt human needs: "What we call world history, that is a kind of satisfying human needs overpowering life".[13] If this idea of history is lost, Western culture as a whole will be under threat, Lessing claims: its very foundations would be undermined. Nevertheless, the idea that all of humanity forms a whole, and that all nations and cultures somehow are part of this whole became dominant only after Vico published his *Scienza nuova* in 1725. Subsequently, it was spread by a number of other thinkers: Lessing, Herder, Kant, and Fichte in Germany, Voltaire, Montesquieu, and Condorcet in France, Buckle and Lecky in England. Afterwards, three great men – but "nevertheless the real forgers and impostors of our time"[14] – raised the buildings of the three main areas of knowledge on the quicksand of this dogma of a linear continuum in time. It concerned the knowledge of culture, of economics, and the one of nature; the three men concerned are, of course, G.W.F. Hegel, Karl Marx, and Charles Darwin respectively. Only science in the strict sense of the word managed to break away from the influence of this way of thinking, Lessing maintains. But we should keep the following in mind, he claims:

> If this idea of history falls, then Hegel, Darwin, and Marx will fall as well. Then Europe's "culture", its "cultural process" and cultural development of mankind will also fall".[15]

---

13   'Was wir Weltgeschichte nennen, das ist eine das Lebendige vergewaltigende Art menschlicher Bedürfnisbefriedigung...'; o.c., 240.
14   'gleichwohl die eigentlichen Verfälscher und Truggeister unseres Zeitalters'; o.c., 241.
15   'fällt dieses Geschichtsbild, dann fallen auch Hegel, Darwin und Marx. Dann fällt auch Europas "Kultur", "Kulturprozeß" und –Entwicklung des Menschengeschlechts".'; o.c., 242.

To keep it short, Lessing claims, he cannot go into all the questions his observations may raise; he focuses on the idea that history conceived as a line in time should be seen as providing a model giving sense to the senseless. Lessing succinctly elucidates this statement as follows:

> Time is a category to understand life; but understanding life is itself: experience. Obviously, there is no other way out but the realization that history only comes into being with man and passes away with man; that its sense cannot (like mathematical truths) be found, but is established, and that its unity thus does not belong to life, but – kills it in consciousness.[16]

Lessing admits that he may give the impression of not only sawing off the branch of the tree on which both his readers and he are sitting, but of cutting down the entire tree. Be that as it may, he thinks his approach is justified in the light of all the confusion concerning the way history is taught at secondary schools. History as taught at school has as little to do with true history as theology has to do with true religion, Lessing argues. How much teachers of history are currently at a loss as regards their own discipline is clearly manifest in the variety of approaches, he maintains, some teachers concentrating on political and military history, others on cultural history, or on social history, some concentrating on the unique achievements of great men, others on collectives, and so on. In short, every single history teacher has his own ideas on how to reform the teaching of history. According to Lessing, none of these ideas is, however, related to what history originally was: "telling stories about occurrences, and the historians of peoples were those who passed on to them the legends of their past, the tidings of their prehistory, the memory of their lineage, and were capable of telling these like epic or rhapsodic poets".[17]

The desire to hear these stories was (and is) bolstered by various motives, and accordingly every story told by a historian emanated (and emanates) from a specific point of view, Lessing asserts. But history in this sense of the word

---

16   'die Zeit ist Vorform zum Erfassen des Lebens; aber Erfassen des Lebens ist selbst: Erlebnis. Es gibt hier offenbar keinen Ausweg als die Erkenntnis, daß Geschichte nur mit Menschen entsteht und vergeht; daß ihr Sinn nicht (wie mathematische Wahrheit) aufgefunden, sondern gestiftet wird, und daß ihre Einheit mithin nicht dem Leben zugehört, sondern – seine Abtötung im Geist'; o.c., 243.

17   'das Erzählen von Begebenheiten, und die Geschichtsschreiber der Völker waren diejenigen, die ihnen die Legende ihrer Vergangenheit, die Kunde ihrer Vorwelt, das Gedächtnis ihrer Gattung überbrachten und sie gleich Epikern und Rhapsoden zu erzählen wußten.'; o.c., 245.

may, apart from reading or listening to the stories of historians, also be experienced when studying old buildings, or when attending traditional feasts, and so on. This implies that any real understanding of history has its roots in the love of the *Heimat*.[18] This means, according to Lessing, that a real sense of history should be protected from too much knowledge of historical facts, and in particular from too much influence of the historical sciences. Telling stories is far more important – although Wilhelm Tell never lived, telling the story of Wilhelm Tell is far more important for the Swiss nation than knowing all the ins and outs of its history. Lessing quotes Johann Wolfgang von Goethe (1749–1832): "The most beautiful thing that history may offer is enthusiasm".[19]

In short, Lessing concludes, the teaching of history is dead. What is being taught at schools is not history:

> What remains as the truly historical essentially is nothing but the terrible wading through political acts of murder and manslaughter and continuously changing rompings between nations, connected with the dispositional lesson that it is good to have *success*. But forest and cloud, cemeteries and old walls, market place and bastion, animals and plants tell a child history, and if it first manages to love the soul of the *Heimat*, it already holds the key to the history of the *world*: man will stay alive only for as long as lives on in him, not overwhelmed: the strength for myth.[20]

With these words Lessing ends his address. Keeping in mind that it was originally intended as a speech for an audience of historians and teachers of history, one cannot but conclude that the content of this address was rather provoking, to say the least. After all, Lessing questions not only the way history usually is

---

18 This word is most difficult to translate in English. It has a number of connotations that 'fatherland' does not cover, in particular a stronger sense of 'where one belongs'; probably 'hometown' comes closer, but a *Heimat* is a region rather than just the hometown.

19 'Das Schönste, was Geschichte zu geben hat, ist Enthusiasmus'; o.c., 247. Lessing does not quote Goethe exactly, as Goethe wrote 'Das Beste, was wir von der Geschichte haben, ist der Enthusiasmus, den sie erregt.' Cfr. J.W. von Goethe, *Wilhelm Meisters Wanderjahre II, Betrachtungen im Sinne der Wanderer*, Kapitel 42.

20 'Was als das eigentlich Geschichtliche bleibt, ist im Kerne nichts als das schreckliche Waten durch politische Mord- und Totschlagsakte und durch immer wechselnde Völkerkatzbalgereien, verbunden mit der Gesinnungsbelehrung, daß es gut sei, *Erfolg* zu haben. Aber Wald und Wolke, Friedhöfe und altes Mauerwerk, Marktplatz und Bastei, Tiere und Pflanzen erzählen dem Kinde Geschichte, und vermag es erst die Seele der Heimat zu lieben, so hat es schon den Schlüssel zur Geschichte der *Welt*: lebendig aber bleibt der Mensch gerade so lange, als in ihm noch unverschüttet fortlebt: Kraft zu Mythos.'; Theodor Lessing o.c., 248. Except for *Heimat*, the italics are Lessing's.

taught at schools, he even questions the very foundations of history as a discipline. Moreover, he recommends teachers of history to tell stories that inspire pupils, regardless of whether these stories are true – as long as they enthuse, these stories serve their main purpose. Lessing's conclusions correspond with the argument as developed in *Geschichte als Sinngebung des Sinnlosen*. In comparison with the book, his argumentation in the address is calm and less emotional, but the underpinning of his vision does not differ from the book. Still, when reading the address one should, I think, keep in mind that it also is a very personal statement, but in a way that markedly differs from *Geschichte als Sinngebung des Sinnlosen*. Lessing's observations on how "forest and cloud, cemeteries and old walls, market place and bastion, animal and plant" tell stories about the past, that is, tell history, correspond to what he would write a few years later about his youth in his autobiography *Einmal und nie wieder* – this was how Lessing himself as a kid had learned about the history of Hanover and its vicinity. Likewise, his description of the way history is taught at school resembles his memories of his own schooldays: the dullness of the history classes and the complete lack of inspiration. So, in a sense this address may be understood as a reckoning with the history education of Lessing's youth. This does not imply, of course, that his criticisms of history and history teaching are unjustified – but possibly they are prompted more by Lessing's personal experiences than one would be inclined to think at first glance.

2 Historian of Hanover

In both *Geschichte als Sinngebung des Sinnlosen* and "Was ist Geschichte?", Theodor Lessing writes on history as a philosopher, that is, as someone who did not have any personal experience with writing history. This inadvertently raises the question what a history book written by Lessing would have looked like – would it have been completely different from the average history book in the tradition of historiography? The obvious answer to this question is that we do not know, and never will know, simply because Lessing did not write any history book. Nevertheless, there is a book by Lessing that might at least give a clue to the answer, as it might be read as a history book, more specifically, as a local history of Hanover: his *Haarmann* – the report on the trial of the serial killer Fritz Haarmann.[21] That it is indeed possible to read *Haarmann* as

---

21   Theodor Lessing, *Haarmann. Die Geschichte einer Werwolfs* (Berlin 1925). I used the reissue *Haarmann. Die Geschichte einer Werwolfs und andere Gerichtsreportagen*, ed. by Rainer Marwedel (Frankfurt a.M. 1989). Cfr. Chapter one, 9.

a local history of Hanover is suggested by an observation Lessing makes on his own approach in the book: "the longer the sessions lasted, the more clearly the conclusion forced itself upon me that one cannot try a snake without at the same time putting on trial the swamp from which alone the snake fed itself".[22] In other words, according to Lessing the society which allowed Haarmann to commit his crimes was at least jointly responsible for these crimes. Consequently, society should be on trial as well – and this is the very reason Lessing discusses this society at length: Hanover in the 1920's. Lessing's approach in this discussion of the society of Hanover is distinctly historical – hence, the book can be read as a local history of the capital of Lower Saxony. The nature of this approach already is apparent from the opening paragraphs of the very first chapter of the book:

> Hanover, the capital of the German province of the same name and the centre of the district Lower Saxony, lies at the remotest offshoots of the German low mountain range, from where the North-German plain with its sandy pine forests and heaths stretches out to the North Seacoast. The little Leine River, coming from Eichsfelde and streaming through the hilly valley of Göttingen in between the Harz and Weser Mountains, reaches the bare North-German plain beneath Elze, appearing between Hildesheimer Forest and Eastern Forest; from Hanover the river turns west and, beyond Hudemühlen, flows into the big swamp. The 'high bank' ['hohen Ufer'], the place where the river absorbs the brooks from the Deister Hills, the Ihme and the Fösse, and hurries, fast-flowingly, through the old city, may have given the place its name which was first mentioned around 1050: 'Honovere'. [...] When in 1866 Hanover was annexed for Prussia by Bismarck, the city had hardly 70,000 inhabitants. But in the era following the victorious war with France between 1870 and 1872, the so-called *Gründerzeit*, industry made its powerful entry, so the little, charming villages in the vicinity, Hainholz, Döhren, Limmer, List quickly transformed into stained industrial suburbs. [...] Anyway, this development towards the reign of money and working classes, which smothered the old culture of nobility and peasantry of Lower Saxony, was not at all

---

22   'Je weiter die Verhandlungen fortschritten, um so klarer drängte sich die Überzeugung auf, daß man eine Schlange nicht richten kann, ohne zugleich den Sumpf mit vor Gericht zu stellen, daraus allein die Schlange ihre Nahrung zog'; o.c., 172. Moreover, in the 'Preface' of the book, Lessing characterizes himself as 'the chronicler of this bit of "cultural history"' ('der Chronist dieses Stückes "Kulturgeschichte"', 49), all be it a reluctant one: he thought both the crimes and the trial of Haarmann were repulsive.

unusual. It was an essential characteristic of Wilhelmine Germany. But a truly infernal chaos broke out when this Prussian superpower collapsed and an in a world war of five years completely corrupted youth, used to killing and 'requiring', shaking off all discipline and manners, returned to the totally impoverished, exploited native region. [...] Unequalled degeneration, impoverishment, confusion. [...] In this so-called 'era of inflation' that started with the collapse of the German armies in the world war and the storms of the German revolution, suddenly the importance of Hanover as an international transit market and black market started to grow.[23]

These paragraphs read as an example of almost classical historiography: like historians already in antiquity not infrequently used to do, Lessing starts his book with an extensive description of the geography of the location where the events took place which form the object of his book. For that matter, paying attention to the geography of historical events is fully in line with a recommendation Lessing makes in "Was ist Geschichte?": "If I were education inspector,

---

23   'Hannover, die Hauptstad der gleichnamige deutschen Provinz und der Mittelpunkt der niedersächsischen Lande, liegt an den letzten Ausläufern des deutschen Mittelgebirges, von welchem aus sich die norddeutsche Ebene mit ihren sandigen Kiefern- und Heidebezirken bis fern zur Nordseeküste hinabzieht. Das Flüßchen Leine, vom Eichsfelde kommend und die zwischen Harz und Weserbergen eingesenkte hügelige Mulde Göttingen durchfließend, erreicht unterhalb Elze, zwischen dem Hildesheimer Walde und dem Osterwalde hervorbrechend, die kahle norddeutsche Ebene; von Hannover ab macht der Fluß einen Bogen nach Westen und mündet hinter Hudemühlen im Großen Moor. Das "Hofe Ufer", dort wo der Fluß die Deisterbäche Ihme und Fösse aufnahm und in schnellen Laufe die Altstadt durcheilt, hat wohl dem um 1050 zuerst erwähnten Orte den Namen gegeben: "Honovere". [...] Als Hannover 1866 durch Bismarck für Preußen annektiert wurde, hatte die Stadt kaum 70 000 Einwohner. Aber in der Zeit nach dem siegreichen Kriege mit Frankreich zwischen 1870 und 1872, in der sogenannten Gründerzeit, hielt die Industrie machtvoll Eintritt, so daß die kleinen lieblichen Dörfer der Umgebung, Hainholz, Döhren, Limmer, List bald zu rußigen Fabrikvororten sich wandelten. [...] Immerhin war diese Entwicklung zu Geldherrschaft und Werkertum, darunter die alte Adels- und Bauernkultur Niedersachsens erstickte, keineswegs ungewöhnlich. Sie war das allgemeine Wesensgepräge des wilhelminischen Deutschlands. Wahres Höllenchaos aber setzte ein, als dies preußische Machtreich zerbrach, und eine an Töten und "Requirieren" gewöhnte, im fünfjährigen Weltkriege verwilderte Jugend, alle Zucht und Form abschüttelnd, in die völlig armgewordene, ausgesogene Heimat zurückkehrte. [...] Entartung, Verarmung, Verwirrung ohnegleichen. [...] In dieser sogenannten "Inflationszeit", anhebend mit dem Zusammenbruch der deutschen Heere im Weltkrieg und den Stürmen der deutschen Revolution, begann die Bedeutung der Stadt Hannover als einen internationalen Durchgangs- und Schiebermarktes plötzlich zu wachsen.'; o.c., 51–53.

I would not allow any history class without a map...".[24] Moreover, he sketches in broad outlines the history of Hanover prior to the time he is going to discuss. The closer he comes to the life and times of Haarmann, the more he goes into details. Finally, Lessing extensively describes the historical context of Haarmann's crimes: the circumstances in Germany, and in particular in Hanover, in the years immediately following the First World War, and the consequences they had:

> Germany had no army. Proletarian youth, excited, depraved, and for years misled and abused in the most irresponsible way, suddenly lacked restraint and guidance. The beaten people hit back. Political murder became habitual. The police force (uniformed police, security police, criminal investigation), limited by the Treaty of Versailles, could not handle these criminal elements, returning from a long life in war, no longer used to being settled. The lower ranks of the police [...] men, who several times a week spend the night on the street until four o'clock in the morning and nevertheless have to be back in the office at nine, were paid so poorly that they became ever more susceptible for the smallest bit of help, for the smallest gift, even from the hands of criminals. One demanded the superhuman from these rightly embittered, only poorly educated officials. In Haarmann's time, the entire vice squad of Hanover consisted of twelve detectives and a police commissioner, who had to monitor around four thousand women living from prostitution (of whom only four hundred are registered prostitutes) and at least three hundred male prostitutes.[25]

---

24   'Wäre ich Schulrat, keine Geschichtsstunde ließe ich zu ohne Landkarte...'; Theodor Lessing, "Was ist Geschichte?", o.c., 245. Lessing puts this recommendation in the mouth of a teacher of history.

25   'Deutschland hatte kein Heer. Die proletarische Jugend, aufgeregt, verwildert, und jahrelang aufs unverantwortlichste irregeleitet und mißbraucht, entbehrte plötzlich der Hemmung und Führung. Das geschlagene Volk schlug zurück. Der politische Mord wurde zur Gewohnheit. Die durch den Vertrag von Versailles beschränkte Polizeimacht (Schutz-, Sicherheits- und Kriminalpolizei) konnte mit den aus langem Kriegsleben Zurückkehrenden, der bürgerlichen Seßhaftigkeit entwöhnten verbrecherischen Elementen nicht fertig werden. Die untere Polizeimannschaft [...], Männer, die mehrmals in der Woche die Nächte bis früh 4 Uhr auf der Straße zubringen und dann noch schon wieder gegen 9 Uhr auf dem Büro sein müssen, war so jämmerlich bezahlt, daß sie für jede kleinste Hilfe und für jedes Geschenk, sogar aus Verbrecherhänden, immer empfänglicher wurde. Man verlangte von diesen mit Recht verbitterten, nur wenig gebildeten Subalternbeamten Übermenschliches. Das gesamte Unzuchtsdezernat der Kriminalpolizei in Hannover bestand zur Haarmanns Zeiten aus 12 Kriminalbeamten und einem Kommissar,

Only at this point, having discussed both the geographical and the historical context, Lessing focuses on the Haarmann-case itself: the crimes Haarmann allegedly committed, and his trial. Lessing describes all twenty-seven cases in which Haarmann was suspected of murder. Mostly, these are quite extensive descriptions; to give an impression of his approach, here is his description – the most concise of all – of one of the murders Haarmann allegedly committed:

> *Wilhelm Schulze from Colshorn, born 31st August 1906, disappeared on 20th March 1923*
> Wilhelm Schulze, apprentice-clerk, a precocious, adventurous lad, sixteen years and a half years old, son of the meanwhile deceased train furniture manufacturer Otto Schulze and his good to a fault, simple wife who now lives in Lehrte, went to his work in the city and one day did not return. Mortal remains have not been traced. The clothes were found with Mrs. Engel. Haarmann had intercepted the boy at the railway station and taken him along.[26]

Having discussed all twenty-seven cases, Lessing reports extensively on the trial itself, to conclude his book with his own view of the matter – that is, both his view on Haarmann's crimes and on the judicial process. Lessing's final verdict on the Haarmann case corresponds with his observations on his approach in this book: a society which allowed Haarmann to commit his crimes is jointly responsible for these crimes. Hence, only substantial changes in politics and society can prevent similar crimes being committed again in the future. And if suchlike reforms will not be carried through, society will be guilty of future crimes. Thus, Lessing's conclusion comes down to an appeal for political and social reform. To remind the inhabitants of Hanover of this very mission, a memorial for Haarmann's victims should be erected in the centre of the city, Lessing suggests. And the inscription should only read: "All of us are to blame!".[27]

---

welche ungefähr 4000 von Prostitution lebenden Frauen (wovon nur 400 eingeschriebene Dirnen sind) und mindestens 300 männliche Prostituenten zu überwachen hatten.'; Theodor Lessing, *Haarmann*, o.c., 75.

26 'Wilhelm Schulze aus Colshorn, geb. 31. August 1906, verschwand 23. März 1923 Wilhelm Schulze, Schreiberlehrling, ein frühfertiger, abenteuer-lustiger Junge, 16½ Jahre alt, Sohn des inzwischen verstorbenen Eisenbahntischlers Otto Schulze und seiner nun in Lehrte wohnenden kreuzbraven, schlichten Ehefrau, fuhr in die Stadt zur Arbeit und kam eines Tages nicht wieder. Leichenreste sind nicht ermittelt. Die Kleider fanden sich bei der Engel. Haarmann hatte den Jungen auf dem Bahnhof abgefangen und mit sich genommen.'; o.c., 131.

27 'Unser aller Schuld!'; o.c., 193.

Now the question is: how does this chronicle of the Haarmann case, this history of Hanover in the 1920's, relate to Lessing's philosophical analysis of history as expounded in *Geschichte als Sinngebung des Sinnlosen* and "Was ist Geschichte?", his address for the *Internationale Geschichtstagung*?

What immediately strikes the eye is that Lessing is deeply committed to establish what exactly happened in the Haarmann case: what did Fritz Haarmann do? To what extent was his accomplice Hans Grans involved? What happened to each and every one of the twenty-seven alleged victims of Haarmann? How did the police proceed when investigating Haarmann? Why did the local police initially try to cover up Haarmann's involvement? These questions guide Lessing's argument, and he tries to answer them as precisely as possible. Indeed, it is no exaggeration to maintain that he tries to establish the truth of the matter in the traditional sense of the word, not in the sense that he himself gave to the notion of truth in *Geschichte als Sinngebung des Sinnlosen*. That is, he strives for correspondence between his report and a past state of affairs, or, as philosophers of history prefer, between his report and what the evidence at his disposal obliges him to believe about a past state of affairs. Lessing does not proudly exclaim "I want it to have been like this!", as he suggested in *Geschichte als Sinngebung des Sinnlosen*; instead he carefully and conscientiously studies the evidence to infer what most probably happened.

Though Lessing's tone in the book is generally quite composed, when he accuses the authorities – both the judiciary and the police – of trying to conceal the truth of the matter, his emotional involvement is obvious. The difference is even striking: Lessing's descriptions of Haarmann's horrible crimes are predominantly non-accusatory, referring to mitigating circumstances which do not, of course, clear Haarmann of his crimes, but which do help to understand how it was possible that he could have committed them. Lessing does not show similar understanding for the authorities, however. Following an arrest for petty crimes, the local police of Hanover had used Haarmann as an informer for a number of years. With some people, Haarmann even had the nickname "Herr Kommissar" ('Mr. Superintendent'). Haarmann derived some privileges from his status as informer; in Hanover station, for example, he had admission to rooms that were open only to the staff of the station and to the police. When Haarmann started to be under suspicion, Hanover police considered it of little importance. As a result, Haarmann was not barred earlier – had the police taken these early allegations seriously, a number of his killings would not have taken place. Later on, when the suspicions against him grew stronger and stronger, the police tried to conceal its use of Haarmann as an informer. According to Lessing, in its turn the court tried to cover the police, keeping its relations with Haarmann a secret. In his reports in the *Prager*

Tageblatt – which form the nucleus of the book on Haarmann – Lessing protested vehemently: he was truly enraged because the authorities attempted to cover up the truth in this trial. Likewise, he was also infuriated when the higher echelons of the police tried to put all the blame for not immediately investigating the allegations against Haarmann on the lower ranks, without taking any responsibility themselves. Therefore, while Lessing in both *Geschichte als Sinngebung des Sinnlosen* and "Was ist Geschichte?" denied that history can establish the truth about the past, in his report on the Haarmann-case he not only considered it possible to establish the truth, but was, moreover, most furious when he was convinced that the authorities tried to cover up this truth. In this respect, there seems to be a contrast between Lessing as philosopher of history, and Lessing as historian of the Haarmann-case.

In both *Geschichte als Sinngebung des Sinnlosen* and "Was ist Geschichte?", Lessing claimed that the main function of history within a culture or nation is to enthuse, that is, to tell inspiring stories about the past and, thus, to spread ideals. Does this hold true for his report on the Haarmann-case as well? In a sense, I think, it does: Lessing tells the story of the crimes and trial of Haarmann expressly with an ideal in view: he wants to see justice done. Both his reports on the Haarmann-case and his other court reports[28] eventually are meant to serve the ideal of justice.

To sum up: Lessing's book on the crimes and the trial of the serial killer Fritz Haarmann may be read as a history of the Haarmann-case, and even as a local history of Hanover in the years following the First World War – one does not, I think, do an injustice to either the author or his book by reading it this way. If one reads the report on Haarmann as a specimen of history, Lessing turns out to be a quite traditional historian, extensively describing the geographical and the historical context of the occurrences that form the object of his book. Moreover, he seems to presume a correspondence theory of truth, contrary to the ideas he developed in both *Geschichte als Sinngebung des Sinnlosen* and "Was ist Geschichte?" – in both these writings he had, after all, emphasized that history by definition cannot be true, and that it is indeed a category mistake to apply the notion of "truth" to history. But, as said, his report on Haarmann serves to spread the ideal of justice, and in this sense the Haarmann book is indeed in line with Lessing's philosophical analysis of history.

---

28 These other court reports are now collected in *Haarmann*, ed. by Rainer Marwedel, o.c., in the section "Leerlauf des Willens. Gerichtsreportagen und Essays" ('Draining away of the will. Court reports and essays'), 219–279.

3 Reply to His Critics

Even though *Geschichte als Sinngebung des Sinnlosen* was the book which brought Theodor Lessing his first success, not all reviews were entirely favourable.[29] Lessing even felt compelled to respond to some of the criticisms as put forward in several reviews. He did so in the "Preface" of the fourth, completely revised edition of the book that was published in 1927, claiming that the 1927 edition even is "a completely new work as compared to earlier editions".[30] Lessing alleges that most criticisms of his book are the result of misunderstandings; in the "Preface", he tries to clarify some of these in a nutshell, but as a matter of fact clarifying the misunderstandings of his philosophical ideas by elucidating his analysis of history was one of the main reasons to publish this fourth edition as such. Moreover, explaining these misunderstandings also gave him the opportunity to define his own philosophical position, acknowledging the influence of in particular Theodor Lipps and Edmund Husserl, but at the same time expounding in what way he differed from these teachers. Yet another reason to publish this revised edition was that according to Lessing himself as well, the first edition was "a fruit of its time",[31] though "not *only* a fruit of its time".[32] As he maintains:

> Time-bound and only too time-bound was the language and the mood of my book: a bitter, agitated language. At one time, desperate about an era of brutalization and stultification. At another time, furious and accusing. A mood which made it easy for opponents to dismiss my strictly well-considered and strictly factual book easily with the slogan: "pessimism" (with which one likes to brush aside all truth). Or to put me off with the characteristic: scepticism (with which one easily devalues all search for rigorous certainty).[33]

---

29   For an overview, cfr. Chapter six, below, 288–304.
30   'Den früheren Auflagen gegenüber ein völlig neues Werk'; *GSS4*, 26.
31   'eine Frucht der Zeit'; o.c., 4.
32   'nicht *nur* eine Frucht der Zeit'; loc.cit.. The italics are Lessing's.
33   'Zeitbedingt aber und nur allzu zeitbedingt war die Sprache und die Stimmung meines Buches: eine bittere, gehetzte Sprache. Bald verzweifelt über ein Zeitalter der Verrohung und Verdummung. Bald zornig und anklagend. Eine Stimmung, die es den Gegnern leicht machte, mein streng durchdachtes und streng sachliches Werk einfach abzutun, mit dem Schlagwort „Pessimismus" (womit man gerne alle Wahrheit beiseite schiebt). Oder mich kurz abzufertigen mit der Kennmarke: Skepsis (womit man alles Suchen nach strenger Sicherheit leicht entwerten kann).'; loc.cit..

Moreover, the atmosphere in which Lessing's book was first published was not very welcoming, the author claims: "It [the book, HS] contradicted the sense of the time when everyone made politics and world history and in which one was hardly inclined to follow lines of reasoning which seem to lead to nothing and to reveal history as a flatulent delusion".[34] This is a reference, of course, to the First World War and its immediate aftermath, and to Lessing's refusal to be carried away, like all too many of his contemporaries, by the fluctuations of the state of mind in everyday politics. In this connection it should especially be noted that shortly after *Geschichte als Sinngebung des Sinnlosen*, with the same Munich publisher *Der Untergang des Abendlandes* ('The Decline of the West')[35] by Oswald Spengler (1880–1936) appeared. Spengler's book was a major success, a true bestseller, and it completely overshadowed Lessing's book. In fact, even though Lessing's and Spengler's book completely differed in their approach to history, nevertheless both were often mentioned in the same breath, Lessing sometimes even being called an epigone of Spengler. Their books were frequently thought to be related with respect to content, this being, though, Lessing claims, completely out of place. He considered Spengler's book an example of the very "biological naturalism"[36] he fought against – "this irresponsible nonsense [that], without any logical explanation of notions, conceives nations, cultures, the arts and literatures of the world as if they can be put on a par with organic forms of life [...]."[37] Or, in the terminology of Lessing's theory of three spheres, Spengler failed to distinguish between the spheres of *vitalité* and *réalité*, and consequently his view on history is fundamentally faulty. Even if there are superficial similarities between *Geschichte als Sinngebung des Sinnlosen* and *Der Untergang des Abendlandes*, both, for instance, discussing Europe and its relation to Asia, the differences between the two books are so basic that Lessing repudiated being associated with Spengler. – Although Lessing does not explicitly refer to this, it is not unlikely that differences in political outlook also played a part: Spengler was distinctly conservative, whereas Lessing was a confirmed leftist. –

---

34   'Es widersprach der Gefühlshaltung von Tagen, in denen jedermann Politik und Weltgeschichte machte und in denen man wenig geneigt war, Gedankengänge zu folgen, welche ins Leere zu führen und Geschichte als windschaffenen Wahn zu enthüllen schienen.'; loc.cit..
35   Oswald Spengler, *Der Untergang des Abendlandes. Umrisse einer Morphologie der Weltgeschichte*, 2 volumes (Munich 1918–1923).
36   'biologischer Naturalismus'; Theodor Lessing, o.c., 6.
37   'diesen unverantwortlichen Unfug, ohne logische Begriffserklärung, die Völker, die Kulturen, die Kunst- und Schrifttümer der Erde so aufzufassen, als seien sie gleichsetzbar mit organischen Lebensgestalten [...]'; loc.cit..

Which, then, are the criticisms that Lessing discusses in the "Preface" of the fourth edition of *Geschichte als Sinngebung des Sinnlosen*? For convenience, Lessing distinguishes four main groups of criticisms, which he discusses in turn.

The first group concern the criticisms put forward by philosophers from the so-called "Baden School" of Neo-Kantian philosophy. Starting point for these criticisms is the alleged distinction between natural sciences and historical sciences – a distinction that was elaborated by, for instance, philosophers like Wilhelm Windelband and Heinrich Rickert. Windelband argued that the natural sciences are aimed at establishing general laws in explaining natural phenomena, whereas the historical sciences are oriented towards the description of singular events. But Lessing rejects on principle this distinction between the natural sciences and the historical sciences, claiming that what they have in common is far more important than the differences they admittedly do have as well. According to Lessing

> both natural reality and historical reality only come into being indirectly and in their directedness towards the human self (idiomorphic) and are neither living nor true, but: construction of the being that at the core of consciousness breaks way into a reflected world that mirrors *undivided* being.[38]

In other words, both the natural reality that is studied by the natural sciences and the historical reality that is studied by the historical sciences eventually are constructions of human consciousness – and this similarity is far more important, Lessing argues, than any differences between the two. This implies that Lessing rejects any philosophy which presupposes a distinction between subject and object – for in all philosophies in which a distinction between subject and object is presupposed, reality is presupposed as something given, a given, moreover, that is only naively believed. For reality is not given, but constructed, Lessing emphasizes, and as such it cannot be separated from the consciousness that constructs it. But, Lessing claims, the approach of the Baden School does not show any awareness of this character of reality: it starts with

---

38 'beides, Naturwirklichkeit wie Geschichtswirklichkeit, durchaus nur mittelbar und menschlich-ichbezüglich (idiomorph) zustande kommt und weder lebendig ist noch wahr, sondern: Zusammenbau des im Schwärpunkt des Bewußtseins auseinandertretenden Seins zu einer das *ungespaltene* Sein spiegelnden Reflexwelt.'; o.c., 11. The italics are Lessing's.

presupposing "historical reality", only to claim on second thoughts that it is relative – that is, it is dependent on the mind that forms it. As Lessing puts it: "he who wants to prove that 'the given world' is mere appearance, just presupposes behind it the world as one that is *not* appearance; because every appearance points at some existence".[39] In Lessing's view, this attitude is typical of European philosophy as a whole, not just of philosophy of history: it habitually tends "to presuppose reality in order to prove it does not exist".[40] Examples may be found in the philosophy of religion, or in the philosophy of art as well. It is what Lessing calls "the ontic trick"[41] – and this is exactly what Windelband, Rickert and their followers did for history. Lessing claims that it eventually is nothing but switching over between the poles of realism and idealism – but he considers it an outdated kind of epistemology that is already dead and buried. Eventually, this epistemology comes down to a simple claim: reality is what we need it to be – and Lessing opposes this very way of thinking, and concludes:

> Only this is right: history is not *knowing* like the natural sciences. History only seems to be a science.
>
> In science, only a continuously renewed checking of what once was calculated is necessary. History, in contrast, has to be experienced anew continuously, and even would not be when it is not "experienced". It is not about continuously checking again, or about new connections between facts that are established once and for all. No! The historical fact only comes into existence in the act of cathartic understanding of an occurrence that makes it into an event. There is no historical reality at all outside of experiencing it. Likewise, there "are" no tones somewhere in space or time outside of "experiencing music".[42]

---

39   'Wer beweisen will, daß die "gegebene Welt" eine scheinbare sei, der setzt eben hinter ihr noch einmal die Welt als eine *nicht* scheinbare voraus; denn jeder Schein deutet auf irgendein Sein.'; o.c., 12. The italics are Lessing's.
40   'Wirklichkeit voraussetzen um zu beweisen, daß sie nicht da sei'; o.c., 13.
41   'den Ontischen Trick'; loc.cit..
42   'Richtig ist nur: Geschichte ist kein *Wissen* wie Naturwissenschaft. Geschichte ist nur scheinbar Wissenschaft.
    Beim Wissen ist lediglich nötig ein immer neues Nachrechnen des schon einmal Errechneten. Geschichte dagegen muß immer neu erlebt werden und wäre gar nicht, wenn sie nicht "erlebt" wird. Es handelt sich nicht um ein immer neues Nachprüfen oder neues Verknüpfen ein für allemal festgestellter Tatsachen. Nein! Die geschichtliche Tatsache entsteht erst mit dem Akt des Aufnehmens von Geschehnis zu Ereignis. Es gibt überhaupt keine geschichtliche Wirklichkeit außerhalb ihres Erlebens. So "gibt" es auch keine Töne irgendwo im Raum oder in der Zeit außerhalb des "Erlebens von Musik".'; o.c., 15–16.

It is noteworthy that while Lessing rejects on the one hand the criticisms of his philosophy of history by the Baden School, because it presupposes a fundamental difference between the natural and the historical sciences, on the other hand in his own argument against the Baden School specific differences between the natural and the historical sciences are pivotal.

A second group of criticisms levelled at *Geschichte als Sinngebung des Sinnlosen* was put forward by the philosopher and theologian Ernst Troeltsch (1865–1923). Troeltsch was a versatile author, who showed interest in philosophy of history as well, and discussed the epistemology of history extensively in his *Der Historismus und seine Probleme* (1922; 'Historism and its problems'). In this book, he mentions Lessing briefly in a footnote, following a discussion of Schopenhauer and Nietzsche.[43] Troeltsch criticized Lessing both in writing and in a conversation, and allegedly admitted Lessing's criticisms of history – or, as Troeltsch called it, his "repudiation of history" – had disturbed him.[44] But the very fact that Troeltsch called Lessing's analysis of history a repudiation indicates, Lessing claims, that Troeltsch naively believes in the reality of the past. In this connection, his repeated objection that Lessing could not possibly deny that it is, for instance, a fact that Goethe was born on August 28th, 1749, just testifies to this naive belief in the reality of the past, Lessing argues. He maintains, however, that he would never want to deny this fact, nor similar facts, for that matter. But the real question is: what does this fact mean? According to Lessing, establishing a fact like the birth of Goethe simply is not (yet) history: it precedes history, providing at most a skeleton for it. But, to hold on to this metaphor, this skeleton has to be made into a body, and life has to be breathed into this body – and this is what history is all about. The fact that Goethe was born on August 28th, 1749, has to be incorporated in a story about, for instance, his life – a story that is told in such a manner that readers "experience" Goethe's life, and are inspired by the story of his life. But a story can inspire only if it is told time and again, tailored for the audience it is told to. This implies that all historical personalities and all historical events "continuously have to be judged and fictionalised anew, partially on the ground of political-economic needs, partially in view of ethical-ideological desires of the group and of human communities".[45] Only a past that thus is brought to life by

---

43   Ernst Troeltsch, *Der Historismus und seine Probleme. Erstes Buch: Das logische Problem der Geschichtsphilosophie* (1922; I used the reprint: Aalen 1961), 577–578.
44   Theodor Lessing, o.c., 16.
45   'sondern fortdauernd neu gerichtet und umgedichtet werden muß, teils auf Grund politisch-wirtschaftlicher Bedürfnisse, teils in Hinblick auf die sittlich-ideologischen Wunschanbilde der Gruppe und der menschlichen Gemeinschaftsverbände'; o.c., 17.

the historian is accessible for experience. This does not imply that the event as such is repeated: it is only repeated as a thought ("Gedanke"). The longer ago the events happened about which the stories are told, the more they turn into a myth: in, say, five hundred years time our present-day reality will have turned into a myth. For this very reason, historians should not want to be investigators of (past) reality: they should want to be better poets of myths, Lessing maintains.

A third group of criticisms of *Geschichte als Sinngebung des Sinnlosen* suggested that the book was nothing but a duplication of *Die Philosophie des Als-Ob* (1911; 'The Philosophy of As-If') by the German philosopher Hans Vaihinger (1852–1933), though being a duplication in Lessing's own words. Lessing was even reproached for not acknowledging his indebtedness to Vaihinger. However, Lessing denied having read Vaihinger's book when he wrote *Geschichte als Sinngebung des Sinnlosen*. When he noted the contents of these criticisms, he did, however – only to conclude that Vaihinger does not discuss either history or the epistemology of history, and that for this reason these criticisms are not to the point at all. Moreover, Lessing claims, there are fundamental differences between Vaihinger's philosophy and his own. According to Vaihinger, truth is relative – an idea Lessing could never endorse: according to Lessing, reality is relative in the sense that it depends on the consciousness that forms it, but truth is not. Truth, after all, is proper to the sphere of *vérité*; the truth of logical deductions does not depend on consciousness. Hence, only those who truly misunderstood his book could suppose he was indebted to Vaihinger, Lessing claims.

Even though several reviews of Lessing's book were not very friendly and even rather sour, there was praise as well – by poets, authors, artists, students, and publicists. But the best review, according to Lessing, was the one by the Austrian writer and dramatist Hermann Bahr.[46] Although Bahr's review was appreciative, it raised an objection against Lessing's approach that induced him to answer – also because Bahr was not the only one to moot the subject. In a nutshell, this objection comes down to the thought that, even if man – as Lessing urges – gives sense to history, it is still possible that there is a higher sense to history, like for instance a divine plan that underlies the historical process. This objection shows, however, Lessing claims, that Bahr and others misunderstood the title of his book. After all, a philosopher by virtue of his profession does not speculate about the past as a whole, but tries to elucidate

---

46   Cfr. Hermann Bahr, 'Tagebuch', in: *Neues Wiener Journal. Unparteiliches Tagblatt*, 27. Jahrgang, Nr. 9195, Sonntag 8 Juni 1919, 7.

what history means – which is neither theology nor metaphysics, at least, not according to Lessing.[47] Moreover, even if Lessing goes beyond the framework of his investigation and tries to answer Bahr's question, his reply would be negative – that is, if the word "sense" is used like Lessing does: "A 'sense' of events may thus only exist in so far as we are conscious of it".[48]

Lessing wonders why some of the reviews of *Geschichte als Sinngebung des Sinnlosen* are so distinctly negative, and even hostile. Why is it, apparently, so controversial to question traditional ideas about history, at a time when so much that always was taken for granted is being questioned? Well, man simply cannot live without delusions, Lessing claims. Man's self-love has been hurt three times, Lessing quotes Sigmund Freud (1856–1939): when he discovered that the earth is not at the centre of the universe; when he discovered that biologically he is not fundamentally different from plants and animals; and when he discovered that his behaviour is not guided by a free and autonomous reason.[49] But these blows are almost insignificant, Lessing claims, in comparison with the fourth blow: the discovery that history is a myth that is, nevertheless, necessary for human life, a discovery, moreover, that has to be notified to a generation that has lost the strength for myth.

4 A New Light on His Own Writings

How does the fourth edition of *Geschichte als Sinngebung des Sinnlosen* relate to the earlier editions, in particular the first one, as the second and third editions were just reprints of the first one? Lessing addresses this question himself in the "Preface" of the fourth edition.[50] He claims that the readers of the first edition regularly misunderstood his presuppositions, especially regarding epistemology, and consequently misunderstood the argument of the book. For

---

47 Of course, there are metaphysical interpretations of history, but Lessing implicitly rejects this approach with this observation.
48 "'Sinn' des Geschehens kann es also gerade nur so weit geben als wir uns seiner bewußt sind.'; Theodor Lessing, o.c., 22.
49 Lessing gives the impression of quoting Freud verbally, but in fact he does not. Freud expounded his theory of the three blows both in 'Eine Schwierigkeit der Psychoanalyse', in: *Imago. Zeitschrift für Anwendung der Psychoanalyse auf die Geisteswissenschaften* vol. V (1917), 1–7; and in '18. Vorlesung: Die Fixierung an das Trauma, das Unbewusste', in his *Vorlesungen zur Einführung in die Psychoanalyse* (1917). Lessing's text does not correspond with either of these texts by Freud, even if the drift of the argument is the same.
50 Theodor Lessing, o.c., 25–27.

this very reason, in this fourth edition Lessing focuses almost exclusively on the epistemology of history – the topic that he discussed in the "first book" of the first edition of *Geschichte als Sinngebung des Sinnlosen*. This implies that he does not discuss the topics of the "second book" – the psychology of history – and the "third book" – history as an ideal – respectively, in this fourth edition. Thus, in comparison with the first edition, the scope of the fourth edition is limited. With this new edition, Lessing hopes to elucidate the argument of the first edition – that is, to cast a new light on his own work. But this does not imply that the earlier edition would no longer be worth reading, Lessing claims: the fourth edition addresses an audience of colleagues, whereas the first edition is addressed to the public at large. For this reason, the first edition does indeed merit to be reprinted in years to come, Lessing maintains. Eventually, the different editions of the book supplement each other – studying the one serves to understand the other, and vice versa.

In what way did Lessing change his mind in the twelve years between writing the first and the fourth edition of *Geschichte als Sinngebung des Sinnlosen*? Over these years, Lessing claims, his repugnance against the human lust for power strengthened continuously, and in particular the way it is habitually dressed up:

> ... everything from which I suffered in this world and what seemed to me malicious and hateful in humans, crude and mean, craving for power or vanity, on my path of life I always met all this in the garment of ideals. In the garment of truth: lies. In the garment of logic: insanity. In the garment of righteousness: every injustice. In the garment of love of one's country: everything that dishonoured the *Heimat*. In the garment of human progress: everything that devaluated humans. And never ever did I see a historical meanness, never a true horribleness that was not committed in the name of some ideal.[51]

But, in Lessing's view, ideals are proper to mankind: nature – that is, animals and plants – has no ideals. This indicates that humans have dissociated themselves

---

51 '... alles das, woran ich auf Erden gelitten habe und was mir am Menschen böswillig und gehässig erschien, brüchig und gemein, machtwillig oder eitel, alles das begegnete mir auf meinem Lebensweg stets im Gewande der Ideale. Im Gewande der Wahrheit: Lüge. Im Gewande der Logik: der Irrsinn. Im Gewande des Rechtes: jegliches Unrecht. Im Gewande der Vaterlandsliebe: alles die Heimat Entehrende. Im Gewande des Menschheitsfortschritts: alles den Menschen Entwürdigende. Und nie sah ich eine geschichtliche Niedertracht, nie eine wirkliche Abscheulichkeit, die nicht geübt wurde im Nahmen irgendeines Ideals.'; o.c., 27. The italics are mine.

from nature: they are no longer "pure" nature. Urged by need, man broke out of nature, and ever since, sees himself outside of or even opposite from nature. Of course, this does not imply that Lessing denies there is a natural or biological side to humans. But besides this natural side, there is consciousness – and human reality, including historical reality, depends on this consciousness. In practice, behaviour is guided by ideals; but ideals are not true: "Ideals, however, are the temporal ideas, which got attained in the world of arbitrariness and in the dirt of the stream of time."[52] The legend of a lost paradise, which one may find in many cultures, is symbolic for the difference between ideals and ideas, Lessing argues: ideas are 'objective' and independent of human consciousness and accordingly true and forever valid, and in this sense proper to paradise. Ideals, in contrast, belong to human reality, which means they depend on human consciousness. In the terminology of Lessing's theory of three spheres: ideas belong to *vérité*, ideals belong to *réalité*. – It is crucial to realize that in the fourth edition of *Geschichte als Sinngebung des Sinnlosen* Lessing changed his vocabulary in this respect in comparison with the first edition. In the latter, he did not strictly distinguish between "ideals" and "ideas", and used the word "ideal" to refer to both. So "ideal" could both refer to eternally valid ideas in the realm of *vérité*, and to their pale shadow that man tries to implement in *réalité*. But the introduction of the term "idea" in the fourth edition of the book implies that hereafter "idea" is proper to *vérité*, and "ideal" to *réalité*.[53] But this is merely a change of vocabulary, not a change of mind. Or, more precisely, it is a refinement of Lessing's vocabulary. The introduction of the term "idea" opens up the possibility of a more differentiated description of the theory of three spheres, enabling Lessing to describe the demarcation between *vérité* and *réalité* more clearly. For it helps to understand why history is proper to *réalité*, whereas the ideas in the realm of *vérité* – being eternally valid and unchanging – have no history. At the risk of stating the obvious, the example of a circle is illustrative. When one asks someone to draw a circle on a blackboard and the circle drawn is not perfectly round, one does not change the definition of a circle: it will rather be concluded that this drawing is not a true circle. In Lessing's terminology, the circle belongs to *vérité*: the idea of a circle is forever

---

52 'Ideale aber sind die zeitlich gewordenen, in die Willkürwelt und in den Schmutz des Zeitstroms hineingeratenen Ideen.'; o.c., 28.

53 Lessing already made a distinction between "ideas" and "ideals" in his address "Volkshochschule als Kulturwert" ('Folk High school as cultural value'), on occasion of the fifth anniversary of the Volkshochschule Hannover: "die Bilder [...] nennen wir (im Theoretischen) Ideen oder (im Praktischen) Ideale" ('these images we call (in the theoretical realm) ideas or (in the practical realm) ideals'); Theodor Lessing, 'Volkshochschule als Kulturwert', quoted from *WeU*, 220–228, at 226.

valid and unchanging, accordingly not having a history. But our efforts to draw a circle belong to *réalité*: the drawing is at best an approximation of a perfect circle, and our efforts to draw a circle do not change the idea of it. This implies that there can be a history of drawing a circle, but not of the idea of a circle: our efforts are proper to *réalité*, the idea of a circle is proper to *vérité*. So, history is proper to *réalité*, while *vitalité* and *vérité* do not know history. As it is put by Lessing: history is proper to

> [...] the world of the reality that is immanent in our consciousness. And only this has history, not the living, not the true.[54]

All this implies, Lessing argues, that man should not be troubled too much over history: man should live! Too much history will only paralyse man, and, moreover, in a thousand years time nothing will remain of the world history that we imagine we are making at present but a few myths, a few anecdotes.

Lessing's observation that history is proper to "the world of the reality that is immanent in our consciousness" may suggest that in this fourth edition of *Geschichte als Sinngebung des Sinnlosen* his main inspiration is the phenomenology of Lipps and Husserl, as it had been in the first edition. This is, after all, the language of phenomenology. And in any case, this fourth edition, again, is not an empirical study of historiography and, again, it hardly contains references to history books. Nevertheless, Lessing claims he has gradually dissociated himself from the influences of his teachers and, in comparison with the first edition of his book, more expressly takes a philosophical position of his own. In an "Appendix" to the first part of the fourth edition of *Geschichte als Sinngebung des Sinnlosen*, Lessing not only gives an overview of his definitions and an explanation of the notions used in the book, but also elucidates his own position. Lessing claims his philosophical position differs from that of all of his contemporaries, saying:

> Hence, it would be best if we divide all the insane bustle of academic science and academic philosophy in "pushers" and "oppressed". [...] Those who currently philosophize *actively* at European and American universities (so, for instance, types like Hermann Cohen, Hans Vaihinger, all Kantians, all pragmatists, all psychologists, all positivists, etc.) let themselves

---

[54] 'die Welt der Bewußtseinsimmanenten Wirklichkeit. Und nur diese, nicht das Lebendige, nicht das Wahre hat Geschichte.'; *GSS4*, 29.'The living' refers, of course to *vitalité*, 'the true' to *vérité*.

unawares be led by the *will*, that is, the European-American practice and factualism that overwhelms the world and dissolves nature.

The other way round: Those who philosophize *passively* at the present European and American universities (so, for instance, types like Edmund Husserl, Henri Bergson, Max Scheler) let themselves unawares be led by Christianity or its churches (Christian science, anthroposophy, and the like).

Every active attitude unrelentingly results in: ethics, axiology, eudemonism, setting aims.

Every passive attitude unrelentingly results in: ontology and metaphysics.

I chose my position in sharp contrast with both these attitudes.[55]

In this connection, the question to be raised is, of course: what exactly is Lessing's specific position? In the "Appendix" just quoted, he does not dwell on this question, so his position has to be inferred from his observations on the philosophers he resists and, of course, from his other writings. As we have seen in Chapter Two, as a philosopher Lessing developed in dialogue with in particular the German language tradition of philosophy. At secondary school he read and discussed Schopenhauer and Von Hartmann with his teacher Max Schneidewin; while reading medicine he got acquainted with the somewhat idiosyncratic Neo-Kantianism of Alois Riehl; and in Munich Theodor Lipps introduced him to his own version of phenomenology. With Edmund Husserl, he subsequently went deeply into phenomenology. In my opinion, the conclusion is justified that Lessing's publications up to 1920 – bearing in mind

---

55   'Somit teilen wir denn auch das ganze irrsinnige Getriebe der Schulwissenschaft und Schulphilosophie am richtigsten auf nach "Stoßenden" und "Bedrückten ". [...] Die an den gegenwärtigen Universitäten Europas und Amerikas *aktiv* Philosophierenden (also z.B. Typen wie Hermann Cohen, Hans Vaihinger, sämtliche Kantianer, sämtliche Pragmatisten, sämtliche Psychologen, sämtliche Positivisten usw.) hängen selbunbewußt im Schlepptau des *Willens*, das will sagen der weltübermächtigenden naturauflösenden europäisch-amerikanischen Praktik und Faktik.

Umgekehrt: Die an den gegenwärtigen Universitäten Europas und Amerikas *passiv* Philosophierenden (also z.B. Typen wie Edmund Husserl, Henri Bergson, Max Scheler) hängen selbunbewußt im Schlepptau des Christentums oder seiner Kirchen (christian science, Anthroposophie u. dgl.).

Jede aktive Einstellung mündet unerbittlich in: Ethik, Wertlehre, Eudämonie, Zielsetzung.

Jede passive Einstellung mündet unerbittlich in: Ontologemen und Metaphysiken.

Ich wählte meinen Standpunkt in scharfen Gegensatz zu diesen beiden Einstellungen.'; o.c., 120.

that a number of these were written during the war, but only published afterwards – belong to the tradition of early phenomenology. But his position was never an orthodox one: as his "Philosophie als Tat" (1907) testifies, in Lessing's eyes philosophy should eventually make a difference to the world, and should change it. So even before the First World War, his position was more "activist" than that of "orthodox" phenomenology. After the war, Lessing gradually dissociated himself from this tradition, the main reason supposedly being the attitude of prominent representatives of early phenomenology towards the war. In Lessing's opinion, Edmund Husserl stood aloof from politics, and wrongly gave priority to developing his philosophical ideas even when the world was on fire. Max Scheler, even worse, not only supported the war, but even tried to justify it in what Lessing considered a truly horrible book. For Lessing himself, however, the confrontation with need and suffering during the war strengthened his conviction that philosophy should make a difference to the world. Hence, for instance, the increase of his distinctly political writings during the Weimar Republic,[56] but also, for instance, his unselfish commitment to Hanover's *Volkshochschule*, and the observation in his autobiography *Einmal und nie wieder*: "The last message of my wisdom is: 'diminish the need!'".[57] Lessing's dissociation from early phenomenology therefore implies an increased emphasis on activism, social commitment, and social responsibility. But Lessing wanted to keep firmly aloof from the attitude that in his view is characteristic of European-American science and of large parts of European-American philosophy: the attitude of overwhelming the world and dissolving nature. This attitude is activist as well – but Lessing's activism actually is of a different nature. That is, Lessing's activism aims at diminishing the effects of the other, dominant activism. In other words: the dominant European-American attitude in science and largely in philosophy generates need and suffering – for humans, and for nature as well –, and Lessing is aimed at diminishing this very need, that is, to make life more bearable for those who suffer from the dominant European-American activism. All this implies that at least after the First World War – but in the germ it was already present before the war –, the guiding principle of Lessing's philosophy is ethical. This should not be conceived, however, as an attempt at developing an ethical theory of his own, but rather as Lessing being of the opinion that his philosophy, directly or indirectly,

---

56   Cfr. Martin Rethmeier, *Theodor Lessing – Politische Aspekte seiner Philosophie und Publizistik in der Zeit der Weimarer Republik, 1918–1933* (unpublished Schriftliche Hausarbeit RWTH Aachen, Aachen 1984), *passim*.
57   'Der letzte Bescheid meiner Weisheit lautet: "Mindere die Not!"'; *Eunw*, 252.

should ultimately contribute to the very practical aim of diminishing the need of those who suffer.[58]

To sum up, at the time when he wrote the fourth edition of *Geschichte als Sinngebung des Sinnlosen*, Lessing had dissociated himself from early phenomenology, because in his eyes it wrongly kept aloof from everyday reality – from politics and from the war. In Lessing's philosophy, however, everyday reality is crucial: it is what he wanted to be changed. He wanted to change it as regards diminishing the effects of the dominating European-American attitude in science and large parts of philosophy that overwhelms the world and dissolves nature. This is indeed a philosophical position of his own – and this is the very position that underlies the fourth edition of his critique of historical reason.

Like the first edition of *Geschichte als Sinngebung des Sinnlosen*, the fourth edition as well consists of three "books". But apart from this, the general plan of the fourth edition is completely different. In contrast to the first edition, the fourth one does not have a "constructive" part – the overall aim of the book as a whole is "destructive", that is, Lessing wants to disprove the delusion that history, in his opinion, actually embodies: the misconception of providing knowledge of past reality. So in this fourth edition, he does not – as he did in the first edition – discuss the function history, despite its delusive character, nonetheless may have in a culture or nation: telling stories that inspire communities. Even if Lessing claimed that the fourth edition of his book is more of an academic nature than the first one, his argument is not always strict, and sometimes he is not able to resist yielding to his sparks of wit.

Of the three "books" of the fourth edition of *Geschichte als Sinngebung des Sinnlosen*, the first one, entitled "Vorlogische Betrachtungen" ('Pre-logical reflections'), has a preliminary character. Lessing discusses on the one hand several aspects of man's belief in history, and on the other hand a number of general notions he is going to use in the following chapters of the book. The second book, "Logische Betrachtungen" ('Logical reflections'), deals with the categories of history, like for instance time and causality. The third and conclusive book of the fourth edition of *Geschichte als Sinngebung des Sinnlosen* is entitled "Paralogische Betrachtungen" ('Para-logical reflections'); Lessing discusses in it topics like historical reputations, images of the past, and the sense of history. Of the three books, the middle one is the largest.

---

58   Cfr. Uwe Kemmler, *Not und Notwendigkeit. Der Primat der Ethik in der Philosophie Theodor Lessings* (Oldenburg 1999), *passim*.

5 Pre-logical Reflections

The first chapter of the first book of the fourth edition of *Geschichte als Sinngebung des Sinnlosen* is entitled "Der Mensch und sein Wahn" – 'man and his delusion'. This title may be seen as programmatic for the entire book, being a concise summary of the aim of this fourth edition as a whole: Lessing tries to prove that it is a delusion that history could give true knowledge of past reality. It is a delusion, however, that is necessary for man to believe in.

The delusion of a past reality and possible knowledge thereof rests on a number of interrelated presuppositions, Lessing argues. These include that history is conceived as a sequence of events in time, imagined as a line; this sequence of events in time is progressive by nature; mankind develops like an organism, from youth to adulthood to old age; mankind is ultimately one. Eventually, all these interrelated presuppositions express the very same thought, Lessing claims: man is the measure of all things – and all these presuppositions reflect human consciousness. In other words, these are not characteristics *of* history, they are characteristics that man assigns *to* history. For example, the idea of seeing history as a line is only one of a number of possible images of history – but for modern man it is so self-evident that he is not even aware it is just one possible image of history among others. But we can only imagine history as a chain of successive events because we presuppose history being a line in time – and this very idea of history as a line in time is nothing but a historical – and in this sense: arbitrary – given, and not a logical truth. This implies, Lessing claims, that ultimately there is no reason why we should presuppose this idea of history: we simply do it, apparently because it fits our psychic needs and our scientific worldview.[59] But even if we imagine history as a line in time, "as a one-dimensional sliding forth from point in time to point in time",[60] it does not necessarily have to be continuously progressive, like "the European-American man of progress dreams".[61] One might also imagine it, for instance, as indeed one-dimensional, but as one showing a continuous decline: there is no reason to prefer the one to the other, except that the idea of linear progress fits the wants of our current worldview. But this worldview is not very generous towards history – one might even say it opposes history, Lessing claims. And the very same holds true for academic historians:

---

59 GSS4, 33–39.
60 'als eindimensionales Fortgleiten von Zeitpunkt zu Zeitpunkt'; o.c., 43.
61 'wie der europäisch-amerikanische Fortschrittsmensch es träumt'; loc. cit..

And in fact I do not hesitate to call the historians at European and American universities the true enemies of history. And consequently the ones who damage nature and the soul of peoples too. They especially are only at the service of the each time dominating aims of the will. Possessed and paid by these idols and ideals of the time, they incite and confuse, poison and entangle the souls of man.[62]

History is not knowledge of the past, Lessing maintains: history is time and again reborn out of myth – but it does not at all make sense, though, to look for myth in contemporary historical sciences, Lessing argues. Contemporary historical sciences dissolve myth, they destroy nations and their dreams, because they try to be the mechanical sciences of what happened in the past. Ultimately, these efforts come down to the same delusion, however: the delusion that history mirrors the (past) world, and that history itself is (past) reality. And all what modern historians strive for is nothing but abstract knowledge of this alleged reality:

> The historian no longer even has the ambition to be a good narrator. He is determined (with alleged "scholarship") to establish "realities".[63]

That is, history no longer is a myth nor a symbol, but bears the stamp of abstract knowledge. This implies, Lessing argues, that the current science of history – "that is, history insofar it claims to be: *science*"[64] – is nothing but the soft side of mechanical science. To underpin this assertion, one simply has to show that our modern historical worldview and our technical (mathematical-scientific) worldview ultimately are nothing but fruits from the very same tree. And, in fact, they are, Lessing maintains, referring to the work of for instance Leibniz,[65]

---

62   'Und so stehe ich in der Tat nicht an: die Historiker an den Universitäten Amerikas und Europas als die eigentlichen Feinde von Geschichte zu bezeichnen. Mithin aber auch als die Schädlinge an der Natur und an der Seele der Völker. Sie vor allem stehen durchaus nur im Dienste jeweils herrschender Willensziele. Besessen und bezahlt von diesen Idolen und Idealen der Zeit verhetzen und verwirren, vergiften und verfeinden sie die Menschenseelen'; o.c., 46.
63   'Der Historiker hat nicht einmal mehr den Ehrgeiz, ein guter Erzähler zu sein. Er will durchaus (mit vermeintlicher "Wissenschaftlichkeit") "Wirklichkeiten" feststellen.'; o.c., 49.
64   'd.h., Geschichte, soweit sie behauptet: *Wissenschaft* zu sein'; o.c., 50. The italics are Lessing's.
65   Lessing adds that Leibniz lived in Hanover – "the same place where I try to unmask modern science with it's world history as a kind of necessary insanity" ('an der selben Stätten, wo ich diesen Versuch mache, die moderne Wissenschaft mitsamt ihrer Weltgeschichte als eine Art notwendigen Irrsinns zu entlarven.'); loc.cit..

who claimed that history and mechanistic thought stem from the same intuition, and Descartes, who was of the same opinion.

According to Lessing, the key question of current history is: "how did it come about?". But this is not a truly scientific question: that can only be "what is it?". The question "how did it come about?" ultimately originates from man's pragmatic attitude – it uncovers the human urge to influence things, and to make things happen, the latter eventually being what science is about. As such, science is proper to *réalité*: and as such, it should be distinguished from on the one hand *Ahmung* (the cathartic understanding that is proper to *vitalité*) and on the other hand "reines Schauen" (pure view that is proper to *vérité*). So, characteristic for science, including current history which tries to be a science, is that it is concerned with human reality, which in its turn depends on human consciousness; and that it tries to change human reality. Thus, it is man who lurks behind current history, Lessing argues; to be specific: *homo faber*

> who for three thousand years has destroyed the vegetable world, overwhelmed the animal world, covered the world with gigantic cities, restrained streams with turbines and bridges, put the wind, the air, the light at his service and has taken apart the preconscious nature that is ruled by feelings and instincts, awaked it and finally replaced it with the realm of institutions and artefacts, the realm of works, words and values, which prevents a chaos of all instincts and completely blocks off the natural regulation [...]⁶⁶

Only for this kind of man, history could become a kind of religion, Lessing argues, using the word "religion" in its original sense, that is, a force (i.e., a story) that knits a group together. Man won the future in the sense that all his life is directed towards the future, but he lost the moment in the sense that he no longer can live by the moment. Hence, he needs history to quiet his tormented soul.

Subsequently, Lessing discusses the distinction between the natural and the historical sciences as it was commonly made in German philosophy at the time.

---

66 'welcher seit dreitausend Jahren die Pflanzenwelt vernichtet, die Tierwelt übermächtigt hat, die Erde überzog mit riesigen Städten, die Ströme bändigte mit Turbinen und Brücken, den Wind, die Luft, das Licht in seine Dienste spannte und die durch Gefühle und Triebmächte geregelte vorbewußte Natur zerlegt, wachgemacht und schließlich ersetzt hat durch das Reich der Institutionen und Artefakte, das Reich der Werke, Worte und Werte, die ein Chaos aller Instinkte hintanhalten und die Naturregelung vollkommen vertreten [...]'; o.c., 54.

In his discussion, he repeats to a large extent the argument of the first edition of *Geschichte als Sinngebung des Sinnlosen*; that is, as both the natural and the historical sciences are proper to *réalité*, both kinds of sciences have more in common than is usually realized, and what they have in common is indeed more important than what separates them.[67] Lessing digresses on this issue by including a fictional dialogue between a scientist and a philosopher of history. This does not really add to his main argument, however, since he actually does not introduce new arguments to support his rejection of the underpinning of the distinction. Neither the natural, nor the historical sciences reflect reality as such, Lessing maintains: both abstract from reality, and this is what matters for him. Strangely enough, though, he observes, the idea that the historical sciences would reflect (past) reality is hardly ever questioned, whereas the idea that the natural sciences reflect reality usually is, because notions like "atom", or "gravity" are generally seen as theoretical constructions. For Lessing, this is incomprehensible: how can mankind be so "superstitious" with regard to one kind of sciences and yet so critical towards another? After all, notions like "historical unity", "connection" or "period" are theoretical constructions too. For this reason, Lessing aims to show there is, at least in this respect, hardly any difference between the historical and natural sciences. Lessing supposes this difference in attitude towards the different kinds of sciences has to be interpreted psychologically. Within the natural sciences doubt as regard the ontological status of theoretical constructions is after all is said and done with considered positively: it advances new research and brings about new insights without the issue of the status of theoretical concepts being involved. With the historical sciences, however, doubt with regard to this issue is considered a threat: it questions as it were the very nature of (historical) thinking itself, and this will inevitably lead to the conclusion that thinking eventually destroys life. But if thinking destroys life, ultimately there is little sense in everything man does. Hence, Lessing argues, in the end there are only two possible attitudes to life: either submerge in being, that is, abstaining from history and development; or being acquiescent to what is happening anyway, which is to abolish thinking by thinking. According to Lessing, eventually this is the choice between Brahmanism and Buddhism,[68] but the question is whether this choice is open for modern man in the Western world: both attitudes are, after all, incompatible with his activist approach to the world. In short, the reason why man shrinks back from a radical critique of the historical sciences, and of historical thinking, is that it threatens a fuddle, the fuddle that forms life:

---

67   Cfr. chapter four above, 158.
68   Theodor Lessing, o.c., 69.

Fuddle however is a creative power of life. Life always rises from fuddle; knowledge always stems from pain.⁶⁹

According to Lessing, this implies that "all self-preservation and all self-justification, yes, one can safely say: all life of mankind as a thinking consciousness risen out of nature, depends on the safeguard of the belief in history".⁷⁰ In other words, life of modern man depends on self-deceit; nothing is more undermining for the very foundations on which all of Western civilisation is built than uncovering this self-deceit. Be this as it may, Lessing argues, the survival of a civilisation neither is nor can be a criterion for truth; his analysis just helps to understand how far-reaching the consequences of his critique of historical reason may be, and accordingly why it is so very controversial.

But first there is another question to answer, Lessing maintains: where does this belief in history originate? Lessing argues that the first author to introduce the ideas of cohesion in history and of progress in time was Giambattista Vico in his *Scienza nuova* (1725). Admittedly, Vico was convinced history develops in cycles and not as a straight line in time; but apart from this, many of his ideas on history proved to be very influential. A number of later thinkers elaborated these ideas, until Darwin, Hegel, and Marx systematized them for the natural sciences, history, and economics respectively. They are

> the three masks that my book uncovers. But what lurks behind them? The face of a most specific kind of man. A haughty, immodest, power-hungry, self-righteous face. On it is chiselled inexorably: "It is *us* who matter!".⁷¹

This is the very face that watched him from his childhood, Lessing claims. But his philosophy is inspired by a different attitude that is not dominated by an "imperious consciousness"⁷² that wants to order and to control all reality. It is inspired by a new attitude, its philosophy implying that history should be seen as neither living nor true, nor considered a science. But this position can

---

69 'Rausch aber ist ein bildende Macht des Lebens. Leben steigt immer aus Rausch, Wissen kommt immer aus Schmerz'; o.c., 70.
70 'Die gesamte Selbsterhaltung und Selbstrechtfertigung, ja, man kann getrost sagen: das ganze Leben der Menschheit, als eines aus der Natur herausgetretenen denkenden Geistes, hängt an der Sicherung des Geschichtsglaubens'; loc.cit..
71 'die drei Masken, die mein Buch entlarvt. Was aber lauert hinter ihnen? Das Gesicht einer ganz bestimmten Menschenart! Ein hochmutiges, demutloses, machtwilliges, selbstgerechten Antlitz. Darauf steht ehern eingeschrieben: "Auf *Uns* kommt es an!"'; o.c., 72. The italics are Lessing's.
72 'herrischen Bewußtsein'; o.c., 73.

only be understood, Lessing argues, if a number of questions is answered – questions like: what is reality? What is history? What is the sense of history? In discussing these questions, his starting-point is the European-American idea of history, "that 'world history' which conceives history as happening in time, stemming from a natural condition, and ending in a consciousness that wants aims".[73]

To make sure his readers will not misunderstand him, Lessing explains the terminology he will hereafter use in his book, emphasizing that history should be distinguished from life on the one hand, and from truth on the other.

> What history books contain and transmit, is life in the mirror of a wanting by a human consciousness that determines targets, consequently being neither element of the living-as-such nor "true" in the timeless sense. History is temporal reality, and like all contents of consciousness just also actively shaped by those categories of thinking and relating without which contents of consciousness would not exist at all, by the categories of connection in time, of progress of a linear movement, in which "a historical subject" as bearer of history finds itself, maintains itself and preserves itself. But in no way history does directly show a causal connection or a development in time without human supplement. History is rather the foundation of this sense; the definition of this connection; the invention of this development. It does not come upon the sense of the world, it gives it...[74]

This very conception of history is the basis of all of Lessing's subsequent reflections on history. It is, of course, nothing but a rephrasing of his theory of three spheres, a rephrasing with history in mind; but as regards content it is in no sense different from the general phrasing of this theory. This shows how much

---

73   'Jene "Weltgeschichte", welche die Welt betrachtet als Geschehen in der Zeit, entstehend aus einem Naturzustand und endigend in einem Ziele wollenden Geistes.'; o.c., 75.

74   'Was die Bücher der Geschichte enthalten und überliefern, das ist Leben im Spiegel eines menschlich-bewußten zwecksetzenden Wollen, also weder Element des An-sich-Lebenden noch auch "wahr" im zeitlosen Sinne. Geschichte ist zeitliche Wirklichkeit und wie jeglicher Bewußtseinsinhalt eben auch tätig gestaltet durch jene Denk- und Verknüpfungsformen, ohne welche Bewußtseinsinhalt überhaupt nicht da wäre, durch die Formen des Zusammenhangs in der Zeit, des Fortschreitens einer linearen Bewegung, worin ein "historisches Subjekt", als Träger der Geschichte sich selber hat, hält und erhält. Keineswegs aber wird durch Geschichte ein Zusammenhang von Ursachen, eine Entwicklung in der Zeit unmittelbar und ohne menschliche Zutat offenbar. Sondern Geschichte ist die Stiftung dieses Sinnes; die Setzung dieses Zusammenhangs; die Erfindung dieser Entwicklung. Sie vorfindet nicht den Sinn der Welt, sie gibt ihn...'; o.c., 76.

Lessing in his well-known, post-war books builds on the philosophy he started to develop well before the First World War.

Subsequently, Lessing discusses the meaning of the word "history". To a large extent, he repeats his argument on the same topic in his "Was ist Geschichte?".[75] Hence, Lessing once more claims that history deals with occurrences in time in chronological order; that these occurrences are not fictional, but real; and that they are one-off, that is, happen only once. In this respect, history differs from the natural sciences, Lessing admits, but this is no reason to assume some fundamental distinction between historical and natural sciences. Nevertheless, it would probably be useful to emphasize certain differences, he argues: it might urge historians to give up their misplaced efforts to transform history into a "real" science (i.e., some kind of natural science of the past). Finally, Lessing repeats the argument that establishing what happened in the past is not (yet) history: true history connects occurrences by putting them in a wider context. – In this way, history gives sense to occurrences that are senseless as such, accordingly making them into events. In Lessing's view, it is precisely this characteristic that distinguishes history from all other intellectual pursuits. It is important to realise, Lessing argues, that this very activity – transforming occurrences into events, or making history out of occurrences – is in no respect a matter of science:

> Shaping history out of occurrences is a poetic process. Imagination, wish, desire, passion, hope, all of these are more involved in it than some sense of science or some will to truth. History never ever was an establishing "sine ira et studio". Because already the alleged facts of history are a matter of *act*.[76]

Thus, ultimately, shaping history out of occurrences is an act of will.

Of course, the will is fundamental for the natural sciences as well – after all, the European-American attitude towards the natural sciences may be aptly summarized in one sentence: "knowledge is power", that is, the power to change the things one wants to change. Still, in this respect there is a fundamental difference between history and the natural sciences. Ultimately, the

---

75 Cfr. above, 213–219.
76 'Das Bilden von Geschichte aus Geschehnissen ist ein dichterischer Vorgang. Phantasie, Wunsch, Sehnsucht, Leidenschaft, Hoffnung, alles das ist mehr daran beteiligt als irgendein Sinn für Wissenschaft oder als der Wille zur Wahrheit. Geschichte war noch niemals ein Feststellen "sine ira et studio". Denn schon die vermeintlichen Tatsachen der Geschichte sind Sache der *Tat*.'; o.c., 82. The italics are Lessing's.

natural sciences are driven by the will to bring about changes in daily life. History, however, is ultimately driven by the will to bring about changes far beyond daily reality – one might even say it tries to free mankind from daily reality by offering images of, say, some "Golden Age" when life was better, as an image of how life can or should be. Thus, history may be driven by, for instance, the desire to offer hope or encouragement; the desire for justification; the desire for power, and so on. But it is of vital importance, Lessing claims, to realise that history by no means starts with

> an already established substratum, of a reality of the past hither and shapes out of this post festum, on the basis of selective points of view once again history and histories. No! History is *nowhere* real but in the events themselves of shaping history. Or, to put it the other way round: only with the shaping of history the shape of history *comes into being*. There is no other reality of history![77]

But once history has come into being, it is no longer possible to evaluate the nature and implications of the historian's picture of the past. That is, we know that the historian actively shaped history, but it is no longer possible to determine the way has this been done.

However, it is clear by now, Lessing argues, that, ultimately, goals and aims underlie the (shaping) activity of the historian, his or her job not being to investigate reality, or to establish facts. The historian

> consciously or unconsciously carries his ideals, even if they are only his biases, to the indeed always merely mediate reality as given in consciousness, and exposes, no, overwhelms the occurrences known to him and important for him, with his ideals as with his eye through which he looks and only can look. And see! Out of the occurrences, raw as such, knitted together, rises the sense, as what the will lies into the occurrences, while knowledge beliefs to come across it. The driving force therefore would be called: ideal.[78]

---

77 'ein schon feststehendes Substrat, an eine Wirklichkeit der Geschichte heran und schafft aus ihr post festum an Hand von selektiven Wertgesichtspunkten nochmals Geschichte und Geschichten. Nein! Die Geschichte ist *nirgendwo* wirklich als in den geschichteschaffenden Vorgängen selber. Oder umgekehrt gesagt: Mit dem Bilden von Geschichte *ersteht* erst das Bild der Geschichte. Eine andere Wirklichkeit von Geschichte gibt es nicht!'; o.c., 89. The italics are Lessing's.

78 'trägt [...] bewußt oder unbewußt seine Leitbilder, und seien das auch seine Vorurteile, an die ja immer nur mittelbare Bewußtseinswirklichkeit heran und beleuchtet, nein

The function of ideals is twofold: on the one hand, they motivate people to act, on the other they are the criterion that is used to judge the past.

In Lessing's opinion, his argument thus far leads to an incontestable conclusion – a conclusion, however, that in his eyes disproves all traditional ideas on history:

> History is not living, immediate, elementary. Nor is history true, logical, rational.[79]

History is, however, "the *flowing image* of reality, fictionalised and dreamed of in view of desires".[80] And it is only as such that history makes sense. But what is meant with the sense of history, that is, what does this notion imply?

When we use this concept, Lessing maintains, we use it in the sense of ratio, that is, in its logical or ethical sense. This sense is proper to *réalité*. After all, *vitalité*, i.e., nature, knows neither logic nor ethics. But the concept does not relate to *vérité* either, that is, to a sense of the world that would exist whether man is aware of it or not. – This is the very argument Lessing used in his refutation of the criticism by Hermann Bahr. In theory, it is not impossible that there is a, say, God-given sense to the whole of history, but this sense would be known only unto God. But when Lessing speaks of the sense of history, he only speaks of reality as given in consciousness or *réalité*.[81] This implies that it is possible to rephrase the title *Geschichte als Sinngebung des Sinnlosen* as "Geschichte als Werteverwirklichung am Wertfreien" – 'history as the realisation of values on what is free of value'.[82] If this alternative title clarifies what he intends to claim in his book, Lessing argues, simply use this title instead of the present one. – Fortunately, his publisher did not follow him in this, as *Geschichte als Sinngebung des Sinnlosen* is a more appealing title by far; the alternative one indeed might well have helped the book fall into oblivion. –

---

vergewaltigt die ihm bekannt gewordenen und für ihn bedeutungsvolle Geschehnisse mit seinen Ideal als mit dem Auge, durch das er blickt und einzig blicken kann. Und siehe da! Aus den an sich selber brutalen geballten Geschehnissen springt hervor der Sinn, als welchen der Wille in das Geschehen hineinlügt, indessen das Wissen wähnt, ihn vorzufinden. Die treibende Macht hieß somit: Ideal...'; o.c., 91.

79 'Geschichte ist nicht lebendig, unmittelbar, elementar. Geschichte ist auch nicht wahr, logisch, rational.'; o.c., 92.
80 'das *fließende Bild* der Wirklichkeit, erdichtet und geträumt an Hand von Wünschen.'; o.c., 93. The italics are Lessing's.
81 Cfr. above, 231–232.
82 Theodor Lessing, o.c., 96.

A good example of what he means with "Sinngebung des Sinnlosen" – 'giving sense to the senseless'–, Lessing argues, is the way we commemorate the dead. Remembering the dead "always is an actively creative, even though unconsciously creative process, a comforting gilding and embellishing, straightening out and correcting, reshaping and shaping once more and above all a healingly and reconcilingly forgetting of passing occurrences".[83] Characteristic of this process is that only those occurrences are included which fit the complete story. This is what Lessing calls the conserving function of remembrance. A second function is the rejecting one: remembrance always discards what does not fit the story in its entirety, by ignoring, denying, and so on. But sometimes, say, an anecdote about a deceased intrudes so strongly that it cannot be ignored, even if it does not fit the story as told about the deceased. Then the anecdote will indeed be referred to, but without truly being incorporated in the story – like the statue of some hero of the past that stands in a city without ever being looked at. This is what Lessing calls the third function of remembrance: the isolating one. Not surprisingly, he considers these three functions of remembrance also to be functions of history: history as well conserves, ignores, and isolates.

What history does conserve, ignore, or isolate is to a large extent arbitrary, Lessing argues – repeating, sometimes even verbally, what he wrote on the subject in the first edition of *Geschichte als Sinngebung des Sinnlosen*. Reputations in history mostly result from coincidence; and the same holds true as regards the preservation or loss of historical sources. The result of all this ultimately is that "man falsifies the contents of his memory according to the future he desires most".[84] Thus, "what we *expect* of the future, we transfer to the past".[85] Consequently, "it is for instance a quite general rule that each people transfers those characteristics that it desires (and perhaps exactly desires because they are lacking) into its historical past, and continuously praises them as the historically believed in and from early days preserved characteristics of its ancestors".[86]

---

83 'durchweg ein tätig schöpferischer, wenn auch unbewußt schöpferischer Vorgang, ein tröstliches Vergolden und Verschönen, Zurecht- und Richtigrücken, Um- und Neugestalten und vor allem auch ein ausheilendes und versöhnendes Vergessen der vorübergleitenden Geschehnisse.'; o.c., 96–97.
84 'Der Mensch fälscht die Inhalte seiner Erinnerung im Sinne der ihm wünschenswerteste Zukunft.'; o.c., 102.
85 'Was wir von der Zukunft *erwarten*, das verlegen wir in die Vergangenheit.'; loc. cit.. The italics are Lessing's.
86 'So ist es z.B. eine ganze allgemeine Regel, daß jedes Volk diejenigen Eigenschaften, die es sich wünscht (und vielleicht gerade darum wünscht, weil sie ihm fehlen), in seine

However, if one takes a realistic view of history, one cannot but conclude with Johannes Scherr,[87] Lessing claims, that history is a completely pointless tragicomedy of "stupidity, meanness, baseness, in which the heroes needlessly bleed to death and the brutes triumph, in which the high and noble perish without a tray at the edge of the road and the bad and evil, to the extent that it only has successes, is raised to the ranks of the gods".[88] Why, then, should one practice history, "why should one lead the growing youth time and again through this ocean of blood and tears?".[89] If history truly is the study of historical reality, historians can only turn away or be paralyzed in disdain of mankind. But history is not about past reality, Lessing claims, history is myth, or, more precisely: a myth that should inspire: "If I believe in a Golden Age or if I hope to bring about an age of truth and justice in future, nothing helps me better to achieve these goals than the conviction that something like this already once really existed on earth".[90] Ultimately, this is the very beginning of history, Lessing argues, and this is what history really is about.

This leaves the possibility open to write history with a great variety of desires and aspirations for a starting-point – in fact, as many as there are human desires, aspirations, and aims, from the smallest to the most widely ranging. Consequently, it is only possible to classify history writing in a most general way. One may, for instance, write history with particular ambitions in mind, for instance those of the kingdom of Prussia, like Heinrich von Treitsche (1834–1896) did; or one may write history with distinctly moralistic ambitions in mind, like Tacitus (ca. 56–117); or with political ambitions in mind, like Caesar; or with poetic ambitions in mind, like Hippolyte Taine (1828–1893), and so on. But eventually, Lessing claims, suchlike classifications are pointless – after all, they do not bring any important insights, "because there is no intention and no prejudice, no ideal and no kind of value, no interest and no

---

historische Vergangenheit verlegt und als die geschichtlich beglaubigten und altbewährten Eigenschaften seiner Vorfahren unaufhörlich anpreist.'; loc. cit.. The italics are Lessing's.
87 O.c., 103.
88 'aus Dummheit, Gemeinheit und Niedertracht, darin die Helden unnütz verbluten und die Henker triumphieren, darin das Hohe und Edle spurlos am Straßenrand verwest und das Schlechte und Böse, wofern es nur Erfolge hat, in den Rang der Götter gehoben wird.'; o.c., 103.
89 'warum sollte man die heranwachsende Jugend immer wieder hindurchführen durch diesen Ozean von Blut und Tränen? '; loc. cit..
90 'Wenn ich an ein goldenes Zeitalter glaube oder wenn ich künftig einmal ein Zeitalter der Wahrheit und des Rechts zu verwirklichen hoffe, so verhilft mir zu diesem Ziele nichts besser als die Überzeugung, daß dergleichen schon einmal auf Erden wirklich gewesen sei.'; loc. cit..

system of relationship that could not serve the eye for the shaping of history from the angle of an age or an individual, a group or a nation".[91] Hence, there is actually a competition between various constructions of history, one of which will become at least for the time being the dominant one in a certain age or for a certain nation. This only proves, Lessing argues, that it is pointless to speak of *the* history of the world, *the* development of culture, *the* progress of mankind, and so on: there is not one single history of the world, but only various different possible histories, because history simply does not have a fixed object.

Taking into consideration how history is currently practiced, one has to draw the conclusion that there is a truly overwhelming number of possible sources available to the historian, it indeed being completely impossible to study all of them. Hence, it is likewise impossible to reconstruct historical reality, even the reality of a single day. So what could possibly justify studying all of these sources, or at least as many as possible? The underlying assumption of this approach is, of course, that there would be some kind of historical reality that has to be reconstructed by studying all the sources concerned. This assumption is shared, Lessing claims, by thinkers as divergent as Hegel, Rickert, Windelband, and Spengler. But there does not exist something like a historical reality, and consequently it makes no sense trying to study as many sources as possible. Yet another implication of the position that there is no historical reality, Lessing argues, is that history does not originate in history[92] – for that could only be possible if there is a fixed historical reality that subsequently is described by various historians. Of course, this is not to deny the possibility that historians may influence each other, but eventually this is not essential for history, according to Lessing. What is essential, is that the historian time and again gives sense to what as such is senseless apart from his or her particular point of view.

Many misunderstandings about history, Lessing writes in conclusion of the first book of the fourth edition of *Geschichte als Sinngebung des Sinnlosen*, result from the ambiguity of the word "history". The word has at least twenty different meanings, and the problem is that people often thoughtlessly assign certain characteristics of one meaning of the word to another, Lessing argues. It is often this that causes confusion; one ascribes, for instance, the cohesion of the historian's narrative about the past to the past itself. For this reason,

---

91   'Denn es gibt keine Absicht und kein Vorurteil, kein Ideal und keine Wertgattung, kein Interesse und kein Beziehungssystem, das nicht zum Auge dienen könnte für die Geschichtsgestaltung von seiten [sic!, HS] eines Zeitalters oder eines Einzelnen, einer Gruppe oder ein Volkschaft.'; o.c., 105.

92   O.c., 109.

keeping apart various meanings of words like "history" or "past" more carefully would, in Lessing's view, prevent many misunderstandings.

6 Logical Reflections

In the second book of the fourth edition of *Geschichte als Sinngebung des Sinnlosen*, Lessing discusses the categories of history – that is, those categories without which the contents of consciousness that the historian studies would not even exist.

The first one of these is time. Historical time is proper to *réalité*, Lessing claims: in *vitalité* there is no time, in the sense that nature simply lives by the moment, and in *vérité* there is by definition no change, so there is no time either. This implies that historical time only comes into being with consciousness: the time of the clock is not a given that man comes upon, but invented by man. That is, time itself is man-made, made as a way to order the contents of consciousness. This means, Lessing argues, that history ultimately is a hotchpotch made by human consciousness: a transient, passing effort of thinking. But

> nature did not know development, progress, culture, tradition, intention, end and purpose. It rather is and remains the ever present, neither old nor young, neither living nor dying, building, shaping, forming essential element.[93]

So why does man need history? History is like the stem of a plant, Lessing claims: a plant needs a stem to grow, but eventually it will lignify, and as a result the growth of the plant will stop and the plant will die. Likewise, history is the backbone of man – but eventually it will kill man, like the stem eventually kills the plant.

Once again, Lessing emphasizes that history by definition cannot be about *vitalité*, but only about *réalité*. History is only possible from the moment that, as a result of need, consciousness breaks out of nature: consequently, history is about experiences which are the contents of consciousness. In this respect it is of vital importance, Lessing argues, to distinguish between experiences as such and established experiences. This is, as we have seen,[94] one of the points

---

93 'Die Natur kennte keine Entwicklung, Fortschritt, Kultur, Tradition, Absicht, Ende und Ziel. Vielmehr ist und bleibt sie das immer gegenwärtige, nicht alte noch junge, weder lebende noch sterbende, bauende, bildende, formende Wesens-Element.'; o.c., 129.
94 Cfr. chapter four above, 180.

of difference between Husserl and Lessing, or rather one of Lessing's criticisms of Husserl. According to Lessing, Husserl claims that it is possible to describe experiences as they occur. But Lessing considers this a misconception, because describing experiences is only possible by using pre-existing linguistic concepts. This implies that the very act of describing experiences is to infringe on the experiences as they occur – that is, the experiences-as-described differ from the experiences-as-occurred, the experience-as-described therefore not mirroring the experience-as-occurred: "Experiences are present: free of time, free of words, free of notions, and totally transcend consciousness".[95] History, on the other hand, presupposes the existence of a reality already shaped by consciousness, which implies the act of processing and shaping. Consequently, history can never be about *vitalité*: it cannot grasp experience-as-occurred, and cannot grasp primordial life.

But if one is not aware of this basic fact, all kinds of problems will arise which in fact are only illusory, like for instance the problem of the relationship between individual and group (state, nation, society, and so on). Though this relationship is often considered problematic, sometimes reflections on it even form the basis of a complete philosophical system, like Karl Marx's. But, Lessing argues, one should realize that these notions are proper to *réalité*: the distinction between individual and group is made by consciousness, while in *vitalité* there is no such distinction: "Hence, the notion of the individual, of the singular I or unique is exactly as remote from life as the dead notions state, nation, society, club".[96] Once we realize this, it is clear that eventually the relationship between individual and group is not a genuine problem, but just reflecting a lack of clarity in thought about these phenomena, a lack of clarity, moreover, that can be overcome.

To complicate matters further, Lessing points out that categories like time, space, and causality are usually conceived as being fixed. But there is no warrant that these categories themselves would not change as well. As Lessing puts it: "Who warrants that time is established a priori?".[97] In fact, there is no good reason to assume it is, and the same holds true, of course, for the other categories:

> Terrible embarrassment! This consideration should suffice to show that history is built on quicksand, since the categories on the basis of which

---

95 'Erlebnisse sind Gegenwart: zeitfrei, wortfrei, begriffsfrei und durchaus bewußtseins-transzendent.'; Theodor Lessing, o.c., 131.
96 'Somit ist der Begriff des Individuums, des Einzel-Ich oder Einzigen genau so lebensfern wie die toten Begriffe Staat, Nation, Gesellschaft, Sozietät.'; o.c., 135.
97 'Wer bürgt dafür, daß die Zeit als Apriori feststeht?'; o.c., 137.

history is realized, still must have a *history* themselves, and when the categorical shapes are only dreams... how could beyond sleep the building be fixed?[98]

Moreover, if, for the sake of argument, we would assume that time exists in *vitalité* like some kind of pre-phenomenal time, we would necessarily have to assume the existence of some kind of categories proper to *vitalité* as well – but this would only imply that we are still not capable to grasp *vitalité* as such. So the problem still would not be solved. Thus, Lessing argues,

> There is no solution but the insight that history only emerges and perishes with man; that its sense is not come upon but established, and that its unity is therefore not proper to life, but to its killing in consciousness.[99]

This implies, of course, that every division of history in periods, eras or ages is man-made, that is, proper to *réalité*. But this has not always been realized. In fact, there are numerous examples of thinkers who hold on to the idea that, for instance, the division of history into various periods is just a given that only had to be determined. Some examples verge on the ridiculous, Lessing argues, for instance the claim made by F.-Ch. Barlet, one of the pen-names of the French occultist Albert Faucheux (1838–1921; Lessing erroneously gives the pen-name as V.W. Barlet), in his *L'astrologie et la guerre* (1918) that because of the rhythm of the stellar constellation, in 1914 war was inevitable. In the first edition of *Geschichte als Sinngebung des Sinnlosen*, Lessing mentioned more, comparable examples – all of which share the same underlying, utterly wrong, assumption that the rhythm of history would somehow be a given. Remarkably enough, the criteria mostly used in these interpretations are external to history (like in the example mentioned of the rhythm of the stellar constellation). This even holds true for Hegel's dialectics: for this as well is, in Lessing's view, a principle external to history. Thus, in his opinion, eventually suchlike interpretations of history have nothing at all to do with history, not even with history as the would-be science that it is currently all too often alleged to be. But, Lessing argues, as these interpretations of history are always formulated *post festum*, it is all too easy to develop them:

---

98   'Grauenhafte Verlegenheit! Diese Überlegung dürfte genügen, um zu zeigen, daß Geschichte auf Flugsand gebaut ist, da die Kategorien, auf Grund deren Geschichte zustande kommt, selbst noch *Geschichte* haben müssen, und wenn die Bauformen nur Träume sind, ... wie soll jenseits des Schlafes das Gebäude feststehen?...'; loc.cit.. The italics are Lessing's.

99   'Es gibt hier keinen Ausweg als die Erkenntnis, daß Geschichte nur mit Menschen entsteht und vergeht; daß ihr Sinn nicht aufgefunden, sondern gestiftet wird und daß ihre Einheit mithin nicht dem Leben zugehört, sondern seiner Abtötung in Geist...'; o.c., 144.

while it would be truly doubtful whether someone systematically and on the basis of laws can describe as regards *content* and not just formally what in fifty years from now will be historical reality... Whenever there are accidents, catastrophes, acts of violence, deaths, there are always thousands of people who can demonstrate they had premonitions of or predicted the event, and moreover it is perfectly easy to prove post festum for every event that it necessarily *had* to happen.[100]

But behind all these interpretations of history lurks "a moralistic *will*".[101] In this connection, it is for Lessing beyond all reasonable doubt that time, including the division of history into periods, is the result of the way human consciousness orders reality.

Lessing's observations on time imply his position as regards *vitalité*, in the sense that he clarifies what *vitalité* is not. That is, in *vitalité* there is no time, no space, no causality, and no opposition, nor even a distinction between "I" and "other". But it is almost impossible to say more on *vitalité*, i.e. to describe what it is:

> The reader should bear in mind, however, that we thus embark on secrets which are forever impenetrable for *thinking*; on that great mystery to which the facts of experience may well *refer*, but which cannot further be grasped in words, names and notions.[102]

Hence, Lessing can only confine himself to trying to adumbrate these secrets. It is, he claims, a fact, for instance, that two intimately related souls can influence each other even if they are not in the same room. But in this case there is no *causal* explanation for this phenomenon. This, and similar phenomena are of a "meta-logical kind",[103] Lessing argues; it is by definition impossible to

---

100 'während es doch recht zweifelhaft wäre, ob irgendwer gesetzmäßig und auf Grund von Gesetzen *inhaltlich* und nicht nur formal angeben kann, was heute in fünfzig Jahren historisch wirklich sein wird... Bein Unglücksfällen. Katastrophen, Gewalttakten, Todesfällen gibt es immer Tausende, welche nachweisen können, daß sie das Geschehnis geahnt oder vorausgesagt haben, und vollends ist es kinderleicht, von einem jeden Geschehnis post festum nachzuweisen, daß es notwendig kommen *mußte*.'; o.c., 148–149. The italics are Lessing's.
101 'ein moralistischer *Wille*'; o.c., 149. The italics are Lessing's.
102 'Der Leser bedenke aber, daß wir damit vor Geheimnisse treten, auf ewig undurchdringlich für das *Denken*; vor jenes große Mysterium, auf welches wohl noch die Erfahrungstatsachen *hin-weisen*, das aber nicht mehr faßlich ist in Worten, Namen und Begriffen.'; o.c., 152. The italics are Lessing's.
103 'meta-logischer Art'; o.c., 153.

explain them causally. All efforts to understand these phenomena will necessarily cross the threshold of mysticism. Thus, Lessing would not want to deny the possibility that there might be a connection between the fly on the wall in his room, the cold that the emir of Afghanistan is suffering from, and the position of the stellar constellation; but if there is such a connection it cannot be explained causally, "it *cannot* be grasped, explained, measured, substantiated".[104] It is, as Lessing calls it, "the face of the world".[105] Anyway, if we suppose that there is a sense to this *vitalité*, that is, a sense apart from human ordering, then this sense will necessarily be of a completely different kind: it will have nothing at all to do with human values, aims, wants, and desires. As Lessing explains his viewpoint:

> The question of the worth or worthlessness of life, the sense or senselessness of the world is merely a human question. It only arises and can only arise with the experience of the *need* of this world and thus with the postulate of the *deliverance from this need*. It arises only and can only arise with the suffering from this life and thus with a splitting off from and stepping out of this life. As long as man lives in panic, cosmically, intertwined with nature, he cannot whatsoever complain and quarrel, because the deaths and downfalls like the births and blisses of nature still all are *his*. Only when we *suffer* and this means become *consciousness*, we appear complaining *out* [of nature, HS] as an I [...][106]

If, on the other hand, we would suppose that some eternal logic would govern life on earth, what difference would that make? None, Lessing claims: "The *sense* of what is, thus always remains rooted in *human experiences!*".[107] Without human experience there would be neither history nor time, neither past nor future. Human experience is basically twofold: fear and hope – "Fear with

---

104 'kann *nicht* erfaßt, erklärt, gemessen, begründet werden.'; o.c., 155. The italics are Lessing's.
105 'Gesicht der Welt'; loc.cit..
106 'die Frage nach Wert oder Unwert des Lebens, Sinn oder Sinnlosigkeit der Welt ist nur eine Menschenfrage. Sie tritt erst auf und kann erst auftreten mit dem Erlebnis der *Not* dieser Welt und somit dem Postulate der *Erlösung von dieser Not*. Sie tritt erst dann auf und kann erst auftreten mit dem Leiden an diesem Leben und somit einem Abspalten und Heraustreten aus diesem Leben. Solange der Mensch panisch, kosmisch, natureinverschlungen lebt, kann er gar nicht hadern und rechten, denn die Tode und Untergänge wie die Geburten und Seligkeiten der Natur sind noch alle *sein*. Erst dann, wenn wir *Leiden* und das heißt *Geist* werden, treten wir hadernd als Ich *heraus* [...]'; o.c., 156. The italics are Lessing's.
107 '*Sinn* des Seienden bleibt somit immer verwurzelt in *Menschenerlebnissen!*'; o.c., 158. The italics are Lessing's.

regard to what has been suffered formerly, hope with regard to what is desired in the future".[108] Consciousness, Lessing argues, is both disease and remedy: it is the result of suffering, but it can also find the way out of suffering, by formulating ideas, setting aims, and so on. Thus, human history is *the revolt of consciousness against nature*".[109] But life is, and always will remain more comprehensive than consciousness, Lessing argues – most likely, human consciousness is controlled by sleep and dreams.

The next category of historical reason that Lessing discusses is "the unity of history", that is, history as considered a "coherence of events". It is only possible to speak of a suchlike coherence if there is some unity being the bearer of this coherence, Lessing claims, following Kant: "One cannot [...] think history without a 'historical subject'".[110] That is, history always is the history of something or someone, which accordingly may be almost anything. Once we have chosen this historical subject, we relate everything that happened to this subject, as if all of it is its history. Of course, the choice of the subject implies that differences will occur: "For the history of Germany, the years from 1914 to 1919 have a different meaning than for the history of the United States".[111] This already indicates that historians do not come upon the subject of history: these subjects are actually man-made reference points that the historian uses to order history. That is, they are not proper to experience, they are the patterns the historian needs to be able to think about and to write history at all.

Eventually, these subjects of history are nothing but the mirror-image of the image we have of ourselves, Lessing claims, repeating, if not verbally, what he wrote on the same topic in the first edition of *Geschichte als Sinngebung des Sinnlosen*. That is, the historical subject always is an image of man, having aims, the will to survive, the desire for happiness, in short, the typical characteristics of human self-centredness. This image of man is an abstraction of innumerable individuals – men and women – by suppressing as many individual characteristics as possible. Thus, an image of man emerges with the least possible contents, similar to the way a mathematical formula is an abstraction from reality. Subsequently, the historian may use his or her personal strivings, sufferings, wants, love and hate to fill in the abstract image with life – with his

---

108 'Angst in Hinblick auf ehemals Erlittenes, Hoffnung in Hinblick auf künftig Ersehntes'; loc.cit..
109 'der *Aufstand des Geistes wider Natur*.'; o.c., 159. The italics are Lessing's.
110 'Man kann [...] nicht Geschichte denken ohne ein "geschichtliches Subjekt".'; o.c., 160.
111 'Für die Geschichte Deutschlands haben die Jahre 1914 bis 1919 eine andere Bedeutung als für die Geschichte Amerikas'; o.c., 161.

or her own life. Thus, history always becomes the very own story of the historian: "the historical subject always has to let merge itself with my personal loving or hating".[112] Only in this way historical coherence is feasible, Lessing argues. This implies, of course, that historical coherence is dependent on the shaping consciousness. Hence, as regards all that happened in the past, giving retrospectively sense to it, and in relation to the "I" of the historian, are features that underlie all history. But in this sense, history does not differ from the other sciences, Lessing claims. For both the historical and the natural sciences deal with reality in relation to the "I" of respectively the historian and the scientist. Of course, the historical and the natural sciences differ in the way they deal with reality – but as we have seen, according to Lessing this difference ultimately is of little importance.

Lessing points out that his analysis of the bearer of the unity of history is incompatible with the view of those who criticize metaphysics, wanting "to dispose of metaphysics". Characteristic of this war on metaphysics is the idea that in science everything that may be branded as being "not scientific" should be abolished. Lessing compares this attitude with the study of boiling water: one is only interested in "pure boiling", simply ascertaining "it boils" – but the question "what boils, and why?" is strictly considered out of order. This attitude and effort to overcome metaphysics is still widely spread both in science and philosophy. But ultimately, it is nothing but an effort to disguise the true character of Western science and civilization, Lessing argues:

> Thus, one has to guard against taking the war of science against metaphysics seriously. All these discrepancies Europe-America is preoccupied with – discrepancies like those between science and church, physics and metaphysics –, only are illusory discrepancies like the discrepancies between competing merchants who all want the *same*.[113]

Even European-American religion ultimately is rooted in what consciousness aims for, and not in submitting oneself to some higher force. Likewise, in Lessing's view, presupposing a bearer of the unity of history is not the introduction

---

112   'Das historische Subjekt muß sich immer verschmelzen lassen mit meinem persönlichen Lieben oder Hassen'; o.c., 163.
113   'Man muß sich somit hüten, den Krieg der Wissenschaft gegen Metaphysik wichtig zu nehmen. Alle die Gegensätze, von denen Europa-Amerika erfüllt ist – Gegensätze wie die von Wissenschaft und Kirche, Physik und Metaphysik –, sind doch nur Scheingegensätze wie die Gegensätze konkurrierender Händler, welche alle das *Selbe* wollen.'; o.c., 170. The italics are Lessing's.

of a metaphysical notion; for it simply is not possible to think or write about history without a historical subject – the two necessarily go hand in hand.

According to Lessing, any bearer of the unity of history necessarily has some continuity: it could not exist if every single moment history started anew. This is an additional reason why there is no history in *vitalité*: nature indeed lives by the moment, Lessing argues; the notion of continuity is, like time itself, one of the categories to order reality as given in consciousness. In this connection, one of the problems historians face is that they are part of the very same continuity that they study: the historian does not stand outside history. But this problem may be overcome by isolating the historical subject, that is, by treating it as if it is on its own. Hence, Lessing does not see this as a genuine problem. In other words, the solution is that the historian has to leave out of consideration innumerable possible relationships the historical subject may have had, and focuses on what is relevant in his or her eyes. Thus, history time and again may have a new image: after all, the reign of, say, king Henry VIII appears differently if it is discussed in the context of e.g. English constitutional history, English religious history, or the history of international politics, and so on, the bearer of historical unity being conceived differently in each of these histories. In all his reflections on history thus far a number of seemingly insolvable contradictions is involved, Lessing argues. One may, for instance, claim that human consciousness thinks about history, but also that human consciousness itself is (part of) history. Or one may claim that both nature and the way nature is ordered is a representation, but also that representing nature and the way it is ordered is (part of) nature, in the sense that it is part of human nature that humans order nature. Again, one may claim that values, logic, and ethics kill life (i.e., they infringe on life as it is), but also that the ultimate aim – nirvana – itself still is a fact of life. And, finally, one may claim that all acts of mind that shape history are themselves historical in character. Thus, we seem to find ourselves at a dead end – there is no way to make one's choice between these various assertions. But this conclusion is mistaken, Lessing claims: the contradictions mentioned are just illusory. That is, not either one *or* the other assertion is right, but in each case both are, they accordingly not being alternatives we have to choose from. Consequently, it is, for example, not relevant whether we describe a famine as the result of natural conditions ("the weather was exceptionally dry") or as the result of human errors ("farmers should have watered the land more often") – both are right. Ultimately, this is nothing but a pointless conflict of notions, Lessing argues. So one simultaneously thinks about history and is part of history: both assertions are right, and one does not have to make one's choice between them.

An analysis of these illusory contradictions is nevertheless necessary, Lessing maintains, because they often are the source of misunderstandings, and various usually hardly underpinned opinions that are presented as ideals. But eventually, life in the Western world is not guided by ideals, but actually directed by utilitarianism and Machiavellianism. Much would be won if this was frankly admitted, Lessing argues. But this it is not the case: instead, all kinds of ideals are presented as cover-up. Even the so-called *Realpolitiker* do not appeal to reality, however, they just take their own ideology for granted and present it as the only sound and "realistic" one. But it is always the policy that has been successful that is retrospectively praised as being "realistic". Eventually, in the Western world success, and success only, is what matters, and the more people acknowledging this success the better.

If we assume that history is aimed at establishing how the past really was – Lessing's phrase "wie es wirklich gewesen ist" is an echo of Ranke's famous "wie es eigentlich gewesen" ('how it in fact was')[114] –, and manages to do so, we could only come to the conclusion that the past as it really was is pointless, nothing but a boring sequence of shifting balances of power, resulting in a lot of casualties and suffering. In the second place, history is an inscrutable brood of lies, falsifications, and wrongs – and, moreover, all facts and connections between facts might always have been completely different. Hence, in the third place, history exhibits no logic whatsoever. Lessing underpins these assertions with a number of examples, some of which he already discussed in the first edition of *Geschichte als Sinngebung des Sinnlosen*. To give but one: "at their death, terrible beasts like Ivan IV and Henry VIII were more sincerely mourned for by their people than Jesus and Buddha [...]".[115] Lessing concludes from all this that "all organized states (in whose history Hegel sees the incarnation and the coming into the world of God) are the result of robbery, theft, deceit, and murder".[116] So what, eventually, is history? As Lessing explains:

> But history *is* simply not reality! It is *liberation* from reality. It is dream, myth, for all I care: comforting lie. Everything: but not reality...

---

114 O.c., 181; cfr. L. von Ranke, *Geschichten der romanischen und germanischen Völker von 1494 bis 1514* (Dritte Auflage, Leipzig 1885), vii. Ranke's phrase is often read as an epistemological claim, but it was not. He wanted to contest the traditional idea that history would have an exemplary function. He denied this, adding that history only tries to establish what happened.

115 'scheußliche Bestien wie Iwan IV. und Heinrich VIII. sind bei ihrem Tode von ihren Völkern ehrlicher betrauert worden als Jesus und Buddha'; Theodor Lessing, o.c., 185.

116 'Alle Staatsorganisationen (in deren Geschichte Hegel die Verleiblichung und Weltwerdung Gottes sieht) sind aus Raub, Diebstahl, Betrug und Mord hervorgegangen.'; o.c., 188.

Thus, an epistemological critique of history does not at all come down to an *epistemological critique of science*. It has nothing at all to do with investigations into the foundations of the belief in reality. It deals with the nowadays still new investigations into the foundations of human idols, of human illusions.[117]

This is how we should understand in particular the fourth edition of *Geschichte als Sinngebung des Sinnlosen*: it is Lessing's investigation into the foundations of human illusions – because, according to Lessing, it is an illusion to believe that history is, or for that matter: reflects, past reality. As we have seen, Lessing argues that the bearer of history is "an abstract, empty, general man", some kind of formula that has to be filled with everything human – passion, love, hate – that ultimately regards the historian's own person. Of course, there are all kinds of entities of what Lessing calls "sub-bearers" of history: states, nations, political parties, cities, organisations of all sorts, and so on, to which the historian assigns all kinds of (human) characteristics. The more comprehensive such a sub-bearer is, the farther away it is from true life. Thus, the biography is the most authentic kind of history, Lessing claims – and the autobiography is the most authentic one amongst the biographies –, whereas universal history is the most hollow one. Ultimately, universal histories are no more than collections of individual histories of countries. Some people believe the era of great personalities – and consequently the era of biographies – is over: all that matters in future is the history of the masses, of millions of forgotten and unknown people. So no more biographies of great men and women! Lessing argues that this claim rests on a misunderstanding. History only knows individuals because they represent larger groups. Moreover, what is a mass, except a big number of individuals? Thus, the issue whether history is made by outstanding individuals or by the masses is simply inappropriate: one may always approach history from both sides, from that of the individual and that of the masses.

Subsequently, Lessing once more criticizes the approach of, among others, the historian Heinrich von Treitsche, when he speaks of "the spirit of German

---

117 'Aber Geschichte *ist* eben keine Wirklichkeit! Sie ist *Befreiung* von Wirklichkeit. Sie ist Traum, Mythos, meinethalb [sic! HS]: tröstend Lüge. Alles: nur nicht Wirklichkeit!...
Eine Erkenntniskritik der Geschichte kommt daher überhaupt nicht hinaus auf *Erkenntniskritik der Wissenschaft*. Sie hat es durchaus nicht zu tun mit Untersuchungen über die Grundlagen des Wirklichkeitsglaubens. Sie hat es zu tun mit heute noch neuen Untersuchungen über die Grundlagen der menschlichen Idole, der menschlichen Illusionen.'; o.c., 192. The italics are Lessing's.

history", or of Hegel declaring "the objective mind" to be the bearer of human history. In these and similar interpretations of history, "the spirit" or "the mind" respectively are not only seen as the bearer of history, but also considered exhibiting the ultimate sense of history: "it underlies her and it is *expressed* as history".[118] This shows how "Geschichtsmetaphysiker" – 'metaphysicians of history' – turn things upside down. As Lessing observes:

> Consequently it would be incomprehensible why world history as enumeration of countless stupidities or acts of violence by all nations and in all countries would nevertheless as a whole have more "sense" than even inhabits the top minds. This assumption is no less incomprehensible than if one assumes that the more madmen are locked up in a madhouse, the more it will approach "organic self-control".[119]

According to Lessing, "every people, every community, indeed, already every family and eventually every individual human being needs an accompanying loadstar of itself".[120] This is a "better I", a kind of mythical second life guiding us. This accompanying loadstar is the result of "the conversion of the real into the legendary".[121] If one realises how desire or memory may distort our image of reality, one can imagine how strong the influence of such a loadstar may be. Our image of a deceased never corresponds with the image we had of the same person when he or she was still alive. Does this imply we retrospectively shape this image? Or do we only get the true image retrospectively? Of course, considerations like these are relevant for history as well – similar observations and questions hold true for history too. And, Lessing argues,

> [i]t would be possible that all judgments err, as long as we still are runners towards the same goal, fighters for the same laurel, and eaters from

---

118 'Es liegt ihr zugrunde und kommt als Geschichte zum *Ausdruck*'; o.c., 200. The italics are Lessing's.
119 'Es wäre somit unbegreiflich, warum die Weltgeschichte als Aufsummierung zahlloser Torheiten oder Gewaltakte bei allen Völkern und in allen Ländern dennoch als Ganzes mehr "Sinn" haben soll, als selbst den Gipfelgeistern innewohnt. Diese Annahme ist nicht minder unbegreiflich, als wenn man annehmen wollte, daß ein Irrenhaus, je mehr Irre darin eingesperrt werden, der "organischen Selbststeuerung" immer näher komme.'; o.c., 201.
120 'Jedes Volk, jede Gemeinschaft, ja schon jede Familie und schließlich jeder einzelne Mensch bedarf eines begleitenden Leitbildes seiner selbst.'; o.c., 203.
121 'Die Umwandlung des Wirklichen ins Sagenhafte.'; loc. cit..

the same dish. Only estrangement lets the truth appear from reality. One could say that reality stands in the way of knowing its own truth.¹²²

All of this changes, Lessing claims, once our everyday reality is reborn as history, and the longer ago something is, the less controversial it is, and accordingly the easier to assess:

> Our reality is forgotten. And to the same extent as it is forgotten, the true image behind reality appears from time in pure intuition of essence.¹²³

The longer the origin of an image is forgotten, the clearer the image will be, Lessing maintains, adding – rather surprisingly –: "This is the way religion emanates from history."¹²⁴ This implies that myths, fairy tales, and legends ultimately somehow all go back to some historical kernel, one way or another, they all have an actual relationship with the past.

The development from history into myth, fairy tale or legend is obviously a complicated process. Lessing observes that he cannot discuss this process in detail in this fourth edition of *Geschichte als Sinngebung des Sinnlosen* in which he, after all, focuses his attention on epistemological questions. But he discussed it at greater length in the first edition of the book. Still, he cannot resist clarifying in this fourth edition a quite common misunderstanding of the first edition of his book. A number of critics of the latter edition blamed Lessing for trying to prove that it is ideals that make history. But Lessing denies ever having made this claim: what he tried to prove is that "the materialized history is a materialized ideal".¹²⁵ However, he argues that this should not be understood as implying that ideals themselves are the true driving forces of history. For this issue eventually relates to a correct understanding of his theory of three spheres, Lessing maintains: if one understands this theory properly, the misunderstanding simply will not arise. In summary, it comes down to the following:

---

122 'Es wäre möglich, daß alle Urteile irren, solange wir noch sind Läufer nach dem selben Ziel, Ringer um den selben Kranz und Mitesser aus der selben Schüssel. Erst die Entfernung läßt aus der Wirklichkeit die Wahrheit hervortreten. Man könnte sagen, daß das Wirkliche dem Erkennen seiner eigenen Wahrheit im Wege steht.'; o.c., 204.
123 'Unsere Wirklichkeit ist vergessen. Und im selben Maße, als sie vergessen ist, tritt das wahre Bild hinter der Wirklichkeit in reiner Wesensschau aus der Zeit hervor.'; loc. cit.. It is noteworthy how Lessing in this quotation sticks to the language of phenomenology.
124 'Dies ist der Weg, auf welchem Religion aus Geschichte hervorgeht.'; loc. cit..
125 'die verwirklichte Geschichte [ist] ein verwirklichtes Ideal'; o.c., 206.

It is just the case that we transform something that once has been in the sense of our ideal desiderata. On the other hand, our ideal desiderata are always realized anew in life. In other words: out of reality our consciousness abstracts a realm of images. The other way round, the realm of images also serves consciousness, however, for the construction of reality. By transforming our reality into a world of poetry, the other way round the world of poetry becomes reality again.[126]

This implies that "everything in which a human believes sometime once has been reality, and that the other way round, only that in which a man believes can become reality".[127] Hence, it does indeed make quite a difference whether man believes in a conqueror or a preacher: Western civilization has become what it is today, because it believes that God has become man, Lessing claims – man developed, to give but one of the examples he mentions, artificial food only because he believed that God could feed thousands with a few leafs of bread. Eventually, he argues, this continuous interaction between reality and ideal is what the process of history is about.

According to Lessing, this implies that we can only understand the question of the meaning of history, if we leave out of consideration the issue of the reality or unreality of history. Consequently, the question forces itself upon us what the role of history as a discipline is in the process of transforming reality into myth. Lessing, not very flatteringly, compares historians with earthworms that eat lots of dead matter only to excrete it again, transforming this matter in this very process, however, into raw material for possibly new life. Likewise, this is what historians actually do: processing reality and excreting it as raw material for a possible new reality – that is, making loadstars from reality that direct man in building a new reality. Or, to put it otherwise, giving sense to the senseless...

Why was this poetic function of history hidden for so long a time? Lessing presumes it might be because the horizon of Western man has become considerably limited. For Western man is so much focused on the present that he simply is not aware of the transformation of reality into myth over time – a process

---

126 'Es ist einmal so, daß wir etwas Gewesenes umbilden im Sinn unserer nationalen Wunschbilder. Es ist andererseits so, daß unsere idealen Wunschbilder immer neu am Leben verwirklicht werden. Oder anders gesagt: Aus der Wirklichkeit abstrahiert unser Geist ein Reich der Bilder. Umgekehrt dient aber auch das Reich der Bilder dem Geiste zum Aufbau von Wirklichkeit. Indem wir unsere Wirklichkeit umbilden in eine Welt der Dichtung, wird auch wieder umgekehrt die Welt der Dichtung neu zu Wirklichkeit.'; o.c., 206–207.
127 'alles woran ein Mensch glaubt, irgendwann einmal wirklich gewesen ist, und daß umgekehrt nur wirklich werden kann woran ein Mensch glaubt.'; o.c., 207.

which, after all, takes centuries, if not thousands of years. But one can truly understand the nature of history only if one is able to develop an overview over a long range of time. And, Lessing argues, this analysis conclusively shows that

> [h]istory should not work at accumulating ever more facts of reality, but it should deliver man from his reality. For this reason, the most qualified guardians of history are: the poets.[128]

This is because all that ultimately remains of reality is a symbol; eventually, history is a "world poem and myth".[129]

Subsequently, Lessing focuses his attention on the third category of historical thinking: causality – the most important one of all. After all, perceptions are only made into experience by relating them causally, as a first step toward scientific investigation. However, one should note instantly, Lessing observes, that the idea of history being a science – a science *because* it makes causal connections – only is the fruit of modern times, that is, of the era of mechanistic thinking. After all, mankind always has had a memory and remembrance, without always having the idea of a science of history. History only developed into an (alleged) science when it started to relate occurrences causally, in Greek antiquity with Herodotus, and in Roman antiquity with Polybius. This mechanistic way of thinking has become increasingly dominant ever since, in the natural sciences as well as in historiography.

According to Lessing, modern man lives in causality like a snail lives in its shell. As a result, everything that enters consciousness does so in the form of causality or, in other words, in the form of a necessary relationship. That is, human consciousness processes all events in order to explain them as something that had to happen as it did and, indeed, could not have happened otherwise. This characteristic of causal explanations has become sophisticated, while originally it was rather primitive, comparable to, for example, children that blame and punish the door they ran into. Over time causal explanations have become increasingly sophisticated. But regardless of their condition of complexity, Lessing maintains, ultimately these explanations are nothing but a means to overpower, shape, and order life. Consequently, they do not express knowledge in any sense of the word, but are merely an expression of

---

128 'Die Geschichte sollte nicht daran arbeiten, immer neue Wirklichkeitstatsachen aufzuspeichern, sondern sie soll den Menschen von seiner Wirklichkeit erlösen. Darum sind die berufensten Verwalter der Geschichte: die Dichter.'; o.c., 209.
129 'Weltgedicht und Mythos'; o.c., 210, footnote.

the will. For this very reason, causal explanations are ultimately of a moral nature. The Greek word αἰτία does not distinguish between "cause" and "culpability", but unites both meanings – which proves, Lessing argues, that every causal judgment is actually a moral judgment. The main lines of his argument are identical with his argument as developed in the first edition of *Geschichte als Sinngebung des Sinnlosen*. That is, man asks for causal explanations not because he seeks after knowledge, but because he is aimed at becoming reconciled to what has happened in the past – because he wants to convince himself that he either can prevent or bring about a particular result in future.

We should realize, Lessing emphasizes, that in every causal judgment one makes, one singles out one or at most a few reasons and/or conditions out of a possibly countless number. Which ones one singles out, depends on one's kind of approach, which may be biographical, psychological, political, and so on; nevertheless, this process of singling out causal factors is a kind of roulette. Once one has singled out specific reasons and/or conditions, one *post festum* establishes a law to explain that what happened indeed had to happen as it did. After all, *post festum* it is always possible, and even rather easy, to find an appropriate law to explain what happened. Lessing compares this process with the way we understand our own parentage: even if we do know that it might well have been possible that our father would have married a different wife, or that we were born at a different place or country, we cannot truly realize this. The parentage we actually do have is taken for granted to such an extent that we experience it as being necessary. This is exactly what history implies, Lessing claims. Thus, history plays a prominent part as regards humankind's need for giving meaning to its existence, and the notion of causality is an important element with this: "This need for history providing meaning is so strong that every human being imagines itself that a mystical necessity is directed at precisely *his* life and *his* death".[130] After all, we simply cannot believe that what befalls us – and often moves us deeply – is nothing but the result of chance: there simply must be some logical explanation! Moreover, for most human beings, life in a world that is merely determined by chance would be completely unbearable, Lessing claims. Hence, we explain everything retrospectively as necessary, as our destiny or karma – as long as it was not chance, it is fine... But ultimately, these explanations are nothing but the means to quiet our souls: they do not offer any knowledge, and eventually simply reflect our own needs and aims.

---

130   'Dieses sinngebende Geschichtsbedürfnis ist so stark, daß jeder Mensch eine mystische Notwendigkeit just auf *sein* Leben und *sein* Sterben gerichtet wähnt.'; o.c., 214–215. The italics are Lessing's.

Remarkably enough, this need for causality has the very same root as the need to refer to fate or destiny that is widespread in the Eastern half of the world, Lessing observes. At first sight, they may appear different, but both serve to satisfy the desire for reconcilement with what happened in the past. Once one realizes that this is the basic function of our need for causality, certain misunderstandings may be avoided. There is no need, for instance, to introduce a notion like "mass delusion" to explain group behaviour. What matters, is the unwarranted belief in causal laws being operative in history, regardless whether we try to explain the behaviour of individuals or groups. Eventually, what it comes down to is the human need to discern a logical-moral sense in all that happens.

The search for causal relationships in history usually focuses primarily on the motivations of people, in order to explain their deeds. However, the question by what motives someone is driven is most difficult to answer, Lessing claims: in this connection, all kinds of thoughts, feelings, ideals, circumstances and conditions are relevant. Usually, when we try to explain something we have done, we retrospectively put one of these factors at the centre of the account given. But there is every reason to seriously question this practice, according to Lessing: there is no valid reason to suppose that our actions would be driven by a single motive – even though the names given to them , like "love", "hate", "jealousy", "revenge", "bloodlust" – are most suggestive. However, if we seriously try to consider what prompts our very own actions, we directly realize how artificial these explanations are. And this holds true even more so for the explanations we give of the behaviour of groups, for example nations: when one speaks, for instance, of "the pride of Japan" as the cause of war, what exactly is meant with these words? Could Japan indeed be proud, France be angry, or England be jealous? "I believe that no man and no God would be able to unriddle exhaustively everything that mingles in mass occurrences, which retrospectively will be unloaded simply and simplifying on a complex subject, and on an alleged motive in the soul of this subject", Lessing maintains.[131] Moreover, historians are hardly ever good judges of human beings, nor do they possess much wisdom of the world. Usually, they also judge too rashly. For historians, heydays are periods in which much has happened and there being a lot to tell about – albeit mainly stories about violence and suffering. In

---

131   'Ich glaube, kein Mensch und kein Gott könnte erschöpfend enträtseln, was alles in Massenvorgängen zusammenquirlt, welche von nachhinein einfach und vereinfachend auf ein erklittertes Subjekt und einen vermeintlichen Beweggrund in der Seele dieses Subjekts abgeschoben werden.'; o.c., 222.

contrast, periods in which not much happened – usually times when people were relatively happy – are usually not paid attention to.

However, Lessing argues, "everyone who once was in the midst of mass movements has to become a sceptical about time and history".[132] He can only be astonished by the way others retrospectively interpret these great times... Though Lessing does not dwell on this subject, it is tempting to read it as an autobiographical statement – and to conclude that Lessing's experiences in the autumn of 1914 have been decisive in the development of his philosophy of history.

His reflections on causality confirm, Lessing claims, that reason by definition cannot be a driving force in history, "because reason can always only post festum judge occurrences and history".[133] Conscious mind appears both as contemplating mind ("Vernunft") and wanting mind ("Verstand"). Contemplating mind can indeed only contemplate: it stands outside of time, and can neither overcome nor promote life. Wanting mind, however, is capable of either overcoming or promoting life. But "true and reliable in this comedy of history is nothing but need, suffering, and joke!",[134] Lessing observes, and neither of these is in any way linked to reason. Hence, it is rather easy to infer from this what the historian ultimately does: "Because the whole matter of historians consists in making fate, which actually has no sense, look as if it is meaningful and understandable to human character".[135] In a sense, this procedure is quite simple: as the historian always knows the result of the process he or she is describing – indeed, the result is the logical starting point of his or her account –, it is rather easy to find all kinds of factors that contributed to this result. But the explanations of historians are completely arbitrary, Lessing argues, in the sense that it is always possible to refer to a completely different set of causes to explain the very same result. And this alternative account could indeed be equally plausible. It is accordingly not surprising that modern historians refer to different causal arrangements as compared with historians of, say, two centuries ago. Historians are aware of this, realizing that their stories about the past are not, nor can be, true. But they also know that human

---

132 'Wer jemals mitten in Volksbewegungen stand, der muß Zweifler werden an Zeit und Geschichte.'; o.c., 223.
133 'Denn Vernunft kann immer nur post festum Geschehen und Geschichte beurteilen.'; o.c., 224.
134 'Wahr und glaubwürdig an dieser Komödie der Geschichte ist nichts als die Not, das Leiden und der Scherz!'; o.c., 225–226.
135 'Denn das ganze Geschäft der Historiker besteht darin, das eigentlich sinnlose Fatum so erscheinen zu lassen, als wenn es nach Menschenart sinnvoll und begreiflich wäre.'; o.c., 227.

beings need stories about the past, and cling to the illusion that these stories are true."This belief in history is the rock on which humanity builds its temporary and earthly cities", Lessing claims.[136] And if someone turns up proving that this belief in history is nothing but an illusion, he will be killed or locked up in an asylum. Be that as it may, ultimately causal explanations by historians are nothing but a Procrustean bed, into which life is forced by consciousness. In fact, historical causal explanations come down to a very simple formula, Lessing argues: because life apparently is like this, it has to be like this.

The history of art shows how arbitrary these causal explanations by historians actually are. For instance, the sequence "early renaissance – high renaissance – baroque" suggests that there is some logic in this development, as if the latter period springs from the former. But this is in fact something that is assigned to this development, and one might as well claim that for example high renaissance was something completely new in comparison with early renaissance, and not being related to it. The same argument holds true for the history of music. Today, we honour Johann Sebastian Bach as the founding father of an important tradition in music, but in mid nineteenth century he was almost completely forgotten – and at that time the history of music told an entirely different story than at present. Of course, the same holds true for history in general, it ultimately being nothing but an arbitrary story. In the first edition of *Geschichte als Sinngebung des Sinnlosen*, Lessing had given several examples in support of this claim; in this fourth edition, he adds a few more. All of these lead to the conclusion that history eventually is "a fiction of the mind".[137] The very same holds true for notions like race, landscape, *Zeitgeist*, style, nation – they all are fictions of the mind, and not based on experience. They are the means by which man orchestrates (past) reality. It is a perception shared by many people, Lessing argues, that the present is chaotic and confused; but in, say, a few hundred years time historians will characterize our time with a few keywords – and thus, the image of our time will be as clear as the image we now have of past times. This implies, Lessing emphasizes, that there are no essences in history: there is no pre-existing, given "Romanità" in Roman history, but historians retrospectively assign a specific Roman character to Roman history.

But, Lessing emphatically claims, this does not imply that historians may invent history at will or arbitrarily, for the stories they tell are neither invented

---

136 'Dieser Geschichtsglaube ist der Felsen, auf dem die Menschheit ihre zeitlichen und irdischen Städte baut.'; o.c., 229.
137 'eine Dichtung des Geistes'; o.c., 234.

at pleasure nor the result of free, unrestrained imagination, but are always based on tradition as their starting point.

Both in the first and the fourth edition of *Geschichte als Sinngebung des Sinnlosen*, Lessing argues that a moral sentiment ultimately underlies all causal explanation, since causal judgments always imply the idea that we can bring about or prevent a particular result, or, for that matter, a different one, in future. We catch a cold because of a draught, but this judgement implies the idea that we may prevent catching a cold in future by, say, closing the window to avert a draught. Lessing claims that this very same moral character underlies all *logificatio post festum*, that is, the process of retrospectively giving sense to a past that as such does not have a sense. Sometimes it is claimed that this process of retrospectively giving sense to the past is typical for Western culture. Lessing doubts this, however, claiming it to be characteristic of mankind in general, the only difference being that what Western man calls "causes" is called "spirits" or "demons" in other cultures. Be this as it may, the common reflex of someone being confronted with some disaster is to look for a scapegoat: a specific person or condition that may be blamed for the disaster concerned. This is the way humans deal with disasters: one raises the question "who is to blame?", and is reassured if this question can be answered. This holds true in general, but it is also the way jurisdiction works, according to Lessing: almost always a single person is held accountable for evils in which, in one way or another, numerous others are involved as well. This obviously reminds of Lessing's criticisms of the judicial process at the Haarmann-trial, where all the blame was put on Haarmann, and none on the society that afforded him the opportunity to commit his crimes.[138] – It is just customary that a single person is blamed or punished in order to quiet our own souls. A similar mechanism is operative with causal judgments in history, and the way they evolve, as Lessing explains with the following example:

> When in 1914 the German people went to war, German historians justified this with the guilt of others, they indeed representing it as an ideal that the sick world should heal through the German substance. But when in 1918 the war changed into a revolution, one started the other way round to consider the *German* substance being sick or guilty, even though the people behaved much more heroically at the moment of defeat than at the moment of the outbreak of its will to be supreme. This alternation

---

138   Cfr. above, 219–226.

of: "you are guilty" and "I am guilty" is something that returns time and again in history.[139]

The very way history is written implies that history always makes sense, Lessing claims: "So it is not at all clear how one could ever draw up a history that would *not* make sense".[140] In this respect, historical thinking corresponds to evolutionary thinking in biology, Lessing maintains: both stem from the very same American-European will to power, and both make success the measure of significance, implying that what is successful *necessarily* makes sense. Hence, Treitschke rightly characterized historians as "prophets turned backward",[141] that is, historians start with the result and subsequently "predict" how it came about. But anybody who has been involved in historical occurrences will realize and admit that history as experienced by contemporaries is completely different from history as written by historians. Lessing himself, of course, experienced the days of August 1914 – but the accounts given by historians do not tally at all with his involvement with this period.

What future does history as a discipline have? According to Lessing, there at least three possibilities. In the first place, history continues in the direction it has taken, and continues as an alleged investigation of (past) reality. This might well imply that history eventually will be nothing but an auxiliary science for other sciences, and might even disappear in time. That is, by trying to be what it is not, history might eventually bring about its own disappearance by becoming superfluous. Secondly, history is recognized for what it is: the way to myth. This implies that eventually the very idea of historical reality might disappear, and what will ultimately matter is nothing but the truth and value that is implied in myth. Lastly, man might gradually learn to abstain from ideas and ideals, and learn to live life as it happens – that is, yield to a life without goals, aims, and values, by accepting that it is not mankind that ultimately

---

139   'Als im Jahre 1914 das deutsche Volk zum Kriege aufstand, da begründete das die deutsche Geschichtsschreibung mit der Schuld der anderen, ja sie stellte es als ein Ideal hin, daß am deutschen Wesen die kranke Welt genesen müsse. Als aber im November 1918 der Krieg in Revolution übergegangen war, da begann man umgekehrt das *deutsche* Wesen krank oder schuldig zu befinden, obwohl das Volk im Augenblick der Niederlage sich ungleich heldischer bewährte als im Ausbruch seines Übermächtigungswillens. Dieser Wechsel von: "Du hast die Schuld" und "Ich bin schuldig" ist ein immer wiederkehrender Vorgang der Geschichte.'; Theodor Lessing, o.c., 240. The italics are Lessing's.
140   'so ist es überhaupt nicht einzusehen, wie man jemals Geschichte aufstellen könnte, die *nicht* sinnvoll wäre.'; o.c., 241. The italics are Lessing's.
141   'rückwärts gewendeten Propheten'; o.c., 242.

matters. If humanity stops being a self-directed creature, history as we know it might indeed disappear.

In his day and age, Lessing argues, people have started to realize that causal explanations are artificial. As a result, a new kind of history did arise: history as a science of forms, that is, a descriptive and classificatory science of phenomena: "cultures, works of art, literatures, nations are seen as one sees the different species of animals or the different kinds of trees".[142] Lessing does not oppose this approach as long as one understands what one is in fact doing: "Youth, blooming, maturity, old age, downfall, death of cultures or nations... yes, what does this in fact *mean*?"[143] That is, Lessing emphatically warns against the tendency to take these descriptions and classifications for essences. After all, these descriptions and classifications ultimately are the mirror image of human consciousness, and the way it orders what is given to it. Moreover, what are the criteria which allow someone to call a nation young, or a culture mature?

> What does it in fact come down to when one speaks of blooming or downfall? To power? Happiness? Holiness? To force? To achievement? To the accumulation of goods?[144]

In short, historians should be aware that it simply does not make any sense to apply unthinkingly the notions of biology to history.

Lessing concludes his analysis of the categories of history with a short reflection on the human condition. The kernel of the human condition is suffering and need; the essence of all individuation is the tension between will and consciousness that is born out of need. That is, Lessing claims that he managed to prove that reality as given in consciousness is generally of a negative nature, the historical world of mankind accordingly having this negative character as well. As Lessing puts it:

> Thus, every random conscious, that is, logical or moral or shaping reaction is an attempt "to make a virtue out of need " [...] Thus, logic is a

---

142 'Kulturen, Kunstwerke, Dichtungen, Völker werden betrachtet, wie man die Arten der Tiere oder die Gattungen der Bäume betrachtet.'; o.c., 249.
143 'Jugend, Blüte, Reife, Alter, Niedergang, Tod von Kulturen oder Völker... ja was *heißt* denn das eigentlich?'; o.c., 250. The italics are Lessing's.
144 'Worauf eigentlich soll es denn ankommen, wenn man von Blüte oder Niedergang spricht? Auf Macht? Glück? Heiligkeit? Auf Stärke? Auf Leistung? Auf Anhäufen von Gütern?'; o.c., 251.

cleansing from a mental obstruction and mental contradiction, ethics and morals, a pushing away of discomfort on something being addressed as "guilty".[145]

This implies that the fundamental fact of the human condition is pain: all logic, all ethics, actually all of conscious life of humans, may eventually be reduced to pain. In other words, behind all ethics lurks the delusion that one has to look for causes of the pain one suffers, whereas the pain in fact is within the "I" of the one who suffers. As Lessing argues, it is only when mankind manages to liberate itself from its human perspective, that is, when it no longer judges morally nor evaluates ethically, but manages to look from a "panzoistic" ('panzoistisch') perspective, all suffering will vanish – because human consciousness itself will be vanished.

7 Para-logical Reflections

The third and final book of the fourth edition of *Geschichte als Sinngebung des Sinnlosen* consists of three chapters. They serve more or less as an – admittedly long – afterword to the reflections in especially the second book of this fourth edition. In the first chapter of the third book, Lessing discusses images. For a start, he again argues against the idea that history somehow deals with, or even would mirror past reality. However, man tends to cling to his belief in historical reality, because "here are his hopes and comforts, his aims and plans, his aspirational dreams and giving meaning".[146] This implies that it might well be possible that man lives thanks to his superstitious belief in historical reality. The way someone thinks – either mechanistically or teleologically, dialectically or intuitively, psychologically or logically, reflectively or speculatively – might well be determined by preconscious prejudices, Lessing claims. However, in his opinion, knowledge of prejudices still is in its infancy. The only philosopher who seriously studied prejudices and presumptions is Francis Bacon, resulting in his theory of "idols". But his approach merits elaboration, according to Lessing. Eventually, its conclusion will be clear: it will show that – with the

---

145 'So ist denn jede beliebige geistige, d.h. logische oder moralische oder formschaffende Reaktion ein Versuch "aus der Not eine Tugend zu machen" [...] So ist Logik ein Entwirken seelischer Stauung und seelischen Widerspruchs, Ethik und Moral ein Abschieben von Unlust auf etwas als "schuldig" angesprochenes.'; o.c., 255.
146 'Hier legen seine Hoffnungen und Tröstungen, seine Absichten und Pläne, seine Zielträume und Sinngebungen.'; o.c., 260.

exception of the sphere of *vérité* – everything that humans know is prefigured by their urge to live and to survive. The subsequent question will be whether humans can cling to their prejudices in the knowledge that they are indeed prejudices, or have to leave them behind, only to live from then on half a life. We do not know what the answer to this question will be – that is for the future to decide. What is clear, however, Lessing argues, is that if we strip European science of its scientific language and abstract form, what one will meet with is a desire, an ideal – based on an image that we want to be materialized. For a culture consists on the one hand of images we managed to materialize, on the other hand of images we want to be realized in future.

Subsequently, Lessing reiterates his views on historical thought in the terminology of his theory of cathartic understanding, involving his notion of *Ahmung*. In a nutshell, this comes down to the following:

> The historian faces his subjects not otherwise than the way a lover faces his beloved. The bare fact that he chooses for depiction precisely *this one* out of millions of subjects of equal merit, must be reduced to a matter of sentiment (predilection). The very same relation holds true when the subject of history is chosen out of antipathy (that is, a prejudice in *another* direction). Also this allegedly "critical history" is already controlled beforehand by idol and ideal. [...] One misunderstands the essence, indeed one impedes the possibility of history if one demands that the historian should neither love nor hate, because love or hate makes one sharp-eyed or blind. – Love and hate make *seeing* [...][147]

Thus, man writes history, according to Lessing, projecting our idols and ideals on a past they are not proper to. Or, in the terminology of his theory of *Ahmung*: if we feel a predilection for our subject, we "understand" our subject in a process of *Aufahmnung*, that is, we make the most of our subject, like a lover makes the most of his beloved. In contrast, if we feel a preconscious

---

147 'Der Historiker steht zu seinen Gegenständen nichts anders, wie der Liebende zu seiner Geliebten. Schon daß er aus Millionen gleichwerter Gegenstände gerade *diesen* zur Darstellung ergreift, muß auf eine Gefühlseinstellung (Prädilektion) zurückgeführt werden. Ganz das selbe Verhältnis liegt vor, wenn aus Abneigung (d.h., aus Voreingung nach einer *anderen* Richtung hin) der Geschichtsstoff ergriffen wird. Auch diese vermeintliche "kritische Historie" ist schon von Idol und Ideal vorbeherrscht [...]. Man verkennt das Wesen, ja man unterbindet die Möglichkeit von Geschichte, wenn man fordert, der Historiker solle weder lieben noch hassen, weil Liebe oder Haß überscharfsichtig oder blind mache. – Liebe und Haß machen *sehend* [...]'; o.c., 267–268. The italics are Lessing's.

antipathy towards our subject, we "understand" it in a process of *Gegenahmung*: we do not make the most of the subject concerned, but do exactly the opposite.

In Lessing's view, it is not possible, however, to use all of the past to project our idols and ideals on. First of all, history ultimately is not written by individuals who choose a subject at random, for historians always belong to a particular tradition and community. Current knowledge that is incorporated in this background is accordingly always the starting point for a historian:

> No individual writes history. First of all, for history is only under consideration – what attains to knowledge. And that is indeed doubtlessly only what *can* have success and effect.[148]

This implies that, otherwise than often believed, history will usually fail to do justice by, say, pointing at someone or something that has been unjustly forgotten. For it are success and effect that matter; and besides this, the human need to appreciate. Thus,

> [...] in world history, on this "theatre of life" [...] already completed facts of success and power are *given*, and now the need of the hearts for justice and sanctification has to *convert* these facts of power into facts of value, has *to see into them* a worth and a sense, an ethos and a value.[149]

Which facts become "facts of success and power" is completely coincidental and unpredictable, Lessing argues.

To underpin this claim, Lessing gives a number of arguments. Firstly, it generally is individuals being at the centre of history, traditionally mostly kings and noblemen. They do indeed have success and effect in history, but not because of their outstanding abilities, but because of their parentage. Secondly, if truly important persons appear in history, this is mostly not because of their importance, but because of some minor side effect, or owing to coincidence. Nietzsche, for instance, mainly achieved fame because his work was

---

148   'Kein Einzelner schreibt Geschichte. Zunächst kommt für Geschichte nur in Betracht – was zur Kenntnis gelangt. Und das ist doch zweifellos nur das, was Erfolg und Wirkung erlangen *kann*.'; o.c., 269. The italics are Lessing's.
149   '[...] in der Weltgeschichte, auf diesem "Theater des Lebens" [...] sind schon fertige Erfolgs- und Machttatsachen *gegeben*, und nun muß das Bedürfnis der Herzen nach Gerechtigkeit und Heiligung diese Machttatsachen in Werttatsachen *umglauben*, muß eine Würde und einen Sinn, ein Ethos und einen Wert *in sie hineinschauen*.'; o.c., 269–270. The italics are Lessing's.

misunderstood. Likewise, historical tradition is often the result of particular misunderstandings. Thirdly, if a person becomes successful there usually is something wrong with him or her, that is, he or she must be controversial or neglected, subsequently only on second thoughts becoming a historical figure. In the fourth place, success and effect as such do not matter: they only do when people are aware of them. In the fifth place, the facts of history may change overnight: "there nowhere is an established body of historical facts".[150] Hence, it is customary that historical reputations may change; thus, "there is a very large succession of different Bonaparte, Socrates, Bismarck, Goethe".[151] And their reputation ultimately is determined by the outcome of history:

> Or let one assume that Wilhelm II of Germany thanks to some happy coincidences had brilliantly won the 1914–1918 war; – exactly the same historians who now (1927) cannot do enough to damn his government and who look for and find reasons why such a ruler eventually *had* to lose, would have put this figure next to the figures of the great Hohenstaufen.[152]

Moreover, the past contains a countless number of facts, names, books, and documents, it being impossible to study all of them; thus, history necessarily has to confine itself to a few symbolic, particular or random facts. For that matter, history can never grasp what is really essential in life. Yet another argument is that one is usually not inclined to acknowledge the greatness of others, if only because it implies the recognition of a great historical figure being greater and more important than oneself. The very idea that someone else would be more important, intelligent or stronger, is sufficient to arouse painful feelings with most people. Hence, the reputation of a historical figure is often explained by referring to coincidence: had Providence not chosen Spinoza but John Doe to be a great philosopher, today we would all know John Doe but not Spinoza – thus, John Doe in fact is hardly different from Spinoza, and not less important, it is just that Providence happened to choose Spinoza and not John Doe... For the very same reason, most people are interested in gossip

---

150 'Es gibt nirgendwo eine feststehende historische Dinglichkeit.'; o.c., 273.
151 'Es gibt eine sehr große Reihe verschiedener Bonaparte, Sokrates, Bismarck, Goethe.'; loc. cit..
152 'Oder man nehme an, Wilhelm II. von Deutschland hätte den Krieg 1914–1918 dank irgendwelcher glücklicher Fügungen glänzend gewonnen; – genau die selben Historiker, welche gegenwärtig (1927) sich nicht genug tun können in der Verdammnis seiner Regierung und die Gründe suchen und finden, warum ein solcher Herrscher schließlich unterliegen *mußte*, hätten diese Gestalt neben die Gestalten der großen Hohenstaufen gestellt'; o.c., 274. The italics are Lessing's.

about famous people: it proves that ultimately they are not really different from you and me, Lessing argues. When history debunks great historical figures by pointing to petty facts of their life, it puts itself at the service of exactly this inclination. Only if one does not succeed in reducing a historical figure to the ranks of ordinary men and women, he or she will be recognized as a great historical figure – but then that person will be almost deified, and in order to distinguish him or her from ordinary men and women their uniqueness will be emphasized. Finally, if someone happens to become a historical figure in his or her lifetime, Lessing argues, one will feel compelled to meet his or her developing reputation, with the result that the reputation will increasingly take over, while the original person gradually disappears. In short, whether someone will have influence and success in history is the product of sheer coincidence, and historical reputations do not provide any indication of the real value of the person concerned, according to Lessing.

Fame originally means that someone (or something) is being talked about, Lessing observes; it does neither imply a judgment on worth nor on value. Likewise, history cannot judge true worth or value: it simply shows that someone (or something) from the past is still being talked about. Hence, Schiller's famous *dictum* that "world history is the world court of justice" ('die Weltgeschichte ist das Weltgericht') is utterly mistaken, according to Lessing.

Lessing repeats his observation that it is always possible to approach history from two sides: from that of the individual or the group. Again he argues that there is no contradiction between these approaches, since on the one hand an individual always has relations with others, on the other hand a group consists of individuals. Moreover, an individual only enters into history because his or her acts affect others – a recluse who abstains from all contacts with other people is not a likely candidate to play a part in history: "the complete solitary cannot become historical".[153] However, all of this does not imply the denial of the possibility that there could be an area of tension between individual and group. For as Immanual Kant has explained in his *Idee zu einer allgemeinen Geschichte in weltbürgerlicher Absicht*, the tension between individual and group is not only characteristic of the human condition, but even plays a pivotal part in its development. This insight relates to a number of problems, some of which Lessing subsequently addresses.

Lessing points out that an individual may only become a representative of a group – i.e., a historical figure in relation to that group – if he or she is every inch a member of it. This holds true in the cultural sense, but in Lessing's

---

153   'Das völlig Abseitige kann nicht historisch werden.'; o.c., 282.

view probably in the biological and racial sense as well. That is, it is not very likely that an American will become a historical figure in, say, China. – This is a rather peculiar argument. Apparently, Lessing felt he could not ignore the debates on "race" that were quite prominent in public opinion at the time. Still, his argument, in particular the use of notions like "biological" and "race", does not seem to be very well-considered. – According to Lessing, the tragic fate of the Jews proves his point: no matter how long they live in a certain country, they still are seen as being different or considered strangers. Hence, "wherever Jews acquire historical significance their tragic end is completely inevitable".[154] A related issue concerns the circumstance that history is often represented as relying on some kind of "national metaphysics" ('Nationalmetaphysik'), that is, the idea that history should necessarily be the history of a nation. That is, the nation is considered supreme; if, in this connection, in a national mythology an outsider enters the stage, this person only functions to increase the self-love of the nation.

Lessing claims that the argument as developed thus far in his book implies that history may start from reality, but definitely ends with symbols. The most important method historians follow to escape from reality into the realm of symbols is personification, that is: historical forces are presented as if they are persons. Figures like Romulus and Remus are emblematic, being symbols in the history of the city of Rome and the Roman Empire. But the same holds true for, say, Tiberius or Nero – whether these symbolic figures tally with the actual personalities of Roman antiquity is not a relevant question. The question who Nero "really" was is as inappropriate as the question whether Wilhelm Tell "really" existed. Their importance lies in their symbolic function, this symbolic "truth" accordingly being far more significant than their alleged reality:

> Figures arise through transferring desires of the heart into the realm of time and being sensualized in the reality one is conscious of. Thus, the as such insignificant and always coincidental factuality of history is elevated to truth by the fictionalising spirit of the people and its spokesman, the historian.[155]

---

[154] 'Wo immer Juden zu geschichtlichen Größen werden, da ist ihr tragischer Ausgang ganz unvermeidlich.'; o.c., 283.

[155] 'Gestalten entstehen, indem Wünsche des Herzens auf die Ebene der Zeit übertragen und an der bewußtgewordenen Wirklichkeit versinnlicht werden. So wird die an sich gleichgültige und immer zufällige Tatsächlichkeit der Geschichte vom dichtenden Volksgeist und seinem Fürsprecher, dem Geschichtseschreiber, zu Wahrheit erhoben.'; o.c., 286.

We have to keep in mind, Lessing claims, that man, whenever he loves or hates, has no other means available than personification. Whether these are called "Mother Russia", "Uncle Sam", "the state" or "the economy", makes no difference. Without personifications like these, there simply cannot be history. According to Lessing, the "growth" of personified figures is almost identical to the rise of religious symbols. Both concern, after all, the symbolizations of material that is ultimately given by life, by means of a vision that is nourished by desire and need. In this sense, there is no difference between the Muses of Greek antiquity and the figures created by historians. This shows that man needs symbols, and cannot really do without them. The often heard argument that history deals with occurrences in time, whereas religion deals with the timeless, does not apply, Lessing argues. For the images of history will eventually turn into timelessness, while the images of religion ultimately started in time. This similarity explains why history is a kind of religious force in a society – in the original sense of the word, that is, a force that unites a group.[156] This implies that history tells truths – though not in the traditional sense, that is, stories that "correspond" with some kind of reality, but in the sense of "higher" and enduring truths.

In the second chapter of book three of the fourth edition of *Geschichte als Sinngebung des Sinnlosen*, Lessing discusses some fundamental issues that underlie history. Referring to what he discussed in the previous chapter – to wit that individuals from the past gradually change into symbols and only as symbols appear in history – Lessing argues that this is the very moment mass psychology enters the stage. For mass psychology changes fact into fate, that is, it makes what happened into a necessity. When this happens, two possibilities arise. Either one accepts fate, and respects it, or one thinks fate may still be changed and influenced, and thus disrespects it. If fate is accepted, it is canonized – like a deceased will be canonized, and thus is reborn for a second life in the memory of those who remember a person. This again shows the similarities between history and religion, Lessing claims. But if fate is not accepted, man revolts against, and thus desecrates, the values that are implied in fate.

In this way, history may be seen as a continuous pendulum between canonization and disrespect. In daily life, one may recognize this very process in the way a group relates to its leaders: if this leader is powerful and has success he or she will be canonized even during his or her life; if, on the other hand, this

---

156 The Latin word "religare", from which the English words "religion" and "religious" stem, literally means "to tie together".

leader fails and is powerless he or she will instantly lose respect. As we have seen, if someone dies he or she will be canonized, according to Lessing. This may be explained because of the invisibility of a deceased, it being an important factor in this process. For this very reason, political or religious leaders are often kept from the public eye. Likewise, aloofness is a feature that increases power, while closeness decreases power – again something that can be experienced in daily life. Hence, elected representatives are on the one hand akin to the people who elected them, but may on the other hand serve as a leg up to something that is looked for. Again, if the leader of a group gets too close to its members, he or she will lose authority, Lessing maintains. The most powerful force a leader has at his or her disposal is anxiety: fear of those in power against whom one cannot defend oneself. This force is even more fundamental than the will, or whatever values. Subsequently, Lessing returns to the difference between history and religion, claiming that history mainly differs from religion in deifying humans, and actually making them the most powerful creature on earth. But woe be unto anyone in power who fails, Lessing argues: his or her group will see him or her as the scapegoat on which all the blame may be put for everything that went wrong. This is what happened in Germany after it lost the Great War; and only when the German people did not manage to find a foreign scapegoat, it started to blame itself.[157]

According to Lessing, these insights from mass psychology help to understand what is implied in commanding and obeying, or in overpowering and surrendering. Both of these drives continuously interact. Quite a lot is known about their impact on sexuality, Lessing claims, but they are important in history as well, though it has been hardly recognized. Nevertheless, a large number of historical phenomena may be understood by relating them to the interaction between these drives. Lessing cannot discuss these issues at length, he writes apologetically, but he refers for instance to Nietzsche who had similar ideas when he pointed out that history may always be seen either from the perspective of the bird or from that of the frog, from the perspective of the master or from that of the slave. But it is important to realize this is a psychological truth, Lessing emphasizes, and not – as Nietzsche seemed to think, at least according to Lessing – a historical fact.[158]

Another couple of notions that may help to understand history is the one of acting and undergoing: in Lessing's view, history may be seen as a continuous interaction between acting and undergoing. That is, in history, some people play an active role, while others the one of mainly awaiting and undergoing

---

157 O.c., 292–296.
158 O.c., 297–298.

what happens. As a result, the facts of history always show a Janus face: one that looks differently whether one sees it from the perspective of those who make history, or from the perspective of the substance out of which history is made. Closely connected to these perspectives are two basic attitudes with regard to history as a process: optimism and pessimism. Those who are focused on the perspective of performer usually are optimistic about history, while those who take up the perspective of merely undergoing history usually are pessimistic. Closely related to both of these attitudes is another couple of outlooks: people who are optimistic about history usually are directed towards the future, and have only a limited sense of history, while people who are pessimistic about history, in contrast, tend to cling to the past and do not expect much from the future:

> Fear always looks back, but its backwards is indeed merely lie. Hope always looks forward, but its forwards is indeed merely imagination.[159]

The life of humans eventually is a pendulum between hope and fear, with now hope, and then again fear as the dominating power. But the very same applies to history at large, Lessing argues. People without a sense of history live by the day, hoping for the best. In contrast, people with a sense of history have a broader perspective of time, involving an awareness of the future, though they usually are not optimistic about its nature. Sometimes people wonder whether this difference in attitude does not simply reflect a difference in character. Though Lessing raises this question, he gives no answer, merely pointing out that it regards a typically human issue: in the entire creation, it is only humans that struggle with this dualism. Eventually, this is, Lessing maintains, because humanity itself is dual by nature, being both nature and mind. According to Lessing, fear relates to man as a natural being, the awareness of this condition implying the notion of being mortal. Hope, in contrast, relates to man as a spiritual being, implying the idea that mind will somehow be stronger than nature. All this means that it is possible to describe history as a continuous balancing between fear and hope, with a conceivably happy present as the middle.

Lessing begins the third and final chapter of the third book of the fourth edition of *Geschichte als Sinngebung des Sinnlosen* with the observation that it is a mistake trying to transfer the typically human linear conception of time to the realm of the non-human. This implies that his analysis of the categories of

---

159 'Die Furcht blickt immer nach rückwärts, aber ihr Rückwärts ist ja nur Lüge. Die Hoffnung blickt immer nach vorwärts, aber ihr Vorwärts ist ja nur Imagination.'; o.c., 303.

historical thinking is not, and should not be understood as, being an account of a particular historical development. In his critique of history, the categories of historical thinking are a given, and asking for the history of these categories would amount to demanding the philosopher to jump over his own shadow. Thus, the linear order only bears on reality as given in consciousness. Or, in the terminology of Lessing's theory of three spheres: human knowledge relates to *réalité*, but does not imply anything as regards *vitalité*. Indeed, it is not even possible to conclude anything with respect to *vitalité*, except for what it is not. That is, we may safely assume that "time" as a typically human way to order reality as given in consciousness does not exist in *vitalité*. Likewise, we may also be sure that "causality" does not exist in *vitalité*. Again, the sense of history as well is proper to reality as given in consciousness or *réalité* – and, again, we may accordingly be sure that the sense of history does not exist in the past itself. The writing of history is the way man orders the past, which amounts to giving sense to it; the sense of history is therefore not proper to the past itself, but assigned to it. In a nutshell, this is what Lessing's philosophy of history is about, and articulates its essence. According to Lessing, it is not possible for man to go beyond the sense of history as it is given by man himself in *réalité*, even though some people claim they can by transcending the merely human point of view. Though Lessing does not say so explicitly, it is most likely that he has in this connection in particular the philosophy of G.W.F. Hegel in mind, which indeed adopts a point of view that transcends the merely human. Lessing, however, strongly opposes this idea, it being essential for him to consider and elaborate the way man orders the past and thus giving sense to it.

In contrast to quite a number of his contemporaries, Lessing does not want to revolt against reason: he emphatically claims to adhere to the tradition of rationalism and intellectualism. He is aimed at resisting the abuse of reason, not reason itself. Lessing observes that culture is often defined as a reshaping of nature, but in his opinion it is rather the opposite of nature, going at the expense of it, even to the degree that, in Lessing's view, one could declare that culture kills nature. Thus, one should ask: "Is, where cultural activity no longer is the expression of nature, this human work somehow the tomb and death of all nature?".[160] Lessing raises a number of similar general questions – questions which, he thinks, should be asked, even if they cannot be answered instantly, and in fact are not even understood by most people.

A final thought Lessing puts forward for consideration is that "the development of man and his unstoppable progressive cultural process will with

---

160 'Ist dort, wo das Kulturwerk nicht mehr Ausdruck der Natur ist, dieses Menschenwerk etwa Grabmal und Tod aller Natur?'; o.c., 315.

irresistible certainty end in – madness".[161] As we have seen, *vitalité* does have neither ideals nor values, both being proper to *réalité*, that is, to the reality that humans are conscious of, and as it is ordered by them. Hence, history is proper to *réalité*, and "this is the path of history: a victory of an alert ideal and a conscious wanting up to the complete enervation and demolition of the myth of nature in favour of human ideology".[162] But, as said, in Lessing's view, this path will lead to madness, referring in this connection to, among other things, the biblical story of the Tower of Babel, also being a story about human pride leading to the downfall of man. Lessing wonders whether he is the only one to comprehend this imminent danger, and the only one who recognizes the symptoms of the impending madness. Modern megacities, for example, Lessing considers anthills of madness, in which even the most sensible people do nothing but trying to make as much money as possible at a deadly pace. And similar developments may be noticed everywhere, he observes: in art, politics, economics, and philosophy. They all bear witness to this human megalomania, coupled with an ever increasing madness. It would be easy to digress endlessly on this issue, Lessing argues. Another symptom is that a nation may totally renounce everything in which it devotedly believed, and for which it passionately fought for four years – like the German nation completely repudiated the Great War after it was lost. This increasing madness even shows in love, according to Lessing: most of his contemporaries do not really understand what love implies, confusing love with, for instance, utility.

Lessing claims that the development, of which he has only given a sketch, may also be noticed in the changes in flora and fauna under the influence of human intervention. Domesticated animals are an outstanding example: they lose the certainty of their instincts, especially their sexual drive, and, moreover, the strength of all their natural urges decreases, they consequently becoming largely disorientated. In his book *Meine Tiere* ('My animals')[163] Lessing discusses numerous examples of this very development. But, he emphasizes, in a natural state none of this would occur: it is the effect of domestication, and happens when flora and fauna are cultivated. Culture has the very same effect on mankind, Lessing claims: human's natural urges lose strength, and people become disorientated. But there is no way back: mankind cannot return to its

---

161 'Die Entwicklung des Menschen und sein unhemmbar fortschreitender Kulturprozeß mündet mit unverweiglicher Sicherheit in den – Irrsinn.'; loc.cit..
162 'Das ist der Weg der Geschichte: ein Sieg wachen Ideals und bewußten Wollens bis zu voller Entseelung und Ausödung des Naturmythos zugunsten der Menschheitsideologie.'; o.c., 317.
163 Berlin 1926.

natural state, not even partially. So all suggestions and appeals for mankind to return to nature are in vain. For mankind is preordained to do only one thing, and, indeed, one thing only: to continue the development of culture. Hence, Lessing suggests a "radicalism of reason"[164] in order to save coming generations from a downfall into senselessness. This implies that "logic and ethics are thus indeed a disease, but also at the same time cure".[165] Thus, eventually, "the goal of mankind is: rational self-adjustment of an anarchic madhouse...".[166]

In conclusion of this fourth edition of *Geschichte als Sinngebung des Sinnlosen*, Lessing duplicates – albeit with some minor stylistic improvements – his "Philosophie als Tat", the text of the inaugural lecture that he delivered in 1907 at the *Technische Hochschule* in his native Hanover.[167] In this way he emphasizes the fundamental continuity in his thinking: the author of *Geschichte als Sinngebung des Sinnlosen* still endorses the main lines of the argument as developed in his inaugural lecture. In this lecture of 1907 he argued that his philosophy is not to be found in his writings, but in his deeds. That is, what in his opinion eventually matters is whether he could manage, albeit only marginally, to diminish the suffering in the world. Hence, his philosophy of history as exposed in *Geschichte als Sinngebung des Sinnlosen* may ultimately be considered merely instrumental: it should contribute to the decrease of suffering in the world – after all, that has been the goal Lessing was truly striving for.

---

164 'Radikalismus der Vernunft'; *GSS4*, o.c., 324.
165 'Logik und Ethik sind somit zwar eine Krankheit, aber auch zugleich Genesung.'; loc.cit..
166 'Das Ziel der Menschheit ist: Rationale Selbstregulation eines anarchischen Irrenhauses...'; o.c., 325.
167 Cfr. Chapter one, above, 21.

CHAPTER 6

'Es Wird Zum Denken Anregen'
The Reception of Lessing's Philosophy of History

Theodor Lessing expounded his ideas on the philosophy of history mainly in two books, both entitled *Geschichte als Sinngebung des Sinnlosen*.[1] In the first, published in 1919, he addresses the public at large; in the second, published in 1927 – formally the fourth edition of the book, as the first edition was reprinted twice without alterations –, a public of peers. Accordingly, the tone of both books differs: in the first, it is at times quite emotional, in the second predominantly academic. Despite this and other differences, Lessing's general position in both books is the same. How may it be characterized? First and foremost, Lessing's philosophy of history evidences a radical epistemological scepticism concerning history: Lessing claims that it is impossible for the historian to know the past as it really happened, that is, the study of history does not, and indeed cannot, result in knowledge of the past. To underpin this thesis, he brings forward all kinds of arguments. In the first edition of *Geschichte als Sinngebung des Sinnlosen* he advances these arguments rather spontaneously, in the fourth more systematically by discussing what he considers the specific categories of historical thought: the "bearer" of history that provides its unity, time, and causality. As regards these categories of historical thought, his analyses lead up to one and the same conclusion: these categories are the way consciousness orders the reality of which it is conscious, or, in Lessing's terminology, *réalité*. The categories concerned consequently are not proper to the past, but to (present) consciousness. Hence, history can neither know nor mirror past reality as such: the image of the past is, even if one claims that this ordering is the ordering of something given, at least partially the result of the ordering by consciousness in the present – and it is impossible to determine which part. Moreover, the ordering of *réalité* by consciousness is guided by present needs and ideals. Thus, history reveals present needs and beliefs as they appear from the very way *réalité* is ordered. This implies that according to Lessing, attempts to justify political acts and decisions retrospectively by appealing to past reality lack all credibility: as we cannot know past reality, it is not possible to justify acts and decisions retrospectively by appealing to past

---

1 A translation of the chapter title is, 'It will incite thinking'.

reality. However, for Lessing this does not imply that history is worthless or useless, for it is in his view definitely of great value within a culture. Historians have to tell inspiring stories to the communities to which they belong, in particular stories that serve the primary ethical purpose of decreasing the need in the world. Ultimately, this is what Lessing's reflections on history lead up to: history has no intrinsic value, but only instrumental value at the service of an ethical ideal. As such, however, it is vitally important within society.

Lessing unfolded his ideas on history not only through *Geschichte als Sinngebung des Sinnlosen*, but also numerous stray observations scattered through his other writings. For instance, in 1925 Lessing published a brief portrait of the actor and publicist Maximilian Harden, it being the pseudonym of Felix Witkowski (1861–1927). Harden was the founder and editor of the weekly *Die Zukunft* ('The Future'), in which he frequently published his comments on contemporary politics. As such, he was a quite influential voice in late Wilhelmine Germany. As a schoolboy, Lessing greatly admired Harden, and even went to visit him in Berlin, which he described in his autobiography *Einmal und nie wieder*.[2] He would include a more comprehensive portrait of Harden in his *Der jüdische Selbsthaß* (1930).[3] In his 1925 portrait of Harden, Lessing observes in passing:

> History comes, history goes. The legend of the historical and public person is spun from envy and hatred, need and hope. What do we know about the real person? As often as we get to know a highly controversial person more closely, we discover the delusion of all judgments we made in our life. It indeed is always completely different.[4]

This observation is, of course, easily understandable within the context of this short essay on Harden. But for readers familiar with *Geschichte als Sinngebung des Sinnlosen* it provides moreover a succinct summary of Lessing's view of an issue he discussed at length in the book itself. Similar allusions to his philosophy of history may be found frequently in Lessing's writings. Sometimes, it is no more than a casual remark, for instance when Lessing refers to "Clio,

---

2 Cfr. *Eunw*, chapters 17 and 18, 223–234.
3 *DjS*, 167–207.
4 'Geschichte kommt, Geschichte geht. Die Legende des historischen und öffentlichen Menschen wird von Neid und Haß, Bedürfniss und Hoffnung gesponnen. Was wissen wir von den wirklichen Menschen? So oft wir einen Vielumstrittenen aus menschlicher Nähe kennen lernen, da entdecken wir den Wahn all unserer im Leben gefällte Urteile. Es ist ja doch alles immer ganz anders.'; Theodor Lessing, 'Maximilian Harden', in: *Prager Tagblatt*, December 12th, 1925, reprinted in: *IFEG*, 389–393, there 393.

the laughable Muse".⁵ But then again, he sometimes presents an aspect of his philosophy of history in a short accessible essay, like for instance "Alles wäre anders gekommen..." ('Everything would have been different...'). In this essay, Lessing tells a couple of anecdotes, all with the same lesson: had a detail in the story been different, the outcome would have been different – had he not left a classmate alone but kept him company, the boy would not have committed suicide. These anecdotes – and, Lessing claims, it would be very easy to give many more examples – testify to what he calls the "Kausalitätswahnsinn" ('the causal madness') of mankind:

> But this establishment of causal chains, this discovery of cause and effect, without exception hides an act of will and of superstition, yes, essentially it is nothing but a single unwittingly awful artificiality. Because as we can very well connect everyone with everything, we can never run against facts, occurrences, acts, with respect to which could not be said: "When this or that had not happened, everything would have been different".⁶

Thus, had not general Emmanuel Grouchy (1766–1847) misunderstood an order by Napoleon, the latter might have won the Battle of Waterloo, and all subsequent European history would have been entirely different."But what if this entire chain of cause-effect is solely cheat and delusion, stemming from the psychology of human thought, a linearly directed, intentional thought?", Lessing asks.⁷ Again, this is a most concise summary of the analyses of causality in *Geschichte als Sinngebung des Sinnlosen*, adjusted to a general public: a causal judgment ultimately is the result of human arbitrariness, not of scientific research, and accordingly not being "objective". Likewise, the essay "Es ist nur ein Übergang" ('It only is a transition') summarizes another aspect of Lessing's philosophy of history. It is often and easily said, he argues, that

---

5 'Klio, die lächerliche Muse'; Theodor Lessing, 'Letzte Worte', in: *Prager Tagblatt*, March 25th, 1926, reprinted in: *IFEG*, 205–207, there 205.
6 'Aber diese Stiftung der Ursachketten, dieses Finden von Ursache und Wirkung, verbirgt ausnahmslos einen Akt des Wollens und des Aberglaubens, ja im Kerne ist es nichts anderes als eine einzige ahnungslose ungeheuerliche Unnatur. Denn da wir sehr wohl Jeder mit Jedem in Verbindung setzen können, so können uns niemals Tatsachen, Ereignisse, Handlungen begegnen, angesichts derer sich nicht sagen ließe: "Wenn dies oder jenes nicht gewesen wäre, so wäre eben alles anders gekommen".'; Theodor Lessing, 'Alles wäre anders gekommen...', in: *Prager Tagblatt*, March 4th, 1928, reprinted in: *IFEG*, 341–345, there 344.
7 'Wie aber wenn die ganze Kette Ursache-Wirkung ein einziger Betrug und Trug wäre, hervorgehend aus der Psychologie des menschlichen Denkens, eines linear gerichteten, intentionalen Denkens?'; loc. cit..

occurrences are nothing but a transition, and that next year or, for that matter, in five years time, everything will be changed for the better. But this is a delusion, Lessing claims:

> There is no progress and there is no decline. There is no beginning and there is no end. There are no periods and there is no history.[8]

The only thing that is, is man – and for man, everything is a transition, or nothing is. To give one more example, in 1930 Lessing retorted against an address by dr. J. Goebbels, then "Gauleiter" (district leader) of the NSDAP for Berlin and responsible for propaganda by this party, in which the latter reproached Lessing for having compared president Hindenburg with Fritz Haarmann, the serial killer from Hanover. Lessing, however, never did: virtually everything Goebbels said to accuse Lessing was in fact wrong. Hence, Lessing retorted:

> In the history of culture, the history of religion, doxography, numerous historical images, for instance the image of Socrates, only rest on a few sentences that were passed on by contemporaries. Who guarantees that it was not a "tangle of association" like the foregoing that was passed on? What if everything that remains from me will be the sentence in the address of dr. Goebbels, as all that remains from Catalina is nothing but the address by Cicero? Terrible! And one still fights against the scepticism of my *Geschichte als Sinngebung des Sinnlosen*?[9]

Thus, Lessing uses a short text on a personal experience not only to refute the false accusation by Goebbels, but at the same time to explain an aspect of his philosophy of history: the sheer fortuity of the evidence that is handed down from the past, and that which is lost. As a result, the image of the past can only be arbitrary.

---

8 'Es gibt keinen Fortschritt und es gibt keinen Rückschritt. Es gibt keinen Anfang und es gibt kein Ende. Es gibt keine Perioden und es gibt keine Geschichte.'; Theodor Lessing, 'Es ist nur ein Übergang', in: *Prager Tagblatt*, May 28th, reprinted in: *IFEG*, 346–349, there 348.
9 'In der Kulturgeschichte, Religionsgeschichte, Doxographie beruhen zahlreiche Geschichtsbilder, etwa z.B. das Bild des Sokrates, einzig auf ein paar Sätzen, die von Zeitgenossen überliefert sind. Wer gibt Gewähr dafür, daß da nicht "Assoziationsknäuel" überliefert werden, gleich den obigen? Wenn nun alles, was von mir übrigbleibt, der Satz aus der Rede des Dokter Goebbels wäre, so wie vom Catalina nichts übrigblieb als die Rede des Cicero? Schrecklich! Und da bekämpft man noch die Skepsis meiner *Geschichte als Sinngebung des Sinnlosen*?'; Theodor Lessing, 'Über einen Ausspruch von Doktor Goebbels', in: *Das Tagebuch* 11 (1930), reprinted in: *IFEG*, 73–74, there 74.

Even in the last substantial publication to appear during his lifetime, the booklet *Deutschland und seine Juden*,[10] Lessing repeatedly expresses his ideas on history, for example when he claims that "I am convinced that the whore 'world history' one day will lie [...] sense into the 'German Revolution'."[11] After all,

> One can justify every crime in history retrospectively. Indeed, all of so-called world history is nothing but retrospectively giving sense to chance or crimes.[12]

Moreover,

> Europe's best minds will retrospectively justify all current barbarities. Because history was and is nothing but giving sense to the senseless. A myth, spun from desires, tears and the projection of desires.[13]

How were Lessing's ideas on history as expounded in both his books entitled *Geschichte als Sinngebung des Sinnlosen* and in his stray observations in other writings received at the time? And which positions do they imply in debates within the tradition of philosophy of history? These are the questions that will be addressed in this chapter.

1 *Geschichte als Sinngebung des Sinnlosen* Reviewed

In the "Preface" of the fourth edition of *Geschichte als Sinngebung des Sinnlosen*, Theodor Lessing discusses the reception of the first edition of the book." Only a few works of philosophy may have been disparaged and undervalued so much at their appearance", he observes.[14] Lessing blames his critics for not discussing the main questions he addresses in his book, and for not going into the logical

---

10   *DusJ*.
11   'Ich bin überzeugt, daß die Hure "Weltgeschichte" einst [...] Sinn der "deutschen Revolution" einlügen wird.'; o.c., 242. The 'German Revolution' refers to the rise of the NSDAP.
12   'Man kann jeden Frevel der Geschichte von Nachhinein rechtfertigen. Ja, die ganze sogenannte Weltgeschichte ist nichts anderes als ein nachträgliches Sinngeben von Zufällen oder Freveln.'; o.c., 229.
13   'Die besten Geister Europas werden alle Barbareien von heute nachträglich rechtfertigen. Denn Geschichte war und ist nichts als die Sinngebung des Sinnlosen. Ein Mythos, gewoben aus Wünschen, Tränen und Wunscheinblendungen.'; o.c., 237.
14   'Nur wenige Werke der Philosophie dürften bei ihrem Erscheinen so herabwürdigt und so verkannt worden sein.'; *GSS4*, 4.

presuppositions of his analyses. He mentions the example – unfortunately without giving any details – of a philosophical journal that returned the review copy of the book it had received, because on principle it only reviewed new scientific publications which, in its opinion, Lessing's book apparently was not.[15] Subsequently, in his "Preface" Lessing replies to some of the criticisms of his book, again without giving any bibliographical details.[16] On the other hand, as Lessing himself maintains, the first edition of *Geschichte als Sinngebung des Sinnlosen* was the book which brought him his first success as an author: it was quickly reprinted twice and, moreover, Lessing was awarded the Strindberg Prize for it. Besides, he was invited to address the *Internationale Geschichtstagung* that was organised by the *Bund Entschiedener Schulreformer* in the autumn of 1924.[17] Hence, the question arises: were the reviews of *Geschichte als Sinngebung des Sinnlosen* indeed by and large dismissive, as Lessing seems to suggest?[18]

The first edition of *Geschichte als Sinngebung des Sinnlosen* was reviewed well over twenty times, in both newspapers and journals, including much respected journals like the *Annalen der Philosophie* ('Annals of Philosophy'), the *Kantstudien*, the *Historische Zeitschrift* ('Historical Journal'), and the *Historische Vierteljahrschrift* ('Historical Quarterly'). Hence, it can hardly be claimed that Lessing's book was ignored at its appearance. And even if the reviews were mixed, they definitely were not unequivocally dismissive. One of the first to review the book was the Austrian author Hermann Bahr, who was quite appreciative, calling Lessing an author he had been watching curiously for some years, to see whether he would manage to free himself from the tendency always having to have the last word. With this book, he had indeed managed to do so, Bahr claims, even if he does include some critical questions in his review as well.[19] Bahr's generally appreciative tenor is rather remarkable – he was, after all, one the intellectuals who, in August 1914, had been most enthusiastic about the outbreak of the war and exuberantly praised the alleged sense of unity of the German people at the time.[20] Thus, Bahr was one of the very intellectuals Lessing vehemently opposed both during the war

---

15   O.c., 5.
16   Cfr. chapter five, 212.
17   Cfr. chapter five, 213–219.
18   In answering this question, I benefit from the results of a Master-thesis written under my guidance: Elma Nelissen, *De receptiegeschiedenis van* Geschichte als Sinngebung des Sinnlosen *van Theodor Lessing*, Master-thesis Open Universiteit Nederland (not published, Heerlen 2011).
19   Hermann Bahr, 'Tagebuch', in: *Neues Wiener Journal. Unparteiliches Tagblatt*, 27. Jahrgang, Nr. 9195, Sonntag 8 Juni 1919, 7; cfr. chapter five, above, 218.
20   Cfr. chapter 3, 109–110.

and in *Geschichte als Sinngebung des Sinnlosen*. Nevertheless, Bahr was quite sympathetic. He was one of the critics Lessing answered in the "Preface" of the fourth edition of the book. Both Bahr's critical observations and Lessing's reply clearly show that Bahr indeed had not fully understood what Lessing meant with the expression "Sinngebung des Sinnlosen". Bahr wondered whether Lessing really meant to exclude the possibility of a given, "objective" sense of history, in particular a religious, i.e. God-given sense of history. The very suggestion shows, Lessing argues, that Bahr had misunderstood him: he did not address this question in his book, as he rightly claims, for his book is about the way human consciousness orders *réalité*, that is, the reality of which it is conscious. Lessing simply did not express any opinion on the issue that Bahr raises. In answering Bahr, however, he emphasizes that even in the unlikely case that such an "objective" sense of history would exist, it is not for mankind to know. Mankind, after all, lives in *réalité*, even if, at times, it is, in the process of *Ahmung* or cathartic understanding, in touch with *vitalité*; and even if, at times, it can comprehend *vérité*. But if there indeed is a God-given sense to history, it is only God who knows it, and not mankind. Bahr's suggestion therefore indeed misses the point of Lessing's notion of "Sinngebung des Sinnlosen".

Another review already published in 1919 is by Ernst Koetzsche, in *Der individualistische Anarchist*, an anarchist bimonthly that appeared only for a short period of time. Koetzsche states that he read *Geschichte als Sinngebung des Sinnlosen* several times because he really wanted to understand it; nevertheless, he has to admit he does not truly know what to think about the book. One the one hand, he maintains, there is a number of possible and very serious objections that may be raised against Lessing's book. For instance, it is neither a new insight that historical knowledge is imperfect, nor that historians depend on the availability of evidence. But according to the reviewer this does not necessarily imply the radical scepticism that Lessing advocates. After all, no kind of science whatsoever could be possible if perfection were the norm, Koetzsche argues: natural scientists as well cannot claim to know everything, but this does not mean they cannot strive for truth. Moreover, Lessing's terminology as made up by himself is quite difficult to understand, and his repeated references to his other writings are rather overdone. But on the other hand, Koetzsche did at times really enjoy studying the book: "To many of those who did not yet engage in the problems discussed in it, it will bring something new, it will incite thinking, and even where it provokes contradiction, it will not be read without benefit".[21] All in all, it is not light reading – it demands serious study, but this is worth the effort, Koetzsche concludes.

---

21 'Vielen, die sich mit den in ihm behandelten Problemen noch nicht beschäftigten, wird es Neues bringen, es wird zum Denken anregen, und selbst wo es zum Widerspruche

In a short review in *Der Tag*, the pastor and novelist Kurt Engelbrecht (1883–1960) characterizes Lessing's book as exceptionally interesting, even though it will incite serious opposition. People, after all, are in the habit of believing in history – whatever happens this moment, in the end the objective judgment of history will distinguish between the good and the bad, the right and the wrong. But Lessing expels history from this throne: he completely denies the possibility of objective history, and argues that the stories historians tell eventually are the arbitrary product of human will. Engelbrecht believes that Lessing is right, and argues that the examples given by the philosopher are very convincing. Engelbrecht concludes: "his understanding, his view on history [is], however, the purest historical pragmatism",[22] even though he is fully aware that Lessing himself rejects being called a pragmatist. Be that as it may, Engelbrecht states that he seldom read a more inspiring book.

A similar assessment is given by the jurist dr. Kurt Imberg in the literary magazine *Nord und Süd*: he disagrees with Lessing in most respects as regards his view on history and historical research, but nevertheless thinks *Geschichte als Sinngebung des Sinnlosen* is a most interesting book and thus "an enrichment for philosophy of history".[23] For this reason, it is a readable book for both historians and philosophers.

In his review of *Geschichte als Sinngebung des Sinnlosen* in *Der Zweemann*, a Dadaist magazine for poetry and art, Rolf Reißmann tries to understand Lessing's book in the light of his former publications, notably *Studien zur Wertaxiomatik* and *Europa und Asien*. Thus, he is one of the few critics who addresses Lessing's theory of three spheres. According to Reißmann, Lessing's analyses are crushing for modern belief in progress and evolutionary optimism. All this eventually is nothing but the superstition of humans who, poor creatures they are, consider themselves to be the crown and purpose of all creation. But Lessing does not confine himself to exposing history, Reißmann argues: in the last part of the book he develops a new idea of history – history as a necessary illusion, functioning as an emergency valve for human wants. As such, it helps humans to bear the misery of life, and is an inspiration for life. Reißmann concludes:

> his [Lessing's] works are the natural, self-evident product of his being. A philosophical system in most concentrated form and full with acute

---

herausfordert, wird es nicht ohne Nutzen gelesen werden.'; E. Koetzsche, Review of *Geschichte als Sinngebung des Sinnlosen*, in: *Der individualistische Anarchist* 1 (1919), 439–441.

22 'sein Verständnis, Seine Auffassung von Geschichte [ist] doch reinster historischer Pragmatismus.'; Kurt Engelbrecht, 'Auch eine Entthronung', in : *Der Tag*, March 26th, 1919.

23 'eine Verreicherung der Geschichtsphilosophie'; dr. Kurt Imberg, Review of *Geschichte als Sinngebung des Sinnlosen*, in: *Nord und Süd*, April 1919, 106.

clarity is leavened with the living breath of a strong, warm man who did not lapse into European intellectualism.[24]

In his review of Lessing's book in *Psychische Studien* ('Psychological Studies'), Max Seiling (1852–1928), an engineer with a great interest in parapsychology, as well is quite appreciative, calling it an important, deeply disturbing book, as it questions many traditional notions of history. But, Seiling warns, it is not easy reading: Lessing's way of expressing his ideas is not easily accessible.[25]

Dr. Hans Taub (1880–1957), in a short review in the newspaper *Münchener Neueste Nachrichten* ('Munich Latest News'), observes that Lessing vehemently places "the especially in Germany highly overrated science of history"[26] in its true perspective, thus continuing the effort by Nietzsche in his *Vom Nutzen und Nachteil der Historie für das Leben*. Lessing's book is dominated by one idea only, Taub argues: history is in essence an uninterrupted chain of value judgments. It is impossible for the historian, no matter how hard he strives for objectivity, to reflect occurrences exactly as they happened in the past. If we only try to describe our own past experiences, we have to admit Lessing is right, Taub concludes, adding that as Lessing's findings are quite controversial, it is likely that he either will be ignored or arouse strong opposition.

The critic in *Evangelische Freiheit* ('Evangelical Freedom'), a theological monthly, "F.N.", observes that *Geschichte als Sinngebung des Sinnlosen* is full with examples and ideas, and exceptionally baroque in style. But it deserves serious attention, as it raises some very fundamental questions, which, however, cannot be discussed within the limits a short review.[27]

In his review in the journal *Vergangenheit und Gegenwart* ('Past and Present'), a monthly on history teaching and political education, O. Braun[28] characterizes Theodor Lessing as a maverick, with some resentment against

---

24 'seine Werke sind der natürliche, selbstverständlicher Ausfluß seines Seins. Ein philosophisches System in konzentriertester Form und voll schärfster Klarheit ist durchzittert von dem lebendigen Hauch eines blutvollen warmen Menschen, der nicht europäischer Intellektualität verfiel.'; Rolf Reißmann, 'Über ein Buch Theodor Lessings', in: *Der Zweemann. Monatsblätter für Dichtung und Kunst* 2 (December 1919), 19–20, there 20.
25 M. Seiling, Review of *Geschichte als Sinngebung des Sinnlosen*, in: *Psychische Studien* 46 (1919), 261–262.
26 'die gerade in Deutschland weit überschätzte Geschichtswissenschaft'; dr. Hans Taub, Review of *Geschichte als Sinngebung des Sinnlosen*, in: *Münchener Neueste Nachrichten*, August 30th, 1919.
27 F.N., Review of *Geschichte als Sinngebung des Sinnlosen*, in: *Evangelische Freiheit* (1920), 230–231. "F.N. "probably was the theologian Friedrich Niebergall (1886–1932), one of the co-editors of *Evangelische Freiheit*.
28 Possibly the philosopher Otto Braun (1885–1922).

academic philosophy. Moreover, his basic ideas are not that original – there have been philosophers before him who argued that the sense of all reality stems from humans themselves. The same holds true for Lessing's scepticism, Braun observes. Still, *Geschichte als Sinngebung des Sinnlosen* contains many an interesting idea, and striking notions like "Willenschaft". But Lessing's work would have risen in importance when he would have abstained from the tendency to resist contemporaries; and if he acknowledges similarities with philosophers from Kant to Simmel, and with Rickert.[29]

The philosopher Theodor Litt (1880–1962), in his review of Lessing's book in the journal *Sokrates*, argues that Lessing is a contemporary representative of the tradition of historical scepticism, who does not manage to escape, however, the argument against each and every form of scepticism: why should one believe the sceptic's argument, and not the arguments of those he opposes? Lessing argues, for instance, against the credibility of causal reasoning by historians, but in his refutations he himself relies on alternative causal judgments. His scepticism seems therefore not to be directed against history as such, but against some specific historical interpretations. According to Litt, these discrepancies result from the fact that Lessing confuses three different themes: a critique of history as such, a critique of some specific interpretations of history, and a critique of Western man as the product of history. But, Litt claims, it is impossible to treat these three themes in one book: after all, if Lessing indeed manages to prove that history as such is impossible – that is that it would indeed be impossible to know the past –, why discuss the second and third themes? And if history indeed is nothing but a subjective story, why should one prefer one story over another? Why Lessing's story over the stories of those he criticizes? Especially when Lessing discusses causality, the problematic nature of his effort is obvious, Litt argues. Of course, one may question the very idea of causality as such, but this cannot be a reason to disqualify specific causal judgments by historians in actual history books as "subjective" – in doing so, Lessing confuses two different levels of his argument. That is, the practising historian has to underpin his specific causal judgments, but one cannot, of course, expect him to underpin the notion of causality as such. Moreover, the historian does not establish causal relations, Litt claims, but finds them. Usually, this is a quite difficult process, but it is regulated by strict methodical requirements. Hence, the historian is not comparable to the artist, for the artist is free to create in a sense the historian is not. In conclusion, Litt does not want

---

29 O. Braun, Review of *Geschichte als Sinngebung des Sinnlosen*, in: *Vergangenheit und Gegenwart* 10 (1920), 171–172.

to deny that Lessing's book is useful as food for "academic doubt", but he thinks that Lessing did not succeed in achieving his objective.[30]

Litt's review is not only interesting as such, but also because he would discuss Theodor Lessing's philosophy of history again, many years later, in his book *Wege und Irrwege geschichtlichen Denkens* ('Ways and Wrong Ways of Historical Thinking').[31] Litt's ideas on history in this book are coloured by his experiences in National-Socialist Germany. He was an outspoken and courageous opponent of National-Socialism, already before 1933 arguing in defence of academic freedom and fighting political interference in both teaching and research. He continued to do so even after National-Socialism took power and, moreover, openly criticized the National-Socialist ideology through the spoken and written word. Because of this, he was banned from public speaking by the authorities and, later, confined to his house. In *Wege und Irrwege geschichtlichen Denkens*, Litt opposes irresponsible notions of history, arguing that the abuse of history is one of the pillars of totalitarianism. Characteristic of these irresponsible notions of history is the arbitrariness of the interpretations given of history, a subjectivism that Litt vigorously opposes. Of course, he is fully aware that history cannot be objective. But he distinguishes two kinds of subjectivism, one he accepts, and one he rejects. The one he accepts is the subjectivism that is proper to all historical understanding, to "Verstehen", to use the German word. This subjectivism is not arbitrary, according to Litt: it is strictly restrained by the demands of historical method. That is, the historian has to answer his peers, for example by showing what evidence he uses, and explaining why he thinks this evidence leads to his conclusions. But Litt opposes any arbitrary subjectivism in which historical interpretations are dictated by political demands, calling this "voluntarist subjectivism". The National-Socialist interpretation of history is, of course, an example of this kind of subjectivism, Litt claims, but so is Theodor Lessing's, he argues.[32] Thus, for both Lessing and Litt as outspoken critics of National-Socialism, the idea of history is pivotal in their critique of contemporary politics, but they come to completely contrary conclusions. Both agree that history cannot be objective – but whereas Lessing concludes "if so, then let us consciously and proudly be subjective", Litt proposes to restrain subjectivism by relying on historical method, that is, on

---

30   Th. Litt, Review of *Geschichte als Sinngebung des Sinnlosen*, in: *Sokrates. Zeitschrift für das Gymnasialwesen* (1920), 100–103.
31   Th. Litt, *Wege und Irrwege geschichtlichen Denkens* (Munich 1948), especially chapter three: 'Die Vergegenwärtigung der Vergangenheit' ('The representation of the past'; 'Vergegenwärtigung' here is an untranslatable pun, meaning both 'representation' and 'making [the past] into the present'), 78–110.
32   Loc. cit..

intersubjectivism. Even if Litt does have a point in his criticisms of Lessing's position, he shows remarkably little understanding for the latter's commitment: both were, after all, fighting the same abuse of history, and the same enemy – an enemy that got Litt into serious trouble, but that killed Lessing.

In his review of *Geschichte als Sinngebung des Sinnlosen* in the *Frankfurter Zeitung*, one of its editors, the journalist dr. Rudolf Brandl (1884–1957), claims that Lessing's book should be seen in the light of Oswald Spengler's *Der Untergang des Abendlandes*, like Lessing's book published by the C.H. Beck'sche Verlagsbuchhandlung in Munich. A direct influence of Spengler's book on Lessing's is not demonstrable, however, and Lessing's views at times even contradict Spengler's. Nevertheless, Spengler addressed some fundamental issues in his book, and following him other authors have dealt with these as well; thus, it is interesting to compare Spengler and Lessing in this respect. Brandl is quite critical about Lessing's book, claiming, among other things, that the latter's self-made terminology mainly serves to distinguish himself from philosophers with whom he actually is congenial, though he apparently does not want to admit this. Lessing's ambitions result in a very eclectic book, which seems to show all kinds of influences, from Husserl and Lipps to neo-Kantianism, even if Lessing is not very open on this. Brandl observes that "the years of the world war and the German revolution, from which the book originated, greatly nurtured the author's contempt of man",[33] but this does not, of course, imply that Lessing's conclusions are always justified. Only in the third part of his book, Lessing finally explains what history in his opinion really is: the story of what one wants the past to be from a particular point of view. All in all, Brandl concludes, Lessing's book is rich in ideas, but it lacks discipline, his arguments going in all directions. Moreover, the representatives of idealist philosophy at German universities do not deserve the mocking criticisms of their peer Theodor Lessing, Brandl considering their work too valuable to deserve this treatment.

"G.K.", the author of the review in the *Literarischer Zentralblatt* ('Literary Central Review'), writing about the second, unaltered edition of *Geschichte als Sinngebung des Sinnlosen*, maintains that it is remarkable that a philosophical book is reprinted in such a short span. All the more since in his opinion both the argument and, in particular, the terminology of the book are rather peculiar. Still, he considers it a stimulating read, at the very least because Lessing is a capable author, whose prose evidences the influence of both Schopenhauer

---

33 'Die Jahre des Weltkrieges und der deutschen Staatsumwälzung, in denen das Buch entstanden ist, gaben der Menschenverachtung des Autors reicher Nahrung.'; dr. Rudolf Brandl, 'Zur Problematik der Geschichte', in: *Frankfurter Zeitung*, April 30th, 1920.

and Nietzsche. Like Nietzsche, at least to some extent, Lessing wants to free Western civilization from the tyranny of history over life. And "what makes Lessing's expositions valuable, is the emphasis on the 'poetic' element in history, which is so readily overlooked through the scientific character of history", the author argues.[34] The review is not unambiguously appreciative, however: "G.K." considers it a major flaw that Lessing flatly denies that history is a kind of craft, that is, a particular kind of research with its own methods, which is aimed at the objective-scientific comprehension of unique, individual occurrences. This position of Lessing is even basically faulty, the author claims, arguing that Lessing's notion of "poetic" history and the one of objective, scientific history are by no means mutually exclusive. Lessing would have disputed this standpoint, of course, for his position involves that history is in essence giving sense to what is senseless as such, and not establishing simple facts like, for instance, the birthday of Goethe; and, moreover, that historians, whatever their methods and aims, can never know the real past.

According to the philosopher Max Frischeisen-Köhler (1878–1923), who reviewed *Geschichte als Sinngebung des Sinnlosen* in the *Historische Zeitschrift*, the book conveys an impression of two kinds. On the one hand, it is the work of a courageous and acute thinker, on the other hand the argument is quite unsystematic and aphoristic – even to the extent that it does excite, but not convince the reader. Hence, it cannot be claimed that the author achieved the goal he set himself: to develop a theory of historical categories. Moreover, Lessing, like many of his contemporaries, apparently is not inclined to acknowledge the work of authors with similar ideas, for instance Georg Simmel, who did as well fight the naive realism that all too many historians still tend to adhere to. According to Frischeisen-Köhler, Lessing fails to prove why his idea that history as such does not have sense should be preferred over alternative ideas. Eventually, historians probably will be inspired by Lessing's book, but not shocked.[35]

The philosopher Heinz Heimsoeth (1886–1975), in the *Deutsche Literaturzeitung* ('German Literary Review'), argues that in recent years one could witness history in the making, obviously referring to the world war and the German revolution. But what was really going on? Those interested in this and similar questions should study *Geschichte als Sinngebung des Sinnlosen*, Heimsoeth observes. But even if one may have doubts about Lessing's interpretations of

---

34   'Was die Ausführungen Lessing's wertvoll macht, ist die Betonung des "dichterischen" Moments in der Geschichte, der über dem wissenschaftlichen Charakter der Geschichte so gern übersehen wird.'; G.K., Review of *Geschichte als Sinngebung des Sinnlosen*, in: *Literarischer Zentralblatt* 30 (1921), 571–572, there 572.

35   M. Frischeisen-Köhler, Review of *Geschichte als Sinngebung des Sinnlosen*, in: *Historische Zeitschrift* 124 (1921), 517–518.

both the recent past and history as a discipline – as Heimsoeth does –, one has to admit that his book is rich in ideas and thoughts, in observations and striking criticisms. It offers, in his view, sharp weapons against superficial evolutionary optimism, and against the worship of success.[36]

In the *Sozialistische Monatshefte* ('Socialist Monthly'), Walther Koch observes that the shocking experience of the recent world war brought the question "why, what for?" with regard to the historical process again to the attention of philosophers of history. With respect to this, Koch considers Lessing's *Geschichte als Sinngebung des Sinnlosen* of importance, "that originated during the war from the strongest inner aversion to the nationalist war lies of newspaper journalists and professors".[37] In Koch's view, the book is significant: "Even if one often has to raise objections to his basic attitude, one still has to welcome it as an at present exceptionally courageous and independent work, it being worthwhile to be engaged in."[38]

According to the philosopher dr. Georg Morgenstern (1892–1975), reviewing *Geschichte als Sinngebung des Sinnlosen* in the *Annalen der Philosophie* ('Annals of Philosophy'), Lessing argues against the naive realism that in his opinion is still dominant in contemporary thought on history. Morgenstern calls this into question: after all, philosophers like Rickert, Simmel, and Vaihinger have been fighting this naive realism for some time now. Still, there is every reason to be thankful to Lessing for the passionate presentation of his ideas in this book, Morgenstern maintains – his digressions on the historical subject or on the way historians give sense to the past that is senseless as such, henceforth have to be considered an important element of the tradition of philosophy of history that cannot be ignored. Nevertheless, there is much in this book that demands opposition as well, for example the strict distinction between *réalité* and *vérité* (Morgenstern does not use Lessing's terminology, but this is what his observation comes down to). Hence, there still remains a lot to elaborate upon in philosophy of history, even if Lessing's book is a valuable first step, Morgenstern concludes.[39]

---

36 H. Heimsoeth, Review of *Geschichte als Sinngebung des Sinnlosen*, in: *Deutsche Literaturzeitung* 42 (1921), 269–272. As a philosopher, Heimsoeth published on the history of philosophy and in particular on Kant.

37 'das im Weltkrieg aus stärkstem innern Widerstreben gegen nationalistische Kriegslügen der Zeitungsschreiber und Professoren geboren ist.'; Walther Koch, Review of *Geschichte als Sinngebung des Sinnlosen*, in: *Sozialistische Monatshefte* 21 (1921), 571–572, there 572.

38 'Auch wenn man häufig Widerspüch gegen Seine Grundeinstellung erheben muß, muß man es doch als ein in der heutigen Zeit selten tapferes und selbständiges Werk begrüßen, mit dem es sich verlohnt sich auseinanderzusetzen.'; loc. cit..

39 Georg Morgenstern, Review of *Geschichte als Sinngebung des Sinnlosen*, in: *Annalen der Philosophie* 2 (1921), 275–276.

The linguist and sociologist H.L. Stoltenberg (1888–1963), the reviewer of Lessing's book in *Schmollers Jahrbuch für Gesetzgebung, Verwaltung und Volkswirtschaft im Deutschen Reiche* ('Schmoller's Annual for Legislation, Administration and National Economy in the German Empire'),[40] observes that Theodor Lessing is highly ambitious, as he claims that he wants to do for history what Immanuel Kant did for the sciences: to develop a theory of categories. Stoltenberg aptly summarizes Lessing's book at some length, adding his comments at the end of the review, the most important one being that in his opinion Lessing's argument against the notion of history as a science is too simple and accordingly not convincing. Finally, he points out particular similarities between Lessing and Theodor Lipps, as well as between Lessing and both Kurt Breysig and Oswald Spengler.[41]

The philosopher Hans Leisegang (1890–1951) is quite critical of Lessing's book in his review in the *Historische Vierteljahrschrift* ('Historical Quarterly'), calling it "extravagant" and "constantly straining for effect".[42] Lessing's main idea in *Geschichte als Sinngebung des Sinnlosen* is the notion of *logificatio post festum*, according to Leisegang, but he passes over all insights of contemporary philosophy of history – notably the ones developed by Windelband, Rickert, and Husserl – in favour of this idea. Leisegang blames Lessing for being bluntly one-sided in his approach to philosophy of history. For instance, he argues, Lessing ignores that besides a *logificatio post festum*, there is also a *logificatio ante festum* that precedes action. Lessing, for sure, would have disagreed with this suggestion, however, which for that matter Leisegang did not elaborate upon. For it evidences a misunderstanding of the notion of *logificatio post festum*, if he indeed meant to claim that *logificatio ante festum* is a mirror-image of *logificatio post festum* in being related to future expectations.

The philosopher Gerhard von Mutius (1872–1934) claims that the experience of the recent world war urges his generation to rethink history: "Does history, world history, look like this if one experiences it oneself?".[43] One effort

---

40 The name refers to the influential economist Gustav von Schmoller (1838–1917), who was its editor from 1877. In honour of his commitment, in 1913 the annual was named after him.

41 H.L. Stoltenberg, Review of *Geschichte als Sinngebung des Sinnlosen*, in: *Schmollers Jahrbuch für Gesetzgebung, Verwaltung und Volkswirtschaft im deutschen Reich* 45 (1921–1922), Heft 4, 268–271.

42 'extravagant' and 'ständig nach Effekt haschenden Buches'; H. Leisegang, Review of *Geschichte als Sinngebung des Sinnlosen*, in: *Historische Vierteljahrschrift* 20 (1922), 234–235, there 234.

43 'Sieht so Geschichte, Weltgeschichte, aus, wenn man sie selber durchlebt?'; Gerhard von Mutius, Review of *Geschichte als Sinngebung des Sinnlosen*, in: *Preussische Jahrbücher* 188 (1922), 357–359, there 357.

to rethink history is Spengler's *Untergang des Abendlandes*; this book implies a turn to a scientific-deterministic interpretation of history. An opposite interpretation of history is developed by Theodor Lessing, von Mutius maintains, it being a sceptic interpretation expressing a widespread feeling, and as such deserves the special interest of both contemporary and future historians. Von Mutius cannot accept Lessing's scepticism, however: he thinks historical consciousness is a normal and naive memory function of man, which is not glossed over by Lessing's analyses. But one has to grant him that historical knowledge differs from the natural sciences, and that there is every reason to be modest as regards the capacity of history. Von Mutius is critical of Lessing's theory of three spheres: he thinks that Lessing does not realize that *vitalité* itself implies the possibility of being ordered by consciousness. – Von Mutius seems to hint at some kind of pre-figuration which is proper to *vitalité*, being a kind of pre-categorical ordering; he does not elaborate upon this point, however. Lessing would have refused this suggestion, of course: it shows a misunderstanding of what *vitalité* in his theory implies. – Von Mutius claims that this is a weakness in Lessing's argument, being in his opinion an example of the one-sidedness that is typical for his book as a whole. What eventually matters for Lessing is the act, von Mutius maintains, and in this sense his approach is a-historical. – For his part for that matter, Lessing might well have applauded this observation: as history ultimately only has instrumental value at the service of a primary ethical ideal, the present indeed is more important for him than the past. – Nevertheless, *Geschichte als Sinngebung des Sinnlosen* is a profound, highly unconventional and sincere book, von Mutius concludes.

In her short review of Lessing's book, the historian Ermentrude von Ranke (1892–1931), granddaughter of Leopold von Ranke, very concisely summarizes his conclusions: the historian cannot know the past as such, and writing history essentially is giving sense to what is senseless *in se*. Therefore, the historian should write *cum ira et studio,* and not deplore the epistemological impotence of his discipline, but inspire his people. Ranke concludes:

> Many certainly will shake their head. And yet! no serious researcher may ignore Lessing's senselessness. I do not know another book which will stir his inner life so much that it can force him to ask for the justification and the foundations of his work, like this one.[44]

---

44 'Gewiß schüttelt mancher den Kopf. Und doch! an Lessings "Sinnlosigkeit" darf kein ernster Forscher vorübergehen. Ich kenne kein zweiter Buch, das ihn innerlich so aufwühlen, das ihn so dazu zwingen kann, nach der Berechtigung und nach den Grundlagen seiner Arbeit zu fragen, wie dieser.'; Ermentrude von Ranke, Review of *Geschichte als Sinngebung des Sinnlosen*, in: *Vierteljahrschrift für Sozial- und Wirtschaftsgeschichte* 16 (1922), 450.

The psychologist and philosopher Friedrich Seifert (1891–1963) reviewed *Geschichte als Sinngebung des Sinnlosen* along with Lessing's *Die verfluchte Kultur*. The first book typically is, he maintains, an expression of "the spiritual condition of the time".⁴⁵ As such, it is close to Spengler's *Untergang des Abendlandes*, which also testifies to feelings of decline and downfall, and of the idea that Asian wisdom might prove to be the deliverance. Lessing's *Die verfluchte Kultur* is the best introduction to his ideas, Seifert argues, as in this booklet the author at length explains the dualism between *vitalité* and *réalité*. In *Geschichte als Sinngebung des Sinnlosen*, Lessing tries to develop a theory of historical categories, but actually it is rather a denial of these, as he tries to destroy the "legend" of history as a science, Seifert argues. In the third part of his book, Lessing offers a way out of this negativity, by presenting history as a "fictionalising *Willenschaft*". Seifert claims that within the limits of his review, he cannot present a complete critical appreciation of Lessing's work, but he thinks the relation between the first two parts of *Geschichte als Sinngebung des Sinnlosen* and the third part is not that clear, and demands further elaboration.

In his very short review of Lessing's book in *Theologische Literaturzeitung* ('Theological Literature News'), the theologian Horst Stephan (1873–1954) emphasizes that it is a quite peculiar mixture of all kinds of influences, from the modern sciences to Nietzsche and Asian wisdom. It really deserves a serious, more lengthy discussion than is feasible within the limits of a review, Stephan maintains.⁴⁶

Otto Bauer (1881–1938), reviewing Lessing's book in the *Deutsches Philologenblatt* ('German Linguists' Journal'), claims that Lessing continues a line of thought that had begun by Dilthey with his idea of the construction of the historical world. Bauer argues that Lessing's theory in the end proves no more than the alternatives he rejects. He emphasizes that, in Lessing's view, the sense of history is not found, but established by historians. In this connection, he especially values Lessing's digressions on *logificatio post festum* and on the development of historical reputations. All in all, the book is an interesting counterpoise to dominant trends in historical thought, Bauer concludes.⁴⁷

Drawing up the balance of these reviews of the first, second and third editions of *Geschichte als Sinngebung des Sinnlosen*, one may conclude that

---

45 'der geistigen Situation der Zeit'; Friedrich Seifert, Review of *Geschichte als Sinngebung des Sinnlosen* and *Die verfluchte Kultur*, in: *Kantstudien* 27 (1922), 190–191, there 190.
46 Horst Stephan, Review of *Geschichte als Sinngebung des Sinnlosen*, in: *Theologische Literaturzeitung* 1922, Nr. 1, column 18.
47 Otto Bauer, Review of *Geschichte als Sinngebung des Sinnlosen*, in: *Deutsches Philologenblatt* 32 (1924), 413.

Lessing seems somewhat to overstate his case in the "Preface" of the fourth edition of the book. For judging from the number of reviews, it was definitely not ignored. Moreover, even if not all of the reviews were appreciative, quite a number indeed was. Some critics actually misunderstood one or more of Lessing's ideas, but the reviewers almost all seem to have sincerely tried to judge the book fairly. Thus, Lessing's complaint possibly reveals his feelings of being misunderstood, notwithstanding the fact that in general his critics were not unfavourable.

The fourth edition of *Geschichte als Sinngebung des Sinnlosen* was reviewed less frequently than the first one, which is, of course, hardly surprising. After all, it is less customary to review reissues of a book, and, moreover, not all journals and newspapers will have realized that this new, fourth edition was in fact more or less a new book, only sharing its title with the earlier editions. Still, the fourth edition as well was reviewed a number of times.

Thus, there is a short notice in the *Annalen der Philosophie*, which had reviewed the earlier edition as well. The reviewer, "S.", points at the differences between this new edition and the earlier one, and concludes: "It is a pity that this highly interesting work that everyone practising history or theory of history should have read, is so deformed by the author's lamentations on his being misunderstood".[48]

The critic in *Biologische Heilkunst* ('Biological Medicine'), A. Baginsky,[49] observes that the scandal over Lessing's satire on Hindenburg[50] may have had positive effects as well, liberating Lessing in a sense. Only since then his work evidences his unrestricted greatness. This greatness in particular evidences in the consistency of his writings from his first publications onwards. The main question in Lessing's new book concerns the nature of history; as a philosopher he fights the delusion that history is real, or providing the mirror-image of (past) reality, it accordingly in his opinion not being qualified to be scientific or objective. Moreover, Lessing fights the historical delusions implied in the ideas of Darwin, Hegel, and Marx. Eventually, history is myth – a fabricated version of what once was reality. According to Baginsky, the book is clearly and simply written, and thus very accessible.[51]

---

48 'Es ist schade, daß das hochinteressante Werk, das jeder, der Geschichte oder Theorie der Geschichte treibt, gelesen haben sollte, durch die Lamentationen des Verfassers über sein Verkanntsein, so verunschönt wird.'; S., Review of *Geschichte als Sinngebung des Sinnlosen*, in: *Annalen der Philosophie und philosophische Kritik* 6 (1927), 156–157, there 157.
49 Possibly this is the physician dr. Arnold Baginsky (^{0}1887).
50 Cfr. above, chapter one, 8–9.
51 A. Baginsky, Review of *Geschichte als Sinngebung des Sinnlosen*, in: *Biologische Heilkunst* 34 (1927), 985.

In his notice in the journal *Die Literatur*, the historian Hans F. Helmholt (1865–1929) observes that the very fact that the philosopher and biologist Hans Driesch (1867–1941) included this new edition of Lessing's book in the series "Metaphysik und Weltanschauung" ('Metaphysics and World View), being the editor of it, justifies reviewing *Geschichte als Sinngebung des Sinnlosen*, even if it is a fourth edition. Moreover, in his "Preface", Driesch praises the sincerity of Lessing's book. Helmholt, however, definitely does not endorse the arguments used in Lessing's book, calling him a principled sceptic and denier, who developed a philosophy of history of unprecedented desolation. Be this as it may, Helmholt flatly rejects the drift of Lessing's argument in general.[52]

The chemist prof. dr. Sigm. von Kapff (1864–1946), reviewing Lessing's book in the magazine *Der Umschau* ('The Survey'), as well refers to the recommendation by Hans Driesch in "Metaphysik und Weltanschauung". Von Kapff is quite appreciative of this book by "a martyr of his conviction",[53] obviously referring to the notorious Hindenburg affair which did cost Lessing his job at the *Technische Hochschule* in Hanover. According to von Kapff, Lessing did do quite a lot to make himself rather unpopular, but he considers this no argument against the drift of his book. In *Geschichte als Sinngebung des Sinnlosen*, Lessing at times exaggerates, and some of his statements seem false or at least questionable, accordingly provoking contradiction, von Kapff argues. Nevertheless, his conclusion is quite positive: everyone somehow involved in history should study this book, and it will prompt many a reader to revise his ideas on history.

In his review in the newspaper the *Vossische Zeitung*, Leo Matthies acknowledges a certain ambiguity towards Lessing and his book, sometimes accepting, but also rejecting certain of his arguments. In this new edition of his book, the author presents his basically unchanged views in a new form. The revision of the book certainly clarified some problematic issues, but Matthies still wonders what Lessing eventually hopes to achieve with his philosophy of history. The new edition as well confronts its readers with some extraordinary difficulties, the critic opines.[54]

According to Richard Strathmann, reviewing Lessing's book in the journal *Philosophie und Leben* ('Philosophy and Life'), the latter's writings seem very

---

52   Hans F. Helmholt, Review of *Geschichte als Sinngebung des Sinnlosen*, in: *Die Literatur* 30 (1927), Heft 2, November 1927, 119.
53   'eines Märtyrers seiner Überzeugung'; Sigm. von Kapff, Review of *Geschichte als Sinngebung des Sinnlosen*, in: *Der Umschau* 31 (1927), 1061.
54   Leo Matthies, 'Geschichte als Sinngebung des Sinnlosen. Zu Theodor Lessings Werk', in: *Vossische Zeitung*, August 28th, 1927.

accessible and at first sight easily understandable.⁵⁵ But on second thoughts, a complete philosophical system underlies these writings, which cannot be separated from its author. Hence, Lessing's book should be read otherwise as compared with scientific books: it is the expression of the personality of the philosopher. As a result, Lessing's work sometimes seems to invite misunderstandings. The one thinker with whom he really seems to be congenial is, Strathmann claims, Ludwig Klages – in their youth a close companion of Lessing's, but they developed completely differently, Klages' philosophy testifying to an obsessive rigidity, whereas Lessing's to a flexible playfulness. The main problem underlying Lessing's philosophy seems to be the issue of "knowledge out of need", that is, the relation between need and consciousness. The fourth edition of *Geschichte als Sinngebung des Sinnlosen* again addresses this topic, it being Lessing's most personal theme: knowledge out of suffering. It results in a scepticism regarding all philosophical thought presupposing a dichotomy between subject and object. The main elements of Lessing's alternative are the theory of *Ahmung* and the theory of three spheres. The latter is quite hard to understand, even for those being familiar with Lessing's writings. It is all too easy, Strathmann claims, to find contradictions in Lessing's work, but this is not the right approach to his writings, he argues. *Geschichte als Sinngebung des Sinnlosen* should be read as the direct expression of the life of its author – a human being with inner contradictions, like everyone. But it is quite likely that Lessing will not be appreciated: the philosopher himself is an outsider who, moreover, proclaims solidarity with the oppressed. For this reason, Strathmann wishes Lessing unprejudiced and unsophisticated readers, both now and in the future.⁵⁶

In his review in the *Blätter für deutsche Philosophie* ('Papers for German Philosophy'), the philosopher Th. Haering (1884–1964) observes that the first edition of Lessing's book was both highly praised and slated. This new edition of the book should, according to its author, clarify some of the misunderstandings the first one apparently incited. Haering thinks Lessing did not manage to do so completely, though he is of the opinion that Lessing's argument should indeed be taken seriously. After all, beneath Lessing's surface pessimism is an optimism, and beneath his scepticism a deep belief in the truth as he himself conceives it, the critic claims. But Haering wonders if Lessing's philosophy of history is not too much the product of its times, that is, he questions whether

---

55 In his review, Strathmann refers to conversations he has had with Lessing, so they must have been acquainted.
56 Richard Strathmann, 'Theodor Lessings Geschichtsbild', in: *Philosophie und Leben* 4 (1928), 22–25.

it holds true generally or merely in this day and age, from which it stems. In the latter sense, it might well prove to be primarily the product of Lessing's particular need. And if so, it is not at all clear why Lessing's philosophy of history should be preferred over alternative philosophies of history.[57]

Like the earlier editions of *Geschichte als Sinngebung des Sinnlosen*, the fourth one was not ignored by reviewers and critics. Again, the judgments were varied, some critics praising the book, some, on the other hand, being rather negative. But by and large, all reviewers agree that Lessing's book is a serious contribution to philosophy of history, even if some of them do not share Lessing's ideas, or even outspokenly reject them.

2 Lessing's Philosophy of History Discussed

Apart from the reviews of *Geschichte als Sinngebung des Sinnlosen*, Theodor Lessing's philosophy of history was not very much debated. Already in 1921, though, it was the subject of an essay by the theologian Th. Steinmann (1869–1950).[58] In his article, Steinmann compares the ideas of Theodor Lessing, Oswald Spengler, and Heinrich Rickert. Starting point of his argument is the observation that Lessing's *Geschichte als Sinngebung des Sinnlosen* is an outstanding example of a consequently elaborated world view, and for this reason already meritorious and informing; moreover, this philosopher forces his readers to see problems that usually are overlooked. In discussing Lessing's philosophy of history, Steinmann mainly focuses on two aspects: the view on historical reality, and the rejection of evolutionary constructs of history. According to Steinmann, Lessing might well be right: a sober look at the facts of human history simply shows it to be a muddle. This holds true for political history, from which Lessing derives most of his examples, but no less for intellectual history: "here as well a continuous and coherent development, through which an inner sense would be exposed ever more concretely, cannot be shown."[59] Here, Lessing and Spengler agree, the author argues: Spengler as well opposes this naive idea of evolutionary progress. As a great number

---

57 Th. Haering, Review of *Geschichte als Sinngebung des Sinnlosen*, in: *Blätter für deutsche Philosophie* 4 (1930), 246–248.
58 Th. Steinmann , 'Sinn und Tatsächlichkeit bei Spengler, Lessing und Rickert', in: *Zeitschrift für Theologie und Kirche*, Neue Folge 11 (1921), 348–372.
59 'auch läßt sich hier nicht eine fortlaufende und zusammenhängende Entwicklung aufweisen, durch welche es einen in ihm selber gelegenen Sinn immer greifbarer herausstellte.'; o.c., 350.

of people in the Western world still naively believes that history is a progressive process that eventually leads to themselves, Lessing's and Spengler's criticisms are completely justified, and even necessary, Steinmann maintains. But most likely, Lessing will reject Spengler's alternative to this view on history as a progressive process as well – that is, the division of history into the story of a number of independent cultures – as yet another example of "Sinngebung des Sinnlosen", which assumes far too much, instead of realizing what history actually is like. Still, Steinmann argues that Lessing's views have more in common with Spengler's than one might think at first sight. Both, after all, assign a pragmatic value to history writing; and according to both, history writing establishes a reality of which one is conscious, it being beyond mere fact. And this imaginary reality of which one is conscious is necessary in order that mankind may bear the chaos of factuality. Of course, this implies that according to Lessing, history is relative: "It is an illusion for a specific objective; and therefore only significant as long as it is needed."[60] But this does not imply that for Lessing truth does not exist: after all, in his opinion, at times man is aware of the imaginary character of reality. Moreover, apart from this awareness, Lessing assumes the existence of a sphere of logical and ethical truth that is independent of the knowing subject. – Steinmann refers to the sphere of *vérité* in Lessing's theory of three spheres, without, however, adopting his terminology. – But in Lessing's philosophy there is a gap between this sphere and the reality of which one is conscious, and "only through the modification of the factuality of all things human in the writing of history, a quasi-overcoming of this tension succeeds".[61] Mankind needs this quasi-overcoming, since it simply cannot bear to live in a world without the illusion of causality, and the illusion that history makes sense. In this way, Lessing ultimately confronts his readers with senselessness, all sense attributed to history eventually being an illusion. According to Steinmann, Lessing is definitely right when he claims that reason and ethics are not proper to history. But this does not imply that his argument as a whole is right: Steinmann doubts whether the gap between *réalité* and *vérité* – to use Lessing's terminology, which Steinmann does not apply – is as unbridgeable as Lessing claims. That is, Steinmann thinks ideals can indeed motivate behaviour. Thus, Steinmann argues, in West-European culture the notion that in science one has a duty to speak the truth is stringent: this is an unconditional norm that holds true, and obliges scientists to a

---

60 'Sie ist Illusion zu bestimmten Zweck; und darum nur so lange von Bedeutung, als man ihrer bedarf.'; o.c., 359.

61 'Lediglich durch die Umdichtung der Tatsächlichkeit der menschlichen Dinge in der Geschichteschreibung gelingt eine Scheinüberwindung dieser Spannung.'; o.c., 362.

particular kind of behaviour. This ultimately implies, Steinmann claims, that Lessing is right when he argues that every empirical sense assigned to history is illusionary; but he is not, if he denies the possibility of attributing a transcendent sense to history. – Lessing would have rejected this argument, however, for in his view, even in case of a possible transcendent sense being attributable to history, one would not be able to know it, and accordingly this transcendent sense could not be binding. –

The comparison between the philosophies of history of Spengler and Lessing is further developed by Wolf Goetze in his dissertation *Die Gegensätzlichkeit der Geschichtsphilosophie Oswald Spenglers und Theodor Lessings* ('The Contrast between the Philosophy of History of Oswald Spengler and Theodor Lessing').[62] Goetze's supervisor was Hans Driesch, the biologist and philosopher who had included the fourth edition of *Geschichte als Sinngebung des Sinnlosen* in the series "Metaphysik und Weltanschauung", being its editor. Goetze claims that thus far, the essay by Steinmann was the only effort to compare Spengler's and Lessing's ideas. Steinmann's article, though valuable, is not exhaustive, however, he maintains, there being more to say on the subject. Spengler and Lessing judged the World War completely differently, Goetze observes, and this is of significance for a better understanding of their philosophies of history.[63] In contrast to Spengler's metaphysics, which is rather mystical and can neither be proved nor disproved, Lessing's is logical: it is carefully thought out, and not the result of a flash of inspiration. This is an indication of the difference in their notion of metaphysics, Goetze maintains. Despite this difference, however, both agree on the relativity of reality, or rather – as reality is a term with various connotations – the relativity of what happens. This conclusion raises the question how Spengler and Lessing see the main notions of history writing, like the position of the observer, time, the bearer of history, causality; etc. According to Goetze, referring to an essay by the theologian Karl Heim (1874–1950), entitled "Gedanken eines Theologen zu Einsteins Relativitätstheorie" ('Thoughts by a theologian on Einstein's theory of relativity'),[64] Spengler's position is comparable to Isaac Newton's. Following Heim, Goetze claims that like in Newton's theory, for Spengler time and space are independent of the observer's perspective, but the observer's perspective itself has become relative. But Lessing took the step Einstein did, for in his view not only the observer's perspective, but time and space as well have become relative, like in Einstein's theory of relativity. In other words, Goetze claims,

---

62   Leipzig 1930.
63   O.c., 15–16.
64   It was published in the *Zeitschrift für Theologie und Kirche*, Neue Folge 1 (1920).

in Lessing's philosophy of history all main notions are relative: it is no longer possible to describe the process of history independently of the perspective of the historian – time, causality, and the bearer of history all depend on the perspective of the historian, and this perspective itself is relative too. Hence, Lessing's philosophy of history is far more radical than Spengler's. Lessing's position implies that history is not a science, and does not have a solid method. In the alleged historical process, there is no time and no causality, and neither does it have a purpose. All interpretations of the historical process eventually relate to the "I" of the historian. Accordingly, causal judgments in historiography, for instance, only serve to quiet the souls of the historian and that of the members of his or her community: the notion of causality answers to a psychological need, to the idea that one can either achieve the same result again, or avoid it. Ultimately, history writing is founded on nothing but delusions, prejudices and premonitions – this is how Goetze summarizes Lessing's analyses of history writing. In comparison with Spengler, Lessing pushes matters to the extreme: he always draws the most radical conclusions possible. Hence, Goetze claims, "we have to realize that history with this is deprived of all firm ground, an orientation has become impossible, because wherever we want to flee to acquire an attitude toward the historical process, we are followed by anticipations, prejudices, and premonitions".[65] That is, "needs of the soul and mind are thus according to Lessing what forges [the process of] history into historical science".[66] The historical process is nothing but chance to which retrospectively a sense is attributed in accordance with human needs.

In summary, Goetze argues, Lessing does not deny that there is a method of historical inquiry, but he claims that this very method gives a false, or rather illusionary, picture of the historical process. Thus, it is impossible to understand the past as such. The past as such has no sense, for any sense is retrospectively attributed to history in the very process of ordering the past. But the sense that thus is assigned to history should put history at the service of the all-embracing ethical ideal of diminishing the need in the world.

In his dissertation *Geschichtsphilosophie und Kulturkritik Theodor Lessings*[67] ('The Philosophy of History and Cultural Criticism of Theodor Lessing'), Hans Dieter Hüsgen focuses on Theodor Lessing's critique of European culture.

---

65 'Wir müssen uns darüber im klaren sein, daß damit Geschichtswissenschaft jeden festen Boden beraubt ist, eine Orientierung ist unmöglich geworden, denn wo wir uns hinflüchten, um eine Eistellung zu dem Geschichtsablauf zu gewinnen, überallhin folgen uns Vorgefühle, Vorurteile und Vorwertungen.'; o.c., 47.

66 'Bedürfnisse der Seele und des Verstandes sind es also nach Lessing, die Geschichte in Geschichtswissenschaft fälschen.'; o.c., 48.

67 (Mainz 1961).

Hüsgen rightly emphasizes that Lessing's views on European culture and historiography are part of his philosophy in general, and for this reason he gives an exposition of Lessing's theory of three spheres, his theory of need, and the one of *Ahmung* at some length. Subsequently, he discusses Lessing's idea of culture, rightly underlining that culture according to Lessing by definition is a restraint against nature, it indeed being at the expense of nature. Nowhere in the world culture has developed like in Europe, and nowhere in the world it is as distant from nature like in Europe. According to Lessing, there is a close connection between religion and culture; hence, there is a link between Christianity as the dominant religion in Europe and this particular development of culture. It is characteristic of Christianity to put man at the centre of creation, and even to consider man its crown. This very attitude allegedly reverberates in Darwin's theory of evolution, and in Hegel's philosophy of history: for both, mankind ultimately is what matters. Hüsgen points out that in historiography as well, all of history ultimately relates to the "I" of the historian. Lessing's analyses of the categories of historical thinking corroborate this point of view. Hence, historiography either is the expression of the urge for self-justification, or it is the expression of the urge to liberate oneself from the past. Thus, Hüsgen argues, for Lessing history is not a science ("Wissenschaft") but a "Willenschaft": it creates a past as the historian wants it to have been.

The studies by Steinmann, Goetze, and Hüsgen may be read as efforts to expound and elucidate particular aspects of Theodor Lessing's philosophy of history. In his contribution to the collection *"Sinngebung des Sinnlosen"*, the philosopher Friedrich von Petersdorff chooses a somewhat different approach.[68] Von Petersdorff aims at understanding Lessing's specific position in the context of debates in twentieth century philosophy of history, especially as regards the historian's perspective. After all, Lessing emphasizes time and again that history is always written from the perspective of the historian, historiography retrospectively giving sense to the past. This emphasis on the historian's perspective is not new – it was not even so in Lessing's time, Von Petersdorff claims – but it still is a topical subject in current philosophy of history. It was discussed, for example, by the American philosopher Arthur Danto (1924–2013), the Finnish philosopher Georg Henrik von Wright (1916–2003), and Paul Ricoeur. All three – each in his own way – underline that historians always judge the past from a posterior point of view, that is, they know the

---

68 Friedrich von Petersdorff, 'Die perspektivische Konstruktion von Geschichte in Lessings beide Büchern „Geschichte als Sinngebung des Sinnlosen"', in: Elke-Vera Kotowski (ed.), *"Sinngebung des Sinnlosen". Zum Leben und Werk des Kulturkritikers Theodor Lessing (1872–1933)* (Hildesheim etc. 2006), 201–214.

result of the process they are studying, if only the preliminary result. Hence, for all three, the truth of history is always relative, the view on the past changing continuously in the light of later developments. Thus, to underpin his argument, Danto argues that the characteristic narrative sentences of historians – for example: "The Thirty Years War started in 1618" – always refer to two points in time, in the example 1618 and 1648, even if they mention only one. Von Wright emphasizes that historiography is by definition incomplete, because the historical process continues, and the view of the past is accordingly continuously revised in the light of later developments. According to Ricoeur, matters are even more complicated: history actually refers to three moments in time – the occurrence which is described, the later moment in time in the light of which it is judged, and the historical context of the historian. Lessing's philosophy of history by and large corresponds with these ideas of Danto, Von Wright, and Ricoeur, Von Petersdorff claims. They all agree that it is impossible to give a definitive description of the past, and, moreover, that one cannot ignore the historian's involvement in his or her narrative. Of course, Lessing's argument in support of this position differs in details from the ones by Danto, Von Wright, and Ricoeur. Lessing's argument is, after all, closely related to his critique of contemporary Western culture, whereas the approach of the other three philosophers is predominantly analytical. Moreover, Lessing rejects the idea that history is a science, whereas the other authors seem to endorse the notion of a scientific historiography. Be this as it may, from his outsider's point of view Lessing offers a challenging approach to the problems of historiography that deserves to be taken seriously, Von Petersdorff concludes.

With his essay, Von Petersdorff takes a first step to answering a question that has been hardly raised thus far, let alone answered: what is the significance of Theodor Lessing's philosophy of history within the tradition of philosophy of history? Of course, this question is far too comprehensive to answer in this study, but in the remainder of this chapter I will try to start at addressing it, by making some observations on successively Lessing's opposition against realism, his ideas on the unity of history, on causality, and, finally, on his idea that history first and foremost has to tell inspiring stories.

The most remarkable characteristic of Theodor Lessing's philosophy of history probably is that it bears evidence of a radical scepticism with regard to history. Lessing claims that it is impossible for the historian to know the past as it really happened, that is, he argues that history can never reflect the past as it really has been. The historian therefore does not discover and report on the past, but makes a construction of it. This construction, in its turn, rests on evidence that only by chance has come down from earlier ages, which implies an additional argument for Lessing's scepticism. This scepticism is directed against the naive realism that according to Lessing is characteristic of all too many historians, an example being Ranke with his famous dictum that historians simply want to show "wie es eigentlich gewesen" ('as it actually has been'). Of course, this opposition against realism among historians is at least partially a product of its times: it was a fight against the way realist interpretations of history were used to justify the German position in the 1914–1918 war. But in the fourth edition of *Geschichte als Sinngebung des Sinnlosen*, Lessing holds on to this view: his scepticism thus definitely is not only the product of its time, but a view on history that he continued to adhere to in later years.

Scepticism with regard to historical knowledge has not been widely discussed – after all, most historians just assume that it is possible to have knowledge of the past, even if they are well aware that the story they tell does not simply reflect the past; and most philosophers of history as well seem inclined to assume that, one way or another, knowledge of the past is possible. Historical scepticism was the subject, however, of a well-known study by the American philosopher Jack W. Meiland (1934–1998), *Scepticism and Historical Knowledge*.[69] Like Lessing, Meiland claims that there are convincing arguments in favour of historical scepticism, and he also maintains that the historian does not discover a given past, but makes a construction of it – hence, he characterizes his position as "constructivist". To underpin this constructivist position, Meiland refers to the ideas of philosophers of history like Benedetto Croce, R.G. Collingwood, and Michael Oakeshott (1901–1990).[70] In his discussion of Croce, Meiland points out that according to the Italian philosopher historical scepticism is indeed unavoidable if one thinks historians are concerned with bringing their narrative correspondent with past events. Croce claims this is simply impossible, one of the reasons being that the evidence of the historian is by definition questionable, in the sense that it never is a reflection of the past, but merely a reference to it.[71] This corresponds by and large with Lessing's argument. The alternative developed by Croce is meant to evade this very scepticism by claiming that history is not about past events, but about the significance of present evidence for the current historian. That is, the present historian interprets available evidence in the light of present questions, which in their turn are the result of present interests. Again, this alternative seems to be closely related to Lessing's position. Both, after all, bear evidence of a

---

69   New York 1965.
70   The American philosopher Leon J. Goldstein (1927–2002) worked in line with these, but his book *Historical Knowing* only appeared in 1976.
71   Meiland, o.c., 33.

radical scepticism as regards the idea of history providing knowledge of the real past; and both nevertheless do not want to abolish history for this reason, but develop an alternative idea of history, in which history is of importance because of its significance for the present. So, even if Lessing's terminology is somewhat idiosyncratic, and his manner of arguing not very systematic, but rather associative, his approach to the problems of philosophy of history is quite akin to the constructivist approach as advocated by Croce.

Another philosopher discussed by Meiland in his study of historical scepticism is Michael Oakeshott. Oakeshott as well claims that there are convincing arguments in favour of historical scepticism if history is conceived of as knowledge of the real past. The English philosopher argues that the distinction between the real past and the past as constructed by the historian on the basis of evidence is meaningless, because there just does not exist a "real past". The only past that exists is the past as constructed by the historian:

> The historian's business is not to discover, to recapture, or even to interpret; it is to create and construct. Interpretation and discovery imply something independent of experience, and there is nothing independent of experience.[72]

Again, this by and large corresponds with Lessing's argument, for Lessing as well claims that there is no past besides the image of the past as created by the historian.[73] And as there is no real past, the very idea that the historian's narrative should somehow correspond to a real past is simply meaningless, Oakeshott claims. So even if there is a particular connection between present evidence and the past, this connection can never imply a correspondence between the historian's narrative and the past. Does this imply that history is meaningless? Not so, according to Oakeshott, but history should be redefined, he argues. History is, he maintains, "what the evidence obliges us to believe".[74]

---

72 Michael Oakeshott, *Experience and its modes* (Cambridge 1933) 93, quoted from Meiland, o.c., 42.

73 It might well be worthwhile to elaborate upon a comparison between Lessing's ideas and Oakeshott's. For example, Oakeshott distinguishes between "sensations" and "experiences", claiming that sensations become "determinate" by having made judgments about them, and only after having in this way become determinate, a sensation may be experienced. This seems to correspond with Lessing's ideas, in particular as regards his criticisms of Husserl. Lessing, after all, as well claims that "pure experience" cannot be described, and that the very act of describing infringes on the alleged "purity" of the experience.

74 Oakeshott, o.c., 108, quoted from Meiland, o.c., 50.

That is, statements that seem to be about the past actually are statements about present evidence. Thus, Oakeshott's alternative to the idea of history as a narrative about the real past is even more radical than Croce's; but both firmly oppose the idea of a real past. And in this sense, Lessing's position is very similar to theirs.

It is notable that the very expression "what the evidence obliges us to believe" was used by R.G. Collingwood as well, independently of Oakeshott's use of it.[75] Collingwood used the expression to develop a position that is very similar to Croce's. That is, according to Collingwood as well, it is not possible to know the real past: the activity of the historian consists in answering present questions and reasoning from present evidence. Hence, history is by definition inferential, the image of the past being based on questions about the past that are inferentially answered from evidence. As compared with Lessing, Collingwood definitely puts more trust in the methods of history, that is, the Oxford philosopher is confident that the historian is not at the mercy of the evidence, because in his view the use of evidence is always related to the questions asked by the historian. For this reason, an accomplished historian may even use evidence to come to conclusions the evidence was not meant to yield up.[76] Collingwood's position is hardly different from Croce's: knowledge of the real past is impossible, the only past that exists is the past as inferred from evidence.[77] For this reason, Collingwood maintains that the past is "ideal", that is, it is something that is being thought and in no sense "real", calling it "the doctrine of the ideality of history".[78] Hence, Lessing's position is quite similar to Collingwood's: both deny the possibility of knowledge of the "real past",

---

[75] Collingwood used the expression in a manuscript of 1928 that was only published in 1993, saying in the table of contents: "Historical truth = *what evidence obliges us to believe*". Cfr. R.G. Collingwood, *The Idea of History*, revised edition, edited with an introduction by Jan van der Dussen (Oxford etc. 1993), there 438.

[76] Cfr. the example of Caesar's invasion of Britain, discussed in Chapter four above, 185.

[77] My discussion of Collingwood differs from Meiland's, as his is, I would maintain, highly unsatisfactory. Meiland claims, for example, that according to Collingwood it is possible for the historian to know the past directly, "as opposed to being known indirectly through the use of evidence" (Meiland, o.c., 77), apparently thinking that Collingwood's notion of re-enactment implies a way of knowing the past directly. This claim is, of course, completely out of place, since for Collingwood, history is firmly rooted in evidence: no evidence, no history! The nature of Collingwood's re-enactment doctrine is another subject, and is dealt with in his manuscript "Outlines of a Philosophy of History", referred to above (Cfr. Collingwood, *The Idea of History*, rev. ed. (1993), 439–50).

[78] Cfr. Jan van der Dussen, 'A Quest for the Real Past. Ankersmit on Historiography and (Sublime) Historical Experience', in: Jan van der Dussen, *Studies on Collingwood, History and Civilization* (Cham etc. 2016), 220.

and conceive of history as a present construction based on evidence. Lessing emphasizes, however, the political and social function of this construction in a present community, whereas Collingwood places more confidence on the methods used by historians. So there are definitely differences between both philosophers.

Nevertheless, I would maintain the conclusion is justified that, in his fight against the idea that knowledge of the real past would be possible, Lessing's position is akin to that of Croce, Collingwood, and Oakeshott, they being the most prominent theorists of the constructivist view of history. As such, Lessing's philosophy of history is still of topical interest, not in the least because realist notions of history – unlikely as they may be – occasionally still crop up again. Admittedly, they usually no longer concern the kind of naive realist notions of history as Lessing encountered in his time, but more sophisticated versions. An example is the American historian Hayden White, who in his influential *Metahistory* seems to take an ambiguous position with respect to the question of the reality of the past. For as regards singular statements, White appears to accept realism, arguing that a singular statement about the past relates to a real past. As White puts it: "[...] historical works are made up of events that exist outside the consciousness of the writer".[79] A statement like "Caesar crossed the Rubicon" therefore refers to the real past. But the narratives historians construct on the basis of singular statements do not refer to a real past, White argues: by using their "poetic insight", historians transform singular statements into narratives, making use of literary categories to interpret the singular statements concerned. As a result of the interpreting activity of the historian the historical narrative does not relate to the real past. This means that the question whether White's view on history is realist or constructivist, cannot be answered unambiguously: he seems to adhere to both positions, and thus to contradict himself. After all, the past cannot be both real and ideal. Anyhow, the observation that White's narrative constructivism is inadequately thought out seems to be appropriate.

Following in White's tracks, the Dutch philosopher of history F.R. Ankersmit in his *Narrative Logic* demonstrates the very same ambiguity. For he as well claims that singular statements about the past refer to the real past, whereas the narratives historians construct out of singular statements do not.[80] But Ankersmit did not keep to this position, his flirt with realist notions of history

---

79   Hayden White, *Metahistory: The Historical Imagination in Nineteenth-century Europe* (Baltimore 1973) 6, footnote.
80   F. R. Ankersmit, *Narrative logic. A Semantic Analysis of the Historian's Language* (The Hague 1983) 54–55, 102–103.

developing in rather unexpected ways. In his subsequent book *Historical Representation*,[81] he claims that the narratives historians write about the past should be conceived metaphorically as representations of the real past, accordingly implying that a specific relation with the real past is indeed feasible. And in his book *Sublime Historical Experience*,[82] Ankersmit even claims that it is possible to experience the past directly. This very claim, however, gets him entangled in all kinds of contradictions and difficulties.[83] Again, the conclusion is warranted that any ambiguity as regards the question whether it is possible to know the real past is inappropriate. For the real past may either be known or not known: it is not possible to reconcile these contradictory positions.

In his *Scepticism and Historical Knowledge*, Jack Meiland concludes that the theory that historians are aimed at exposing an independently existing past on which they report, makes history vulnerable to the most devastating sceptical criticisms, which are almost impossible to refute satisfactorily. For this very reason, he advocates the alternative constructivist theory of history. Theodor Lessing's idea of history as expounded in both the first and the fourth editions of *Geschichte als Sinngebung des Sinnlosen* is undoubtedly a constructivist one, which has significant characteristics in common with the views on history of leading representatives of the constructivist view, such as Croce, Oakeshott, and Collingwood. Hence, Lessing's view is still of current interest, not in the least because realist notions of history still emerge occasionally, notwithstanding the overwhelming sceptical criticisms of realist notions of history that have been put forward.

But it is, I would argue, not only Lessing's general position that is still relevant for current debates in philosophy of history, but also some of the specific arguments used by him. An example is his observations on the historical subject or, in Lessing's terminology, the bearer of history. To recapitulate, Lessing claims that history is always considered a "coherence of events", that is, history is conceived of as a particular unity. But this is only possible if some bearer of this unity or coherence is presupposed as the historical subject. This historical subject is not a given, however, as something that would exist independently and being "discovered", but is a manmade frame of reference used by the historian to order history. Once the historian has established such a frame, he or she

---

81   Stanford 2001.
82   Stanford 2005.
83   For a profound critique of Ankersmit's successive positions, cfr. Jan van der Dussen, o.c., 213–253.

relates the relevant data to it, ignoring tacitly what is not considered pertinent. In other words, the historical subject actually is a man-made means to order history; and everything of which a history may be written may function as a historical subject.

Notwithstanding its significance, Lessing's views on the historical subject have not been discussed in philosophy of history in later years, neither in the German-speaking, nor in the English-speaking world. Nevertheless, they are in a remarkable way in line with what the British philosopher W.H. Walsh (1913–1986) called "colligatory concepts in history". Walsh first developed this notion in his classic *Philosophy of History: An Introduction*.[84] He borrowed the concept of colligation from the nineteenth-century English logician William Whewell (1794–1866), who had introduced it to describe the way scientists relate seemingly independent facts by using specific concepts. Whewell characterizes this as "the colligation of facts", and claims this term may be applied "to every case in which, by an act of the intellect, we establish a precise connexion among the phenomena which are presented to our senses".[85] In history, Walsh argues, this is "the procedure of explaining an event by tracing its intrinsic relations to other events and locating it in its historical context".[86] Walsh discusses the example of the German reoccupation of the Rhineland in 1936; an historian will try to explain this by describing it as part of a more comprehensive policy, to wit "a general policy of German self-assertion and expansion which Hitler pursued from the time of his accession to power".[87] By subsuming the single event or action – the reoccupation of the Rhineland – under a more comprehensive notion, the historian establishes a relation between various events, thus establishing a certain unity in history. According to Walsh, this is common practice in history: notions like "Enlightenment", "Napoleonic wars", "Industrial Revolution", "the Great Crash", etc. are the means by which historians establish relations between various events, and thus express a particular historical unity. In a later essay, "Colligatory concepts in history",[88] Walsh elaborated upon this notion. He observes that he initially discussed colligation as an explanatory process; but now he is inclined to see it more comprehensively, as the way

---

84   (New York 1967). The first edition of the book was published in 1951.
85   William Whewell, *The Philosophy of the Inductive Sciences Founded upon their History* (New York 1967 [1847]), vol. 2, 36.
86   Walsh, o.c., 59.
87   Loc. cit..
88   W.H. Walsh, 'Colligatory concepts in history', in: W.H. Burston and D. Thompson (eds), *Studies in the Nature and Teaching of History* (London 1967), 65–84; reprinted with minor alterations in: P. Gardiner (ed.), *The Philosophy of History* (Oxford 1974), 126–144. I use this reprint.

historians interpret: "But we use [colligatory concepts] for other purposes too, to characterize and analyze, and in doing so commonly aim at producing understanding and enlightenment".[89] But these colligatory concepts are not proper to the period studied, Walsh emphasizes: we use these concepts retrospectively, to summarize developments over a longer period of time. But this does not epitomize, at least not necessarily, an anachronistic approach: history, after all, may only be understood on the basis of contemporary concepts. When, Walsh asks, is a colligatory concept successful? He claims that it is successful if a historian manages to correlate a great number of seemingly unrelated phenomena by using a particular concept, without however forcing the issue. That is, a colligatory concept should not be a Procrustean bed; and, moreover, it should not ignore contradictory evidence. In the end, the success of a colligatory concept depends on the professional skills and cogency of the historian introducing it – and of the approval of the community of his or her peers. A second criterion mentioned by Walsh is that a colligatory concept should clarify matters: it should make the past "intelligible *to us*",[90] that is, it should increase our understanding of the past. Walsh maintains that colligatory concepts have a temporal and a spatial scope; moreover, what they refer to always is in a process of continuous change, which depends on what humans do, or fail to do.

The similarities between Lessing's notion of the historical subject and Walsh's of colligation are obvious. Both the historical subject and the colligatory concept bear upon any object of which a history may be meaningfully written. Both serve to accomplish a certain unity within history. But neither the historical subject nor the colligatory concept is a given: both are constructed by the historian in order to increase our (contemporary) understanding of history. And, finally, both imply that history bears upon processes of continuous change brought about by humans.

Unlike Lessing's observations on the historical subject, Walsh's notion of colligation in history has been discussed in contemporary philosophy of history. Ankersmit, for example, elaborates in his *Narrative Logic* upon Walsh's notion of colligatory concepts, using it in the context of his own narrative approach of historiography.[91] Instead of colligatory concepts, Ankersmit prefers the term "narrative substances", but a narrative substance is basically the same as

---

89   O.c, 136–137.
90   O.c., 140. The italics are Walsh's.
91   Ankersmit, o.c., 93: "In fact, this book might be looked upon as an attempt to elaborate Walsh's notion of the "colligatory concept". "

a colligatory concept,[92] or, for that matter, a historical subject in Lessing's terminology. Like these, a narrative substance is constructed by the historian as a means to order the past, and aimed at increasing our understanding of the past; it is not proper to the past itself, but a means that is used retrospectively. However, Ankersmit subsequently rather pointlessly complicates matters by claiming that every single interpretation by a historian is a narrative substance by itself, like a monad in the philosophy of Leibniz.[93] Hence, there is no such narrative substance as "the French Revolution", but only "the French Revolution according to Georges Lefebvre", "the French Revolution according to François Furet", "the French Revolution according to Simon Schama", etc., and it is not even possible to compare these various narrative substances. Here, the philosopher of history is out of touch with the practice of historiography: he fails to appreciate that historiography is not a solitary undertaking, but a collective one. That is, the single historian does not write in isolation, but as a member of a community of peers that is having an ongoing discussion. Thus, there is most definitely a narrative substance "the French Revolution", and debates among historians are efforts to clarify it. If they result in new interpretations of this revolution, these are not new narrative substances, but rather efforts to elucidate a "shared" or common narrative substance. In Ankersmit's view, debates between historians are actually impossible, because they do not, and even cannot, discuss the same narrative substance. This viewpoint simply ignores, however, the value of the ongoing debates between historians for the development of historiography, and moreover is also in flagrant contradiction with the practice of historiography. What Ankersmit does not take into account is that what he calls a narrative substance or a colligatory concept has rather the character of a working paper: it is a suggestion to a community of peers to see the past in a certain way, and an invitation to discuss this suggestion.

Summing up, it is obvious that Lessing's observations on the historical subject correspond with Walsh's notion of colligatory concepts and Ankersmit's one of narrative substances. In this respect, Lessing's position may accordingly be considered a precursor of current debates in philosophy of history.

The same holds true, I would maintain, for Lessing's observations on causality in history, a theme that has been amply discussed by philosophers of history in the previous century. As W.H. Walsh pointed out, the notion of a cause in historiography differs from that in the natural sciences: "We may suppose that the notion of cause was introduced into history from everyday life, which means that a cause in history was, originally, an event, action or omission but

---

92 O.c., 93–94.
93 O.c., 109–111, and *passim*.

for which the whole subsequent course of events would have been significantly different."[94] But, Walsh adds, this is not as clarifying as it might seem at first sight: for how can the historian assess which particular event, action, or omission did have this decisive impact? For this reason, historians usually resort to listing a series of factors that are considered of importance in bringing about a particular effect, subsequently focusing on a specific one as having been decisive, consequently being the "real" cause. The main issue is, of course, how to decide which factor has been the decisive one. In this connection certain positions may be involved. A Marxist historian, for instance, will mainly refer to economic factors. Walsh, however, presents a different approach by referring to R.G. Collingwood's analysis of causality as explained in his *An Essay on Metaphysics*.[95] Collingwood argues that in the case of human actions usually various perspectives are involved. To illustrate his point, he discusses the plain example of a car crash. For the driver of the car, the cause of the accident is his failure to slow down sufficiently, and thus losing control of the car in the bend of the road. But for the constructor of the road the cause is that mistakes have been made when constructing the upper road structure. And for the designer of the car, the cause is that the centre of gravity of the car is inadequate, as a result of which the road-holding of the car is insufficient. Thus, what is selected as the cause of the car crash depends on the perspective chosen, it being the one that could have been influenced by an agent in a particular situation. Hence, the driver of the car will not consider its design to be the cause of the accident, as he was not in the position to have influence on it. Collingwood argues that historians single out the cause of an event in the same way as with this example, that is, they also focus on a factor that could have been influenced from the perspective of the agent – be that a person or a group – in a particular situation. This analysis of historical causality by Collingwood corresponds remarkably with Lessing's observations on causality in history. For he frequently emphasized that in history a causal judgment amounts to a moral judgment, in the sense that it is a statement on how an agent could have brought about or, for that matter, prevented a certain result. One blames a draught for catching a cold, to use one of Lessing's examples, but implied in this causal judgment is the idea that one may prevent catching a cold in future by closing the window. Thus, both Lessing and Collingwood emphasize that a causal judgment in history always presupposes the perspective of human agency, that is, a cause in history is always considered something done

---

94 W.H. Walsh, 'Historical Causation', *Proceedings of the Aristotelian Society*, New Series, 63(1962–1963), 217–236; reprinted in Walsh, *Philosophy of History*, 188–206, there 190.
95 Oxford 1939.

or failed to do by humans. Of course, this does not imply that there always is only one possible cause, for in a particular situation there usually is more than one agent involved, there accordingly being various possible perspectives and ditto possible causes. Which one is singled out, depends on the perspective selected by the historian. This implies that neither for Lessing nor for Collingwood there are "objective causes" in history – a causal judgment by a historian is indeed an interpretation that depends on the perspective selected, it being the bench-mark for the judgment concerned. For Lessing, this is an argument in favour of scepticism with regard to history as a discipline, for Collingwood, however, it is not. But as regards the notion of causality Collingwood corresponds with Lessing in not adhering to a realist view on it.

In his *Philosophy of History*,[96] the Canadian philosopher of history W.H. Dray (1921–2009) observes that it "may be of interest to look in a little detail at the varying causal judgments which historians have actually made about some widely studied event",[97] as many debates on causality in history tend to ignore the practice of history. Dray himself studied various examples of particular cases, one of them being an investigation how historians have interpreted the causes of the American Civil War. One of the results of his study of particular cases is that Dray as well emphasizes that causal judgments by historians depend on the chosen perspective, and that this always implies "the standpoint of moral appraisal (rather than that of manipulability)".[98] In this sense, Dray is even closer to Lessing than Collingwood, who emphasizes that the historian always chooses the perspective of the agent and that of manipulability, to use Dray's terminology. According to Dray, there will always be a wide variety of causal judgments in history, simply because there is a wide variety of standpoints of moral appraisal. Hence, the conclusion is inevitable that in history there are no "objective" causes, and that a variety of causal judgments relating to the very same phenomenon will be made. In Dray's view, however, this does not imply, at least not necessarily, that different causal judgments in history mutually exclude each other, for it is often the case that a question of emphasis is involved. Moreover, it is also often the case that it is impossible to single out a decisive factor, it being again, of course, dependent on the chosen perspective.

These considerations over causality in history again correspond to a remarkable extent with Lessing's observations. For Lessing as well emphasizes that causes in history are selected from almost endless possible causes, and that the choice of a cause ultimately depends on the approach and perspective applied.

---

96   Englewood Cliffs 1964.
97   O.c., 47.
98   O.c., 55.

In his *Laws and Explanation in History*[99] as well Dray discusses (causal) explanations in history. In this book too he argues that as regards causality, historians apply a pluralist approach. That is, a broad variety of possible causes may be put forward to explain a particular historical phenomenon and, moreover, these various causes are not necessarily mutually exclusive. But one kind of explanation is of special importance in history, Dray claims: explaining behaviour by understanding what motivated a particular agent to do what he or she did. In suchlike explanations, motives are considered a special kind of cause. Dray elaborated upon this insight with his notion of "rational explanation" – that is, an analysis of what, in his view, an explanation in the sense of motives implies.[100] Dray's analysis to a large extent is, as he himself acknowledges, based on R.G. Collingwood's notion of "re-enactment" in the sense that – as Collingwood claims – a (past) thought may be "re-thought" as regards its purport. Like Dray, Lessing also considers assigning motives to agents in history a kind of causal explanation historians have a specific predilection for. But, unlike Dray, for Lessing this is an additional reason for historical scepticism. As Lessing maintains, we cannot even be sure about what motivated our own behaviour in the past – so how could we ever know what motivated others, living centuries ago? Especially in the first edition of *Geschichte als Sinngebung des Sinnlosen*, Lessing gives a number of historical examples of reasons being assigned to agents, all of which are highly questionable. And historians not only blatantly assign motives to individuals, he argues, but to social classes, political parties, governments and peoples as well! Lessing's criticisms of this kind of explanation are devastating indeed if one adheres to a realist notion of history, that is, if one supposes that one may discover what "really" motivated "real" people of the "real" past. But if one does not adhere to this notion of history, but to an idealist one, his criticisms do not hold true. Within an idealist notion of history, assigning reasons to an agent in order to explain his or her behaviour is assigning reasons which make this behaviour intelligible *to us*: as the historian does not make up these reasons, but infers them from the evidence at his or her disposal, it is possible to justify an explanation in terms of motives, and to discuss it with one's peers. But as there is no "real" past, there neither are "real" reasons that would explain past behaviour. Thus, explaining behaviour by assigning motives for it to agents in history – be they individuals or groups – by definition is a construction by the historian, not the discovery of some independently existing fact.

---

99   Oxford 1957.
100 Cfr. especially o.c., 118–155, chapter 5: The rationale of actions.

Be this as it may, Lessing's observations on causality show a number of interesting similarities with debates on the same subject by later philosophers of history, and thus deserve being paid attention to.

Lessing's reflections on history eventually lead him to conclude – rather surprisingly, in view of his devastating criticisms of the epistemological claims of historians of his day and age – that history is vitally important within a community. It is important, not because it offers knowledge of the "real" past, but because of the religious function it has within a community. Lessing uses "religion" here in the original sense of the word, that is, "religion" as a force that ties together a group of people. In this connection, the function of history within a community is to tell stories about its past that unite its members or, to put it otherwise, stories about the past of a community that articulate or rather provide the identity of this particular community. Whether these stories are true – in the traditional sense of the word – or not, is not relevant, Lessing argues. An example he mentions in this connection, is the story told in Switzerland about Wilhelm Tell, it being in Lessing's opinion of no importance whether Wilhelm Tell "really" did exist or not. What is actually is of importance, is that the story of his life is told convincingly, and thus unites the Swiss nation into a community that is convinced of its shared identity, or rather truly feels it as such. What it amounts to is that the story of Wilhelm Tell really inspires the Swiss nation. Lessing claims that this holds true, not only for the story about Wilhelm Tell, but likewise for stories about Nero or Napoleon, Charlemagne or czar Peter the Great, the Victorian Empire or Mother Russia, indeed for all history. Hence, what history ultimately boils down to is telling attractive and convincing stories that inspire the community to whom these stories are told.

In focusing attention on history as essentially being a story told about the past within a particular community, Lessing actually foreshadows certain developments in philosophy of history from the second half of the twentieth century onwards. For in his *Laws and Explanation in History* Dray argues that historical explanations typically differ from scientific explanations in that they do not require a reference to universal laws or law-like statements. But he also claims that historical explanations are not presented in the form of a model, but are rather smoothly interwoven in a story about the past and in this way incorporated in it.[101] One could therefore maintain that the subsequent debates on historical narratives actually originate in the debates on historical explanation that started with Dray's classic *Laws and Explanation in History*.

---

101 Dray, *Laws and Explanation in History*, passim. Cfr. W.H. Dray, 'Explanatory Narrative in History', in: *The Philosophical Quarterly* 4 (1954), 15–27.

These subsequent debates on the narrative aspect of history developed a dynamics of their own, in which their origin gradually got out of sight.

The debates on history being in essence a story about the past are usually qualified as the "narrative approach" of history. This approach originates in the claim that history as a story does not incorporate historical explanations, but is rather a form of explanation in itself – that is, telling a story provides in itself a kind of explanation.[102] An additional claim in these debates is that it is the story as a whole that explains. As a result, the focus shifted to the question what characterizes historical "narratives" – as the stories told about the past now usually are called – in general. As Ankersmit points out, this attention for the historical narrative resulted in two different approaches, one concentrating on "the relationship between the historian's language and the past recounted in it",[103] the other on the rhetorics of history. The first one ultimately deals with the question whether the stories told about the past by historians are reports on something that exists independently (whether these stories are told or not), or that these stories are mere constructions by the historian in which both the past and the stories themselves come about. Lessing, of course, would have taken the latter position, for he is very outspoken in his claim that history is being constructed in the stories told about the past. That is, in Lessing's view there does not exist a past besides the stories told about it. Accordingly, all history is a construction, he argues – a construction, moreover, that is guided by present needs and wants; thus, history ultimately is what we want it to have been.

The second approach mentioned by Ankersmit focuses on the rhetorics of history: history, after all, usually is a written story about the past. Hence, the question is: which literary means does the historian use to tell his or her story as convincingly as possible? The most influential representative of this approach in the philosophy of history is Hayden White, who was greatly inspired by literary theory in his efforts to analyze how historians construct their texts about the past. But, as noted above, White clings to the notion of a past that "really" exists as regards singular statements about the past – in his own words: historical narratives are verbal fictions, "the contents of which are as much *invented* as *found*".[104] White puts the element of invention entirely in the process of writing, that is, in the use of literary techniques in telling stories about the past. The constitutive elements of these stories, in contrast, – singular statements

---

102 Idem.
103 F.R. Ankersmit, 'Narrative and Interpretation', in: A. Tucker (ed.), *A Companion to the Philosophy of History and Historiography* (Malden MA 2009), 199–208, there 201.
104 Hayden White, 'The Historical Text as Literary Artefact', in: Hayden White, *Tropics of Discourse*, 81–100, there 82. The italics are White's.

about the past – are ultimately found. Lessing surely would have rejected this ambiguity: he claims that there is in no way a past to be "found" involved, but only a past as constructed by the historian in the story that he or she tells about the past. Thus, in his philosophy of history Lessing is unambiguous and more outspoken in his rejection of realist notions of history than White or, for that matter, other representatives of the rhetorical approach within the narrative one in the philosophy of history.

Again, one could therefore maintain that Lessing in a kind of way foreshadows the narrative approach in the philosophy of history, in the sense that he discusses related questions. But he pushes his analyses to the extreme: his conclusions are consistent, unambiguous, and radical. As a result, the position he takes represents a constructivist notion of history that is maintained more consistently than any of the major representatives of the narrative approach.

But it is not only representatives of the narrative approach in philosophy of history, who put the idea that history in essence is telling a story about the past at the centre of attention, for so do postmodernist authors."Postmodernism" is, of course, a highly contested concept – and every effort to define it seems only to increase controversy. Be that as it may, postmodernist theorists of history appear to agree in the emphasis on the contrast between their idea of history and the traditional or "modernist" one. – In general, postmodernist theorists are in the habit of focusing on what they are opposed to rather than what they adhere to. – According to the postmodernist theorists of history, the traditional or modernist idea of history implies that history is an intellectual undertaking that models its procedures after those of the sciences, and thus claims to be able to discover and describe what actually happened in the past."Historiography as thus understood has been widely valued as providing supposedly reliable foundations for personal and national identities and, where religious belief has eroded, as supplying a secular replacement for the conveyance and confirmation of existential meaning", the English historian of ideas Beverly Southgate argues.[105] Moreover, she claims, this traditional or modernist idea of history would imply the idea that there is a direction in history, usually conceived of as progress. But this idea has been questioned and rejected by postmodernist theorists of history: they deny that history has a direction, accordingly progress in history being out of the question. Connected with this postmodernist denial of direction and progress is yet another claim, Southgate maintains: there is no meaning in history – the meaning of what happened in the past is imposed

---

105 Beverly Southgate, 'Postmodernism', in: A. Tucker (ed.), o.c., 540–549, there 541. The literature on postmodernism is overwhelming. Here, I confine myself to this handy overview by Southgate.

upon history rather than found in it, and is articulated in the story the historian tells about the past. But the historian necessarily writes this story from his or her particular perspective that is limited and partial: there is no "view from nowhere", to use the expression of the American philosopher Thomas Nagel,[106] from which an impartial historian could write about the past. According to postmodernist theorists of history, Southgate argues, this implies that it is not possible to tell the truth about the past. One of the consequences of the claim that history is necessarily written from a partial and limited perspective is the rise of numerous new approaches within historiography, all presupposing a perspective that hitherto allegedly has been neglected, for example labourers, feminists, ethnic and sexual minorities. All these approaches are meant to correct and complement the hitherto dominant perspective, challenging the objectivity of the dominant tradition.

Quite a number of these criticisms of the traditional or modernist idea of history put forward by postmodernist theorists were raised already by Theodor Lessing in both editions of *Geschichte als Sinngebung des Sinnlosen*. Thus, Lessing criticized the idea that history would discover and describe the past as it actually happened, and likewise opposed the idea that some direction or trend would be proper to history itself, accordingly denying the idea that history is the story of progress. He further claimed that the sense of history is imposed upon the past by the historian, and that this sense is articulated in the story that the historian tells about the past. Finally, Lessing argued that history is always written from a limited and partial perspective, almost without exception being the "victorious" one. And this implies a criticism of Eurocentrism as well that is so dominant in of Western historiography and, for that matter, philosophy.

In this connection, two comments are called for. In the first place, these criticisms of history by both Lessing and postmodernist theorists of history mainly concern the realist view on history in general. In this they concur with the adherents of the constructivist idea of history – philosophers like Croce, Collingwood, and Oakeshott – who claim that history is not found, but constructed by the historian. They also claim that, for this reason, the story told about the past by the historian is not, and cannot be, "objective", but is written from a partial and limited perspective. And they argue moreover that if the notion of "truth" can be upheld with regard to history, it has to be defined not as a correspondence between a statement about a past state of affairs and the original state of affairs itself, but in a different way, namely by evidence

---

[106] Thomas Nagel, *The view from nowhere* (Oxford 1986). Nagel describes an objective perspective as the view from nowhere.

being involved. It is the latter aspect in which constructivists differ from postmodernists.

In the second place, as Southgate rightly argues, practising historians tend to be unfavourably disposed towards the postmodernist challenge, which they see – and not without reason – as a threat to history as it is usually conceived of.[107] The same holds true, I would maintain, for the reactions to Lessing's criticisms of history. Though the reviews of both editions of his *Geschichte als Sinngebung des Sinnlosen* were not unkind, his observations on history have since then not been seriously discussed. Of course, this is not inexplicable. Lessing's *Geschichte als Sinngebung des Sinnlosen* is not easily accessible for readers not familiar with its underlying philosophical system. Moreover, the Third Reich with its long shadow was not an atmosphere in which intellectual debates on competing views on history prospered. Besides, from the 1950's, international debates in philosophy of history were dominated by questions originating in the analytic philosophy of science. Finally, Lessing's book was, and is, not available in an English translation. Be that as it may, his argument too implies a threat to history as traditionally conceived of. As Southgate observes with regard to postmodernist criticisms of historiography, both practising historians and a number of philosophers of history are inclined to defend traditional notions of history:

> Most important is a continuing assumption that the acquisition of historiographic *knowledge* is still possible, so that a concept of *truth* survives towards which it is the function and duty of historians to strive. The means to attain such truthful knowledge is essentially *scientific*, empirical and rational or logical; and it can, it is argued, readily be validated by appeals to *common sense* and professional *consensus*.[108]

This implies that there is a gulf between postmodernist critics of historiography on the one hand, and practising historians and a number of philosophers of history – Southgate mentions for example contemporary philosophers of history like C. Behan McCullagh, M.C. Lemon, and A. Tucker[109] – on the other, with adherents of a constructivist view on history taking up a middle

---

107   Southgate, o.c., 545.
108   O.c., 546. The italics are Southgate's.
109   Loc.cit.; cfr. C.B. McCullagh, *Justifying Historical Descriptions* (Cambridge 1984); C.B. McCullagh, *The Truth of History* (London 1998); C.B. McCullagh, *The Logic of History. Putting postmodernism in perspective* (London 2004); M. C. Lemon, *Philosophy of History: A Guide for Students* (London 2003); and A. Tucker, *Our Knowledge of the Past: A Philosophy of Historiography* (Cambridge 2004).

position. Philosophers like Croce, Collingwood and Oakeshott share some of the criticisms of traditional historiography by postmodernist theorists, but nevertheless tend to cling to the idea of truth in history, if not conceived of realistically, and to the importance of historical method and professional consensus. Lessing's position seems to be most akin to that of postmodernist critics of traditional historiography, although he definitely has ideas in common with constructivist philosophers of history as well. Be that as it may, his observations on history in both editions of *Geschichte als Sinngebung des Sinnlosen* foreshadow most debates in philosophy of history in the second half of the twentieth, and the first years of the present century, and are accordingly highly relevant for these debates.

Finally, it should be emphasized that for Lessing history ultimately has only instrumental value. His primary commitment was ethical: in the last resort, history has in this respect to contribute to the ethical ideal of diminishing the need in the world. In his view, history should tell convincing and inspiring stories about the past of a particular community, and thus create and affirm its identity, in this way binding this community into a unity. But ultimately, these stories have to support his all-embracing ethical ideal of diminishing the need in the world. For Theodor Lessing, this ethical ideal was what his philosophy, and his very life was all about.

Conclusion

In his review of *Geschichte als Sinngebung des Sinnlosen*, the philosopher dr. Georg Morgenstern claimed that with this book – in particular with his expositions on the historical subject and on the way historians give sense to the past –, Theodor Lessing made a lasting contribution to the tradition of philosophy of history.[1]

Lessing's philosophy of history as expressed mainly in the first and fourth editions of his *Geschichte als Sinngebung des Sinnlosen* should be considered an elaboration of the philosophical system of his own that he developed from his adolescence onward. It is therefore questionable whether his philosophy of history is indeed comprehensible when it is not seen within the context of this system. Lessing maintained that this philosophical system of his own reflected his most personal experiences – and that accordingly this system was indissolubly related to his life and person. In Lessing's view, this is what distinguishes philosophy in the true sense of the word from the academic philosophy which had become increasingly dominant in the Western world: academic philosophy is usually involved with details in the interpretation of the works of, say, Plato or Aristotle, whereas philosophy in the true sense of the word is driven by an inner necessity reflecting the philosopher's inner life. As Lessing experienced his youth mainly as one of suffering – as can be inferred from his autobiographical *Einmal und nie wieder*, and from stray autobiographical observations in his other writings –, for him to be was to be in need. Hence, he called the philosophical system of his own "the philosophy of need". Lessing claimed that the basic intuition of this system – his so-called theory of three spheres – suddenly struck him when he, still a schoolboy, was walking on the bank of a river in his native Hanover. In the following years, he would elaborate this basic intuition into a system, initially using the terminology of the philosophy of life, but from the late 1890's increasingly that of early phenomenology. Lessing got first acquainted with phenomenology when he attended lectures by Theodor Lipps in Munich, and later on studying with Edmund Husserl in Göttingen. *Geschichte als Sinngebung des Sinnlosen* clearly evidences the influence of early phenomenology. Indeed, Lessing eventually should be seen as a representative of the phenomenological tradition – though not an orthodox one, in view of his self-professed activist attitude – rather than of

---

1 Georg Morgenstern, Review of *Geschichte als Sinngebung des Sinnlosen*, in: *Annalen der Philosophie* 2 (1921), 275–276. Cfr. chapter six, 297.

the philosophy of life, he so often is associated with in encyclopaedia's and textbooks (if he is mentioned at all).

Pivotal in Lessing's philosophical system is the idea that consciousness is born out of need: "in the beginning" mankind was one with nature or, one might say, it actually was nature. But as a result of need, mankind dissociated itself from nature, and mankind started to see itself as distinct from, or even opposite to nature – which in Lessing's philosophy is the very same thing as the birth of consciousness. Hereafter, one has to distinguish two spheres: the sphere from which mankind dissociated itself, called *vitalité* by Lessing; and the sphere of the reality of which mankind is conscious, called *réalité* by him. It is characteristic of *réalité* as the sphere of the reality of which mankind is conscious that it is by definition ordered by consciousness: this sphere is not a given, but the result of an ordering process by man. Apart from *vitalité* and *réalité*, Lessing distinguishes yet another sphere, the one of *vérité*, which is the sphere of logical and mathematical truth, and of eternally valid notions like Kant's categorical imperative. In Lessing's view, these three spheres exist independently of each other. Humans are subconsciously aware of the separation of these three spheres, and indeed experience it as an imperfection that somehow should be reconciled, which is impossible, however. Quite rarely, in the process of *Ahmung* or cathartic understanding, man is in direct contact with *vitalité*, for instance when someone is so much taken up with a stage play or a piece of music that all distinctions between him- or herself and the outer world disappear. The sphere of *vérité* in its turn may serve as a loadstar for *réalité*, it being an unattainable truth, which may be valuable, however, for orientation in *réalité*. The dissociation of mankind from *vitalité* is an incomplete and ongoing process, but it is nowhere evolved as in Europe (– which for Lessing is not a geographical term, but refers to a cultural unity that includes the United States, Canada, etc.). This process of dissociation from nature by definition goes at the expense of nature; hence, Lessing argues that due to consciousness the earth will eventually collapse. This is, however, no reason for pessimism, he maintains: it simply is something that comes about...

Lessing claimed that he completed this philosophical system of his own on the eve of the First World War. As a result of the outbreak of the war, however, he never did manage to put his system down in writing: there were more urgent problems to deal with, both practically – surviving the war with his wife and children – and intellectually – how to respond to the war, in particular as regards the enthusiasm the war was welcomed with by all too many of his compatriots. Hence, his philosophical system has to be reconstructed from stray observations in his various publications. This system is presupposed however in his essays and books written and published both during and after the First World War.

The outbreak of the war in August 1914 made an overwhelming impression on Lessing. He saw the war as a confirmation of a basic intuition of his philosophical system – that to be is to be in need. Because of this, there was in his view every reason to bring up his philosophical system. Moreover, he was bewildered and even appalled by the way a great majority of German intellectuals endeavoured to justify the war. These justifications frequently implied an appeal to history, that is, historical arguments were used in order to claim that Germany was right in its policy, and its enemies were to blame for the war. These appeals to history induced Lessing to rethink history as a discipline, and to address questions like: can we know the past? Can history be true? Can history be objective? What does the notion of causality in history mean and imply?

Lessing published his views on history mainly in two books, both entitled *Geschichte als Sinngebung des Sinnlosen*, the second one being formally the fourth edition of the first one. The first edition, by and large written during the war, but only published in 1919, addresses the public at large; it is an, at times rather emotional, outburst against efforts to justify the German position in the Great War historically, in particular against the idea that history would prove objectively that Germany was fighting a just war. In the fourth edition of the book, published in 1927, Lessing addresses a public of peers, his argument accordingly being of a more academic nature as compared to the first edition, though he does allow himself an occasional emotional outburst. For Lessing himself, the first and fourth editions of the book were complementary, and he did not consider the first edition to be superseded by the last one – one the contrary, he rather hoped that both editions would be available side by side in future.

The drift of the argument in both versions of *Geschichte als Sinngebung des Sinnlosen* is identical. In Lessing's view, history is proper to *réalité*, that is, it is proper to the reality of which mankind is conscious and which is ordered by consciousness. Thus, in accordance with Lessing's philosophical system, history is not about *vitalité* nor about *vérité*. This implies that history cannot be true, for in Lessing's view truth is limited to the sphere of *vérité*, that is, the sphere of provable truth of mathematics and logic and of eternally valid notions. As history is proper to *réalité*, Lessing argues that history by definition is ordered by consciousness, that is, history as known by mankind is the result of a process of ordering by consciousness that takes place in the present. Hence, history cannot reflect the past as it actually happened, Lessing claims: what is taken for historical reality in fact is a construction put up in the present. Consequently, in both versions of *Geschichte als Sinngebung des Sinnlosen*, Lessing persistently opposes the claim that historians can have knowledge of the past as it actually happened, or that history simply describes, mirrors, or even equals past reality. This realist view of history, however, underlies the efforts to justify the German position in the Great War historically, it being the very reason Lessing so strongly rejects it.

In support of his scepticism as regards the claim that historians can know the past as it actually happened, Lessing advances a number of arguments. In the first edition of *Geschichte als Sinngebung des Sinnlosen*, Lessing's discourse is associative: he gives numerous examples, all leading to the same conclusion: whatever historians may maintain, it is impossible to know the past as it really happened. In the final part of this edition of the book, he develops his alternative view of history. In this connection, he argues that history plays a most important part within a society or culture not, however, because it offers knowledge of the past, but because of what he calls its "religious" function. With this he means that history is of importance because it tells stories that establish or affirm the identity of a society or culture, and thus unites a particular society or culture. A favourite example of Lessing's is the story about Wilhelm Tell as told in Switzerland: it is important because it confirms the Swiss national identity, no matter whether it is true or not, and even no matter whether Tell actually existed or not. According to Lessing, all history works like in the example of Tell: history is important because of its religious function, not because it offers knowledge of the past, let alone knowledge of the past as it actually happened.

In the fourth edition of *Geschichte als Sinngebung des Sinnlosen*, Lessing mainly limits himself to rebutting the claims that history would in one way or another describe or give a picture of the "real" past. In this version of the book, his approach is more systematic: he examines the historical categories that are the means consciousness uses to order *réalité*, specifically when it shapes the past. These categories include what Lessing calls the "bearer" of history (or the historical subject) that gives history a particular unity; time; and causality. His analyses of the functioning of these categories all result in the same conclusion: they are proper to (present) consciousness and not to the past, and thus history does not and indeed cannot describe or mirror the past as it actually happened. As regards causality, Lessing pays special attention to a particular kind of causality that is characteristic of history. For historians often give causal explanations by assigning reasons or motives to particular historical agents. For Lessing, this is an additional reason for scepticism with regard to the claim that it is possible to know the past as it actually happened. After all, we often do not even know ourselves what moved us to do something we have done in the past, he argues, so how could we possibly know what really moved people centuries ago?

The dominant feature of Theodor Lessing's philosophy of history therefore implies a radical scepticism as regards the claim that history would describe or provide a mirror image of the past as it actually has been. How should this philosophy of history be assessed? Lessing's criticisms of the realist view of history are most convincing, and even devastating. For a realist view of history is indeed not tenable, since history is just not capable of displaying the past as it actually has been. Though Lessing's opposition to the claims of the realist view of history may have been prompted by the efforts of leading German intellectuals to justify the German position in the Great War historically, his conclusions do hold true apart from this particular context. The observation should be made, however, that as Lessing's position is explicitly based on his rejection of the realist view of history, it does not justify a general scepticism as regards the possibility of historical knowledge in general. After all, not all historians and philosophers of history adhere to a realist view of history. For philosophers of history like Benedetto Croce, R.G. Collingwood, and Michael Oakeshott – to mention but a few – have explicitly developed a constructivist view of history as an alternative to the realist one. Lessing's sceptical criticisms of the realist view of history for the greater part do not touch upon the arguments used within this constructivist position. Indeed, there are some striking similarities between Lessing's observations on history and the constructivist view of history. This regards for instance the notion of history as telling stories that establish and affirm the identity of a society or culture.

But there are major differences between the adherents of a constructivist view of history and Lessing as well. For whereas both agree that history by definition cannot be objective, the conclusion they they draw from this position is quite opposite. Lessing's conclusion implies a recommendation to historians to be explicitly and proudly subjective, if objectivity is not possible. Adherents of the constructivist view of history, on the other hand, do not resort to subjectivism: they want to restrain subjectivism by inter-subjectivism, relying on the methods and (formal and informal) rules of history to warrant the inter-subjectivity of the historian's conclusions. – For that matter, a similar argument was developed by Theodor Litt in his discussion of Lessing's philosophy of history.[2] – Yet another difference between the adherents of a constructivist view of history and Lessing relates to the idea of truth. While Lessing argues that history cannot be true, adherents of the constructivist view of history do not want to give up the notion of truth in history. Of course, the latter are fully aware that a traditional correspondence theory of truth does not apply

---

2   Cfr. Chapter six, above, 293–295.

to history, and that if the notion of truth can be used with respect to history, it has to be defined differently, for instance as a specific relation between the historian's statements and the evidence at his disposal.[3]

Thus, Lessing's scepticism seems to be somewhat overstated, since his criticisms of history for the greater part do not touch upon the constructivist position, neither does his scepticism. The constructivist view of history thus seems to be tenable despite Lessing's more far-reaching criticisms of history. But this does not mean that Lessing's philosophy of history is no longer of interest, nor that it is superseded. After all, realist notions of history are at the present day still upheld, though not the more naive ones that Lessing primarily opposed, but more sophisticated variants as defended by for instance influential philosophers of history like Hayden White or F.R. Ankersmit. As a corrective to these eventually untenable realist notions of history, Lessing's arguments against realism are still not only of importance but also cogent. Besides this, it is important to realize that this issue does not concern a merely academic question: after all, Lessing's critique of realist notions of history was prompted by the way German intellectuals tried to use history for political reasons in the late summer and autumn of 1914, illustrating with this how an erroneous view on history may definitely have serious political implications. Indeed, the mistaken notion of history underlying the ideas of 1914 ultimately contributed to the instability of the Weimar Republic, which in its turn was a decisive factor in the rise of National-Socialism and its assumption of power in Germany. Hence, the way we think about history and its possible consequences is not an idle or speculative question, but an issue of critical importance that should be considered seriously and carefully. The way Lessing has made this clear as a result of a vital period in European history may be considered a major contribution to philosophy of history, though it is an aspect that until now has hardly been noticed.

But Lessing's observations on the function of history within a society are also of interest in that he focuses on the role of history in establishing and affirming the identity of a society. It is actually this aspect of history that makes it at times the subject of sometimes heated debates, for history indeed directly touches on how humans perceive themselves as social beings. This is what often makes history into a sensitive subject, it being a subject that deserves to be taken into consideration by both historians and philosophers of history. Lessing's warnings that history tends to assume the position of the "victors" in history and consequently to endorse the status quo, and according excluding

---

3 But not, of course, in the realist sense in which White and Ankersmit define it. Cfr. Chapter six above, 313–314.

the "losers" – be they colonized peoples, labourers, women, sexual or ethnic minorities –, are still most relevant too. Since the 1960's, several new types of history developed, like labourers' history or women's history, precisely to correct this tendency of history. Lessing's observations both foreshadow and justify this development.

Hence, Morgenstern was right when he claimed in his review of *Geschichte als Sinngebung des Sinnlosen* that Lessing made a lasting contribution to the tradition of philosophy of history.

The framework of this study on Theodor Lessing's philosophy of history is twofold. First, it is argued that his philosophy of history is a specific elaboration of the philosophical system of his own that he had developed in the years before the First World War. Secondly, this elaboration of his philosophical system was prompted by the outbreak of the First World War, in particular by the way the majority of German intellectuals justified Germany's policy by appealing to history. The significance of Lessing's philosophy of history is not limited to this context of origin, however, but it is also relevant beyond this context, and is of importance for contemporary debates within philosophy of history as well. Thus far, both aspects mentioned did not get the attention they deserve, and neither have they been seen as being related. That is, Lessing's philosophy of history has not been the subject of a study that explicitly aims at explaining it within the context of his philosophical system, and elaborates on the specific context of its genesis. In this study an effort has been made to expound both aspects. Besides this, the relevance of Lessings's philosophy of history for current debates on the subject is discussed.

A more exhaustive discussion of various aspects of Lessing's philosophy of history, in particular as regards its relevance for contemporary debates within philosophy of history, is certainly desirable. The same holds true for a thorough investigation of the notes and writings that Lessing left, which could not be undertaken within the limits if this study. However, it is not very likely that this would result in radically new interpretations of his philosophy of history. After all, Lessing's view on history by and large did not undergo major changes between his first and last published statements on the subject. Though it is possible that there will be more evidence that gains an insight into his philosophy of history, or particular aspects of it, it is not very probable that it will support a substantially new interpretation of his philosophy of history. Over the years, his thought on history was, after all, remarkably consistent; it is therefore not to be expected that the notes and writings he left will contain radically different ideas on history.

Finally, for Lessing himself his philosophy of history, like his philosophy in general, was only of instrumental value. What ultimately mattered to him, was his all-embracing ethical ideal of diminishing the need in the world. Eventually, his commitment to this ideal did cost him his life – even after he fled Germany, he felt he had to fight National-Socialism by publicly criticizing it and by standing up for the persecuted German Jews, which incensed the National-Socialist regime to such an extent that he was murdered in his place of exile at Marienbad. But his ideal did not die with him. Today, the ideal to diminish the need in the world is hardly less relevant than it was in Lessing's days and age. Thus it is, to use a favourite metaphor of his, the message-in-a-bottle that he threw in the frozen sea of history, hoping that one day it would be picked up and inspire those who find it.

Bibliography

A. Works by Theodor Lessing[1]

a. Books

Der Fall Panizza. Eine kritische Betrachtung über 'Gotteslasterung' und künstlerische Dinge vor Schwurgerichten (Munich 1895)

Weiber! 301 Stoßseufzer über das 'schönere' Geschlecht (Berlin 1897)

African Spir's Erkenntnislehre (Phil. Diss. Erlangen, Gießen 1900)

Schopenhauer - Wagner - Nietzsche. Einführung in moderne deutsche Philosophie (Munich 1906)

Theater-Seele. Studie über Bühnenästhetik und Schauspielkunst (Berlin 1907)

Der Bruch in der Ethik Kants: Wert- und willenstheoretische Prolegomena (Bern 1908)

Der Lärm. Eine Kampfschrift gegen die Geräusche unseres Lebens (Wiesbaden 1908)

Madonna Sixtina. Ästhetische und religiöse Studien (Leipzig 1908)

Weib, Frau, Dame. Ein Essay (Munich 1910)

Samuel zieht die Bilanz und Tomi melkt die Moralkuh oder Zweier Könige Sturze. Eine Warnung für Deutsche, Satiren zu schreiben (Hanover 1910); reprinted in *Th-STM*.

Der fröhliche Eselsquell. Gedanken über Theater, Schauspieler, Drame (Berlin 1912)

Studien zur Wertaxiomatik. Untersuchungen über Reine Ethik und Reines Recht (Leipzig 1914)

Philosophie als Tat (Göttingen 1914)

Europa und Asien (Berlin 1918)

Geschichte als Sinngebung des Sinnlosen (Munich 1919)

Jäö. Studienblätter (Hannover 1919)

Die verfluchte Kultur. Gedanken über den Gegensatz von Leben und Geist (Munich 1921)

Feind im Land. Satiren und Novellen (Hanover 1923)

Volkshochschule als Kulturwert. Ansprache bei der 5. Jahresfeier der Volkshochschule Hannover - Linden (Hannover - Linden 1923); reprinted in *WeU*, 220–228 and in *Bis*, 110–118

Europa und Asien oder Der Mensch und das Wandellose. 6 Bücher wider Geschichte und Zeit (second edition, Hanover 1923)

Haarmann. Die Geschichte einer Werwolfs (Berlin 1925); reprinted as *Haarmann. Die Geschichte einer Werwolfs und andere Gerichtsreportagen*, ed. by Rainer Marwedel (Frankfurt a.M. 1989)

Meine Tiere (Berlin 1926)

---

[1] I confine myself to works by Lessing used in this study. An updated bibliography of Lessing's writings is a desideratum; although the bibliography by Luitger Dietze in Ekkehard Hieronimus, *Theodor Lessing. Eine Lebensskizze* (Hanover 1972) still is a good starting point, it is not complete.

Prinzipien der Charakterologie (Halle 1926)
Geschichte als Sinngebung des Sinnlosen oder die Geburt der Geschichte aus dem Mythos (fourth edition, Leipzig 1927)
Blumen (Berlin 1928)
Dämonen (Berlin 1928)
Der jüdische Selbsthaß (Berlin 1930)
Deutschland und seine Juden (Prag - Karlin 1933), reprinted in: *Wmnm*, 217–240
Einmal und nie wieder. Lebenserinnerungen (Gütersloh 1969 [first edition Prag 1935])
Ich warf eine Flaschenpost ins Eismeer der Geschichte. Essays und Feuilletons, ed. by Rainer Marwedel (Darmstadt and Neuwied 1986)
Wortmeldungen eines Unerschrockenen. Publizistik aus drei Jahrzehnten, ed. by Hans Stern (Leipzig and Weimar 1987)
Bildung ist Schönheit. Autobiographische Zeugnisse und Schriften zur Bildungsreform, ed. by Jörg Wollenberg (*Ausgewählte Schriften*, vol. 1, Bremen 1995)
Wir machen nicht mit! Schriften gegen den Nationalismus und zur Judenfrage, ed. by Jörg Wollenberg (*Ausgewählte Schriften*, vol. 2, Bremen 1997)
Theater-Seele und Tomi melkt die Moralkuh. Schriften zu Theater und Literatur, ed. by Jörg Wollenberg et.al., (*Ausgewählte Schriften*, vol. 3, Bremen 2003)
Nachtkritiken. Kleine Schriften 1906–1907, ed. by Rainer Marwedel (Göttingen 2006)
Eindrücke aus Galizien, edited by Wolgang Eggersdorfer (Hanover 2014)

b.   Essays

'Studien zur Wertaxiomatik', in: *Archiv für systematische Philosophie*, Neue Folge, 14 (1908), 58–93, 226–257
'Leibniz in Hannover. Ein Stück Autobiografie' (1908), in: *PaT,* 452–473
'Philosophie als Tat', in: *Archiv für systematische Philosophie*, Neue Folge, 15 (1909), 23–39; reprinted in: *PaT*, 1–29
'Wissenschaft als Kraftökonomie' (1907), in: *PaT*, 30–73
'Darwin. Kritik des Entwicklungs-Glaubens' (1909), in: *PaT*, 157–208
'Galizien. Zur Abwehr', in: *Allgemeinen Zeitung des Judentums*, Heft 7, (1910), reprinted in: Theodor Lessing, *Eindrücke aus Galizien*, edited by Wolgang Eggersdorfer (Hanover 2014), 40–45
'Theodor Lipps' (1910), in: *PaT*, 253–262
'Moralische Noten. Fragmente einer Ethik, aus den Jahren 1900–1913', in *PaT*, 74–110
'Eduard Pflüger. Erinnerungen' (1909), in: *PaT*, 218–240
'Samuel zieht die Bilanz', in: *Die Schaubühne* 6, 1 (1910), 65–73; reprinted in: *Th-STM*, 17–27
'Ferdinand Lasalle' (1911), in: *PaT*, 396–419
'Afrikan Spir' (1911), in: *PaT*, 353–373

'Psychologie der Ahmung', in: *Archiv für systematische Philosophie*, Neue Folge, 18 (1912), 209–223; reprinted in: *PaT*, 127–151
'Omar al Raschid Bey' (1912), in: *PaT*, 374–395
'Note über Religion' (1912), in: *PaT*, 118–126
'Der neue Sudermann', in: *Die Schaubühne* 8, 2 (1912), 691–692
'Georg Simmel. Betrachtungen und Exkurse' (1912–1913), in: *PaT*, 303–342
'Carl Gustav Carus. Gedenkblatt' (1913), in: *PaT*, 204–217
'An den Nerven krank und dem Zusammenbruch nahe – Tagebuchnotizen August 1914', in: *Wmnm*, 21–25
'Et si omnes ego non', in: *Wmnm*, 27–46
'Europa und Asien', in: *Die Aktion* 7 (1917), col. 317–319, 347–350, 365–370, 449–454, 506–508, and 550–551
'Die schönen Sünderinnen', in: *Prager Tagblatt*, October 28th, 1923
"Erinnere Dich…", in: *Prager Tagblatt*, December 25th 1923, reprinted in: *IFEG*, 349–354
'Wie werde ich gebildet?', in: *Prager Tagblatt*, January 20th, 1924
'Schopenhauer gegen Kant', in: *Jahrbuch der Schopenhauergesellschaft* 12 (1923–1925), 3–25
'Hindenburg', in: *Prager Tagblatt*, April 25th 1925; reprinted in: *IFEG*, 65–69
'Ausflug nach Goslar', in: *Prager Tagblatt*, December 6th, 1925
'Maximilian Harden', in: *Prager Tagblatt*, December 12th, 1925, reprinted in: *IFEG*, 389–393
'Antwort auf die Rundfrage: Wie Sie Mussolini sehen', in: *Prager Tagblatt*, December 25th 1925
'Deutsche Studentenschaft um 1925', in: *Die neue Erziehung* 7 (1925), 637–643; reprinted in: *IFEG*, 75–82
'Was ist Geschichte?', in: *Die ewige Revolution, Ergebnisse der Internationalen Geschichtstagung, 2.-4.x.1924*, ed. by Siegfried Kawerau (Berlin 1925), 17–34; reprinted in: *WeU* 229–248
'Gerichtstag über mich selbst', in: *Junge Menschen* 6 (1925), Heft 10, 238–244; reprinted in: *BiS*, 57–68
'Worüber ich mich immer wieder ärgere. Antwort auf eine Enquête', in: *Das Stachelschwein* 2 (1925), Heft 14, 15–22; reprinted in: *IFEG*, 145–154
'Letzte Worte', in: *Prager Tagblatt*, March 25th, 1926, reprinted in: *IFEG*, 205–207
'Gerichtstag über mich selbst', in: *Prager Tagblatt*, June 13th 1926; reprinted in: *Eunw*, 316–322
'Jüdisches Schicksal', in: *Der Jude* (1926), Sonderheft 3 – Judentum und Deutschtum, 11–17, reprinted in: *Wmnm*, 121–128
'Es ist nur ein Übergang', in: *Prager Tagblatt*, May 28th 1926; reprinted in: *IFEG*, 346–349
'Ein deutscher Gelehrter', in: *Prager Tagblatt*, February 15th, 1927

'Schmerzensruf einer Normalen', in: *Prager Tagblatt*, December 20th, 1927; reprinted in *IFEG*, 198–202

'Die 'Kulturmission' der abendländischen Völker', in: *Das Flammenzeichen vom Palais Egmont*, published by the Liga gegen Imperialismus und für nationale Unabhängigkeit, Berlin 1927, 205–214; reprinted in: *WeU*, 248–259

'Meine Beziehungen zu Ludwig Klages' (1928), reprinted in: *Eunw*, 413–446

'Alles wäre anders gekommen...', in: *Prager Tagblatt*, March 4th, 1928, reprinted in: *IFEG*, 341–345

'Es ist nur ein Übergang', in: *Prager Tagblatt*, May 28th, reprinted in: *IFEG*, 346–349

'Zwei Gräber', in: *Prager Tagblatt*, July 29th 1928; reprinted in: *IFEG* , 402–406

'Das Lazarett', *Prager Tagblatt*, February 10th 1929; February 17th 1929; March 2nd 1929; March 7th 1929; March 23rd 1929; April 6th 1929; April 19th 1929; reprinted in: *IFEG*, 354–386

'§ 297: Gewerbsmäßige Unzucht. Antwort auf eine Rundfrage', in: § 297: *'Unzucht zwischen Männern'? Ein Beitrag zur Strafgesetzreform*, ed. by R. Linsert (Berlin 1929); reprinted in: Theodor Lessing, *Haarmann. Die Geschichte eines Werwolfs und andere Gerichtsreportagen*, ed. by Rainer Marwedel (Frankfurt a.M. 1989)

'Der deutsche Aufsatz', in: *Die neue Erziehung* 13 (1930), 904–909; reprinted in: *BiS*, 184–191

'Antwort auf die Rundfrage: 'Die Intellektuellen haben das Wort'', in: *Die Linkskurve*, September 1930; reprinted in: *WeU*, 346–347

'Konservative Tendenzen in der Sozialdemokratie? Eine Rundfrage', in: *Mitteilungsblatt des sozialdemokratischen Intellektuellenbundes*, Juli 1930, Heft 5, 9–13; reprinted in: *IFEG*, 96–102

'Der Tag der Tiere', in: *Prager Tagblatt*, October 2nd, 1930; reprinted in: *IFEG*, 275–277

'Irrende Helden', in: *Prager Tagblatt*, November 27th, 1930; reprinted in: *IFEG*, 82–87

'Über einen Ausspruch von Doktor Goebbels', in: *Das Tagebuch* 11 (1930), reprinted in: *IFEG*, 73–74

'Ein Buchhandler', in: *Prager Tagblatt*, March 17th, 1931; reprinted in: *IFEG*, 394–398

'Wie es kommen wird', in: *General-Anzeiger für Dortmund*, June 19th 1932; reprinted in: *IFEG*, 108–111

'Nur wer die Waffen hat, kann Frieden schaffen', in: *General-Anzeiger für Dortmund*, March 2nd 1932

'Nein!', in: *Volkswille*, January 31st, 1933; reprinted in: *WeU*, 347–353

'Deutschland', in: *Aufruf. Streitschrift für Menschenrechte* 3 (1933), Special issue, 'Judenverfolgung', March 1933, Heft 6; reprinted in: *WeU*, 356–358

'Gnade dem Maultier', in: *Selbstwehr*, August 31st 1933; reprinted in: *Wmnm*, 129–134

'Vermächtnis an Deutschland', in: *Die Wahrheit*, 1933, Heft 19; reprinted in: *WeU*, 367–372

'Ein Mensch schreibt Erinnerungen', in: *Die Kritik* 2 (1934), nr. 10; reprinted in: *IFEG*, 411–414

'Mein Kopf', in: *Uni Hannover. Zeitschrift der Universität Hannover* 10 (1983), Heft 1, 29 ff; reprinted in: *BiS*, 69–71

B. Works on Theodor Lessing

Baron, Lawrence, 'Noise and Degeneration: Theodor Lessing's Crusade for Quiet', in: *Journal of Contemporary History* 17 (1982), 165–178

Baron, Lawrence, 'Discipleship and Dissent: Theodor Lessing and Edmund Husserl', in: *Proceedings of the American Philosophical Society* 127 (1983), no. 1, 32–49

Baule, Bernward, *Kulturerkenntnis und Kulturbewertung bei Theodor Lessing* (Hildesheim 1992)

Böhm, Peter, *Theodor Lessings Versuch einer erkenntnistheoretischen Grundlegung von Welt. Ein kritischer Beitrag zur Aporetik der Lebensphilosophie* (Amsterdam s.d. [1986])

Goetze, Wolf, *Die Gegensätzlichkeit der Geschichtsphilosophie Oswald Spenglers und Theodor Lessing* (diss. Leipzig 1930)

Goodyear, John, 'Viel Lärm um Theodor Lessing', in: *Angermion* 4 (2011), 95–112

Hartwig, Jochen, *'Sei was immer du bist'. Theodor Lessings wendungsvolle Identitätsbildung als Deutscher und Jude* (Oldenburg 1999)

Henrich, Johannes, *Friedrich Nietzsche und Theodor Lessing. Ein Vergleich* (Marburg 2004)

Heppner, Christian (ed.), *Wissen ist Macht, Bildung ist Schönheit. Ada & Theodor Lessing und die Volkshochschule Hannover.* Katalog zur Ausstellung des Stadtarchivs zum 75 jährigen Bestehen der VHS. 26.1. – 4.3.1995 in der VHS Hannover (Hanover 1995)

Hieronimus, Ekkehard, *Theodor Lessing - Otto Meyerhof - Leonard Nelson. Bedeutende Juden in Niedersachsen* (Hanover 1964)

Hieronimus, Ekkehard, *Theodor Lessing. Eine Lebensskizze*, Bibliography by Luitger Dietze (Hanover 1972)

Hiller, Kurt, 'Der Denker im Spiegel', in: *Die neue Weltbühne* (1936), Heft 3, 77–82; reprinted in: Kurt Hiller, *Köpfe und Tröpfe. Profile aus ein Vierteljahrhundert* (Hamburg 1950), 301–308

Hüsgen, Hans Dieter, *Geschichtsphilosophie und Kulturkritik Theodor Lessings* (diss. Mainz 1961)

Kaufmann, Herbert L., *Essai sur l'anti-progressisme et ses origines dans la philosophie allemande moderne* (diss. Sorbonne, Paris 1936)

Kemmler, Uwe, *Not und Notwendigkeit. Der Primat der Ethik in der Philosophie Theodor Lessings* (Frankfurt a.M. 2004)

Kotowski, Elke-Vera, *Feindliche Dioskuren. Theodor Lessing und Ludwig Klages: Das Scheitern einer Jugendfreundschaft* (Berlin 2000)

Kotowski, Elke-Vera (ed.), *"Sinngebung des Sinnlosen". Zum Leben und Werk des Kulturkritikers Theodor Lessing (1872 – 1933)* (Hildesheim 2006)

Kotowski, Elke-Vera et.al., *"Ich warf eine einsame Flaschenpost in das unermessliche Dunkel". Theodor Lessing 1872 – 1933* (Hildesheim 2008)

Kotowski, Elke-Vera, *Theodor Lessing (1872–1933): Philosoph - Feuilletonist – Volksbildner* (Berlin 2009)

Küchler, Manfred, *Die literarische und philosophische Entwicklung Theodor Lessings* Staatsexamensarbeit Technische Hochschule Hannover (not published, Hanover 1976)

Lentz, Matthias, '„Ruhe ist die erste Bürgerpflicht". Lärm, Großstadt und Nervosität im Spiegel von Theodor Lessings „Antilärmverein"', in: *Medizin, Gesellschaft und Geschichte* 13 (1994), 81–105

Mann, Thomas, 'Der Doktor Lessing, followed by Berichtigungen, followed by An die Redaktion der „Staatsbürgerzeitung"', in: Thomas Mann, *Gesammelte Werken in Zwölf Bänden*, ed. by Hans Bürgin, vol. 11. *Reden und Aufsätze* 3 (s.l. [Frankfurt a.M.] 1960) 719–731

Marwedel, Rainer, *Theodor Lessing 1872–1933. Eine Biographie* (Darmstadt and Neuwied 1987)

Mayer, Hans, 'Berichte über ein politisches Trauma', in: Hans Mayer, *Der Repräsentant und der Märtyrer. Konstellationen der Literatur* (Frankfurt a.M. 1971), 94–120

Mechler, Wolf D., *Albert Einstein und Theodor Lessing: Parallelen. Berührungen. Begleitband zur Ausstellung des Historischen Museums Hannover* (Hannover 2005)

Nelissen, Elma, *De receptiegeschiedenis van* Geschichte als Sinngebung des Sinnlosen *van Theodor Lessing*, Master-thesis Open Universiteit Nederland (not published, Heerlen 2011)

Petersdorff, Friedrich von, 'Die perspektivische Konstruktion von Geschichte in Lessings beide Büchern „Geschichte als Sinngebung des Sinnlosen" ', in: Elke-Vera Kotowski (ed.), *"Sinngebung des Sinnlosen". Zum Leben und Werk des Kulturkritikers Theodor Lessing (1872–1933)* (Hildesheim etc. 2006), 201–214

Poetzl, Herbert, *Confrontation with Modernity: Theodor Lessing's Critique of German Culture* (unpublished PhD-thesis, University of Massachusetts 1978)

Rethmeier, Martin, *Theodor Lessing – Politische Aspekte seiner Philosophie und Publizistik in der Zeit der Weimarer Republik 1918 – 1933*, Schriftliche Hausarbeit RWTH (not published, Aachen 1984)

Schmid, Hans-Dieter, 'Theodor Lessing und die Israelitische Gartenbauschule Ahlem - eine Legende', in: *Hannoversche Geschichtsblätter*, Neue Folge 52 (1998), 289–295

Schröder, *Hans Eggert, Theodor Lessings autobiografischen Schriften. Ein Kommentar* (Bonn 1970)

Schwake, Ruth, 'Von den Volkstümlichen Hochschulkursen zur Gründung der Freien Volkshochschule Hannover Theodor Lessing in Linden', in: *BiS*, 85–98

Segel, Binjamin, *Die Entdeckungsreise des Hernn Dr. Theodor Lessing zu den Ostjuden* (Lemberg 1910)

Siegrist, Maja I., *Theodor Lessing – Die entropische Philosophie. Freilegung und Rekonstruktion eines verdrängten Denkers* (Bern 1995)

Steinmann, Th., 'Sinn und Tatsächlichkeit bei Spengler, Lessing und Rickert', *Zeitschrift für Theologie und Kirche*, Neue Folge 11 (1921), 348–372

Stern, Hans, 'Theodor Lessing (1872–1933) ', in: *WeU*, 7–48

Wiersma-Verschaffelt, F., *Een tragische vriendschap. Ludwig Klages en Theodor Lessing* (Leiden 1968)

Wollenberg, Jörg, 'Schönheit durch Bildung – Theodor Lessing als Bildungsreformer und Volkshochschulgründer', in: *BiS*, 10–50

Wollenberg, Jörg, '"14 Jahre Volkshochschularbeit... das lasse ich nicht aus der Geschichte Hannovers löschen". Ada Lessing als geschäftsführende Leiterin der Volkshochschule Hannover von 1919–1933', in: Paul Ciupke and Karin Derichs-Kunstmann (ed.), *Zwischen Emanzipation und 'besonderer Kulturaufgabe der Frau'. Frauenbildung in der Geschichte der Erwachsenenbildung* (Essen 2001), 133–148

Wollenberg, Jörg, 'Ada und Theodor Lessing: Rückkehr unerwünscht', in: *Sozial. Geschichte* 21 (2006), 52–66

Wysling, Hans, '„Ein Elender". Zu einem Novellenplan Thomas Manns', *Quellenkritische Studien zum Werk Thomas Manns*, ed. by P. Scherrer and H. Wysling (Bern and Munich 1967), 106–122

C. *Reviews of* Geschichte als Sinngebung des Sinnlosen

Editions 1, 2 and 3

An., in: *Friedensblätter / Völkerfriede* 19 (1919), 79

An., in: *Evangelische Freiheit* (1920), 230–231

An., in: *Faust. Eine Rundschau, Kunst und Mythos* 1 (1922), 55

An., in: *Literarisch Centralblatt für Deutschland* 72 (1921), 571–573

An., in: *Theologie der Gegenwart* 16 (1922), 13–15

Bahr, Hermann, 'Tagebuch', in: *Neues Wiener Journal. Unparteiliches Tagblatt*, 27. Jahrgang, Nr. 9195, Sonntag 8 Juni 1919, 7

Bauer, Otto, in: *Deutsches Philologenblatt* 32 (1924), 413

Brandl, R., 'Zur Problematik der Geschichte', in: *Frankfurter Zeitung*, April 30th, 1920

Braun, O., in: *Vergangenheit und Gegenwart* 10 (1920), 171

Engelbrecht, K., 'Auch eine Entthronung', in: *Der Tag*, Beilage Grundbesitz und Realkredit, March 26th, 1919

Frischeisen-Köhler, M., in: *Historische Zeitschrift* 124 (1921), 517–518

Heimsoeth, H., in: *Deutsche Literaturzeitung* 42 (1921), 269–272

Imberg, K.E., in: *Nord und Süd*, April 1919, 106

Koch, W., in: *Sozialistische Monatshefte* 21 (1921), 571–572

Koetzsche, E., in: *Der individualistische Anarchist* 1 (1919), 439–441

Leisegang, H., in: *Historische Vierteljahrschrift* 20 (1922), 234

Litt, Th., in: *Sokrates. Zeitschrift für das Gymnasialwesen* (1920), 100–103

Morgenstern, G., in: *Annalen der Philosophie* 2 (1921), 275–276

Mutius, Gerhard, von, in: *Preussische Jahrbücher* 188 (1922), 357–359

Preuss, H., in: *Theologische Literaturblätter* 42 (1921), 171
Ranke, Ermentrude, von, in: *Vierteljahrschrift für Sozial- und Wirtschaftsgeschichte* 16 (1922), 450
Reissmann, Rolf, in: *Der Zweemann. Monatsblätter für Dichtung und Kunst* 2 (December 1919), 19–20
Seifert, Friedrich, in: *Kantstudien* 27 (1922), 190–191
Seiling, M., in: *Psychische Studien* 46 (1919), 261–262
Stephan, Horst, in: *Theologische Literaturzeitung* 1922 Nr. 1, Spalte 18
Stoltenberg, H.L., in: *Schmollers Jahrbuch für Gesetzgebung, Verwaltung und Volkswirtschaft im deutschen Reich* 45 (1921–1922), Heft 4, 268–271
Taub, Hans, in: *Münchener neueste Nachrichten*, August 30th, 1919
Weber, in: *Theologische Literaturberichte* (1923), 2

Edition 4

An., in: *Annalen der Philosophie und philosophische Kritik* 6 (1927), 156–157
An., in: *Der Mittelschullehrer* (1927)
Baginsky, A., in: *Biologische Heilkunst* 34 (1927), 985
Haering, Th., in: *Blätter für deutsche Philosophie* 4 (1930), 246–248
Hegenwald, H., in: *Grundwissenschaft. Philosophische Zeitschrift der J. Rehmke-Gesellschaft* 9 (1929), 315
Helmholt, Hans, F., in: *Die Literatur* 30 (1927), Heft 2, November 1927, 119
Kapff, S. von, in: *Die Umschau* 31 (1927), 1061
Matthies, Leo, 'Geschichte als Sinngebung des Sinnlosen. Zu Theodor Lessings Werk', in: *Vossische Zeitung*, August 28th, 1927
Strathmann, Richard, 'Theodor Lessings Geschichtsbild', in *Philosophie und Leben* 4 (1928), 22–25

D.   Other Works

An., *Verhandlungen des Reichstags, Stenographische Berichte, 1914/16,* Bd. 306 (Berlin 1916)
An., 'Der Strindberg Preis', in: *Die Fackel* 23 (1921), column 568–571
Ankersmit, F. R., *Narrative logic. A Semantic Analysis of the Historian's Language* (The Hague 1983)
Ankersmit, F. R., *Historical Representation* (Stanford 2001)
Ankersmit, F. R., *Sublime Historical Experience* (Stanford 2005)
Ankersmit, F.R., 'Narrative and Interpretation', in: A. Tucker (ed.), *A Companion to the Philosophy of History and Historiography* (Malden MA 2009), 199–208

Anschütz, Gerhard, 'Gedanken über künftige Staatsreformen', in: Klaus Böhme (ed.), *Aufrufe und Reden deutscher Professoren im Ersten Weltkrieg* (Stuttgart 1975), 113–124
'Aufruf an die Kulturwelt', in: Klaus Böhme (ed.), *Aufrufe und Reden deutscher Professoren im Ersten Weltkrieg* (Stuttgart 1975), 47–49
'Aufruf Bonner Historiker', in: Klaus Böhme (ed.), *Aufrufe und Reden deutscher Professoren im Ersten Weltkrieg* (Stuttgart 1975), 50–51
Bahr, Hermann, 'Das deutsche Wesen ist uns erschienen!, Bayreuth, 12 August 1914', in: Georg Gellert (ed.), *Das eiserne Buch. Die führenden Männer und Frauen zum Weltkrieg 1914/15* (Hamburg 1915), 73–76
Barker, Ernest et al., *Why we are at war. Great Britain's case* (Oxford 1914)
Beck, Lewis White, 'Neo-Kantianism', in: Donald M. Borchert (ed. in chief), *Encyclopaedia of Philosophy* (Second Edition, Detroit 2006), vol. 6, 539–545
Bergson, Henri, *La signification de la guerre* (Paris 1915)
Bethmann-Hollweg, Von, Untitled contribution, in: Georg Gellert (ed.), *Das eiserne Buch. Die führenden Männer und Frauen zum Weltkrieg 1914/15* (Hamburg 1915), 131–132
Böhme, Klaus (ed.), *Aufrufe und Reden deutscher Professoren im Ersten Weltkrieg* (Stuttgart 1975)
Bowie, Andrew, *Introduction to German Philosophy: From Kant to Habermas* (Cambridge 2003)
Bruendel, Steffen, *Volksgemeinschaft oder Volksstaat. Die „Ideen von 1914" und die Neuordnung Deutschlands im Ersten Weltkrieg* (Berlin 2003)
Collingwood, R.G., and J.N.L. Myres, *Roman Britain and the English Settlements*, Oxford History of England, part I (second edition, Oxford 1937)
Collingwood, R.G., *An Essay on Metaphysics* (Oxford 1939)
Collingwood, R.G., *The Idea of History*, revised edition, edited with an introduction by Jan van der Dussen (Oxford etc. 1993)
Collini, Stefan, *Absent Minds: Intellectuals in Britain* (Oxford 2006)
Croce, Benedetto, *Teoria e storia della storiografia* (second revised edition, Bari 1920)
Dove, Richard, *He was a German: A Biography of Ernst Toller* (London 1990)
Dray, W.H., 'Explanatory Narrative in History', in: *The Philosophical Quarterly* 4 (1954), 15–27
Dray, W.H., *Laws and Explanation in History* (Oxford 1957)
Dray, W.H., *Philosophy of History* (Englewood Cliffs 1964)
Dussen, Jan van der, 'A Quest for the Real Past: Ankersmit on Historiography and (Sublime) Historical Experience', in: Jan van der Dussen, *Studies on Collingwood, History and Civilization* (Cham etc. 2016), 213–253
'Erklärung gegen die Oxforder Hochschulen', in: Klaus Böhme (ed.), *Aufrufe und Reden deutscher Professoren im Ersten Weltkrieg* (Stuttgart 1975), 54–56
Eucken, Rudolf, *Die Sinn und Wert des Lebens* (Leipzig 1908)

Eucken, Rudolf, *Die weltgeschichtliche Bedeutung des deutschen Geistes* (Stuttgart and Berlin 1914)

Fain, Haskell, *Between philosophy and history: the resurrection of speculative philosophy of history within the analytic tradition* (Princeton 1970)

Ferguson, Niall, *The Pity of War. Explaining World War One* (London 1998)

Flasch, Kurt, *Die geistige Mobilmachung. Die deutschen Intellektuellen und der Erste Weltkrieg* (Berlin 2000)

Freud, Sigmund, 'Eine Schwierigkeit der Psychoanalyse', in: *Imago. Zeitschrift für Anwendung der Psychoanalyse auf die Geisteswissenschaften* vol. V (1917), 1–7

Friedrich Wilhelm, Kronprinz des Deutschen Reiches, 'Deutschland in Waffen', in: Georg Gellert, (ed.), *Das eiserne Buch. Die führenden Männer und Frauen zum Weltkrieg 1914/15* (Hamburg 1915), 101–108

Fries, Helmut, *Die große Katharsis. Der Erste Weltkrieg in der Sicht deutscher Dichter und Gelehrter*, 2 vols., (Konstanz 1994–1995)

Gellert, Georg (ed.), *Das eiserne Buch. Die führenden Männer und Frauen zum Weltkrieg 1914/15* (Hamburg 1915)

Gierke, Otto von, 'Krieg und Kultur, 1915', in: Klaus Böhme (ed.), *Aufrufe und Reden deutscher Professoren im Ersten Weltkrieg* (Stuttgart 1975), 65–80

Goebbels, Joseph, 'Rassenfrage und Weltpropaganda', in: *Nürnberg 1933. Die ersten Reichstag der geeinten deutschen Nation* (Berlin 1933), 80–84

Goltz, Freiherr von der, Untitled contribution, in: Georg Gellert (ed.), *Das eiserne Buch. Die führenden Männer und Frauen zum Weltkrieg 1914/15* (Hamburg 1915), 13

Gordon, Mel, 'Hitler's Jewish Psychic', in: *Guilt and Pleasure* 3 (Summer 2006), 58 – 69

Haeckel, Ernst, 'Weltkrieg und Naturgeschichte', in: Georg Gellert (ed.), *Das eiserne Buch. Die führenden Männer und Frauen zum Weltkrieg 1914/15* (Hamburg 1915), 48–63

Harnack, Adolf von, 'Was wir schon gewonnen haben und was wir noch gewinnen müssen', in: Klaus Böhme (ed.), *Aufrufe und Reden deutscher Professoren im Ersten Weltkrieg* (Stuttgart 1975), 89–101

Heidelberger, Michael, 'Kantianism and Realism: Alois Riehl (and Moritz Schlick)', in: Michael Friedman and Alfred Nordmann (eds.), *The Kantian Legacy in Nineteenth-Century Science* (Cambridge, Mass. and London 2006), 227 – 247

Hitler, Adolf, *Mein Kampf. Zwei Bände in einem Band. Ungekürzte Ausgabe* (Munich 1943 [originally 1925, 1927])

Horstmann, Ulrich, 'Im Irrsinnsurwald der Geschichte. Dilettant, Polemiker, Feuilletonist: R. Marwedel legt die Biographie Theodor Lessings vor', in: *Die Welt*, Samstag June 13th 1987, nr. 135, 5

Husserl, Edmund, *Ideen zu einer reinen Phänomenologie und phänomenologische Philosophie* I, ed. by W. Biemel (The Hague 1950)

Jagow, von, 'Über den Krieg mit England', in: Georg Gellert (ed.), *Das eiserne Buch. Die führenden Männer und Frauen zum Weltkrieg 1914/15* (Hamburg 1915), 154–156

Jasper, Willi, 'Die verlorene Ehre der Carla Mann. Wurde die Schwester von Thomas Mann Opfer seiner Fehde mit dem Philosophen Theodor Lessing?', in: *Die Welt*, December 6th, 2012

Kaempf, Dr., Untitled contribution, in: Georg Gellert (ed.), *Das eiserne Buch. Die führenden Männer und Frauen zum Weltkrieg 1914/15* (Hamburg 1915), 139

Kieft, Ewout, *Oorlogsenthousiasme. Europa 1900–1918* (Amsterdam 2015)

Kozljanič, Robert Josef, *Lebensphilosophie. Eine Einführung* (Stuttgart 2004)

Köhnke, Klaus Christian, *The rise of neo-Kantianism: German academic philosophy between idealism and positivism* (Cambridge 1991)

Kuhn, H., et al. (eds.), *Die Münchener Phänomenologie* (The Hague 1975)

Laqueur, Walter, *Weimar. A Cultural History 1918–1933* (London 1974)

Lemon, M. C., *Philosophy of History: A Guide for Students* (London 2003)

Lersch, Philipp, *Lebensphilosophie der Gegenwart* (Berlin 1932)

Lipps, Theodor, 'Rezension von Afrikan Spir, *Denken und Wirklichkeit*', in: *Philosophische Monatshefte* 14 (1878), 352–361

Lipps, Theodor, *Grundtatsachen des Seelenlebens* (Bonn 1883)

Litt, Th., *Wege und Irrwege geschichtlichen Denkens* (Munich 1948)

Lübbe, Hermann, *Politische Philosophie in Deutschland. Studien zu ihrer Geschichte* (München 1974 [first edition: Basel 1963])

Mann, Thomas, Untitled contribution, in: Georg Gellert (ed.), *Das eiserne Buch. Die führenden Männer und Frauen zum Weltkrieg 1914/15* (Hamburg 1915), 41–42

Mann, Thomas, *Tagebücher 1933–1934*, ed. by Peter de Mendelssohn (Frankfurt am Main 1977)

Maier, Hans, 'Ideen von 1914 - Ideen von 1939? Zweierlei Kriegsanfänge', in: *Vierteljahrshefte für Zeitgeschichte* 38 (1990), nr. 4, 525–542

Marcks, Erich, 'Wo stehen wir? Die politischen, sittlichen und kulturellen Zusammenhänge unseres Krieges', in: Klaus Böhme (ed.), *Aufrufe und Reden deutscher Professoren im Ersten Weltkrieg* (Stuttgart 1975), 80–88

Mayr, Ernst, *The Growth of Biological Thought: Diversity, Evolution, and Inheritance* (Cambridge, Mass. 1982)

McCullagh, C.B., *Justifying Historical Descriptions* (Cambridge 1984)

McCullagh, C.B., *The Truth of History* (London 1998)

McCullagh, C.B., *The Logic of History. Putting postmodernism in perspective* (London 2004)

Meiland, Jack W., *Scepticism and historical knowledge* (New York 1965)

Meinecke, Friedrich, *Die deutsche Katastrophe: Betrachtungen und Erinnerungen* (Wiesbaden 1947 [first edition 1946])

Munz, Peter, *The shapes of time. A new look at the philosophy of history* (Middletown CT 1977)

Nagel, Thomas, *The view from nowhere* (Oxford 1986)

O'Hear, Anthony (ed.), *German Philosophy Since Kant* (Cambridge 1999)

Oncken, Hermann, 'Die Deutschen auf dem Wege zur einigen und freien Nation', in: Klaus Böhme (ed.), *Aufrufe und Reden deutscher Professoren im Ersten Weltkrieg* (Stuttgart 1975), 102–112

Paasche, 'Englands Weltherrschaft und der Krieg', in: Georg Gellert (ed.), *Das eiserne Buch. Die führenden Männer und Frauen zum Weltkrieg 1914/15* (Hamburg 1915), 172–173

Plenge, Johann, *1789 und 1914. Die symbolischen Jahre in der Geschichte des politischen Geistes* (Berlin 1916)

Popper, K.R., *Three Worlds. The Tanner Lecture on Human Values, Delivered at the University of Michigan, April 7, 1978*, http://tannerlectures.utah.edu/_documents/a-to-z/p/popper80.pdf

Ranke, Leopold von, *Über die Epochen der neueren Geschichte* (Leipzig 1906 [first edition 1854])

Ranke, Leopold von, *Geschichten der romanischen und germanischen Völker von 1494 bis 1514* (Dritte Auflage, Leipzig 1885)

Ricoeur, Paul, *Temps et récit* (three volumes, Paris 1983–1995)

Ricoeur, Paul, *Soi-même comme un autre* (Paris 1990)

Scheler, Max, *Die Idee des Friedens und der Pazifismus*, ed. by Maria Scheler (Berlin 1931)

Schmitt, Richard, 'Phenomenology', in: Donald M. Borchert (ed. in chief), *Encyclopaedia of Philosophy* (Second Edition, Detroit 2006), vol. 7, 278–299

Schneidewin, Max, 'Lärm im Schulunterricht', in: *Der Anti-Rüpel 1* (1908–1909), nr. 7, 128

Schneidewin, Max, 'Über den Willensentschluß als Hilfe gegen peinigende Lärmempfindung – Schullärm', in: *Der Anti-Rüpel 1* (1908–1909), nr. 8, 150

Schneidewin, Max, 'Vom Lärm in der Schule', in: *Der Anti-Rüpel 1* (1908–1909), nr. 9, 166

Schwerin-Löwitz, Graf von, Untitled contribution, in: Georg Gellert (ed.), *Das eiserne Buch. Die führenden Männer und Frauen zum Weltkrieg 1914/15* (Hamburg 1915), 10

Sloterdijk, Peter, *Kritik der zynischen Vernunft* (2 vols., Frankfurt a.M. 1983)

Smid, Reinhold Nikolaus, '"Münchener Phänomenologie" – Zur Frühgeschichte des Begriffs', in: H. Spiegelberg and E. Avé-Lallemant (ed.), *Pfänder-Studien* (The Hague 1982), 109–153

Sombart, Werner, 'Die andern und wir', in: Georg Gellert (ed.), *Das eiserne Buch. Die führenden Männer und Frauen zum Weltkrieg 1914/15* (Hamburg 1915), 83–100

Southgate, Beverly, 'Postmodernism', in: A. Tucker (ed.), *A Companion to the Philosophy of History and Historiography* (Malden MA 2009), 540–549

Spengler, Oswald, *Preußentum und Sozialismus* (Munich 1920)

Spiegelberg, Herbert, *The Phenomenological Movement. A Historical Introduction* (third and enlarged edition, The Hague etc. 1982)

Steiner, George, 'The Hollow Miracle', in: George Steiner, *Language and Silence. Essays 1958–1966* (Harmondsworth 1979 [first edition 1967]), 136–151

Stevenson, David, *1914–1918: The History of the First World War* (London 2004)
Strachan, Hew, *The First World War: A New History* (London 2003)
Toller, Ernst, *Eine Jugend in Deutschland* (Reinbek bei Hamburg 1984 [first edition Amsterdam 1933])
Troeltsch, Ernst, *Der Historismus und seine Probleme. Erstes Buch: Das logische Problem der Geschichtsphilosophie* (1922; reprint: Aalen 1961)
Tucholsky, Kurt, 'Der Geist von 1914', *Die Weltbühne*, August 7th, 1924, Nr. 32, 204
Tucker, A., *Our Knowledge of the Past: A Philosophy of Historiography* (Cambridge 2004)
Tucker, A. (ed.), *A Companion to the Philosophy of History and Historiography* (Malden MA 2009)
Verhey, Jeffrey, *The Spirit of 1914: Militarism, Myth, and Mobilization in Germany* (Cambridge 2000)
Walsh, W.H., *Philosophy of History: An Introduction* (New York 1967 [first edition 1951])
Walsh, W.H., 'Historical Causation', *Proceedings of the Aristotelian Society*, New Series, 63(1962–1963), 217–236
Walsh, W.H., 'Colligatory concepts in history', in: W.H. Burston and D. Thompson (eds), *Studies in the Nature and Teaching of History* (London 1967), 65–84; reprinted with minor alterations in: P. Gardiner (ed.), *The Philosophy of History* (Oxford 1974), 126–144
Whewell, William, *The Philosophy of the Inductive Sciences Founded upon their History* (New York 1967 [1847]), vol. 2
White, Hayden, *Metahistory: the historical imagination in nineteenth-century Europe* (Baltimore 1973)
White, Hayden, 'Foucault decoded: notes from underground', in: Hayden White, *Tropics of Discourse: Essays in cultural criticism* (third edition Baltimore and London 1985), 230–260
White, Hayden, 'The Historical Text as Literary Artefact', in: Hayden White, *Tropics of Discourse*, 81–100

Index of Names

Ahrweiler, Antoni 37
Ahrweiler, Leopold 36–37, 49–50, 52, 54
Alexander the Great 207
Andrejev, Leonid 134
Ankersmit, F.R. 313, 314, 316–317, 322, 331
Anquetil, Georges 11
Anschütz, Gerhard 123–124
Aristotle 19, 96, 327

Bach, J.S. 268
Bacon, Francis 161, 272
Baginsky, A. 301
Bahr, Hermann 109–110, 112, 231–232, 247, 289–290
Baron, Lawrence 6
Bauer, Otto 300
Baule, Bernward 15, 17, 18
Beethoven, Ludwig von 117
Behan McCullagh, C. 325
Bender, Wilhelm 71
Bergson, Henri 133, 134
Bethmann-Hollweg, Theobald von 103, 125, 126
Bey, Omar al-Raschid 50, 76, 86
Bismarck, Otto von 189
Bloch, Ernst 109
Böhlau, Helene 50
Böhm, Peter 14, 17
Borchardt, Rudolf 193
Brandl, Rudolf 295
Braun, O. 292
Brentano, Lujo 109
Breysig, Kurt 298
Bryusov, Valery 134
Buckle, Henry 216
Buddha 87, 89, 209–210

Caesar 183, 185, 207, 249
Carus, Carl Gustav 30, 66
Charlemagne 321
Christ 87. 89
Class, Gustav 55
Claudius 185
Cohen, Hermann 109, 180
Collingwood. R.G. 171, 185, 310, 312, 313, 314, 318, 319, 320, 324, 326, 331

Comte, Auguste 191
Condorcet 216
Croce, Benedetto 178–179, 310, 311, 314, 324, 326, 331

Dante 86
Danto, Arthur 308–309
Darwin, Charles 69, 70, 143, 159, 191, 216, 243, 300, 308
Dehmel, Richard 133
Deiβmann, Adolf 109
Delbrück, Hans 109
Descartes, René 71, 186, 241
Dietze, Luitger 12
Dilthey, Wilhelm 170, 300
Dönniges, Helene von 47, 159
Dray, W.H. 319, 320, 321
Driesch, Hans 302, 306

Ehrenbaum, Fritz 42
Ehrenbaum, Margarethe 42, 45, 58
Einstein, Albert 16, 109, 306
Engelbrecht, Kurt 219
Epicurus 209–210
Eucken, Rudolf 109, 121–122

Fain, Haskell 19
Falckenberg, Richard 55
Faucheux, Albert 253
Fichte, Johann 197. 216
Flasch, Kurt 108
France, Anatole 133, 192
Frank, Bruno 56
Franz Ferdinand, Archduke 102
Freud, Sigmund 232
Friedrich Wilhelm, Crownprince 125
Frischeisen-Köhler, Max 296
Fukuyama, Francis 190*n*
Fulda, Ludwig 117
Furet, François 317

Galsworthy, John 134
Gauguin, Paul 186
George, Stefan 49, 133
Gierke, Otto von 110–111, 118–119
Goebbels, Joseph, 4, 287

INDEX OF NAMES 349

Goethe, J.W. von   117, 218, 230, 296
Goetze, Wolf   13, 17, 18, 306–307
Goltz, Colmar Freiherr von der   137
Grans, Hans   224
Grothe, Ernst   60
Grouchy, Emmanuel   286

Haarmann, Fritz   8, 24, 66, 219–220, 222, 223, 224, 225, 269, 287
Haeckel, Ernst   109, 126
Haering, Th.   303
Hanussen, Erik Jan   1
Harden, Maximilian   285
Harnack, Adolf von   109, 121
Hartmann, Eduard von   43, 67, 76, 180, 236
Hartwig, Jochen   15
Hauptmann, Gerhard   108, 133
Hegel, G.W.F.   29, 55, 143, 160, 179, 190n, 191, 216, 243, 250, 253, 261, 281, 300, 308
Heidelberger, Michael   69
Heim, Karl   306
Heimsoeth, Heinz   296
Helmholt, Hans F.   302
Helmholtz, Hermann von   72
Henrich, Johannes   18
Henry VIII, king   258
Herder, Johann Gottfried von   191, 216
Herodotus   264
Hertling, Georg Freiherr von   71
Hieronimus, Ekkehard   12
Hiller, Kurt   5
Hindenburg, Paul von   8, 24, 43, 66, 128, 148, 149, 287, 301, 302
Hitler, Adolf   1, 9, 113–114, 150
Homer   86
Hugenberg, Alfred   9
Hüsgen, Hans Dieter   14, 17, 18, 307–308
Husserl, Edmund   33, 59, 60, 73–76, 78, 80, 91, 162, 163, 164, 180, 199, 213, 226, 235, 236, 237, 252, 295, 298, 327

Imberg, Kurt   291

Jacobsohn, Siegfried   66
Jagow, Gottlieb von   126–127
Jordan, Wilhelm   42
Jünger, Ernst   109

Kaempf, Johannes   103

Kant, Immanuel   21, 22, 29, 68, 69, 70, 90, 117, 166–167, 168, 188, 189–190, 216, 256, 276, 293, 298
Kapf, Sigm. von   302
Kaufmann, Herbert L.   13–14
Kemmler, Uwe   15
Kjellén, Rudolf   119–120
Klages, Ludwig   12, 13, 30, 40, 41–42, 43–44, 45, 47, 48, 49, 52–53, 54, 55, 69, 71, 97, 303
Koch, Walther   297
Koetzschke, Ernst   290
Kojève, Alexandre   190n
Kotowski, Elke-Vera   13, 16, 41
Kraus, Karl   109
Küchler, Manfred   14
Kuhn, Thomas S.   157

Laqueur, Walter   58
Lasalle, Ferdinand   47, 123, 159
Lecky, William   216
Lefebvre, Georges   317
Leibniz, Gottfried   71, 240, 317
Leisegang, Hans   298
Lemon, M.C.   325
Lersch, Philipp   30
Lessing-Abbenthern, Ada (*second wife*)   1, 3, 15–16, 33, 57, 61, 62, 66
Lessing-Ahrweiler, Adèle (*mother*)   36, 37, 38, 42, 49, 50
Lessing, Gotthold   36, 216
Lessing, Judith (*daughter*)   55, 61
Lessing, Levy Leiser (*grandfather*)   36
Lessing-Stach von Goltzheim, Maria (*first wife*)   51–52, 54, 55–56, 61, 65
Lessing, Miriam (*daughter*)   55, 61, 65
Lessing, Ruth (*daughter*)   1, 62
Lessing, Sigmund (*father*)   36, 37–38, 42, 44, 45, 46, 49, 50, 58
Lessing, Sophie (*sister*)   37, 50
Lessing, Theodor   *passim*
Lévi-Strauss, Claude   17
Liebknecht, Karl   103
Liebmann, Otto   68
Lietz, Hermann   32, 55
Lipps, Theodor   55, 59, 60, 61, 71–74, 75, 76, 80, 91, 94, 162, 164, 213, 226, 235, 236, 295, 298, 327
Litt, Theodor   293–295, 331
Locke, John   68, 70

Lotze, Hermann   72
Lübbe, Hermann   109
Lublinski, Samuel   7, 64, 65
Ludendorff, Erich   150
Luther, Martin   207

Mann, Carla   65
Mann, Heinrich   109
Mann, Thomas   3, 7, 56, 64, 65, 108, 124
Marcks, Erich   120–121
Marwedel, Rainer   13, 16, 18, 32, 64, 77
Marx, Karl   24, 123, 147, 160, 190, 216, 243, 252, 300
Matthies, Leo   302
Mayer, Hans   11, 18
Meiland, Jack W.   310–314
Meinecke, Friedrich   109, 114–115
Menselssohn, Moses   36
Meyer, J.B.   71
Michelangelo   86
Montesquieu   182, 216
Morgenstern, Georg   297, 327, 333
Mozart, W.A.   206
Munz, Peter   19
Mussolini, Benito   11
Mutius, Gerhard von   298
Mynski, Nikolai   134

Nagel, Thomas   324
Napoleon   175, 286, 321
Nero   277, 321
Newton, Isaac   21, 306
Nicolas II, czar   174
Nietzsche, Friedrich   15, 24, 28, 30, 156–157, 203, 206, 274, 279, 292, 296

Oakeshott, Michael   310, 311, 312, 314, 324, 326, 331
Oncken, Hermann   122–123

Paasche, Hermann   127
Panizza, Oskar   8, 48, 154
Peter, czar   189, 321
Petersdorff, Friedrich von   308–309
Petrarch   86, 158
Pfemfert, Franz   141, 144
Plato   29, 327
Plenge, Johann   111–112, 120
Poetzl, Herbert   12, 17, 18
Polybius   264
Popper, K.R.   86

Ranke, Ermentrude von   299
Ranke, Leopold von   192, 198, 259, 299, 310
Reißmann, Rolf   291
Rethmeier, Martin   14
Reventlow, Franziska zu   48
Rice, Muriel (Mrs. Isaac L. Rice)   62
Ricoeur, Paul   308–309
Rickert, Heinrich   70, 76, 80. 158, 180, 228, 229, 250, 293, 297, 298, 304
Riehl, Alois   68, 69, 70, 76, 80, 236
Rolland, Romain   133, 134
Romulus and Remus   277
Rousseau, Jean-Jacques   146
Russell, B.   134

Schaarschmidt, C.M.W.   71
Schama, Simon   317
Scheler, Max   25, 32, 136–137, 139, 153, 193, 237
Schering, Erich   212
Scherr, Johannes   42, 154, 249
Schiller, Friedrich von   58, 276
Schlegel, Friedrich   28, 30
Schleich, Carl Ludwig   212
Schlick, Moritz   70
Schmid, Hans-Dieter   32, 35
Schmoller, Gustav   109
Schneidewin, Max   43, 67, 68, 76, 236
Schopenhauer, Adele   56
Schopenhauer, Arthur   24, 28, 30, 43, 56, 67, 76, 80, 90, 179, 236, 296
Schröder, Hans Eggert   12, 32, 35
Schwerin-Löwitz, Hans Graf von   137
Segel, Binjamin   63
Seifert, Friedrich   300
Seiling, Max   291
Shakespeare, William   22, 186
Shaw, G.B.   134
Siegrist, Maja I.   15, 17
Simmel, Georg   180, 293, 296, 297
Sloterdijk, Peter   17
Smid, Reinhold N.   59
Socrates   87, 89
Sombart, Werner   125, 139
Sophie, Duchess of Hohenberg   102
Southgate, Beverly   323, 324, 325
Spengler, Oswald   13, 112–113, 227, 250, 295, 298, 299, 300, 304, 305, 306, 307
Spiegelberg, Herbert   74

INDEX OF NAMES

Spinoza, Baruch de   275
Spir, Afrikan   55, 77, 81–83
Steiner, George   122
Steinmann, Th.   304–306
Stephan, Horst   300
Stoltenberg, H.L.   298
Strathmann, Richard   302–303
Strindberg, August   212
Sudermann, Hermann   66

Tacitus   178, 249
Taine, Hyppolite   249
Taub, Hans   291
Tell, Wilhelm   218, 277, 321, 330
Tiberius   277
Toller, Ernst   104–107
Treitschke, Heinrich von   249, 260, 270
Troeltsch, Ernst   109, 230
Tucholsky, Kurt   114
Tucker, A.   325

Vaihinger, Hans   231, 297
Verhey, Jeffrey   107
Vico, Giambattista   198, 216, 243
Voltaire   216

Wagner, Adolph   109
Wagner, Richard   24
Walsh, W.H.   315, 316, 317, 318
Weissmann, August   71
Whewell, William   315
White, Hayden   17, 18, 313, 322, 323, 331
Wiersma-Verschaffelt, F.   40
Wilhelm II   102–103
Windelband, Wilhelm   68, 158, 228, 229, 250, 298
Wright, Georg Hendrik von   308–309
Wysling, Hans   7
Wundt, Wilhelm   72

Zweig, Stefan   105

Index of Subjects

Adult education   15–16, 24, 57
Ahmung   93–97, 188–189, 273–274
Art   85–86
Asia   50, 141–143, 144, 146–147
Autobiography   5–6, 31–35

Causality   171–179, 190–191, 215, 264–271, 281, 286, 293, 317–321
Civilization, Western   19, 23–24, 92–93
Consciousness   81–85, 195
Culture   87, 282–283, 308

Destiny, historical   193–195
Development   143, 149, 167, 179–180, 190–192, 204, 304

Education   32, 39, 217, 218–219, 221–222
Essentialism   171, 268
Europe   141–143, 144–146, 146–147, 308
Evidence, historical   184–185, 287
Eyewitnesses, testimony of   183–184

Feminism   24, 56–57
First World War   102–103
First World War, explanations of   172, 253
First World War, historical justifications   116–128

Galicia   62–64
Geisteswissenschaften   158–159, 165, 228–229, 241–243, 245

Haarmann-trial   7–8, 220, 223–225, 269
Hindenburg-affair   8–9, 43, 68, 128
Historiographical genres   203
History, criticisms of   19–20, 154–161, 274–276
History, politics and   196–197

"Ideas of 1914"   112–115
Ideals   86–87, 199–201, 234, 246–247, 249, 262–268
Intersubjectivity   294–295, 331

Jewish identity   36, 277

Lebensphilosophie   30
Lessing,
   ancestry   36–37
   childhood   36–44
   First World War, on   7, 25, 128, 136, 138–141, 147–150, 151–152, 170, 178, 183–184, 193, 197, 206, 267, 269, 270, 279
   friendship with L. Klages   40–42, 43–44, 47, 49, 52–54
   idea of philosophy   21–23, 28–31
   marriage, first   51–52, 55–56, 65
   marriage, second   61–62, 66
   murder of   1–5
   noise   62
   philosophical education   67–76
   philosophical position   236–238
   philosophical system   81–99
   reputation   5–11
   student years   44–49
   studying with Husserl   59–60
   theatre critic   57–59
   university lecturer   61
Logificatio post festum   97–99, 175–179, 195, 269, 288, 298
Lublinski-affair   7, 64–65

Memory   53–54
Method, historical   277–278, 294, 307
Motives as causes   172–175, 266–267. 319–320
Munich phenomenology   73–74

Narrativism   322–323
National-socialism   9–10, 150–151
Naturwissenschaften   158–159, 165, 206, 228–229, 241–243, 245–246, 257
Need   44, 81–85, 271–272
Neo-Kantianism   68–70, 71, 162, 236
Noise   24, 48, 62

Panizza-case   6–7, 48–49
Past, status of the   54, 166–167, 198–199
Personalities, historical   188–189, 208
Phenomenology   59–60, 73–76, 91, 162–164, 180–181, 213

INDEX OF SUBJECTS

Poetics of history   217, 245, 263, 296, 321–323
Postmodernism   323–326
Progress   143, 193, 216, 304–305

Objectivity   292, 294

Religious function of history   278, 330
Remembrance   248, 278–279
Reputations, historical   186–188, 206–208. 248, 268, 274–275

Scepticism, historical   199, 239–241, 250, 284, 299, 309–314
Sinn   167, 231–232, 247, 255, 270, 281, 288, 290, 306
Sinngebung   182, 190, 208, 231–232, 244, 281, 288, 290, 306

Socialism   178
"Spirit of 1914"   104–108, 109–111, 173
Subject, historical   168–170, 215, 256–259, 261, 314–317
Subjectivity   294

Teleology of history   179–182, 189–190
Theatre   57–59
Three-spheres-theory   88–90, 91–93, 142, 165, 167, 171, 195, 200–201, 207, 231, 234–235, 247, 251, 281, 305
Time   217, 251, 289
Truth   207–208, 244, 247
Truth in history   215, 218, 219, 224, 243, 267–268, 331–332

Volkshochschule Hannover   15–16, 57, 237

Printed in the United States
by Baker & Taylor Publisher Services